The Negative of Capital

Historical Materialism Book Series

VOLUME 308

The titles published in this series are listed at *brill.com/hm*

The Negative of Capital

The Marxian Concept of Economic Crisis

By

Jorge Grespan

Translated from the Portuguese by

Martin Charles Nicholl

BRILL

LEIDEN | BOSTON

Originally published as *O negativo do capital: o conceito de crise na crítica de Marx à economia política*, 2nd ed. (Expressão Popular, São Paulo, 2012).

Library of Congress Cataloging-in-Publication Data

Names: Grespan, Jorge, author. | Nicholl, Martin Charles, translator.
Title: The negative of capital : the Marxian concept of economic crisis / by Jorge Grespan ; translated from the Portuguese by Martin Charles Nicholl.
Other titles: Negativo do capital o conceito de crise na crítica de Marx à economia política. English
Description: Leiden ; Boston : Brill, 2024. | Series: Historical materialism book series, 1570-1522 ; volume 308 | "Originally published as O negativo do capital o conceito de crise na crítica de Marx à economia política, 2nd ed. (Expressão Popular, São Paulo, 2012)." | Includes bibliographical references and index.
Identifiers: LCCN 2024000783 (print) | LCCN 2024000784 (ebook) | ISBN 9789004690714 (hardback) | ISBN 9789004690721 (ebook)
Subjects: LCSH: Marxian economics. | Financial crises. | Capital.
Classification: LCC HB97.5 .G6965 2024 (print) | LCC HB97.5 (ebook) | DDC 335.4/12–dc23/eng/20240326
LC record available at https://lccn.loc.gov/2024000783
LC ebook record available at https://lccn.loc.gov/2024000784

Typeface for the Latin, Greek, and Cyrillic scripts: "Brill". See and download: brill.com/brill-typeface.

ISSN 1570-1522
ISBN 978-90-04-69071-4 (hardback)
ISBN 978-90-04-69072-1 (e-book)
DOI 10.1163/9789004690721

Contents

Preface to the English Edition

The book that the reader has in hand corresponds to my doctoral thesis presented in 1994 in Brazil at the University of Campinas under the supervision of Marcos Lutz Müller (1943–2020). It was first published in Portuguese in 1998 with a second edition in 2012. To them I have now added a postface written in 2019 and an enlarged bibliography referring to the Marxist literature published after the economic crisis that began in 2008. The additions to, and revision of, the Brazilian editions that I have made for the present publication have not substantially altered any of the central ideas of the 1994 thesis, quite the contrary; I believe the events of the 2008 crisis, often referred to, incorrectly in my opinion, as a mere 'financial crisis', actually confirmed and underscored them.

This book sets out to examine the concept of economic crisis as presented in Marx's mature work. In it, crises are defined as a phenomenon which, being inherent to capitalism, manifests the contradictory side of capitalism and capital's chronic tendency to devaluation. However clear and simple this definition might seem, since the beginning of the twentieth century it has nevertheless aroused a long debate that has extended right through to beginning of the twenty-first century. It seems to me that an adequate evaluation of this debate can only be achieved by going back to Marx's original texts and submitting them to a new interpretation of the fundamental questions at stake. For this reason, in the body of the text of *The Negative of Capital* I have concentrated on an analysis of Marx and left the discussion of the main theses being debated to the footnotes, which serve to indicate my position in relation to those theses rather than to reconstruct them in detail.

The first of the fundamental questions raised by Marx's definition of crises refers to their cause. Based on different passages isolated from Marx's work, various authors have deduced explanatory theories which either considered crises to be the result of disproportion among the branches of social capital in its reproduction, or the effect of the chronic under-consumption that capitalism is condemned to, or, lastly, as the innate tendency of the average rate of profit to fall. A second question derived from the cause of crises is the form that they take, which is supposed to be either that of an inexorable collapse of the system or that of a cycle in which a stage of crisis always occurs after a stage of expansion. Be that as it may, it must be noted right away that all these solutions for the question of the causes and the form of crises are based on elements present in Marx's own work. This circumstance raises another question concerning the fragmentary presentation of the concept of crisis in the texts Marx wrote in the 1860s, and especially in the 1861–3 and 1863–7 manuscripts and in Volume I of *Capital*.

Indeed, there is no discernible systematic approach to crises in these texts, a fact that has given rise to doubts as to whether Marx did actually develop a theory of crises at all. After Marx abandoned his plan for the work he had begun to elaborate in 1858, in which crises were to be addressed along with the 'world market' in the last of the intended six volumes, not a single chapter of his writings was devoted exclusively to the theme of crises. In the texts of the 1860s, crises always appear linked to capital in its circulation, production and reproduction processes, and the theme is never addressed specifically on its own.

However, I consider that the lack of an exhaustive treatment of crises by Marx does not mean he held them to be an unimportant phenomenon; on the contrary, I believe that for Marx, crises represent the objective form of critique, that is, a kind of self-criticism of capitalism effectuated by the force of the facts themselves. In his works crises materialise the contradictory nature of capitalism in the form of sudden, profound devaluation: crises are decisive because they reveal capital's negative side.

This is precisely what the title *The Negative of Capital* seeks to emphasise: the negative side, the self-negation that marks capital's very existence. Given the omnipresence of this self-negation, I argue that, instead of reserving a specific part of a book or chapter for the treatment of crises, Marx defines them gradually, in the same gradual way that he defines the concept of capital. Thus, each stage of Marx's presentation confers a given content on the concept of capital while at the same time it confers a corresponding content on the concept of crisis, but in a negative way. As an example, in *Capital*, when capital is defined in the ambit of the process of the immediate production of commodities, crisis is also defined in this ambit; and when capital is defined in the ambits of circulation and reproduction processes, the meaning of crisis changes again to accompany the new definition of capital.

It was also in a gradual way that Marx conceived the adequate form for the presentation of categories. For instance, in the 1857–8 manuscript, edited in 1938 with the title *Grundrisse*, Marx was already aware of the need to define capital based on the money-form and not on the labour substance of value. A few months later, while preparing the first part of the manuscript for publication in 1859, he realised that money itself should be defined based on the commodity-form, and it was on this basis that he composed the book *A Contribution to the Critique of Political Economy*. Subsequently, when he was writing the three volumes of *Capital*, Marx had still not determined all the details of the form of presentation, but he had made considerable progress in this direction. Since this is the most elaborated version left by Marx in his critique of political economy, this is the work on which I have focused in my analysis of the concept of crisis. The preceding versions, almost all of which were in the form of manuscripts, are only cited here when their specific formulations contribute towards a better understanding of some passages in *Capital*.

The symmetrical correspondence between the presentation of the concept of capital and the concept of crisis is the axis that structures the four chapters of *The Negative of Capital*. In the first chapter, 'The World of Commodity Producers', capital is merely a presupposition in the simple circulation of commodities, but crisis already appears in the form of the discrepancy between the sales and purchases that the producers engage in. In the second chapter, 'The Constitution of Capital', capital is defined in the ambit of production and crisis appears as the result of the opposition of capital to labour-power, an opposition that characterises production by the extraction of relative and absolute surplus-value. The third chapter, 'The Figures of Reproduction', addresses the circulation process articulated by capital to reproduce itself and the crisis which presents itself at that point as an interruption in the flow of simple and expanded reproduction. Lastly, the fourth chapter, 'Capital as a Totality', discusses the production and circulation processes as a whole within which crisis is defined as the result of the over-valorisation of capital.

Thus, *The Negative of Capital* proposes that, just as there is a theory of capital in Marx's work, so too is there a theory of crisis. If crises do not form the content of a distinct part of *Capital*, that is because they must be defined as a negative side, always there in all stages of the presentation of the concept of capital and materialised on the basis of capital's affirmative side. In this affirmative side, capital commands the production and circulation processes when it appropriates labour's capacity not only to create value but also to measure value. These processes depend on capital's success in constantly measuring itself, that is, in subordinating the measurement afforded by labour. However, as it relates to labour in a contradictory way, capital frequently fails in this self-measurement task and ends up by devaluating.

The second thesis defended in this book is that the crises express capital's tendency to mismeasurement. The concept of mismeasurement is present in all four chapters described above. Ranging from the simple discrepancy between sales and purchases to the over-valorisation of capital, it always concerns the impossibility of capital's measuring itself adequately. Therefore, at every moment of his presentation of the concept of capital, Marx characterises crisis according to the specific way in which it necessarily frustrates capital's pretension to self-measurement. At each moment, the frustration may have a different cause, but it occurs in all of them.

Thus, apart from the questions of the cause, the form, and the mode of presentation of crisis, a final question arises, posed by the definition of crises:

if the impossibility of self-measurement is inherent to capital, why then is capitalism not always in crisis? Turning that around, how is it possible that there are periods during which capital reproduces itself uninterruptedly? In a way, the theories of crisis developed by the authors committed to Marx's thinking in the twentieth and twenty-first centuries could be seen as responses to these questions. According to the emphasis each author places on a certain cause, crises are conceived as being either a mere possibility or a fatal necessity. The same can be said of the form of crisis that each theory chooses to highlight; generally speaking, collapse is taken to be an inexorable destiny while the cycle is explained either as a possibility or as an inflexible need for alternation between crises and expansions.

Far more than the cause or the form of crises, it is their modality that constitutes my main interest. For me, Marx considered crises to be an intrinsic determination of capitalism which cannot be avoided, but only possibly postponed or moderated in their violence. The fact that crises do not occur by chance, however, does not mean that they are predictable and able to impose themselves definitively. Thus, the specificity of this book is to offer a solution for the dichotomy between possibility and absolute necessity, recovering, from the realms of the history of philosophy, the category of relative necessity. Here conditional or relative necessity stems from the relation between capital's negative and affirmative sides, both of which are inherent to it despite being opposed to one another. For this reason, the realisation of each side depends on the other, is related to it and conditioned by it as well as by conditions that cannot immediately be found in either of them.

When, in the first chapter, I analyse the definition of crisis as a manifestation of a disequilibrium between sales and purchases, my intention is to show that, at this level of presentation, crises are determined as a simple possibility. In the second chapter, crises appear in the sphere of capital's production of commodities, and I explain that they are determined as a necessity, in the sense of an intrinsic disposition but with a reference to the opposite, equally intrinsic disposition of capitalist expansion. The third chapter analyses the apparent return to their being a mere possibility in the sphere of the circulation of capital, but this appearance is dispelled in the fourth chapter in which I expose the most complex forms in which Marx conceives necessity: as a whole, the processes of production and circulation are marked by a tendential fall in the rate of profit and by tendencies that act in the contrary direction. At this level of presentation of the concept of capital, the affirmative and negative sides articulate with one another in mutual opposition. Here it becomes clear that both sides are necessary in a conditional way.

My interest in examining the problem of the modality of crises – and my conviction that relative necessity attains its maximum complexity in Marx's presentation in the ambit of the tendencies and counter-tendencies to a fall in the average rate of profit – led me to leave out altogether the analysis of commercial capital and interest-bearing capital. At the time of writing the first version of this book, I based my decision on two reasons. First, these two forms of capital do not create surplus value; they only appropriate part of the surplus value created by the production sector. The second reason derives from the first: the rate of interest, which nourishes interest-bearing capital, is an even more fetishised form of measurement than the rate of profit which guides production investment. The rate of interest corresponds to a representation of the value that could be generated in the circuit of credit/money capital, hiding the real origin of crises in the production sphere.

However, when I began to prepare this edition of *The Negative of Capital* in 2018, it was necessary to explicitly contest the idea that the 2008 crisis could be reduced to the bursting of a speculative bubble created by the predominance of financial capital over productive capital. The new situation obliged me to include interest-bearing capital as it was addressed in the fifth Part of *Capital* Volume III. I decided to do this in the form of a postface because a new chapter, written twenty-five years after the original book, might appear to be rather artificial or discontinuous, even at the level of style or linguistics. In the postface I further develop the theses defended in the book and show that, in the commercial and financial crises, what particularly stands out are the concepts of mismeasurement and relative necessity. Also, parallel to the fetishism that is typical of interest-bearing capital, crisis appears alternately as being a contingent circumstance or as an inexorable collapse, thereby effectively concealing its roots in the sphere of productive capital.

When writing the postface I was able to count on the valuable resources of the Marx-Engels Gesamtausgabe, the so-called MEGA², with which I had been in contact briefly during the months when I was a researcher at the University of Konstanz in Germany in 1989 and 1990, but which I could actually employ only in another period of research in Berlin in 2012. For this reason, while the thesis I presented in 1994 was based on the Marx-Engels Werke (MEW) edition, the postface was based on the 1863–7 and 1868 manuscripts published by the MEGA² II/4.2 and II/4.3. In the present edition of *The Negative of Capital*, I have maintained the MEW references of the original and I cite extracts from Marx's works according to the English translations indicated in the bibliographical references. Thus, the footnotes identify, first, the work cited in the English translation and then (in square brackets), the work in the German text published by the MEW. In the postface, after the reference to the English translation, the footnotes indicate the equivalent in the MEGA². I must advise the reader, however, that in spite of maintaining Marx's text in accordance with the aforementioned English translation whenever possible, I have introduced some eventual changes when the translations masked a meaning important for the understanding of my argument. In such cases I present the word Marx used in German in italics, in square brackets.

These precautions are justified by the relevance of apparently philological details to the discussions in *The Negative of Capital*. The central theme of the symmetry of the concepts of crisis and capital, for example, is only plausible via a reading that captures the differences in the definitions of crisis and identifies their insertion on the reverse – that is to say, the negative, or implicit – side of the fabric of the presentation woven by Marx. The same goes for the concept of the measureless, whose ambivalence with respect to the positive meaning of vastness and the negative meaning of excess is usually lost in the translations. What is even more important is the precise reconstitution of the texts in the case of 'relative necessity', a concept that Marx does not explicitly enunciate and that only emerges in the interweaving of the opposition between the modalities of the possible and the necessary. The results of such care in the reading are worth the effort.

If the theses defended in this book are right, then economic crises do not have a single cause or a single form and all the various causes and forms presented by Marx must be combined according to the specific social conditions of each historical moment analysed. The same relativity helps us to see how the inherent tendencies of capital materialise. There are no perfectly sequential cycles or inexorable tendencies in history; capital's fatal automatism is a fetish. By reconstructing, as far as possible, the overall design of Marx's often fragmented work, the more context-specific approach developed here creates new openings for critical and revolutionary praxis.

Acknowledgements

In preparing this English version of my book, I was able to count on the help of several people and institutions to which I wish to express here my sincere gratitude.

The revision of the text as well as the addition of the postface and bibliography were made possible by research that I carried out in London in 2019 with the support of a fellowship granted by the Foundation for Research Support of the State of São Paulo (*Fundação de Amparo à Pesquisa do Estado de São Paulo*). I am also grateful to Alfredo Saad Filho for welcoming me so warmly to the School of Oriental and African Studies (SOAS) at the London University during the research period.

I would like to thank Nicolas Allen, who first translated the Introduction and Chapter 1, revised and incorporated by Martin Nicholl into his patient and meticulous work on the rest of the book. My collaboration with Martin was very productive and for that I wish to express to him my deep appreciation.

Finally, special thanks are due to my colleagues in the History Department at the University of São Paulo for their understanding during my research stays in Berlin and London.

Introduction

1 The Double Face of Capital

By characterising bourgeois civil society as a capitalist society,[1] that is, by the fundamental power that capital exercises over it, Marx likewise wished to characterise it as being subject to the crises determined by the contradictory nature of capital. And yet this connection, between capital's power over social relations and the crises intrinsic to capital, remains imperceptible to the extent that the term 'crisis' continues to be used in a customarily vague sense, trivialising and rendering imprecise its meaning by associating the word with notions of simple disintegration and decadence. In order to recover the full meaning of Marx's concept of crisis in all its richness, it is necessary to go beyond the simple negativity implied in its common usage and instead define crisis as the negativity immanent to capital, that is, the manifestation of its constitutive contradiction. It is necessary to provide a rigorous "concept of capital 'that can also account for the meaning of crisis.

Grasping the inherent negativity of capital, Marx was able to understand the dynamic of the economy in terms of a constant movement towards the overcoming and repositioning of its contradictions. As the privileged manifestation of capital's self-negation, crisis cannot be bracketed from the analysis of this general dynamic in which it indeed takes part not as a secondary aspect, but as an essential piece in the comprehension of capital's modus operandi. In that same sense, a proper study of the Marxian conception of capitalism must always offer an account of crisis, just as it must account for the way in which capital's negativity combines with supposedly 'normal' forms of reproduction so as to constitute movements in multiple, different directions, each with their own temporality.

Crisis, understood as the negativity immanent to capital, is at the core of the critique of capitalism in the specifically Marxian sense of 'critique':[2] it is

1 The term *bourgeois* employed by Marx has a long and significant history that distances it from its use and misuse in vulgar Marxism. For more on this history and for a precise definition of Marx's concept, see Riedel 1969. Riedel also wrote the entry 'Gesellschaft, bürgerliche' in volume 2 of the *Geschichtliche Grundbegriffe* published by Reinhart Koselleck, Werner Conze and Otto Brunner (1975).

2 The relation between *crisis* and *critique* is of fundamental importance for an understanding of Marx's theoretical framework. There are several classic texts that shed light on the relation between the two concepts and are obligatory reference points, in particular Habermas 1973, Röttgers 1975 and Koselleck 1988 and 2006.

 | DOI:10.1163/9789004690721_002

not a question of subjective disapproval of a social system that points out its injustices from the outside, but of the exposure of the internal and objective contradictions of that system, contradictions that, as they develop, lead the system to self-negation. However, this development does not present itself directly as the fulfilment of contradictions; it appears as the concealment and transfiguration of those contradictions in the sphere of competition, emerging before the eyes of its economic agents as the very realisation of the equality instituted by capital. It follows that the task before us is to reconstruct the procedures through which Marx was able to discover that movement of inversion and the contradictions presiding over it, and continuing from there, to associate those procedures with the objective critique that the system will perform upon itself through its own crises and the possible critique of its economic agents.

Connecting the concepts of crisis and critique similarly serves to underscore the importance of value theory, beyond even the role that the theory plays in Marx's critique of political economy: through the concept of value, Marx presents the natural, autonomous, and objective character of the categories of political economy as the semblance that capitalism creates for itself, but that it also takes care to negate. Behind that semblance are the historically given social relations that constitute the true content of Marx's economic categories. The theory of value is thus configured as the mode for adequately grasping a contradictory system and, simultaneously, as the mode through which the contradiction and its specific behaviour is presented, associating that operation by necessity with critique.[3]

3 On the definition of bourgeois society as a contradictory reality, it is worth clarifying that this book broadly endorses the point of view on the relation between Marx and Hegel offered by Hans-Friedrich Fulda in his 'These zur Dialektik als Darstellungsmethode (im 'Kapital' von Marx)' (Fulda 1974), as well as Michael Theunissen's 'Krise der Macht. Thesen zur Theorie des dialektischen Widerspruchs' (Theunissen 1974). Rejecting the traditional interpretation that the dialectic should be turned upright after Hegel turned it on its head, the authors find a solution to the problem of the relation between Hegel's and Marx's method by suggesting a different sense of the German word *Umstülpung*: a turning inside-out, as one would a glove, so that what was inside is now outside, exposed; and what was outside is now inside. According to this interpretation, Marx would have criticised the Hegelian dialectic for having turned inside-out the relation between the essence and appearance of reality, asserting that the surface of reality would appear as characterised by differences resulting from an essential unifying identity. By righting what Hegel had inverted, Marx would be asserting that the reality of bourgeois society, specifically, presents itself as the equality of all before the law, an external appearance derived from the hidden essence that is the contradiction and class inequality. Hence the dimension of critique and unveiling of apparent harmonies that the dialectic assumes in Marx's theory.

A number of twentieth-century authors have recognised the conceptual significance that crisis held in Marx's writings. The debates it inspired in Marxist circles, to be reviewed in the footnotes of the following chapters, have their origin in two difficulties: first, concerning the conceptual content of *crisis*, this was defined in varying ways throughout Marx's writings so that later authors would privilege one or another possible meaning; second, for each specific content there corresponds a determinate conception of how crisis would be fulfilled, or, put differently, a conception of how crisis passes from potentiality to actuality. This passage is studied in philosophy as a problem of modal propositions or modalities, part of which I will present and discuss in this Introduction, although the modalities problem will also reappear in all the following chapters due to its importance for resolving both older and current debates in Marxism.

It is precisely the modal perspective that allows one to examine the concept of crisis and establish whether the contents of this concept, isolated or combined in some fashion, can offer explanations about how crisis itself is realised. That is, it makes it possible to establish the potentially self-negating determinations of capital that are enacted through its realisation. For example, according to a given content, crisis will only be fulfilled as a possibility, whereas with another it will necessarily become reality.

The consequences of these modal determinations are decisive. Firstly, insofar as crisis is a basic element of the global capitalist dynamic, a given modality makes it possible to determine whether the boom and contraction cycles of capital accumulation and capital's long-term tendencies are determined necessarily or are simply possible. If they are not necessary, then the very concepts of cycle and tendency must be revised, because a cycle or a tendency that could potentially not occur, or occur otherwise then how it took place, does not correspond with the features generally attributed to those concepts. Secondly, the modalities of crisis are also fundamental to the concept in another, specific sense related to critique. If, according to one of its contents, crisis were to be considered as necessary, it would be possible to foresee the inevitable collapse of capitalism. However, if all its contents were merely possible, capitalism could forestall the impact of its crises and maintain itself indefinitely. This, precisely, was one of the main issues in the Marxist debates around the classical 'theory of collapse' [*Zusammenbruchstheorie*]: would a final crisis of capitalism consummate its self-negation as an objective critique?

This case illustrates nicely how the modalities perspective can complement the study of crises. With that perspective, it becomes possible to establish a limit between what the concept of crisis does or does not authorise in terms of a prognosis of capitalism's future. If according to a given content crisis were merely possible, then explanations and forecasts based on that possibility could not be regarded as inevitable. If according to its content crisis were necessary, in the sense that the contrary occurrence of normal accumulation was impossible, then the realisation of a crisis could be explained or foreseen as inevitable. In fact, what we are outlining here is the limit between what is pronounced as a possibility and what is pronounced as the necessity inherent to capital, because pronouncing the possible as if it were necessary means extrapolating on the limits of explanation or foresight, asserting dogmatically and under scientific pretences the predominance of one possibility over others.

Establishing the limits between what can and cannot be said about the concept of crisis means differentiating between those of capital's cyclical movements and tendencies that possess a necessary character and those that are simply possibilities; it means distinguishing between those elements that are merely possible and those that are necessary in the determination of the real movement of capitalism. Moreover, where the nexus between crisis and critique are concerned, grasping this limit means being able to pinpoint within crisis that which is an expression of the negativity intrinsic to capital; that is, that which could be considered as an objective self-critique of capitalism. By applying this optic, it is possible to shed new light on traditional Marxist debates: instead of questioning the legitimacy of each interpretation, the objective instead becomes to determine to what extent these interpretations are not in fact extrapolations of the prognostic capacity of Marx's theory, conferring upon that theory an exaggerated, erroneous or dogmatic quality.

The latter concern happens to be the main purpose of this book. On the one hand, the undeniable potential of Marx's theory must be duly acknowledged, as much for its analysis of the foundations of capitalist functioning as for its radical critique. On the other hand, those aspects of critique that are capable of preventing exorbitant conclusions need to be equally stressed: in other words, precisely those conclusions not legitimised by Marx's original formulations. In order to establish a limit between legitimate and illegitimate deductions, between what can and cannot be derived from Marxian analysis (cannot, because it extrapolates from its constitutive determinations), it is therefore vital to perform a careful reconstruction that clarifies how Marx's theory itself imposes such limits.

The reasons why this undertaking is so difficult are the same as those that led many Marxist authors to draw exorbitant conclusions: the diverse definitions of crisis throughout Marx's work and the problems related to establishing a modality associated with each of these distinct definitions. Each chapter and subchapter in this book represent an attempt to deal with the variety of definitions and modalities. But even at the outset, here in this introduction, we must deal in some detail with the difficulties involved in this endeavour and the solutions being proposed.

2 Content of the Crisis

The difficulties involved in providing Marx's concept of crisis with a single, definite content stems firstly from the fact that his initial plan had been to only present the concept in a systematic way at the end of his work, as the culminating point in his studies of capital and the principal social relations and institutions of capitalism. When Marx subsequently abandoned his original project to write six volumes, several topics that were intended for development after the first volume (on capital) ended up being incorporated into the finished version of the latter.[4] With that, the presentation of the concept of crisis not only would no longer serve as a conclusive synthesis reserved for the 1857 project, it would also be dispersed throughout the three volumes of the definitive version, acquiring in the process an apparently fragmentary and disordered character.

And yet, this in no way meant that Marx neglected the issue or that it would be impossible to establish a clear and distinct content for crisis, nor, much less, that the concept was demoted by Marx within the broader framework of his theory. We should bear in mind that the concept of crisis, within the original plan of the six volumes, was associated with the study of the world market: crises were to be treated as a phenomenon of global scope that spread across the world economy exactly insofar as capital itself did the same. The crisis of the world market is the negative correlation of capital at the final point of its expansion, and the concept of crisis is here most complex and all-encompassing. But crisis is already at hand in the early stages of presentation

4 Rosdolsky 1978 [1968] was perhaps the first to present a full account of the modifications through which Marx's originally formulated 6-books plan from 1857 went until it arrived in the 3-book version of *Capital*. Crisis would nominally appear, along with the world market, only in the sixth book conceived in 1857, as well as in the manuscripts from 1863. Rosdolsky explains how the content of the final version of *Capital* absorbed most of the content from the second and third book of the original plan, namely, on the rent of land and on wage labour. I argue that at least the concept of crisis from the last book was also absorbed in the 1867 version and spread over its various sections and chapters. This argument is not shaken by the debate that arose after Rosdolsky on the modifications in the structure of Marx's work and the fate of the concept of 'capital in general'; see Heinrich 1989 and 1999, and Moseley 1995 and 2016.

as the negative of capital's impulse to growth. It follows that a reconstruction of the steps through which the concept of capital came to be identified with an expansive and totalising process must necessarily also involve a reconstruction of the steps through which the concept was identified with the potential for capital's self-negation.

In other words, one need not wait patiently until the end of Marx's work to come across the concept of crisis; this concept is present from the beginning and all throughout the development of the concept of capital, although often only implicitly and in an unthematised manner, as the negative element contained within each form that capital assumes. Without the complete and conclusive treatment that Marx had intended for the sixth volume of his 1857 plan, it is difficult to determine the content of crisis, and it can only be accomplished through a successful reconstruction of the concept of *capital*, which for its part only emerges from its systematic presentation. Therefore, this book is divided into four chapters that follow the four basic moments in which I set out to reconstruct the concept of capital in parallel with the concept of crisis.

Before addressing the overall organisation of this book, however, it will be necessary to return once again to the Marxian presentation of the concept of capital. We must clarify how Marx defines this presentation and how its unfolding differs from capital's historical and systemic development.

The order in which the economic categories should be presented became a central methodological concern for Marx when, beginning in 1857, he set out to systematically organise the results of his research on political economy. This was not a simple concatenation of propositions, but instead, and above all else, an attempt to find an adequate definition for capital beyond the apparently autonomous and juxtaposed forms it assumes in everyday phenomena. It was inevitable that through that endeavour Marx would come into confrontation with the works of classic economists. Although he considered David Ricardo as the last great representative of political economy, Marx criticised him because:

> when he analyses the *value* of the commodity, he at once allows himself to be influenced by considerations of all kinds of concrete conditions. On the other hand, one must reproach him for regarding the phenomenal form as *immediate and direct* proof or exposition of the general laws, never *developing* them.[5]

Beyond that:

5 Marx 1969b, p. 106. The German edition will be cited in brackets [1967, p. 100].

> With Ricardo the one-sidedness arises also from the fact that in general he wants to show that the various economic categories or relationships *do not contradict the theory of value*, instead of on the contrary, *developing* them together with their apparent contradictions out of this basis or presenting the development of this basis itself.[6]

Marx's critical methodology thus consists in recognising that Ricardo correctly grasped value as the 'basis' and 'general law' of the capitalist economy, but failed to see it 'developing' according to 'various economic categories or relationships' founded on value as 'basis'. Ricardo, on Marx's reading, would have exposed the 'categories or relationships' in an 'immediate and direct' fashion as the 'phenomenal form' of value, limiting his concerns 'to show that the various economic categories or relationships do not contradict the theory of value'. However, 'developing' categories means 'presenting the development of this basis itself … together with their apparent contradictions'. For Marx, Ricardo should have addressed this contradiction, because only in that way would it be possible to understand the movement of mediations involved in the concept of value, constituted by the forms in which the contradiction appears and is resolved and renewed. This movement, opposite to the 'immediacy' criticised by Marx, follows a path from the contradictory 'basis' to its 'phenomenal forms', that is, the path from the 'development' of the categories themselves, which can only be conceived by accepting that the derived economic categories contradict their own 'basis'. This would all be nonsense if it were not also admitted that the very 'basis' appears in the form of a contradiction whose resolution and constant repositioning produces a successive 'development' of the 'various economic categories'.

The Marxian project of presentation is thus based on grasping the capitalist economic 'basis' – the concepts of *value* and *capital* – as the contradiction that sets in motion a process through which the contradiction develops to the point that it envelops the entire set of economic relations as a totality. In this totality, each economic relation, each category, is linked to another as the 'phenomenal form' of the all-encompassing contradiction. Here, Marx is not far from the Hegelian concept of presentation [*Darstellung*], while at the same time, in order to uphold the possibility of a materialist dialectic, he seeks to untangle the idealist elements involved in Hegel's speculative philosophy.

As will become clear throughout this book, Marx is able to present these categories due to his conception of capital as a double social relation. Firstly,

6 Marx 1969b, p. 146 [1967, p. 150].

capital subordinates labour power, creator of value and surplus value, reducing it to a 'moment' of a totality. Secondly, through that subordination, labour power is impeded from effectively constituting itself as a totality that reduces capital to a simple 'moment'. Capital thus posits labour power as one of its 'moments', although it excludes it and disallows its constitution as a possible whole.[7] By asserting and simultaneously negating the source of value upon which it takes shape and is defined, capital negates itself, entering into self-contradiction precisely due to its tendency to compose an exclusive totality that presides over the sum of economic relations.

Marx discovers in capital's totalising drive a substrate upon which he then defines an autonomous object that can and must be presented independently from external conditions; this same object, according to Marx, tends to subsume the rest of existing social relations while rendering them intelligible. In this way, Marx is not performing a simple construction that would frame a possible object: 'Those who consider the autonomisation of value as a mere abstraction forget that the movement of industrial capital is this abstraction in action'.[8] As will be addressed in chapter 1, section 1.3, the opposition between abstract labour and concrete labour, and consequently between value and use-value, is not the result of an abstract mental practice put forward by the theoretician, but rather a real-effective product of the mode in which capital is constituted as a specific object, where theory must restrict itself to reproducing and presenting that abstraction through concepts.

All this notwithstanding, since capital's totalising tendency takes place in a contradictory form, its presentation can and must reconstitute the stages of the determination of this tendency according to its own logic – that of the contradiction. Marx thus seeks to overcome what he criticises as the superficial mode of presenting the categories in classical political economy. These two essential and interrelated aspects – the tendency to subordinate all social relations and the contradictory form that this subordination assumes – is what configures capital in such a way that its concept must be presented as a series of moments in a dialectical unfolding.

However, while using the expression 'moment', employed here in the context of the presentation, we should take care not to interpret this dialectical unfolding of concepts in such a way that it reproduces the historical development of its corresponding objects, that is, assuming that the conceptual order should

7 For more on this entire line of reasoning and in particular the fundamental concept of *moment* that Marx critically adopts from Hegel's logic, see chapter 2, section 2.1 below.

8 Marx 1978, p. 185 [1963, p. 109].

follow the sequence of historical phenomena and that its validity should be based on its accompaniment of these phenomena. In the words of Marx in *Grundrisse*:

> It would therefore be unfeasible and wrong to let the economic categories follow one another in the same sequence as that which they were historically decisive. Their sequence is determined, rather, by their relation to one another in modern bourgeois society, which is precisely the opposite of that which seems their natural order or which corresponds to historical development. The point is not the historic position of the economic relations in the succession of different forms of society. Even less is it their sequence 'in the idea' (Proudhon) … Rather, their order [*Gliederung*] within modern bourgeois society.[9]

Hence, the presentation of categories in *Capital* does not reflect the 'historically decisive' sequence. It does not reveal the history of capitalism, beginning, as it might, with the pre-capitalist social relations, going on to describe the rise of 'modern bourgeois society'. The presentation of economic categories does however depend on its 'order', on its articulation [*Gliederung*] 'within modern bourgeois society', taking the latter as a consolidated fact. This articulation is expressed in the relation established by the economic categories among one another within the larger framework of the definition of the concept of capital.

The categorical presentation also does not reflect 'their sequence "in the idea"', as if it were a logical deduction of concepts based on concepts, in a dialectic of pure thought independent of its object. Therefore, in a footnote to the *Grundrisse*, as a reminder to himself and as a form of self-admonishment, Marx writes:

> It will be necessary later, before this question is dropped, to correct the idealist manner of the presentation, which makes it seem as if it were merely a matter of conceptual determinations and of the dialectic of these concepts.[10]

While the primary aim of *Capital* is not to create a historical narrative, the concepts deployed in the work take as their reference a historically constituted

9 Marx 1974, pp. 107–8 [1983, p. 41].
10 Marx 1974, p. 152 [1983, p. 85].

object, not the eternal, natural and singular form of social production. For this same reason, many 'moments' of the presentation depend on historical presuppositions, evidencing the impossibility of a mere conceptual-logical deduction.

Hence the radical distinction between Marx's definition of presentation and that of Hegel's *Science of Logic*. In the Hegelian definition, the presentation describes the emergence and development of the concept as simultaneous with its corresponding real object. This is the 'idealist manner' that Marx seeks to avoid, whereby the 'dialectic of concepts' seems to produce and reproduce the effective dialectic of the object. However, here is not the place to discuss Marx's critique of Hegel on this topic; what is relevant here is that Marx drew on this critique to establish his well-known distinction between the 'method of inquiry' and the 'method of presentation', which he outlines in the following terms:

> The latter [*inquiry*] has to appropriate the material in detail, to analyse its different forms of development and to track down their inner connection. Only after this work has been done can the real movement be appropriately presented. If this is done successfully, if the life of the subject-matter is now reflected back in the ideas, then it may appear as if we have before us an *a priori* construction.[11]

For Marx, the real development of the object cannot be reconstituted through the presentation of its concept, since the reality is not governed by the dialectic of the concept that becomes effective in its exposition. This line of thought would apply to the Hegelian philosophical project, in which Reason contains within itself the power to self-realise, consisting precisely in that power of realisation. By contrast, Marx's object – capital – has no consciousness of its power for realisation and its immanent rationality (see chapter 2, section 2.1), which must be uncovered through prior investigation into the 'inner connection' of the object. Moreover, the 'real movement' of Marx's object is given under forms that, in the sphere of commodity circulation and competition, invert and conceal their 'inner connection'. For this reason, 'inquiry' is also tasked with finding an 'appropriate' mode of presentation that would reveal the 'inner connection' behind the forms of concealment and explain the necessary relation between this 'connection' and the inverted appearance of its visible manifestations.

By confirming this inversion, Marx's proposed 'method of inquiry' does not seek to deny the forms in which the object is manifested, nor smuggle within

11 Marx 1976a, p. 102 [1962, p. 27].

the posterior 'method of presentation' any subjective hypotheses added by the researcher; it is solely seeking to present the forms of manifestation as the inverse of the 'inner connection', that is to say, as contradictory rather than harmonious forms.[12] Having done so, the 'method of presentation' can assume the 'appropriate' form for this inversion as is revealed in the immanent rationality of the object. The researcher's task is restricted to tracing the 'real movement' of which the object itself is not conscious. This is the 'life of the subject-matter' being presented. Nevertheless, since the forms of manifestation invert the contradictory 'inner connection' of the object, it appears as if the researcher had imposed on it an external 'dialectic of concepts', applying a dialectical method as 'an *a priori* construction'.

Once this appearance of subjectivity has been discarded, the 'inner connection' is revealed as the contradictory totality that contains within itself the power to subsume the other economic relations that must be presented in that double determination – of a force both totalising and contradictory. It follows that the 'method of presentation' must reconstitute the connection between the variety of social forms as the unfolding of mediating stages through which the definition of capital is gradually enriched, until the point that its definition has reached its most complex, most 'concrete' point,[13] in a movement whose finality is to configure the passage from the 'inner connection' of the object to the forms of manifestation as a deduction of categories.

Here it is important to emphasise that this is not a 'dialectic of concepts', as seen above, nor an immediate relation between things: 'What is at issue here is not a set of definitions under which things are to be subsumed. It is rather determined functions that are expressed in determined categories'.[14] It is the social 'function' that decides what a 'thing' is and what is its conceptual 'definition'. For example, one and the same thing can be defined as the means of

12 This interpretation comes from Marx's critique of Hegel, as I have outlined in footnote 3 above and will explain in this book.

13 'Concrete' not in the sense of the tangible, immediately empirical, but rather the 'concentration of many determinations', according to the Introduction to 1857. See Marx 1974, p. 101 [1983, p. 35].

14 Marx 1978, p. 303 [1963, p. 228]. Translation slightly modified by me. An important explanation appears immediately above the text: 'Just as we have shown how, in the labour process (volume 1, chapter 7), it depends entirely on the role which the objective components play at the time in a particular labour process, on their function, whether they function as means of labour, material of labour or product, so, in precisely the same way, means of labour are fixed capital only where the production process is in fact a capitalist production process and the means of production are thus actually capital, i.e. possess the economic determination, the social character, of capital' (Marx 1978, p. 228 [1963, p. 303]).

production or as a consumption good according to the 'determined function' that capital assigns it in its process of self-constitution, that is, according to its appearance within the framework of immediate production, circulation, or in the unity of both spheres. For this reason, the categories do not refer to things themselves, but instead to the function capital attributes to them according to the specific moment of the constitution of their corresponding concept; and the presentation of these categories assumes the character of a progressive enrichment of their content, because those functions are complexified by degree within capital's totalising movement.

Having shed some light on the presentation in *Capital*, we can return to the opening of this subchapter with a better understanding of why the concept of crisis is also enriched insofar as it refers to progressively more complex 'functions' corresponding to the stages in the development of the concept of capital. Both concepts are presented as closely related, so that when the concept of capital refers to a particular content, so too the concept of crisis must refer to a corresponding content; and when there is a shift from one level of presentation to a higher degree of comprehensiveness or complexity in the content of the concept of capital, the concept of crisis should reflect that same passage. The correspondence between these successive contents permits and defines the method used in this book: the varying concepts of crisis present in Marx's critique of political economy will be interconnected by reconstituting the gradual connection of the content of the concept of capital in its successive stages.

Thus, the following chapters of this book seek to explain the meaning of crisis in what I consider to be the four main moments in the definition of the concept of capital as presented in the last version left by Marx of his most important work. The first chapter deals with the sphere of simple circulation of commodities prior to the constitution of capital in Marx's development of categories, although already presided over by the latter in reality; this topic corresponds to the first part of *Capital* Volume I. The second chapter looks at the remaining parts of Volume I concerned with the sphere of the immediate production of commodities that establishes the fundamental determinations of capital. The third chapter examines the sphere of capital circulation as it appears in *Capital* Volume II. Finally, the fourth chapter addresses the sphere of global capitalist production as presented in the first three Parts of Volume III, which synthesises the determinations of the aforementioned spheres and wherein the concepts proposed by Marx's inquiry attain their highest degree of complexity.

My purpose here is not to undertake a possible development of Marx's theory of crises, applying this theory to specific problems of advanced capitalism or to the diverse debates in recent economic literature; my purpose is even less to empirically verify the truth that the prognoses of crisis might contain. These purposes would require, at the outset, a minimal consensus and an adequate general understanding about Marx's writings on crises, which are a long way off. By limiting myself to reconstituting the concept of crisis in what might be called its immanent presence in *Capital*, I have attempted to assess the potentialities as well as the limits of Marx's critical analyses of the destination and dynamics of capitalism. Only by knowing such limits is it possible to grasp the problems at stake in the recent literature devoted to developing Marxian theory, and, furthermore, it is only with these limits in mind that the eventual imprecisions and exaggerations emerging from that enterprise become intelligible.

3 Crisis and Modality

Discussion of Marx's analysis of crisis has always been characterised by divergence in terms of the concept's content, but also around its explanatory role for capitalist dynamics and this social system's future. However, for the most part, the antagonistic positions share the correct idea that, for Marx, crisis is constitutive and inherent to capital. They recognise that Marx goes against classical political economy, which held that crises are accidental results without any deep connection to the system of economic relations. In fact, Marx sought to define crisis within all the spheres of capital development since the circulation of commodities, in which crisis appears as a disturbance in the course of purchase and sale, that is, in the exchange between the value forms of commodity and money.

Nevertheless, according to Marx: 'These forms alone do not explain why their critical aspect becomes prominent and why the potential contradiction contained in them becomes a contradiction *in actu*'.[15] It must be observed that Marx describes the realisation of crisis here in the traditional Aristotelian philosophical terms,[16] that is, in terms of a passage from *potentia* to *actu*. Marx

15 Marx 1969b, p. 512 [1967, p. 513].

16 As a preliminary historical remark, the issue of the passage from 'potentiality' to 'actuality' emerged in Book Theta of Aristotle's *Metaphysics* and was developed in his book on *Interpretation* in the context of his debate with the Megaric School, especially Diodorus Cronus, concerning the necessity and contingency of that which exists. Against fatalism, Aristotle asserts the freedom of man and natural contingency, defending that certain capacities existing in 'potential' but not yet in 'act' should remain always in potential, as a simple possibility. By contrast, Diodorus Cronus proposes in his 'master argument' to interpret 'potentiality' as necessity and that it would be possible to foresee with certainty

makes it clear that crises – the 'critical' element mentioned in the text – must be explained as a passage to '*actu*' of that which is initially only 'potential', which, in other words, is the 'contradiction contained' in the value-form. The meaning of this passage is made clearer in the second part of the text: 'If one asks what its cause is, one wants to know why *its abstract form*, the form of its possibility, turns from possibility into *actuality*'.[17]

'Potential' here means, above all, 'possibility'. The translation into modern terms of the Latin words, from the first to the second text, suggests that 'potentiality' describes not only the capacity of the contradiction to determine a crisis, but also the 'possibility' of whether this crisis would occur, as opposed to its 'actuality', the '*actu*' in which it already is occurring. The text thus invites us to mobilise the entire spectrum of categories from classical modal logic, where 'actuality' emerges from 'possibility' through the mediation of 'necessity'. In this sense, 'potentiality' corresponds more closely to the capacity to determine something as necessary, that is, something that occurs by excluding the possibility of its non-occurrence.

However, the appearance of modal categories in Marx's texts does not follow the sequence of a logical deduction; there is no application of modal logic at work that would be external to his specific object. As mentioned in the previous subchapter, Marx's object, capital, is conceived as a social relation with the power to subordinate all other social relations, making itself into the totality of which the other relations are simple component parts. In other words, according to Marx's own definition, capital possesses a totalising force, a 'potentiality' for the realisation of its constitutive determinations. It follows that the task before us is to investigate how each of these determinations is realised, or, in other words, if these determinations only possibly 'turn into actuality' or if they do so necessarily. Doing so, the study of modalities will be confirmed not only

future events. For a careful examination of these definitions in ancient philosophy, see, for example, Pape 1956–7, Vuillemin 1984, Gaskin, 1995. In modern philosophy the analysis of modalities must undoubtedly consider the solution proposed by Leibniz (1998), who distinguished between necessary or universal necessity and contingent or singular necessity, concepts from which Hegel developed his own concepts of absolute necessity and relative or real necessity at the end of the 'Doctrine of Essence' (2010). These are the works that must have inspired the way Marx conceived the realisation of the immanent tendencies of capital, including those of crisis. The problem was dealt with in an exemplary way by Michel Vadée (1992), for whom the fundamental modality present in Marx's work is that of the 'possible', associated with freedom in political action. Although I agree with the decisive importance of freedom in Marx's thought, I associate freedom with the modality of 'relative necessity', as will be developed throughout this book.

17 Marx 1969b, p. 515 [1967, p. 515].

for its adequacy in the study of crises, but moreover for its fundamental importance for understanding the nature of crises.

The difficulties involved in this undertaking spring from the lack of a clear and specific methodological reflection in Marx's modal approach: in some passages he refers to the crisis as a 'general possibility' or a 'formal possibility'; by contrast, in others his reasoning undoubtedly suggest that crisis is determined as the realisation of a necessity inherent to capital's self-negating essence. As will be discussed in Chapter 4, by explaining the reasons behind why capital's destructive tendencies do not render its existence immediately unviable, Marx often asserts that in the long-term those tendencies end up being the most prevalent, so that the necessity of crisis would eventually assume an inevitable character.

These apparent oscillations in Marx's text are what authorise the opposed versions of capitalism's final destination, from the classic Marxist polemics of the early twentieth century to the most recent theories of long and short-term cycles. In order to avoid these interminable debates, it is necessary to overcome the unilateral approach with which each version privileges one modality of the crisis, and to overcome the apparent ambiguity of Marx's own text. This in turn requires a differentiation between two levels of problems: first, the way in which the explanation of crisis grows progressively more complex and precise through the categorial presentation in *Capital*; and second, the way in which the explanation of crisis proposed by Marx in *Capital* Volume III tries to synthesise the previous explanations.

Therefore, insofar as the categorial presentation develops the connection between different aspects and stages of the concept of capital, it also develops the stages and modes through which capital realises its 'potential', rendering effective its essential determinations, including the self-negating determination that defines crisis. For example, when focus is placed narrowly on the circulation of commodities and capital, 'possibility' appears as the predominant modality that explains the occurrence of crisis and the one through which the determination of crisis becomes 'actuality'. If, however, focus is placed on the immediate production of commodities by capital, a different modality appears as predominant, explaining crisis as the *necessary* realisation of the inherent determination of capital towards self-negation. Hence, insofar as the presentation of categories reconstructs the concept of capital as a totalising force, it likewise reconstitutes the stages through which this totalising force and its crisis – the contrary, though no less intrinsic force – become effective, passing from mere possibility to necessity.

Many authors who have discussed and still discuss the question of capitalism's final destination on the basis of Marx's theory make the mistake of holding fast to a modality that corresponds to an intermediary stage in the presentation of categories, taking that stage as Marx's definitive explanation of crisis while failing to notice that there is a development of the modal perspective corresponding to the development of concepts. In fact, in the initial and intermediary passages of this development, possibility is the predominant mode through which capital's self-negation is realised in crises. At the final point in the development of the categories, however, when the sphere of circulation and immediate production are united, it is necessity that predominates over possibility, to such an extent that crisis may even seem inevitable, whether that be in the form of collapse or the cyclical return of the negative tendency.

It is important to understand the link between the categorial presentation and the development of modalities through which capital's determinations become effective, because, through this link, it is possible to distinguish provisional from final forms of the Marxian explanation of crisis; one can grasp how such forms are organised together with the development of Marxian theory. Thus, by reconstructing the concept of crisis according to the four levels that form the basis for the four chapters of this book, we will also be reconstructing the order of modalities according to which Marx considered the determination of crisis as the passage from 'potentiality' to 'actuality'.

We shall soon see how by overcoming the 'formal possibility' of crises in the sphere of circulation, Marx is able to repel the idea that crises would be merely contingent, that is, occurrences determined from outside the capitalist system. Instead, he pursues their systemic determination, immanent to capitalism and, thus, 'necessary'. But we shall likewise see that his concept of necessity is complex, not least of all because it allows room for contingency and because it is manifested in everyday economic phenomena as 'formal possibility', but most of all because it refers to opposed determinations that are always coexisting in a contradictory totality formed by capital. If this totality were not permanently contradictory, one given determination could prevail over another and become the only factually necessary one. That is, it would consequently be what I call 'absolute' necessity. But since this is not the case, the necessity for the realisation of crisis is not an absolute necessity, making its inevitability problematic.

This is not merely an issue of whether a crisis is possible or necessary, or between a determination that is internal or external to the capitalist system. The difficulty leading to confusion among those who have studied this issue centres on the status of the necessity of crises and the 'laws' of capitalist movement in general in Marx's writings. My own proposal here is to revisit the concept of 'relative' necessity, with the purpose of understanding how, for Marx, a crisis is necessarily determined by capital. According to this concept, necessity is 'relative' insofar as it depends on elements external to it in order to realise that which is 'potential', elements that are conditioning to the point that necessity would only be necessity through their mediation.[18]

Through the definition of the peculiar necessity regulating capital's movement and crisis, the primary aim of this book will be accomplished by establishing the limit between what can and cannot be said about capital's dynamic, its crises, and its destiny.

While 'absolute' necessity would provide capital with the power to determine the univocal realisation of its potentialities fully and endogenously, 'relative' necessity would mean that, for its realisation, capital would always resolve the conflict between its opposed and equally necessary dispositions. The central difficulty lies in the decision between the two forms. Having solved this difficulty, I will have achieved my main objective. Then I hope to show that Marx's position on the role of contingency, despite certain passages in his writing that suggest the inevitability of crisis, draws critical affinities with the positions of Aristotle and Hegel, although less so for the specific content of his exposition and more in a general sense: like them, Marx too rejects simplistic fatalism.

18 Although 'relative' and 'absolute' are terms not explicitly related to necessity in Marx's texts, I think they are plausible and perfectly suited to the way Marx develops the problem of the realisation of potential tendencies and countertendencies. The origin of these terms is, in fact, the Hegelian interpretation of the corresponding Aristotelian modal categories. See Hegel 2010, pp. 482–8 [1986, II, pp. 207–13]. As I hope to show, the overcoming of 'relative' by 'absolute' necessity is impossible in Marx, for whom the Hegelian determinations of capital must always remain within the framework of the 'relative' necessity because neither tendencies nor countertendencies can dominate one another.

CHAPTER 1

The World of Commodity Producers

1 The Social Division of Labour

1.1 *The Problem of the Beginning*

As heir to England's seventeenth-century liberal-revolutionary tradition, political economy remained optimistic about the capacity of society to adequately allocate its available resources throughout the different branches of social production. To this end, it relied on the division of labour, carried out through the exchange of products on the market. The progressive specialisation would make each individual producer more and more independent of the others as a producer in a particular craft, but would also make him more dependent as a consumer. Therefore, the division of labour and the exchange of commodities would be two opposite and complementary aspects of an integrative process that would guarantee and even promote the development of individuality. This development would in turn allow for an increasingly greater mobilisation of resources across different sectors of the economy, depending on the advantage or disadvantage that each sector provided. Hence Adam Smith's famous theorem of the 'invisible hand', asserting that advantages and disadvantages in specific sectors would be compensated in the overall economy, so that there would never be an excess of production nor a general crisis.

In line with the project announced in the subtitle of *Capital*, 'a Critique of Political Economy', Marx proposes a refutation of the 'invisible hand's' optimism, showing that, even in the terms of classical economics, the system does indeed entail general crises. Such demonstration called for a resumption of these presuppositions in order to reorganise and present them in a different light from that in which political economy had previously shown them. The result of this conceptual reorganisation eventually became the first Part of *Capital* Volume I, in which Marx presents 'the simple circulation of commodities' and describes a system not unlike that of the classical economists, although he reaches surprising conclusions by taking classical concepts, such as the *division of labour* and *value*, to their ultimate conclusion. The analysis of Marx is the focus of the present first chapter, whose objective is to explain the simplest conceptual content of crisis and crisis as a mere possibility.

Nevertheless, to understand the rearticulation undertaken by Marx means going beyond the definition of the concepts and paying close attention to the form in which they are presented. On the one hand, one must examine in

 | DOI:10.1163/9789004690721_003

detail the sequence of deductions through which concepts are defined, from the concept of commodity to that of money in its diverse functions. Following this mode of presentation, exchange emerges as a process constituted by a fundamental opposition and apprehended in increasingly rich determinations as its component phases unfold. The unfolding of this opposition in the exchange process is what will reveal the conceptual content of crisis in the sphere of the simple circulation of commodities. It should then be the subject of a careful analysis.

On the other hand, concepts like *value* and *abstract labour* must be clearly defined, since it is on the opposition that constitutes their content that all formal distinctions and all phases of the presentation undertaken by Marx are derived. Therefore, despite the reciprocal determination of form and content, the analysis of the form in which the concepts are derived in the simple circulation of commodities will be outlined in chapter 1, section 2.1, after chapter 1, section 1.3, where we shall analyse the content of these concepts. Before reaching that point, however, it is still necessary to understand the broader context in which the very content of the two fundamental concepts of the simple circulation of commodities are determined. *Value* and *abstract labour* are key categories for an understanding of the Marxian project of a critical restructuring of political economy, associated with a new perception of the division of labour and the specifically bourgeois forms of sociability. It is this perception that must be grasped as the basis for Marx's critique: beyond the strictly economic dimension, here the social dimension of the Marxian concept of *value* is what matters. In this context, the concept of crisis assumes centrality in the critique of capitalism and for this reason Marx would fault political economy for having relegated crisis to a secondary role.

This first section of Chapter 1 will examine the concept of *value* within the broader framework in which Marx defines the foundations of bourgeois sociability and its peculiar division of labour. This also entails explaining how such foundations are hidden from their beginning at the level of simple circulation, appearing transfigured and inverted before the eyes of economic agents. The modes of transfiguration and inversion conceal crisis and impede agents from perceiving it as being intrinsic to capital already in the elementary forms of commodity and money. Therefore, the analysis must begin by signalling the specific aspect of *value* that relates it to the figures of its self-inversion and discovers the inherently negative aspect proper to it, which it systematically conceals. Only then will it be possible to gain insight into the way in which crisis is already present in the sphere of simple circulation of commodities, defining the content of its concepts and the way in which Marx successively and dialectically deduces these concepts.

1.2 *The Fetishism of Commodities*

The distinctiveness of Marxian theory has always, at its roots, been based on its interest in apprehending bourgeois social relations in their specificity. These relations form a system that is different from all previous or even contemporary ones where the social division of labour is based on other principles. At first sight, the division of labour is something universal, insofar as any economic system must organise the division of tasks and products among its members. The way in which it carries this out and the differences between its principles of social division would be of secondary importance. However, this first impression vanishes as soon as the deeper reasons that preside over the forms of distribution are found. In the well-known *Introduction* of 1857, Marx states:

> before distribution can be the distribution of products, it is: (1) the distribution of the instruments of production, and (2), which is a further specification of the same relation, the distribution of the members of society among the different kinds of production (subsumption of the individuals under specific relations of production). The distribution of products is evidently only a result of this distribution, which is comprised within the process of production itself and determines the structure [*Gliederung*] of production.[1]

The distribution 'of the members of society among the different kinds of production' is a 'further specification' or consequence of 'the distribution of the instruments of production' among them. In order to determine the specialisation of individuals in the diverse branches of the economy, the division of labour first distributes the means of production, defining some individuals as the owners of those means and others as excluded from that ownership. In *Capital* Volume III Marx concludes the reasoning:

1 Marx 1974, p. 96 [1983, p. 31]. It must be observed that the original 'distribution of the instruments of production' 'determines the structure [*Gliederung*] of production', but the latter 'is comprised within the process of production itself'. This apparent paradox is clarified in Marx 1974, p. 97 [Ibid.], so that distribution of ownership of the means of production is initially presupposed for production, but later becomes its 'historic product'. Moreover, Marx distinguishes between immediate production, that is, product-creating activity, and production as a social system in which moments of consumption and distribution are contained. Although, strictly speaking, production is also determined by other moments, in the broader sense of 'mode of production' it embraces conditions and transforms its own presuppositions, turning them into the result of its own process.

> It is in each case the direct relationship of the owners of the conditions of production to the immediate producers … in which we find the innermost secret, the hidden basis of the entire social edifice.[2]

What characterises bourgeois society is that in it are differentiated 'the owners of the conditions of production' and the 'immediate producers', who are not owners. However, at the level of categorial presentation in which Marx outlines the presuppositions of political economy, such a distinction is still not decisive. At this level, producers are defined as owners of the means of production, so that society is basically defined as composed of private producers.

Most importantly, the appropriation of the means of production is already defined here as a form of private property that makes each producer into an autonomous, specialised individual, each one different from all the others. Of course, labour in this 'social edifice' also has a social aspect. Marx pursues this idea in texts immediately following the *Grundrisse*. In 1859's *Contribution to the Critique of Political Economy*, for instance, he writes: 'Labour, thus measured by time, does not seem, indeed, to be the labour of different persons, but on the contrary the different working individuals seem to be mere organs of *this* labour'.[3] What the text presents in the first place is social labour, which realises the 'subsumption of the individuals under specific relations of production' (see text at footnote 1 above) as its 'organs'. As 'organs', however, individuals are differentiated within the totality of social labour and, in second place, their autonomisation is a basic moment in the constitution of that totality. The draft of *Contribution to the Critique of Political Economy*, written towards the end of 1858, states:

> If the individual produces as a private individual – *so that this position of his is itself not in any sense a product of Nature but a refined result* of a social process – the social character reveals itself in that in the content of his labour the individual is determined by the social connection and works only as its member, i.e., to satisfy the wants of all the others – so that the social dependence exists for him …[4]

On the one hand, the individual becomes autonomous according to the private character of the ownership of the means of labour, resulting from the specific social process that determines his individual 'position'. On the other hand, to

2 Marx 1981, p. 927 [1964, pp. 799–800].
3 Marx 1976b, p. 272 [1961, p. 18].
4 Marx 1976b, p. 470 [1980, p. 55].

the extent that labour is immediately private, the 'social character' of labour also acquires a specific form: the 'content of the labour' of the individual, its unique materiality, is defined because the individual 'works only as a member' in the social link, that is, attending to 'the wants of all the others'. Hence, in Marx' terms, 'the independence of individual production is supplemented with a social dependence that finds a corresponding expression in the division of labour'.[5] With the distribution of the instruments of production that autonomise individuals as private owners, the social division evolves, and the individuals become more dependent on the labour of others to fulfil their own needs. Therefore, Marx asserts: 'I produce for myself only by producing for the society, each of whose members, for his part, works for me in another circle'.[6]

Due to the tendency towards increasing specialisation, the product of an individual's labour is less and less directed towards the consumption of its own producer and is more and more determined by the needs of other producers. It follows that the multiple necessities of each producer will be met by the products of others, forming an exchange network. In *Capital* Marx says:

> From this moment on, the labour of the individual producer acquires a twofold social character. On the one hand, it must, as a definite useful kind of labour, satisfy a definite social need, and thus maintain its position as an element of the total labour, as a branch of the social division of labour, which originally sprang up spontaneously. On the other hand, it can satisfy the manifold needs of the individual producer himself only in so far as every particular kind of useful private labour can be exchanged with, i.e. counts as the equal of, every other kind of useful private labour.[7]

The 'social character' attributed to individual labour means firstly that this labour must 'satisfy a definite social need'; in other words, 'social character' refers here to the broad sense that individual labour possesses in any system of distribution of the 'conditions of production'. However, 'social character' has a second and specific sense that takes shape because the 'manifold needs' of each individual are met through exchange, 'only in so far as every particular kind of useful private labour can be exchanged with … every other kind

5 Marx 1976b, p. 465 [1980, p. 51].

6 Marx 1976b, p. 464 [1980, p. 50]. For Marx exchange is not instituted merely through individual want and the division of labour, but rather through private property, which transforms individual producers into commodity owners because it invests their labour with a 'private' character. See Giannotti 1971, pp. 199–200.

7 Marx 1976a, p. 166 [1962, p. 87].

of useful private labour'. This specific character can therefore only correspond to a society in which the ownership of the 'conditions of production' is private.

In this type of society, the bond between the various autonomised labours is established by the exchange of products between private owners, as the only form to correlate the immense variety of individual products and needs that are immediately independent. Marx continues:

> Things are themselves external to man, and therefore alienable. In order that this alienation [*Veräußerung*] may be reciprocal, it is only necessary for men to agree tacitly to treat each other as the private owners of those alienable things, and, precisely for that reason, as persons who are independent of each other. But this relationship of reciprocal isolation and foreignness does not exist for the members of a primitive community of natural origin, whether it takes the form of a patriarchal family, an ancient Indian commune or an Inca state. The exchange of commodities begins where communities have their boundaries ...[8]

Exchange is defined by the 'reciprocal ... alienation' of things between persons, which implies the 'independence' also 'reciprocal' of these persons, that is, a 'reciprocal foreignness' determined by their condition as private owners. According to the *Grundrisse*:

> the reciprocal and all-sided dependence of individuals who are indifferent to one another forms their social connection. This social connection is expressed in *exchange value*, by means of which alone each individual's own activity or his product becomes an activity and a product for him.[9]

This text reveals the crux of the Marxian reformulation of the fundamental principles of political economy. On the one hand, as private owners, individuals appear as if they were isolated from one another, as atoms that eventually are aggregated to form a whole. They remain 'indifferent to one another' in an external relation of which they imagine themselves independent. On the other hand, they have a 'reciprocal and all-sided dependence' that 'forms their social connection', despite their 'indifference'. This connection 'is expressed in *exchange value*', since only through exchange of their products do independent individuals manage to satisfy their necessities. In that sense, they are mutually connected by an 'all-sided dependence'.

8 Marx 1976a, p. 182 [1962, p. 102].
9 Marx 1974, pp. 156–7 [1983, p. 80].

Yet, what constitutes their individuality is not the apparent 'indifference' resulting from the immediate independence as private producers, but rather, to the contrary, the 'social connection' that forces them to consume each other's products. This is the case because the product of each individual is only a 'product for him' when it is used as exchange value in order to obtain the products of others. The exchange of products creates a mediation through which the producer's 'own activity or product becomes an activity and a product for him'. When producer is separated from consumer, the independence of each individual is mediated by the 'social connection' established as a consumer in relation to other producers, and as producer in relation to other consumers. The individual is understood by Marx as the result of a social process of autonomisation through which those engaged in exchange can confront each other as independent individuals to the point that they seem to be 'indifferent to one another'.

This relation, between a totality-mediated difference and the immediate difference, i.e., 'indifference', is essential for understanding the Marxian conception of capitalist society across its various levels. This conception will return in the definition of crises whose basis, as we shall see, is the double dimension of the above-mentioned difference.

The 'social connection' between individuals at first sight 'indifferent' to one another defines 'value', conceived by Marx as the social relation strictly associated with the generalisation of exchange, and not a natural quality of products. The 'social connection is expressed in *exchange value*' only when the relation between producers takes place through the mediation of the exchange of their products. Through exchange each producer is seen to be producing too much or too little for the needs of others; exchange is what defines the parameters to which the producer must adjust, by trial and error, to the existing social demands. If it is advantageous, the producer can become even more specialised in some part of the overall production process. Accordingly, Marx writes,

> The need for exchange and for the transformation of the product into a pure exchange value progresses in step with the division of labour, i.e. with the increasingly social character of production.[10]

---

10 Marx 1974, p. 146 [1983, p. 81]. In the original, 'in step' is 'measure' [*Maß*], a very important word in the vocabulary of *Capital*, as we shall see later in this text. The relation between the division of labour and the 'social character of production' is revisited in the critic of Smith's 'invisible hand': 'The real point [*Witz*] is not that each individual's pursuit of his private interest promotes the totality of private interests, the general interest … The point

As a consequence of this logic, *Capital* Volume 1 draws an important and well-known distinction between the product in general and the product that 'transforms' into exchange value, that is, a commodity:

> A thing can be useful and a product of human labour without being a commodity. He who satisfies his own need with the product of his own labour admittedly creates use-values, but not commodities. In order to produce the latter, he must not only produce use-values, but use-values for others, social use-values (and not merely for others. The medieval peasant produced a corn-rent for the feudal lord and a corn-tithe for the priest; but neither the corn-rent nor the corn-tithe became commodities simply by being produced for others. In order to become a commodity, the product must be transferred to the other person, for whom it serves as a use-value, through the medium of exchange).[11]

Commodity is not just any type of product, according to Engels' decisive supplement in parentheses because commodity is only 'the product ... transferred to the other person ... through the medium of exchange', and it is a very specific type of society that produces goods for exchange.

This definition of commodity allows Marx to establish the concept of 'fetishism', by which social relations appear before economic agents as a relation between things and through which sociability is transfigured into something natural. In other words,

> Men are henceforth related to each other in their social process of production in a purely atomistic way. Their own relations of production therefore assume a material shape, which is independent of their control and their conscious individual action. This situation is manifested first by the fact that the products of men's labour universally take the form of commodities.[12]

---

is rather that private interest is itself already a socially determined interest, which can be achieved only within the conditions laid down by society and with the means provided by society ... It is the interest of private persons; but its content, as well as the form and means of its realization, is given by social conditions independent of all'. Marx 1974, p. 156 [1983, p. 90].

11 Marx 1976a, p. 131 [1962, p. 55]. As is well-known, to this passage of chapter 1 of *Capital* Engels added in the fourth edition of the work the explanation that follows in parentheses to Marx's text.

12 Marx 1976a, p. 187 [1962, pp. 107–8].

Since labour is private and autonomised, the 'relations of production' between the members of mercantile society escape their 'control and their conscious individual action', acquiring a 'material shape' external to them and reified in the commodity form. Exchange is the instance in which the 'relations of production' are manifested; relations which, outside of exchange, are obscured by the independence of private labour.

Why is this the case? Marx's response is a familiar one:

> Since the producers do not come into social contact until they exchange the products of their labour, the specific social characteristics of their private labours appear only within this exchange. In other words, the labour of the private individual manifests itself as an element of the total labour of society only through the relations which the act of exchange establishes between the products, and, through their mediation, between the producers. To the producers, therefore, the social relations between their private labours appear as what they are, i.e., they do not appear as direct social relations between persons in their work but rather as material [*dinglich*] relations between persons and social relations between things.[13]

Exchange 'transfers products' by defining them as commodities, already produced in order to allow their producer access to products he does not produce and that he tries to obtain as use values, that is, only for their intrinsic material qualities. In consequence, exchange 'transfers ... producers' in the specific sense of displacing them [*versetzen*] through the relation among their commodities, so that it appears to them that their own relations are achieved through these 'things'.[14]

Or again, 'since the producers do not come into social contact until they exchange', and since this is an exchange of 'products', of things, it seems that this is a relation among things that only bears on the materiality of their use value, the utility for those who acquire them. Commodities, however, are basically products of human labour, so that exchange is the socialisation of these specific types of private labour. They are what is compared and assessed through exchange. Therefore, the relation among things is social, just as the relation among people is mediated by the exchange of things. This 'transference', this displacement of personal relations into relations of things, imbues

13 Marx 1976a 165–6 [1962, p. 87].

14 These terms refer to words of the German original, such as *versetzen*, which have been modified in the English translation.

the relations among people with a 'shape which is independent of their control and their conscious individual action', for the social connection between private producers is presented as the natural connection between objects being exchanged. Of this 'transference', this displacement, producers are in no way 'conscious'. Marx continues:

> The mysterious character of the commodity-form consists therefore simply in the fact that the commodity reflects the social characteristics of men's own social labour as objective characteristics of the products of labour themselves, as the socio-natural properties of these things. Hence it also reflects the social relation of the producers to the sum total of labour as a social relation between objects, a relation which exists apart from and outside the producers. Through this substitution, the products of labour become commodities, sensuous things which are at the same time supra-sensible or social.[15]

The 'mysterious' aspect stems from the fact that social relations are hidden behind the relations among commodities and move them as if their movement came from the things themselves. Hence their quality as 'social things', as 'sensuous things which are at the same time supra-sensible': the human element manifests itself in tangible things because it has become intangible to itself. Hence the metaphor of fetishism, because in the process of exchange things move about as if they had a life of their own.

The importance of the concept of fetishism in Marx's theory consists in that it explains how bourgeois social relations, from their most elemental forms, appear as external forces guided by their own laws. Marx warns that the magnitudes of value

> vary continually, independently of the will, foreknowledge, and actions of the exchangers. Their own movement within society has for them the form of a movement made by things, and these things, far from being under their control, in fact control them.[16]

Social relations become 'independent' of individuals precisely on account of the independence these individuals keep from one another. This reciprocal independence, which individuals so zealously guard, subjects them to a power

15 Marx 1976a, 164–5 [1962, p. 86].
16 Marx 1976a, 167–8 [1962, p. 89].

over which they have lost control, but which instils in them a sensation of pure liberty, since the rules imposed on their private labour do not appear to them in their dominant social character. Individuals believe that they are not subjected to constraints derived from a 'social connection'; to the contrary, they believe their individual independence is guaranteed by private property.

For Marx, however, this inverted vision is not an illusion of economic agents or political economists, since it is bourgeois reality that configures fetishism. As the above-cited text outlines, for producers the 'relations between their private labours appear as what they are'; and, the text elaborates further on, not as 'as direct social relations between persons in their work, but rather as material [*sachlich*] relations between persons'. The 'mysterious character' of fetishism begins to clarify itself at this point. Labour in bourgeois society is immediately private, preventing the existence of 'direct social relations between persons in their work'. A fundamental opposition is thus born, between the directly private dimension of labour and its only indirectly social dimension, an opposition bringing with it significant consequences for the theory of value. This very topic will be our central concern in the next subsection.

1.3 *Abstract Labour*

The central concern of *Capital* in its first chapters is to know what is it that allows for the exchange of commodities, through which the independent producers of bourgeois society are connected to one another; it is, therefore, a matter of understanding what makes possible the comparison of qualitatively different products. Commodities possess a use value on account of their natural properties and the specific content of the labour that produced them. Marx's argument, however, is that exchange, by presupposing comparison, cannot take place by virtue of that qualitative diversity, but rather by virtue of that which is common to any commodity, that which appears as its exchange value. Referring to commodities, he says:

> But if we abstract from their use-value, there remains their value, as it has just been defined. The common factor in the exchange relation, or in the exchange value of the commodity, is therefore its value.[17]

Thus, value 'presents itself in the … exchange value', but it is the 'common factor' that somehow exists in each individual commodity prior to exchange.

---

17 Marx 1976a, p. 128 [1962, p. 53]. In the translation, a part of the second sentence is missing, which is the object of my analysis. The full original text reads: 'The common factor *that presents itself* in the exchange relation'.

Otherwise, the proportions in the exchange of commodities would not be regular, but rather accidental, casual. As the 'common factor' for all commodities being exchanged, value is obtained negatively – 'if we abstract from their use-value'. How then can the concept of value also be positively defined?

In a first approach, the 'abstraction' operation means for Marx that 'if then we disregard the use-value of the body of commodities, only one property remains, that of being products of labour'.[18] Nevertheless, he must go further, because the 'labour' that produces commodities is useful concrete 'labour' that results in the 'use-value of the body of commodities' that must necessarily be 'disregard[ed]'. Commodities must be 'regarded' then as the product of labour in general. Marx arrives here at one of the central concepts of his analysis of capitalism, the origin of so many difficulties and controversies: abstract labour.

In several passages of his work, Marx defines the labour resulting from the abstraction of specific qualities of each craft based on a basically physiological point of view:

> Let us now look at the residue of the products of labour. There is nothing left of them in each case but the same phantom-like objectivity; they are merely congealed quantities of homogeneous human labour, i.e. of human labour power expended without regard to the form of its expenditure. All these things now tell us is that human labour power has been expended to produce them, human labour is accumulated in them. As crystals of this social substance, which is common to them all, they are values – commodity values.[19]

And further:

> If we leave aside the determinate quality of productive activity, and therefore the useful character of the labour, what remains is its quality of being an expenditure of human labour power. Tailoring and weaving, although they are qualitatively different productive activities, are both a productive expenditure of human brains, muscles, nerves, hands etc., and in this sense both human labour. They are merely two different forms of the expenditure of human labour power.[20]

18 Ibid. [1962, p. 52].
19 Marx 1976a, p. 128 [1962, p. 52].
20 Marx 1976a, p. 134 [1962, 58–94].

These texts define abstract labour as the physiological-mental exertion of human energy 'without regard to the form of its expenditure'. Labour is 'abstract' insofar as it sets aside the concrete qualities that differentiate among the diverse instances of labour according to their 'useful character'.[21] By reducing this quality to the 'social substance ... common to them all', the difference between instances of individual labour becomes simply quantitative, established by the socially necessary labour time for the production of commodities in the 'ordinary state of health, strength and activity; in the ordinary degree of the skill and dexterity' of workers, in the words of Smith quoted by Marx.[22]

The comparison of quantities of value in different commodities is the basic condition of exchange. But the opposite is also the case:

> To measure the exchange values of commodities by the labour time they contain, the different kinds of labour have to be reduced to uniform, homogeneous, simple labour, in short to labour of uniform *quality*, whose only difference, therefore, is *quantity*. This reduction appears to be an abstraction, but it is an abstraction which is made every day in the social process of production. The conversion of all commodities into labour time is no greater an abstraction, and is no less real, than the resolution of all organic bodies into air.[23]

A second definition of abstract labour arises here, whereby it becomes evident that 'abstraction' is not a subjective reduction, performed by whoever analyses the capitalist system, but rather an 'abstraction which is made every day in the social process of production'.

In the type of society in which concrete instances of labour are immediately private labour of autonomised producers, exchange of commodities represents the opposite of the concrete private character: it is a means for socialisation because it realises the abstraction of the concrete aspect of private labour. Thus:

> the production of commodities must be fully developed before the scientific conviction emerges, from experience itself, that all the different

21 'We use the abbreviated expression "useful labour" for labour whose utility is represented by the use-value of its product, or by the fact that its product is a use-value. In this connection we consider only its useful effect'; useful labour 'is determined by its aim, mode of operation, object, means and result'. (Marx 1976a, p. 132 [1962, p. 56]).

22 Marx 1976a, p. 137 [1962, p. 61].

23 Marx 1976b, p. 272 [1961, p. 18]; my italics.

> kinds of private labour (which are carried on independently of each other, and yet, as spontaneously developed branches of the social division of labour, are in a situation of all-round dependence on each other) are continually being reduced to the quantitative proportions in which society requires them. The reason for this reduction is that in the midst of the accidental and ever-fluctuating exchange relations between the products, the labour-time socially necessary to produce them asserts itself as a regulative law of nature. In the same way, the law of gravity asserts itself when a person's house collapses on top of him.[24]

Abstraction of labour is only produced through exchange, which puts the products of diverse types of labour on an equal plane.

The two definitions of abstract labour that are seen by some critics as incompatible and problematic – the generic expenditure of productive energy and the result of the socialisation of private-concrete labour through exchange – are considered by Marx to be complementary.[25] This much can be inferred from the passage where he states:

> By equating, for example, the coat as a thing of value to the linen, we equate the labour embedded in the linen. Now it is true that the tailoring which makes the coat is concrete labour of a different sort from the weav-

24 Marx 1976a, p. 168 [1962, p. 89].

25 The double definition of abstract labour as a physiological reality and as the result of the social process of commodity exchange led some critics of Marx to point out the incompatibility of both, thus casting a shadow over this decisive concept for Marx's critique of capitalism (Petry 1916, Lange 1978, Castoriadis 1978). The debate was taken up several times with the intervention of, for instance, Heinrich 1999, Murray 2017, and Reuten 2019. The problem unfolds in two parts. First, the abstraction that creates 'abstract labour' appears to be a mere generalisation resulting from leaving out that which endows useful labour with its specificity. It would be as if a genus was established based on diverse species. In this case, Böhm-Bawerk's old objection would retain its validity (Böhm-Bawerk 1949 [1896]): genus is not opposed to species, only being differentiated at the analytic level; abstract labour would not be the opposite of concrete labour, only different from it. Fausto's 1986 answer to Castoriadis is decisive here, because he recalls that the opposition between abstract and concrete labour derives from the opposition between the social and the private dimension of commodity-producing labour in capitalism. Second, a purely physiological definition of abstract labour would be asocial, incapable of explaining the character of the specifically capitalist production. Leaving aside the various solutions found to the problem since Rubin 1924, I think it is necessary to recapitulate Marx's effort to define ever more precisely the concept of abstract labour and understand why both definitions have always been compatible: Although a historian can calculate the expenditure of physical and mental energy required for the labour of slaves and serfs in ancient modes of production, this

> ing which makes the linen. But the act of equating tailoring with weaving reduces the former in fact to what is really equal in the two kinds of labour, to the characteristic they have in common of being human labour. This is a roundabout way of saying that weaving too, in so far as it weaves value, has nothing to distinguish it from tailoring, and, consequently, is abstract human labour. It is only the expression of equivalence between different sorts of commodities which brings to view the specific character of value-creating labour, by actually reducing the different kinds of labour embedded in the different kinds of commodity to their common quality of being human labour in general.[26]

Abstract labour is clearly also objectified or materialised in the body of commodities, so that commodities become endowed with value as a quality of their own, derived from the commodity form itself. This quality, however, results from a social process of abstraction of the natural qualities that instil commodities with a utility, for 'only the expression of equivalence', the exchange of the products of diverse types of labour, 'actually reduces' these instances of labour to 'human labour in general' – abstract labour in the physiological sense.

In other words, abstract labour exists as the exertion of 'human labour power expended without regard to the form of its expenditure', but it is not the physiological reality alone that makes abstract labour a 'social substance' of value. Weaving 'equates itself' to tailoring only 'in so far as it weaves value', that is, 'in so far' as it produces a commodity, a product for exchange. Thus, 'only the expression of equivalence' of commodities, their relation in exchange, 'actually reduces' the diverse instances of concrete labour to their being 'really equal'. For Marx, the physiological existence of abstract labour only provides the material basis for the social constitution of value, which is 'actually' produced with the existence of the historical conditions of private production of commodities. As a physiological generalisation, abstraction could also be thought of for other societies in which value is not constituted, but without the existence of private property as the condition of production, abstraction cannot 'really' occur.

It is in this sense that value has a 'reality'. The original German word employed by Marx for 'reality' here is *Tatsache*, a fact [*Tat*] that assumes the char-

expenditure was irrelevant in those modes of production, that is, it was not socially calculated by their own mechanisms and institutions; it only becomes relevant when, with the absolute generalisation of mercantile production in capitalism, this expenditure becomes the 'natural' basis, the tangible ballast that serves to compare the value of any commodity produced and exchanged.

26 Marx 1976a, p. 142 [1962, p. 65].

acter of a 'matter' [*Sache*] as a 'matter of fact'. Following Marx's formulation of fetishism, such a fact withdraws private producers from their condition as controlling subjects of the process in which they take part, making them controlled by that process. In this sense of reality as a 'social thing', value is not only *different* from use-value, but *opposed* to it as a 'social substance', since abstract labour is not a mere genus that would encompass various kinds of concrete-specific labour, distinguishing itself from them on that basis alone, but a process that subordinates, controls and defines them.

For this reason, Marx asserts that abstract labour is the 'direct opposite'[27] of concrete labour and value is in direct opposition to use-value, not merely different from it. The opposition form derives from the character of 'social thing', that is, the character of an autonomous 'social substance' controlling private labour acquired by abstract labour in commodity-producing societies. For this reason, too, from the very first pages of *Capital*, value and use-value are opposed within the commodity itself, defining it as the unity of two opposed and not merely different aspects. For instance, Marx writes on this point: 'The internal opposition between use-value and value, hidden within the commodity ...'; and later, 'Hence the simple form of value of a commodity is the simple form of appearance of the opposition between use-value and value which is contained within the commodity'; and finally, 'The historical broadening and deepening of the phenomenon of exchange develops the opposition between use-value and value which is latent in the nature of the commodity'.[28]

The distinction between 'diversity' and 'opposition' resounds another echo of Hegel's *Science of Logic*: 'diversity' is defined as a form of difference in which the diverse terms are independent and indifferent to each other; the difference is not established by any relation among them; 'opposition' in turn is a form of difference that constitutes its terms through their relation, so that each one is what the other is not, and vice versa.[29] For Marx, the various instances of labour initially appear as being merely diverse, and also abstract and concrete labour similarly appear as diverse, defined as genus and species. However, exchange is capable of establishing that which, for Hegel, is achieved by reflection [*Reflexionsbestimmtheiten*], namely, the passage from diversity to opposition. In the exchange relation, the identity imposed by abstract labour equates the diverse kinds of concrete labour while at the same time determining its difference through the division of labour. The differentiation of abstract and

27 Marx 1976b, p. 275 [1961, p. 21]
28 Marx 1976a, pp. 153 and 181 [1962, pp. 75–6 and 102]
29 Hegel, 2010, pp. 418–27.

concrete labour only comes about because of the division of labour, articulated by the permanent comparison of the diverse kinds of concrete labour in exchange, which proceeds by evaluating what they have in common. The difference between concrete instances of labour is determined by the identity of abstract labour that is its opposite.

As the sequence of this chapter will make clear, it is of fundamental importance that Marx presents the relation between value and use-value in the logical form of opposition, since it allows him to develop the 'expression of equivalence' of commodities and define exchange as a relation in which two given commodities are at opposite poles. He thus deduces not only the equivalent form of value, but also the very possibility of crisis.

2 Money and Crisis

2.1 *Deduction of the Money-Form*

Based on a reformulation of the assumptions of political economy concerning the circulation of commodities, *Capital* performs an analysis of the exchange relation as a fundamental determination of the mercantile system; that is, as the privileged form in which immediately private labour is socialised. As seen at the end of the previous subchapter, in this form of sociability the difference of value and use-value appears as an opposition. For that same reason, exchange is constituted as a process that makes explicit and consecutively unfolds the opposition between value and use-value in the deduction of the money-form, laying the groundwork for a first definition of the concept of crisis.

In Marx's own texts, we find evidence that the analysis of the value relation has as its finality the deduction of the money-form:

> Everyone knows, if nothing else, that commodities have a common value-form which contrasts in the most striking manner with the motley natural forms of their use-values. I refer to the money-form. Now, however, we have to perform a task never even attempted by bourgeois economics. That is, we have to show the origin [*Genesis*] of this money-form, we have to trace the development of the expression of value contained in the value-relation of commodities from its simplest, almost imperceptible outline to the dazzling money-form. When this has been done, the mystery of money will immediately disappear.[30]

30 Marx 1976a, p. 139 [1962, p. 62].

Marx regards as insufficient the classical economists' explanation for the origin of money, because it does not start from the 'simplest, almost imperceptible outline' of the 'expression of value contained in the value-relation of commodities'. Those economists were not concerned with deducing the concept of money from the exchange of commodities and the opposed determinations within the singular commodity. By not doing so, the classical economists would have left the existence and character of money shrouded in a 'mystery' that Marx, in the course of his 'development', seeks to resolve and elucidate. This means 'to trace the development of the expression of value ... from its simplest ... outline', the exchange of two commodities, in which the elements later revealed in the money-form are already present. Thus, Marx's presentation of categories revisits that which is comprised as an 'imperceptible outline' in the exchange of commodities in order to arrive at money in its 'dazzling', visible aspect. This is the purpose of the sequence of deductions making up the third Part of chapter 1 of *Capital* in the 1873 edition.

Marx would only achieve what he considered the most adequate way to reproduce the deduction of the money-form in this second edition of *Capital*, and only after long endeavouring with different attempts, as the *Contribution to the Critique of Political Economy*, published in 1859, and the 1867 first edition of *Capital*. The 1873 formulation would therefore serve as the basis for the following analysis, but the earlier ones will also be considered, insofar as their differences from the final version clarify important aspects of the latter.

For example, the clearest difference between the text of *Contribution to the Critique of Political Economy* and the posterior versions of chapter 1 of *Capital* is that, in the former, use-value appears opposed simply to exchange value. At no point in the 1859 work does Marx establish a clear distinction between the value intrinsic to the singular commodity and its form of manifestation, that is, value as a relation of exchange among commodities – exchange value. In *Capital*, on the contrary, the distinction between value and exchange value is explicitly made through Marx's new procedure, by beginning his analysis with the constitutive elements of the singular commodity. There, Marx writes: 'In fact we started from exchange value, or the exchange relation of commodities, in order to track down the value that lay hidden within it'; but he goes on to add 'we must now return to this form of appearance of value', because, as stated earlier in the text, the singular commodity 'remains impossible to grasp as a thing possessing value', since its 'objective character is purely social', that is, 'can only appear in the social relation between commodity and commodity',[31]

31 Marx 1976a, pp. 138–9 [1962, p. 62].

in exchange. This is why the first text cited in this subchapter asserts that 'the expression of value [is] contained in the value-relation of commodities'. The value of the individual commodity 'expresses' itself, appearing in the 'value-relation' as exchange value.

When the analysis changes its level and passes from the singular commodity to the exchange of commodities, the two opposed poles found in the individual case reappear in another form, but the use-value, which classical economists would have disregarded, is still present. For Marx, by neglecting use-value, they would have left out the qualitative dimension of the commodity and only considered its quantitative dimension, its exchange value. Marx of course recognises that in the exchange of equals there is established an equation, a quantitative proportion among the values of commodities being exchanged. However, he objects that, to the extent that use-values are also considered, exchange assumes a more complex character: a relation between different terms, which is to say, precisely, a 'value-relation'.

Hence, *Capital* observes exchange from a double point of view: as the equation of values of the same magnitude, the traditional approach of political economy; and as the relation among the different roles that the two commodities play as part of the so-called 'simple form of value'. Marx explains:

> the internal opposition between use-value and value, hidden within the commodity, therefore presents itself as an external opposition, i.e. by a relation between two commodities such that the one commodity, *whose own* value must be expressed, counts directly only as a use-value, whereas the other commodity, *in which* that value is to be expressed, counts directly only as exchange value. Hence the simple form of value of a commodity is the simple form of appearance of the opposition between use-value and value which is contained within the commodity.[32]

This movement, through which the 'internal opposition ... presents itself as an external opposition', is the fundamental starting point for the Marxian deduction of the money-form. Each of the two commodities related by the exchange are still the unity of use-value and value. Through their relation, however, the terms of the opposition 'internal' to each of them are differentiated, as if only one of the terms were present in each commodity. Thus, the first commodity becomes that '*whose own* value must be expressed', a value distinguished from use-value, so that value alone appears, and it alone 'counts directly'. In turn, the

32 Marx 1976a, p. 153 [1962, pp. 75–6].

second commodity becomes that '*in which* that value is to be expressed', that is, the commodity necessary for the value of the other to appear, and for this other, 'counts directly' only as its exchange value. Marx continues:

> Here two different kinds of commodities (in our example the linen and the coat) evidently play two different parts. The linen expresses its value in the coat; the coat serves as the material in which that value is expressed. The first commodity plays an active role, the second a passive one. The value of the first commodity is presented as relative value, in other words the commodity is in the relative form of value. The second commodity fulfils the function of equivalent, in other words is in the equivalent form.[33]

Without the commodity that stands in the equivalent form, the value of the first cannot be expressed and assume a relative value-form, because it depends on the relation with the equivalent in order to appear. Nevertheless, despite the fact that the commodity in the equivalent-form 'counts directly' for the first only as its exchange value, its use-value 'serves as the material in which that value is expressed'. Therefore:

> By means of the value-relation, therefore, the natural form of commodity B becomes the value-form of commodity A, in other words the physical body of commodity B becomes a mirror for the value of commodity A. Commodity A, then, in entering into a relation with commodity B as an object of value [*Wertkörper*], as a materialization of human labour, makes the use-value B into the material through which its own value is expressed.[34]

The 'natural form' or use-value of each commodity is still a bearer of its own value, but the use-value of the commodity in the equivalent-form is also 'the material through which … is expressed' the value of the commodity in the relative value-form. Therefore, the use-value at both poles of the relation does not have the same function. As the bearer of the value-expression of the commodity in the relative form, the use-value in the equivalent form is not only opposed to its own value – the 'internal opposition' common to all commodities – but also opposed to the value of the other commodity. Marx then asserts that 'The first peculiarity which strikes us when we reflect on the equivalent form is this,

33 Marx 1976a, p. 139 [1962, p. 63].
34 Marx 1976a, p. 144 [1962, p. 67].

that use-value becomes the form of appearance of its opposite, value'.[35] For that reason too, as already stated, the opposition between use-value and value 'presents ... as an external opposition' what before was 'hidden within the commodity', and the simple value-form itself can be conceived as the 'simple form of appearance of the opposition between use-value and value which is contained within the commodity'.

By appearing in the simple value-form, this internal opposition assumes the figure of an opposition between the two poles in the relation of value:

> The relative form of value and the equivalent form are two inseparable moments, which belong to and mutually condition each other; but at the same time, they are mutually exclusive or opposed extremes, i.e. poles of the expression of value. They are always divided up between the different commodities brought into relation with each other by that expression.[36]

The opposition internal to the commodity in the relative form is only manifested through the relation with the commodity in the equivalent form, and the latter acquires an external character only as the manifestation of the former. Consequently, the two forms are 'inseparable moments, which ... mutually condition each other', even if they are both 'mutually exclusive' as 'extremes' of a relation. This 'mutually belonging' and 'excluding' quality characterises the simple value-form as an opposition, according to the definition previously outlined, leading to the unfolding of new figures.

The distinction between the relative value-form and the equivalent value-form constitutes the basic conceptual pairing with which Marx deduces the money-form. The first moment of this deduction consists in that the two opposed forms 'are always divided up between the different commodities brought into relation', whatever the commodities being exchanged. In fact, generalised market production must allow for as many exchange possibilities as there are available commodities, so that each commodity assuming the relative value-form will have all other commodities as its equivalent. This is the 'total or expanded form' ('form B') of the simple relation of value ('form A'). The second moment of the deduction consists in the inversion of the two poles of the 'expanded form': instead of each commodity having every other commodity as its potential equivalent, it becomes the equivalent of all others, which

35 Marx 1976a, p. 148 [1962, p. 70].

36 Marx 1976a, pp. 139–40 [1962, p. 63].

now appear only under the relative value-form. The unique commodity that comes to occupy the equivalent form Marx calls the 'general equivalent', which determines the 'general form', the 'form C' of the relation of value.

Nevertheless, achieving this 'general equivalent form' supposes a more complex reasoning than that of a mere inversion of the two poles constituting the value-form. In Marx's own words:

> But the opposition between the relative form of value and the equivalent form, the two poles of the value-form, also develops concomitantly with the development of the value-form itself. The first form … already contains this antagonism, without as yet fixing it … Finally, the last form, C, gives to the world of commodities a general social relative form of value, because, and in so far as, all commodities except one are thereby excluded from the equivalent form. A single commodity … therefore has the form of direct exchangeability with all other commodities, in other words it has a directly social form because, and in so far as, no other commodity is in this situation. The commodity that figures as universal equivalent is on the other hand excluded from the uniform and therefore universal relative form of value.[37]

The sequence of the three moments in the relation of value corresponds to the development of the 'opposition between … the two poles' to the extent that the commodities configure a 'world' in which all of them are situated in the relative form, so that the commodity in the equivalent form stands out as the 'general social form' and acquires a 'direct exchangeability with all other' commodities.

This movement, however, only takes place 'because, and in so far as, no other commodity is in the situation' of the general equivalent form, that is, 'because, and in so far as, all commodities except one are thereby excluded from the equivalent form'. The general equivalent commodity in turn is 'excluded from the uniform and therefore universal relative form of value'. In the first two moments in the relation of value, A and B, any commodity can play the role of one or another function, but in the third moment, C, commodities as a whole define only one of them as their equivalent, excluding themselves from that function and, inversely, also excluding the equivalent commodity from the relative value-form. The form of the general equivalent is thus achieved through a principle of exclusion present in the 'opposition between … the two poles'

37 Marx 1976a, pp. 160–1 [1962, pp. 82–3].

of the expression of value, since these poles, as seen above, both 'belong to … each other' and are 'mutually exclusive or opposed extremes'. It is this excluding character, constitutive of any opposition, that unfolds in the opposition between the 'world of commodities' and the general equivalent.

The passage from there to the money-form is simple: 'The universal equivalent form is a form of value in general. It can therefore be assumed by any commodity'.[38] Thereafter, by exposing the reasons why this 'any commodity' happened to be historically fixed as gold, Marx goes on to define form D, money proper. With that, the relation between the 'universal relative form' and the 'universal equivalent form' presents itself as the relation between the commodity and money:

> Since all other commodities are merely particular equivalents for money, the latter being their universal equivalent, they relate to money as particular commodities relate to the universal commodity.[39]

On the one hand, the two terms exclude one another, and doubly so: considering the relation from the point of view of money, commodities are 'particular equivalents for money' and the latter, 'their universal equivalent'; from the point of view of commodities, 'they relate to money as particular commodities relate to the universal commodity'. On the other hand, the terms 'belong to each other' and identify with one another, as mentioned in one of the above-cited texts, since money is the 'universal commodity' and commodities also are the 'equivalents for money'. Marx thus recognises that political economy is correct, in part, when it defines money as a commodity, but is mistaken for viewing only the identity of both forms of value, for the simple identity does not allow the money-form to be deduced from the commodity-form.

Capital thus deduces the money-form and at the same time defines it as a relation established by the logic of the determinations of the commodity. In this context, it is imperative to remember that Marx's project consists precisely in showing the necessity of the determination of money in capitalist market production, presenting it as the result of the unfolding of the value-forms that express the commodity's internal opposition. Then:

> The only difficulty in the concept of the money-form is that of grasping the universal equivalent form, and hence the general form of value as

38 Marx 1976a, p. 162 [1962, p. 83].

39 Marx 1976a, p. 184 [1962, p. 104]. And hence Marx's reference to Pietro Verri (1728–97) in footnote 8 on the same page of *Capital*: 'Money is the universal commodity'.

> such, form C. Form C can be reduced by working backwards to form B, the expanded form of value, and its constitutive element is form A ... The simple commodity form is therefore the germ of the money-form.[40]

Each form, more complex than the last, is contained in the earlier simpler ones, deriving itself from them to the extent that the simpler forms of opposition that constitute them are resolved, only to be restored in new forms.

And yet, Marx denies that the deductive aspect assumed by the presentation at this point corresponds to a simple logic of concepts. Instead, the presentation must reproduce the movement accomplished by the real determinations of the commodity, that is, the externalisation of the internal opposition between use-value and value, or the reciprocal exclusion of the relative and equivalent forms. Hence his emphatic assertion:

> But only the social fact can turn a particular commodity into the universal equivalent. The social action of all other commodities, therefore, sets apart the particular commodity in which they all present their values. The natural form of this commodity thereby comes to the socially recognized equivalent form ... It thus becomes – money.[41]

Following the fetishist movement of the 'social action' of things, *Capital* examines in its first chapter the formal development of commodity's determinations, before addressing in its second chapter the properly social relations among individuals. Marx thus signals the central importance of fetishism: if the commodity is the true agent of the 'social fact', then it has the power to realise its determinations, and what is of interest is to present the development of these determinations. However, before proceeding with the unfolding of the relation between commodity and money, it is worthwhile to examine a decisive figure in the autonomisation of value: the fetishism of money, which, in the analysis of the simple circulation of commodities, has not received its due attention.

2.2 *The Fetishism of Money*

Similar to the deduction of the money-form based on the commodity-form, the fetishism of money is conceived as the development of commodity fetishism. In accordance with the determinations of the increasingly complex expres-

40 Marx 1976a, p. 163 [1962, p. 85].

41 Marx 1976a, pp. 180–1 [1962, p. 101].

sions of value in exchange – from its simple form to the general equivalent form and money – it simultaneously develops the autonomisation of value, which is increasingly governed by the laws of the system that it constitutes beyond the control, consciousness and will of individual economic agents.

Already in the simple value-form the process of the autonomisation of value is presented:

> The simplest value-relation is evidently that of one commodity to another commodity of a different kind, it does not matter which one. Hence the relation between the values of two commodities supplies us with the simplest expression of the value of a single commodity.[42]

Insofar as exchange is a relation in which the value of the first commodity is expressed in the body of the second, this 'value-relation … supplies us with the … expression of the value of a single commodity'. But which commodity? That whose value is expressed in the use-value of the second. It is in that sense that, as we saw earlier, 'The first commodity plays an active role, the second a passive one'.[43] The 'activity' of the first commodity means that, through the relation with the other commodity, it expresses its own value, so that the relation with the other is in fact a relation with itself by means of the other. Thus, as self-relation of the commodity, the relative form is already a first moment in the autonomisation of value that will culminate in the constitution of capital, as will be seen in the next chapter of this book.

Because the commodity in relative value-form defines its relationship with the other commodity as a means to relate back to itself, this second commodity plays the 'passive role' of equivalent of the first. This equivalent role of the second commodity stems solely from the relationship with that commodity which plays an 'active role', that is, from the social relation of exchange. And yet, this is not what appears before the economic agents. Marx explains:

> However, the properties of a thing do not arise from its relations to other things, they are, on the contrary, merely activated by such relations. The coat, therefore, seems to be endowed with its equivalent form, its property of direct exchangeability, by nature, just as much as its property of being heavy or its ability to keep us warm. Hence the mysteriousness of the equivalent form, which only impinges on the crude bourgeois vision

42 Marx 1976a, p. 139, [1962, p. 62].

43 Ibid. [1962, p. 63].

> of the political economist when it confronts him in its fully developed shape, that of money … He does not suspect that even the simplest expression of value, such as 20 yards of linen = 1 coat, already presents the riddle of the equivalent form for us to solve.[44]

Although a commodity is equivalent only in relation to another, it 'seems to be endowed with its equivalent form … by nature' and contains in its own use-value the material qualities that will make it capable by itself to express the value of the other.

This appearance becomes even more evident in the case of the general equivalent. When the equivalence of value is anchored in a specific commodity that functions as money, that commodity seems to be the equivalent of all others only for its natural intrinsic qualities:

> We have already seen, from the simplest expression of value, x commodity A = y commodity B, that the thing in which the magnitude of the value is presented appears to have the equivalent form independently of this relation, as a social natural property. We followed the process by which this false semblance became firmly established, a process which was completed when the universal equivalent form became identified with the natural form of a particular commodity, and thus crystallized into the money-form. What appears to happen is not that a particular commodity becomes money because all other commodities present their values in it, but, on the contrary, that all other commodities universally present their values in a particular commodity because it is money. The movement through which this process has been mediated vanishes in its own result, leaving no trace behind. Without any initiative on their part, the commodities find their own value-configuration ready to hand, in the form of a physical commodity existing outside but also alongside them. These things, gold or silver in its crude state, becomes, immediately on its emergence from the bowels of the earth, the direct incarnation of all human labour. Hence the magic of money … The riddle of the money fetish is therefore the riddle of the commodity fetish, now visible and dazzling to our eyes.[45]

The transfiguration of the social relationship into a natural quality is already present in the logic of the equivalent form of the simple expression of value,

44 Marx 1976a, pp. 149–50 [1962, p. 72].

45 Marx 1976a, p. 187 [1962, pp. 107–8].

resolving the 'riddle' of the equivalent form and, from there, also the 'riddle of the money fetish'. The point is that the real movement that defines the commodity as money, the 'mediated movement' in which the self-relation of commodities goes through their relation with money, 'vanishes in its own result, leaving no trace behind'. The only remaining 'visible' thing is that 'all other commodities universally present their values in a particular commodity because it is money'. Nevertheless, the fetish here is not just a transposition of the social relations of exchange into the material of money – gold or silver – but rather is the manifestation of the social power to command the labour of other individuals, a power that money confers on its possessors.[46] The previous relation is inverted. No longer is the activity of producing commodities responsible for conferring social power on the individual; instead, it is the autonomisation of value in the money-form that makes its possessor powerful.

These enigmatic appearances are explained, however, when one takes into account that autonomisation occurs only because 'all other commodities universally present their values' in money, that is, because the universal character of the equivalent results from the impulse of exclusion of one commodity by all other commodities. In turn, this impulse is also the unfolding of the relative and equivalent value-forms and, ultimately, of the commodity's internal opposition. The fetish of money is thus defined as the independent and perfect power of allocating resources and products among agents and economic sectors. In Marx's own words:

> Hence although the movement is merely the expression of the circulation of commodities, the situation appears to be the reverse of this, namely the circulation of commodities seems to be the result of the movement of the money. Again, money functions as a means of circulation because in it the value possessed by commodities has taken on an independent shape. Hence its movement, as the medium of circulation, is in fact merely the movement undergone by commodities while changing their form.[47]

---

46 In the *Grundrisse* Marx explains this point as follows: 'On the other side, this power that each individual exercises over the activity of others or over social wealth exists in him as the owner of *exchange values*, of *money*. The individual carries his social power, as well as his connection with society, in his pocket'. (Marx 1974, p. 157 [1983, p. 90]). Not as producer, but as the possessor of money, this is how the individual shows his or her power.

47 Marx 1976a, pp. 101–2 [1962, p. 130].

Money is the 'value possessed by commodities ... on an independent shape' through the work of commodities, through the development of their double nature as value and use-value. Hence it 'functions as a means of circulation' through the 'movement undergone by commodities while changing their form', since the passage from use-value to exchange value presents itself as a passage from any commodity whatsoever to the general equivalent and vice versa, determining the 'form' of circulation.

The very form of the circulation of commodities therefore creates the impression that the process of exchange is 'the result of the movement of the money'; that money is the motor of the process. And even when the image of money as the perfect allocator of resources crumbles during times of economic crisis, agents do not cease to believe that this distributive power is an inherent property of money. Fetishism subsists, so that the crisis itself appears to the agents as a transcendent fact whose solution is beyond the individual possibility of social intervention. In a certain sense, crisis is also invested with a 'mysterious' character, sharing with money and commodity a fetishist aspect. By unmasking these fetishes, Marx goes so far as to attempt to solve the 'riddle' represented by crisis. This is what will be seen below.

2.3 *The Metamorphosis of the Commodity*

With the introduction of money, exchange is now conceived in a much more complex manner in *Capital*:

> In so far as the process of exchange transfers commodities from hands in which they are non-use-values to hands in which they are use-values, it is a process of social metabolism [*Stoffwechsel*] ... We therefore have to consider the whole process in its formal aspect, that is to say, the change in form [*Formwechsel*] or the metamorphosis of commodities through which the social metabolism is mediated.[48]

Taking 'form' here as value-form – commodity or money – the 'metamorphosis' of commodities is the passage from one form to another. As discussed in chapter 1, section 2.1, this is the result of the opposition and the 'mutual exclusion' between the relative and equivalent value-forms and between the double internal determinations of the commodity, use-value and value.

The exchange mediated by money passes through two different moments that vary according to the direction of the movement: in the first, the pos-

48 Marx 1976a, pp. 198–9 [1962, p. 119]; for more on the subject, see also Marx 1976b, pp. 323–4 [1961, p. 69].

sessor of the commodity relinquishes that commodity in exchange for money, receiving the universal expression of exchange value, the possession of which, in a second moment, means any other commodity can be acquired. The first moment is the sale, the transition from a particular value-form to the general value-form; the second is the purchase, the inverse transition, from the general form to the particular form:

> The process of exchange is therefore accomplished through two metamorphoses of opposite yet mutually complementary character – the conversion of the commodity into money, and the re-conversion of the money into a commodity. The two moments of this metamorphosis are at once distinct transactions of the owner of commodities – selling, or the exchange of the commodity for money, and buying, or the exchange of the money for a commodity – and the unity of the two acts: selling in order to buy.[49]

Based on the relation between the commodity (C) and money (M), a new relation arises whose terms are the two transitions between C and M, purchase and sale. Both are identical as 'metamorphosis' in general, as 'conversions' of the value-form, but they differ as inverse movements, as sale (C–M) and purchase (M–C). They also constitute the terms of a relation whose unity has the form C–M–C, that is, 'selling in order to buy', the expression that reveals the original finality of exchange as binding private producers of commodities and allowing each of them to purchase the use-value needed with the money obtained through the sale of commodities produced. Beyond this, the sequence of 'selling in order to buy' is characterised in Marx's above-cited text as an opposition, defined as a 'process of exchange' that is 'accomplished through … opposite yet mutually complementary' metamorphosis. The opposition of the metamorphosis is formal: C–M and M–C. However, through its mediation a real process is accomplished, a process whose unity expresses the objective of 'selling in order to buy', since buying without previously having sold is impossible and selling without then buying is contrary to the finality of the simple circulation of commodities.

Despite this unity, the formal separation of the purchase and sale phases suggests that sellers are not automatically buying when they sell, as is the case with the bartering of products without the mediation of money. Marx reminds us that:

49 Marx 1976a, p. 200 [1962, p. 120].

> No one can sell unless someone else purchases. But no one directly needs to purchase because he has just sold. Circulation bursts through all the temporal, spatial and personal barriers imposed by the direct exchange of products, and it does this by splitting up the direct identity present in this case between the exchange of one's own product [*Austausch*] and the acquisition of someone else's [*Eintausch*] into the two opposite segments of sale and purchase.[50]

The relation between buying and selling 'splits up the direct identity' of barter, because the mediation of money distinguishes the opposed movements. The possibility of retaining money after selling, presented in detail in the section on 'hoarding' in chapter 3 of *Capital* Volume 1, involves the temporal and spatial separation between the movement of selling and purchasing. For the individual engaged in exchange, yielding one's own product does not mean immediately acquiring another's product; it only means acquiring money that must be used, but under circumstances not determined by the very act of sale, for selling and purchasing are formally separate.

This mediating and separating role is based on the definition of money itself, according to the explanation given by Marx in the manuscripts later published under the title *Theories of Surplus value*:

> The difficulty of transforming the *commodity* – the particular product of individual labour – into its opposite, money, i.e. abstract general social labour, lies in the fact that *money* is not the particular product of individual labour, and that the person who has effected a sale, who therefore has commodities in the form of money, is not compelled to buy again at once, to transform the money again into a particular product of individual labour.[51]

Since money 'is not the particular product of individual labour', its holders can retain it and purchase the desired commodity whenever they wish to satisfy a specific necessity, because the relation between money and the commodity is not solely a relationship of unity. Money is 'its opposite', that is, it is autonomised value in which 'abstract general social labour' is opposed to 'individual labour' of the private producer of the commodity. Marx stated in the *Grundrisse* that: 'Thus already in the quality of money as a medium, in the splitting of

50 Marx 1976a, pp. 208–9 [1962, p. 127]. This text will be analysed in detail in the next subchapter.

51 Marx 1969b, p. 509 [1967, p. 510].

exchange in two acts, there lies the germ of crisis, or at least their possibility ...',[52] but it is important to recall that the 'quality of money' is the result of the unfolding of the opposition between private labour and social labour constitutive of the commodity-producing society. It is there, in the last instance, that one must go looking for 'the germ of crisis'.

The split between selling and purchasing, explained by Marx through this opposition, is even more far-reaching when money functions not only as a means of circulation, but also as a means of payment. Here, the effective transfer of the commodity to the hands of the purchaser and money to the seller is not simultaneous. Money appears in a merely nominal form, as the measure of value of the commodity at the point of its delivery, only to appear later, as the payment of a purchase previously realised. The generalisation of the process through whereby buyer A has credit with seller B, who will use the money from A to pay C and C to pay D, makes it so that the sum of effective money can be much smaller than the value of the transactions that money merely measures.

Hence, the difference between the ideal existence of money, as the measure of value of commodities, and its real existence, as a means of circulation, presents itself as an opposition that can lead to even deeper crises, due to the leverage effect that money has as a means of payment on the volume of exchanges. According to the *Theories of Surplus value*:

> ... in so far as money functions as *means of payment*, it has two different aspects, it acts as *measure of value* and as *realisation of value*. These two aspects may become separated ... If even for only *a limited period of time* the commodity cannot be sold then, although its value has not altered, *money* cannot function as *means of payment*, since it must function as such in a *definite given period of time*. But as the same sum of money acts for a whole series of reciprocal transactions and obligations here, *inability to pay* occurs not only at one, but at many points, hence a *crisis* arises.[53]

The difference between the number of sellers and the number of buyers of commodities or, in turn, between the number of buyers and the number of sellers of money, who need it to make their payments, is now much greater, highlighting the crisis mechanism as the imbalance in the general volume of purchases and sales.

52 Marx 1974, p. 198 [1983, p. 128].

53 Marx 1969b, p. 514 [1967, p. 514].

The function of money as the means of payment is defined by Marx as the combination of the two opposed functions of money previously presented: the measure of value and the means of circulation. Marx seeks thus to explain a form of crisis of greater power and complexity:

> The crisis in its second form is the function of money as a means of payment, in which money has two different functions and figures in two different phases, divided from each other in time. Both these forms are as yet quite abstract, although the second is more concrete than the first.[54]

The form of the means of payment is 'more concrete' than that of the means of circulation because it incorporates the latter and combines it with the function of money as the measure of value. Together they appear as the terms of a new relation, and they can either harmonise in the continuous flow of normally realised and cleared payments or they can separate and paralyse the whole sequence of transactions, since the effective means of circulation has less value than the value of the commodities previously measured. Following this, Marx states:

> These are the *formal possibilities* of crisis. The form mentioned first is possible without the latter – that is to say, crises are possible without credit, without money functioning as a means of payment. But the second form is not possible *without the first* – that is to say, without the separation between purchase and sale. But in the latter case, the crisis occurs not only because the commodity is unsaleable, but because it is not saleable within a *particular period of time*, and the crisis arises and derives not only from the *unsaleability* of the commodity, but from the *non-fulfilment of a whole series of payments* which depend on the sale of this particular commodity within this particular period of time.[55]

The first form determines the crisis based on the mere eventual impossibility of selling commodities, with the interruption of circulation; the second form is more complex, because it presupposes the first. The 'non-fulfilment of a whole series of payments' originates when there is a failure to sell a 'particular commodity within this particular period of time', interrupting the flow of payments and exacerbating the simple form of the crisis.

54 Marx 1969b, p. 510 [1967, p. 511].
55 Marx 1969b, p. 514 [1967, p. 515].

The foundation of crisis in the sphere of simple circulation resides in the difficulty of selling commodities, a situation revealing the distinctive feature of money as the universal expression of value. As such, it can always be of interest to retain money in the form of a hoard and transport it elsewhere, something that leads, however, to the interruption of current transactions and the series of payments on previous purchases. Thus, analysing the crisis of 1857–8, Marx states that in times

> in which it is impossible to sell all commodities … there are more buyers than sellers *of one* commodity, i.e. *money*, and more sellers than buyers as regards *all other forms of money*, i.e. commodities.[56]

In a crisis, all economic agents wish to obtain the money that allows them to purchase use-values and all wish to get rid of the commodities they have produced, because they have not produced them for their own consumption but to sell them for money. When circulation follows its normal course, money presents itself as a commodity and commodities as forms of money, that is, they are immediately convertible into money. In turn, the crisis manifests and deepens the distinction between the two opposed value-forms.

Nevertheless, as two of the texts we have cited above explain, 'these forms are as yet quite abstract', or, 'these are the formal possibilities of crisis'. Beyond the 'abstract-concrete' conceptual pair, these characterisations also return to the modal status of crises in the sphere of simple circulation of commodities. What do the 'possibilities' of crisis mean in this context? And what is the relation between this 'abstract' mode and the merely 'formal' character of these possibilities? These are the questions that the following examination intends to answer, by way of closing.

2.4 *The Possibility of Crisis*

To the assertion of classical political economists that in commodity circulation there can be no general imbalance between purchasing and selling, the Marxian critique responds with the understanding of circulation as commodity 'metamorphosis'. At the same time, that critique reveals the significance of this understanding:

> The general nature of the metamorphosis of commodities – which includes the separation of purchase and sale just as it does their unity –

56 Marx 1976b, p. 334 [1961, p. 78].

> instead of excluding the *possibility* of a general glut, on the contrary, contains the possibility of a general glut.[57]

The metamorphosis is the 'possibility of a general glut' precisely for being 'the separation of purchase and sale just as ... their unity'. In that case, why should the version of classical economists exclude that possibility? And what is the meaning of the categories of 'separation' and 'unity' in Marx's proposition, so that 'the possibility of a general glut' should be 'contained' in the metamorphosis of commodities? It is necessary to examine more closely some of the topics previously addressed.

The point of Marx's critique here is the reduction of commodity circulation to the barter of products:

> No one can sell unless someone else purchases. But no one directly needs to purchase because he has just sold. Circulation bursts through all the temporal, spatial and personal barriers imposed by the direct exchange of products, and it does this by splitting up the direct identity present in this case between the exchange of one's own product [*Austausch*] and the acquisition of someone else's [*Eintausch*] into the two opposite segments of sale and purchase.[58]

In the first sentence of this text, previously cited, Marx reproduces political economy's assertion of equilibrium and then refutes it by distinguishing two different types of unity between purchase and sale. In both types, 'circulation ... splits up the direct identity' of barter of two commodities (C–C) through the introduction of money, which differentiates sale (C–M) from purchase (M–C). However, in the type of unity expressed in the sentence 'no one can sell unless someone else purchases', sale by an agent is simultaneously the purchase by another agent; they are concomitant acts realised by two different agents. In the other type, expressed in the sentence 'no one directly needs to purchase because he has just sold', there is a temporal succession of sale and purchasing by the same agent, the one who 'has just sold'. Not by accident, just before the above text, Marx explained that:

57 Marx 1969b, p. 504 [1967, p. 505]. Even more openly critical is the following statement by Marx: 'The conception (which really belongs to James Mill) adopted by Ricardo from the tedious Say (and to which we shall return when we discuss that miserable individual), that *overproduction* is not possible or at least that *no general glut of the market* is possible, is based on the proposition that products are exchanged against products, or as Mill put it, on the "metaphysical equilibrium of sellers and buyers"'. (Marx 1969b, p. 493 [1967, p. 493]).

58 Marx 1976a, pp. 208–9 [1962, p. 127].

> Nothing can be more foolish than the dogma that because every sale is a purchase, and every purchase a sale, the circulation of commodities necessarily implies an equilibrium between sales and purchases. If this means that the number of actual sales accomplished is equal to the number of purchases, it is a flat tautology. But its real intention is to show that every seller brings its own buyer to market with him. Sale and purchase are one identical act, considered as an alternating relation between two persons who are in polar opposition to each other, the commodity-owner and the money-owner. They constitute two acts, of polar and opposite character, considered as the transactions of one and the same person.[59]

One can say that 'every sale is a purchase, and every purchase a sale', to the extent that both 'are one identical act ... between two persons who are in polar opposition', the seller at one pole and the buyer at the other. They are, therefore, distinct persons who relate through exchange, so that the opposition between them is determined by the opposition between buying and selling. In turn, 'considered as the transactions of one and the same person' in the buying and selling sequence, 'they constitute two acts of polar and opposite character'; an opposition, thus, between the two component moments of the sequence.

According to Marx, from a situation in which there are two agents and a concomitant act of exchange, classical economists have inferred a rule of equilibrium applicable to the other situation, in which there is one agent and two acts or phases in the exchange process, that is, in which the same producer first sells his commodity in order to later buy another commodity. In the initial situation, the simultaneity of purchasing and selling is clear since they correspond to the inverse direction of a singular movement. However, this does not mean that there is also an equilibrium in the second situation, that the seller has to buy immediately after selling, in a previously determined place and time. For Marx, the equilibrium of the classical economists is then nothing but 'flat tautology' in the initial situation and becomes a great error if transposed to the second situation, in which 'every seller brings its own buyer to market with him'. In that case, the sellers' temporary possession of money could lead them to interrupt the sequence of the metamorphosis of value.

Marx's critique of classical economy shows precisely how he conceives the determination of the crisis in the simple circulation of commodities. The concomitance of the act of one person selling and the other person buying does not

59 Marx 1976a, p. 208 [1962, p. 127].

mean that sales always occur, because eventually there will not be a buyer for all the commodities that must be sold. It is in the sequence of sale by purchase that the crisis can manifest itself:

> In the velocity of circulation, therefore, there appears the fluid unity of the opposed and complementary phases, i.e. the transformation of the commodities from the form of utility into the form of value and their re-transformation in the reverse direction, or the two processes of sale and purchase. Inversely, when the circulation of money slows down, the two processes assert their oppositional separation and autonomy, stagnation occurs in the changes of form [*Formwechsel*], and hence in the metabolic process [*Stoffwechsel*].[60]

The faster money moves between the hands of different agents, the more 'fluid' is the unity of buying and selling, the faster and more smoothly they follow one another. Nevertheless, the disturbance of this 'velocity', its acceleration or its 'slowing down', reveals that such a unity is that of two distinct phases, which can be more or less 'fluid', and even break apart.

Moreover, to the extent that they are 'opposed and complementary phases', purchase and sale are effectively separated to the point that as the circulation of money slows and the metamorphosis is interrupted, 'the two processes assert their oppositional separation and autonomy'; that is, in their opposition, both phases can be separated and autonomised, appearing as independent from one another, as if there were no relation between them. As Marx says:

> In so far as purchase and sale, the two essential moments of circulation, are *indifferent* to one another and separated in place and time, they *by no means need* to coincide. Their *indifference* can develop into the fortification and *apparent independence* of the one against the other. But in so far as they are both essential moments of a single whole, there must come a moment when the independent form is violently broken and when the inner unity is established externally through a violent explosion.[61]

In other words, 'separated in place and time', the two phases of circulation of commodities appear as 'indifferent to one another', without either appearing

60 Marx 1976a, p. 217 [1962, p. 134].
61 Marx 1974, p. 198 [1983, p. 128]. My italics.

as determined by the other. This indifference already suggests a type of difference that 'can develop into the fortification' of each phase as an autonomous moment, as if purchase had nothing to do with sale and vice versa.

And yet, it is not the separation of the two phases alone that defines the crisis. To the contrary, the crisis is explained by Marx because in a crisis 'the independent form is violently broken', revealing that purchase and sale are not in fact indifferent, but rather 'essential moments of a single whole' that distinguishes and combines them at the same time. A crisis occurs 'when the inner unity is established externally', when the 'fortification' of the difference of the two phases shows that they cannot exist independently, since then the finality of the process of selling in order to buy would not be achieved. This finality is what gives circulation the quality of a 'whole'. However, if the two moments of this whole possess an 'inner unity', that is, a fundamental link that integrates them even when this unity is not manifested 'externally', then how is it possible that they appear to be '*indifferent* to one another'? Why is it that this '*indifference* can develop into the fortification' of each moment as an 'independent form'? According to Marx:

> If, for example, purchase and sale – or the metamorphosis of commodities – present the unity of two processes, or rather the movement of one process through two opposite phases, and thus essentially the unity of the two phases, the movement is essentially just as much the separation of these two phases and their becoming independent of each other. Since, however, they belong together, the independence of the two correlated aspects can only *show itself* forcibly, as a destructive process. It is just the *crisis* in which they assert their unity, the unity of the different aspects. The independence which these two linked and complimentary phases assume in relation to each other is forcibly destroyed. Thus the crisis manifests the unity of the two phases that have become independent of each other. There would be no crisis without this inner unity of factors that are apparently indifferent to each other.[62]

Conceiving of circulation as a 'whole' means grasping that it determines both 'the unity of the different aspects' and 'the separation of these two phases and their becoming independent of each other'. Both movements are necessary, so that the autonomy of purchase and sale is not a mere appearance, in the sense of an illusion falsifying a true 'inner unity'. What is illusory is their indifference,

62 Marx 1969b, p. 500 [1967, p. 501].

and not their difference; what is illusory is that purchase and sale appear as different acts without a reciprocal relation when, in fact, they are 'two phases that have become independent of each other'.

The difference between the two phases is thus not prior or exterior to the relation between the two; is not a mere diversity in the sense explained in chapter 1, section 1.3. above. On the contrary, it is determined by the relation itself, by the unity of the process of selling in order to buy. This is why a text already quoted identified the separation 'in place and time' of selling and buying as 'apparent independence of the one against the other'. Both are opposed because they are the result of an 'independence', a process instituted by the unity of circulation. In *Capital* Marx presents this point as follows:

> To say that these mutually independent processes form an internal unity is to say also that their internal unity moves forward through external oppositions. These two processes lack internal independence because they complement each other. Hence, if the assertion of their external independence proceeds to a certain critical point, their unity violently makes itself felt by producing – a crisis.[63]

Independence stems from the fact that an 'internal unity moves forward through external oppositions'; that is, it stems from the unity moving through phases that 'complement each other' but appear in 'external independence'. This is also the sense of Marx's statement in the previous text, in which purchase and sale 'belong together' because each depends on the other and contains the other as a moment, as the means for its own realisation.

The private producer cannot buy commodities from others unless he has previously sold his own commodity. This purchase reinforces the dependence of each producer on the labour of all others and, hence, the growing specialisation and division of labour that dictate to everyone the need to sell. In the capitalist market, which opposes the private aspect and the social aspect of labour, the unity of buying in order to sell that is not only necessary, but a necessity that must be accomplished by a 'process through two opposite phases'. The necessity is as much that these phases 'belong together' and 'complement

63 Marx 1976a, p. 209 [1962, pp. 127–8]. Here, the passage from Hegel's *Science of Logic* on 'diversity' and 'opposition' reappears. In the case of purchase and sale, the initial indifference between the two forms is only the immediate mode of appearance of the difference between them, which in fact is presented as the autonomisation resulting from the process of 'selling in order to buy' in the logical figure of 'opposition', the difference determined by the interior unity.

each other', as that they be differentiated within their unity, exclude each other based on a reciprocal inclusion and configure an opposition. Purchase must follow sale, sooner or later, in order that the finality of simple circulation be accomplished; but it must also be distinguished from it, because private labour does not produce use-values for the producer, who must sell in order to buy. Furthermore, purchase must be opposed to sale, since the mediation of money configures exchange not as a barter of one use-value for another, but rather as a 'transformation of the commodities from the form of utility into the form of value and their re-transformation in the reverse direction' – 'external oppositions' in which the 'internal unity moves'.

Therefore, crisis does not mean the merely possible autonomisation of different moments of the process of circulation. It means that this autonomisation would go against the unity of the moments, a unity without which no distribution of commodities occurs among the members of a market economy; it means, then, that people would not have access to the products they wished to consume. The social connection between them, essentially constituted by relations of purchase and sale, would be broken if purchase and sale were completely separated. It is the unity of 'selling in order to buy' that differentiates selling and buying as moments, and attributes to them opposite functions in the social process. Hence the 'violence' with which that unity 'makes itself felt' if the autonomy reaches 'a certain critical point'. The separation of the two moments of circulation serves only to enable the social connection to be established, despite the privacy and the specialisation of the work of individuals; it cannot go beyond that task. From the opposition between purchase and sale there unfolds the opposition between the unity and separation of buying and selling. This is a system, because the social connection mediated by the opposed moments maintains and spurs the private character of production, relating economic agents only in the sphere of exchange. In such a system:

> the division of labour converts the product of labour into a commodity, and thereby makes it necessary its conversion into money. At the same time, it makes it a matter of chance whether this transubstantiation succeeds or not.[64]

The commodity-form of the product of private labour means that, for the seller, it is 'necessarily its conversion into money'. In turn, the 'necessity' that the pas-

64 Marx 1976a, p. 203 [1962 p. 122].

sage from one value-form to another should flow normally also reveals that their separation, as the requisite for each producer to act autonomously, is a 'necessity' of the system. Given this autonomy, however, and the consequent lack of conscious planning in the individual division of labour, there is no prior guarantee for the reconciliation of private interests. That each member produces exactly what the others desire and in the precise quantity desired, without excesses or shortage, 'makes it a matter of chance whether' the conciliation 'succeeds or not', that is, that the 'fluid unity' of sale and purchase 'succeeds or not'.

The accidental harmonising of the interests of private producers, stemming from the 'necessity' of their mutual autonomy, is expressed in the accident of the general correspondence between purchase and sale. As the opposition between social labour and private labour is reflected in the opposition between the commodity and money and in the opposition between the passage from one value form to another, C–M and M–C, the conciliation of the multiple necessities of autonomised producers appears as the accident of the normal succession of purchase and sale. Hence the importance that the opposition between the two phases appears as a reciprocal 'indifference', maintaining the independence in which economic agents present themselves; for, according to a text quoted above, 'In so far as purchase and sale … are indifferent to one another … they by no means need to coincide'. Indifference leads to the accident of coinciding. Along these lines, Marx wrote in the *Grundrisse*:

> Just as the exchange value of the commodity leads a double existence, as the particular commodity and as money, so does the act of exchange split into two mutually independent acts: exchange of commodities for money, exchange of money for commodities; purchase and sale. Since these have now achieved a spatially and temporally separate and mutually *indifferent* form of existence, their immediate identity ceases. They *may correspond or not*; they *may balance or not*; they *may enter into disproportion* with one another. They will of course always attempt to equalise one another; but in the place of the earlier immediate equality there now stands the constant movement of equalization, which evidently presupposes constant non-equivalence. It is now entirely *possible* that consonance may be reached only by passing through the most external dissonances.[65]

65 Marx 1974, p. 148 [1983, p. 82]. My italics. See also Marx 1969b, pp. 507–8 [1967, pp. 508–9].

The 'indifferent form of existence' adopted by purchase and sale makes it so that both 'may ... or not' occur in 'correspondence ... balance ... or disproportion'. Even their equalisation is not a given, but the fruit of the 'constant movement' to overcome their 'constant non-equivalence'. The 'external dissonances' between purchase and sale turn their 'consonance' into something merely 'possible'.

To understand the status of the 'possibility' of crisis in simple circulation, it is essential to remember that, in this form of circulation, not only is the unity of 'selling in order to buy' affirmed as a 'necessity'; the passage of the process through the two opposing phases is also a 'necessity'. The way in which the modal problem makes its appearance in Marx, that is, the relation between possibility and necessity of crisis, is clarified in a crucial extract of the *Theories of Surplus value*:

> The economists who deny crisis consequently assert only the unity of these two phases. If they were only separate, without being a unity, then their unity could not be established by force and there could be no crisis. If they were only a unity without being separate, then no violent separation would be possible implying a crisis. Crisis is the forcible establishment of unity between elements that have become independent and the enforced separation from one another of elements which are essentially one.[66]

Besides criticising the rejection of crisis by some economists and also reaffirming that crisis is not defined by the mere separation of phases, this text clearly presents a modal treatment of the possibility of crisis.

In fact, it states that, on the one hand, 'If they were only separate ... there could be no crisis'; that is, the unity of the phases would be impossible and separation would be an absolute necessity because it would exclude the possibility of the actualisation of the opposite alternative, unity. There would be no mutual relation between purchase and sale, nor a 'violent', destructive aspect characterising crisis. On the other hand, 'If they were only a unity ... then no violent separation would be possible implying a crisis'; that is, the separation of the two phases would now be impossible because unity would exclude the possibility of the opposite alternative, also configuring an absolute necessity. Since unity constitutes a means to autonomisation, and autonomisation constitutes a means to the affirmation of unity, neither can exclude the other. The

66 Marx 1969b, p. 513 [1967, p. 514].

logic of 'selling in order to buy' implies the necessity of a process mediated by the opposition of two moments, that is, selling in order to be able to buy (or pay) and buying (or paying) only after selling.

Thus, just as much when the simple circulation of commodities follows its course uninterrupted, equally with crises, the unity and separation of the two phases are always present. To think that the normal course is only determined by unity, as if unity meant an immediate identity without distinction of the opposite terms, would have been the mistake of the economists criticised by Marx. Normal circulation also necessarily goes through the two opposed moments, only that in this case their autonomisation does not reach the point in which unity must subject them to a 'violent' enforcement. But it is a symmetrical mistake to suppose that crisis is only determined by the separation of the phases, as if it were not the result of a process in which the 'independent form is violently broken', leading the opposition between purchase and sale to the brink of rupture. Crisis is simply the point at which the separation appears as the autonomy of the moments, and in which the autonomy, being a product of unity, reveals itself to be impossible and is established in a 'destructive' manner. In uninterrupted circulation as in crisis, equally patent is the necessity of the reciprocal determination of the two moments of the mediated unity of 'selling in order to buy'.

It is the complex status of 'necessity' in Marx's work that is opposed to the absoluteness of, on the one hand, the mere exterior difference between purchase and sale, and, on the other hand, their immediate identity. The aspect of unity does not exclude the possibility of an ensuing process of autonomisation leading to crisis; nor does the aspect of separation exclude the possibility of unity continuing to exist and achieve a fluid path, or a 'violent' assertion, that unmasks the illusion of autonomy. For that reason, purchase and sale 'may correspond or not; they may balance or not; they may enter into disproportion with one another'. Crisis and the normal sequence are always concomitant alternatives, two equally possible situations within the logic of the simple circulation of commodities. Based on this characterisation, Marx makes further considerations on the status of the possibility of crisis and on the insufficiency of remaining at the initial level of the categorial presentation, if the aim is to analyse that phenomenon in a manner more fitting to its capitalist form.

It is therefore indispensable to abandon the framework of simple circulation of commodities, in which the explanation of crisis cannot advance beyond the discovery of an extremely restricted definition of 'possibility'. In Marx's terms:

> These forms therefore imply the possibility of crisis, though no more than the possibility. For the development from this possibility into a reality

> a whole series of conditions is required which do not yet even exist from the standpoint of the simple circulation of commodities.[67]

The insufficiency of the explanation in this 'simple' sphere is evidenced because it lacks the 'development from this possibility into a reality'; it lacks 'a whole series of conditions' that make it possible to move from the possible crisis to an actual crisis. These two levels appear separate, without any 'development' being able to relate them, for the metamorphosis of commodities is found to be 'no more than the possibility', rather than the element guiding the explanation of crisis 'into a reality'. Hence Marx's critique:

> Incidentally, those economists are no better, who (like John Stuart Mill) want to explain the crisis by these simple *possibilities* of crisis contained in the metamorphosis of commodities – such as the separation between purchase and sale. These factors that explain the possibility of crisis, by no means explain their actual occurrence. They do not explain *why* the phases of the process come into such conflict that their inner unity can only assert itself through a crisis, through a violent process. This *separation* appears in the crisis; it is the elementary form of the crisis. To *explain* the crisis on the basis of this, its elementary form, is to explain the existence of the crisis by describing its most abstract form, that is to say, to explain the crisis by the crisis.[68]

While in the previous critique, Marx upbraided 'economists who … assert only the unity of purchase and sale', because they thereby 'deny crisis', in the above-cited text he regards the explanation of crisis by these other economists as tautological. A crisis that is occurring is obviously possible, and the explanation of these economists would merely consist in 'describing' the possibility of what already exists, without saying how crisis reaches the point of 'actual occurrence' based on its possibility. In order to obtain the element that integrates actuality and possibility, then, it is essential to move forward in the analysis reaching the determinations of capital itself, those 'whole series of conditions … required, which do not yet even exist from the standpoint of the simple circulation of commodities'.

---

67 Marx 1976a, p. 209 [1962, p. 128]. Also: 'The circulation itself, of course, gives no clue to the origin of the stagnation; it merely presents us with the phenomenon'. (Marx 1976a, p. 217 [1962, p. 134]).

68 Marx 1969b, p. 502 [1967, p. 502].

CHAPTER 2

The Constitution of Capital

1 From Simple Circulation to Capital

1.1 *The Circuit of Capital*

Although it presupposes the analysis of the simple circulation of commodities, the analysis of capitalist production by Marx involves a greater degree of complexity. The relation between the two analyses, the passage from one to the other, constitutes one of the traditional difficulties in the study of *Capital* insofar as it raises innumerable questions. First of all, whether, historically, a simple mercantile society did indeed exist prior to capitalist society and, if so, whether the law of value was also operative in pre-capitalist societies; and following that, to clarify whether capitalist production altered in any way the law of value as it works in simple circulation and whether, for that reason, the form of presentation of concepts relating to capital should be different from that relating to simple circulation. It is not my intention to give definitive answers to those and other possible problematic issues, some of which lie outside the scope of this book's objectives, but, instead, to concentrate attention on the way Marx associates those two fundamental ambits of his economic thinking.

In the passage from simple circulation to capitalist production addressed in chapter four of *Capital* Volume I, even before the meaning of the concepts and their reference to the sociability of economic agents, a problem of form comes to the fore. Marx begins the chapter with the apparent intention of conserving the anterior mode of presentation by means of which he had deduced the money-form based on the commodity-form. Would it be possible, however, to now deduce the capital-form directly from money through the development of the antagonistic determinations that constitute them? The difficulty Marx found and the way in which he got around it will be the present subchapter's object of investigation.

One of the basic results obtained at the last moment of Marx's presentation of the money-form – hoarding and means of payment – is that money already appears to its owner as an end in its own right. From the start, money constitutes itself as the universal form of expressing value and afterwards as a power that goes beyond the mere function of a means of purchasing, subordinated to the objectives of the simple circulation of commodities. With the full development of this autonomy of value, money becomes the actual purpose of circulation and can acquire the determination of 'capital'. Marx concludes that:

 | DOI:10.1163/9789004690721_004

'The first distinction between money as money and money as capital is nothing more than a difference in their form of circulation'.[1] The 'form of circulation' characteristic of the simple circulation of commodities can be expressed by the well-known formula C–M–C whereas the 'form of circulation' of money as capital is expressed by M–C–M. In the latter situation, money goes from being a means to being an end without abandoning circulation or interrupting it, as 'hoarding' does.

In this way Marx presents the general formula of capital which, in a first approach appears to be merely an inversion of the moments of the simple circulation formula. Just as the opposition between money and commodity unfolds in the opposition between purchase (M–C) and sale (C–M) when the order of money-form and commodity-form is reversed, here a new unfolding takes place as the order of purchase and sale is reversed. While in simple circulation the sale precedes the purchase, in that of capital the purchase precedes the sale. Marx states that: 'Each circular path is the unity of the same two opposite phases'.[2] In both those 'circular paths' represented by the formulae, the 'opposite phases', sale and purchase, are the same, but the circuits differ in the form of their 'unity'; a difference, at first glance, in the sequence of phases – sale and purchase or purchase and sale.

However, going beyond the difference in the order of the terms, Marx notes that the 'unity' constituted by each circuit signifies differences in their purpose and content:

> The path C–M–C proceeds from the extreme constituted by one commodity, and ends with the extreme constituted by another, which falls out of circulation and into the consumption. Consumption, the satisfaction of needs, in short use-value, is therefore its final goal. The path M–C–M, however, proceeds from the extreme of money and finally returns to that same extreme. Its driving and motivating force, its determining purpose, is therefore exchange value.[3]

In the preceding chapter we saw how in simple circulation the agent's objective is to sell in order to purchase; rid himself of what he has produced which has no use-value for him. In that way he obtains money to purchase goods produced by other people which have no use-value for them but have use-value for him, a process determined by the conditions of the division of social labour. Yet, in the

1 Marx 1976a, p. 247 [1962, p. 161].
2 Marx 1976a, p. 249 [1962, p. 163].
3 Marx 1976a, p. 250 [1962, p. 164].

circuit that constitutes capital the purpose of the agent is to buy in order to sell, to acquire a commodity not because it has any use-value to him, but, instead, to sell it. The commodity now appears as a means to obtaining exchange value and not as a use-value intended for the 'satisfaction of needs' of its purchaser. However, closer analysis reveals an immediate difficulty:

> In the simple circulation of commodities the two extremes have the same economic form. They are both commodities, and commodities of equal value. But they are also qualitatively different use-values, as for example corn and clothes. The exchange of products, the interchange carried out between the different materials in which social labour is embodied, forms here the content of the movement. It is otherwise in the cycle M–C–M. At first sight this appears to lack any content, because it is tautological. Both extremes have the same economic form.[4]

The fact that in simple circulation the commodities at the two extremes of the C–M–C formula are 'qualitatively different use-values' indicates precisely that the 'content of the movement' is the exchangers' interest in obtaining products from one another for their consumption. So, if money at the beginning and the end of the M–C–M formula is qualitatively identical to its own self, what would be the point of performing this movement? What purpose would the resale of the purchased commodity serve? What is the 'content' of this apparently 'tautological' movement? After all, what is the sense in purchasing in order to sell?

Marx gives us the answer to these questions in the very text under analysis when he says that the commodities at the extremities of the C–M–C formula have 'equal value', differing, then, only 'qualitatively'. On the contrary, in M–C–M the quality of the extreme terms is identical, so that the only possible way they can differ from one another is in the quantity of their value; in other words, the value of money at the end of the 'cycle' must be greater than at the beginning. In Marx's own words:

> The complete form of this process is therefore M–C–M', where M' = M + ΔM, i.e. the original sum advanced plus an increment. This increment or excess over the original value I call 'surplus value'. The value originally advanced, therefore, not only remains intact while in circulation, but increases its magnitude, adds to itself a surplus value, or is valorised. And this movement converts it into capital.[5]

4 Marx 1976a, pp. 250–1 [Ibid.].
5 Marx 1976a, pp. 251–2 [1962, p. 165].

The 'cycle' of capital only makes sense if there is an increase in value, that is, if 'the value originally advanced … is valorised'. Thus, the purpose, the 'content' that was sought for movement of purchasing in order to sell is: purchase to sell dearer. Marx defines 'surplus value', the key concept in his critique of capitalism, as being precisely 'this increment or excess over the original value' for it is the valorisation of the 'value originally advanced' that 'converts it into capital'. That being so, it becomes possible to offer a primary definition of capital as a value that 'adds to itself a surplus value or is valorised'.

But then how does this valorisation occur? The question raises a second difficulty that harks back to the fundaments of Marxian theory:

> If commodities, or commodities and money, of equal exchange value, and consequently equivalents, are exchanged, it is plain that no one abstracts more value from the circulation than he throws into it. The formation of surplus value does not take place. In its pure form, the circulation process necessitates the exchange of equivalents.[6]

On the one hand, it is incoherent to state that capital emerges in circulation, that in circulation it would be possible to purchase in order sell dearer because 'the circulation process necessitates the exchange of equivalents'. As indicated in the preceding chapter, the 'exchange of equivalents' is a basic supposition for establishing equality among the owners of commodities and, hence, for the legal system of bourgeois society. On the other hand, however, if value at the end of the circulation movement has the same magnitude as it had at the beginning, 'the formation of surplus value does not take place' and value does not 'convert into capital'. Here Marx characterises a radical alternative between two mutually exclusive situations: either the exchange is of equivalents and capital does not emerge; or capital emerges with the abandonment of the basic supposition concerning the circulation of commodities. Thus, the existence of capital in the circulation would signify the elimination of the constitutive fundaments of bourgeois society, including therein value, based on which capital is defined. Its mere existence would be incoherent insofar as it would be based on the destruction of its presuppositions.

Nevertheless, Marx has no intention of refuting the principle of equivalence in exchanges and discards any solution that would be implied by such

6 Marx 1976a, p. 262 [1962, p. 174].

a refutation, such as positing that capital could emerge from the difference between the value and the price actually obtained for a given commodity. For the principles of circulation to be maintained, including the law of value, the exchange must be of equivalents. Surplus value cannot simply originate in circulation.

> But can surplus value originate anywhere else than in circulation, which is the sum total of all the mutual relations of commodity-owners? Outside circulation, the commodity-owner only stands in a relation to his own commodity … But his labour … does not present itself both in the value of the commodity and in an excess quantity over and above that value … The commodity-owner can create value by his labour, but he cannot create values which can valorise themselves.[7]

As a singular case of socially necessary labour, the labour process of each private producer creates value in his own product, but it does not create any surplus to that value. It is not in each individual's direct production that surplus value emerges. The incoherence referred to above finds a more precise expression: 'Capital cannot therefore arise from circulation, and it is equally impossible for it to arise apart from circulation. It must have its origin both in circulation and not in circulation'.[8]

Marx defines the incoherence in this clear-cut, radical manner as a necessary resource to arrive at an equally radical solution that reveals the difficulty of maintaining the method of deduction of concepts employed at the beginning of *Capital*. The very presentation of the concepts arrives at an impasse that can only be resolved by incorporating a presupposition that is not developed in it but, instead, based on consideration of the historical circumstances in which capital is formed. In the Draft of *A Contribution to the Critique of Political Economy* this solution was already mature:

> It is made quite definite at this point that the dialectical form of presentation is right only when it knows its own limits. The examination of the simple circulation shows *us* the general concept of capital, because within the bourgeois mode of production the simple circulation itself exists only as pre-posited [*Voraussetzung*] by capital and as pre-positing [*voraussetzend*] it. The exposition of the general concept of capital does

7 Marx 1976a, p. 268 [1962, pp. 179–80].

8 Marx 1976a, p. 268 [1962, p. 180].

> not make it an incarnation of some eternal idea, but shows how only in actual reality, merely as a *necessary* form, it has yet to flow into labour creating [*setzend*] exchange value, into production resting on exchange value.[9]

Capital is not 'an incarnation of some eternal idea'. The way in which 'labour creating exchange value' should lead 'into production resting on exchange value', that is, the way how, based on value, capitalist production arises, generalising the conditions for value production, 'only' reveals itself in the 'actual' specific historical 'reality' in which that emergence takes place.

This historical circumstance can be incorporated in the presentation of the concepts precisely because it has, at one and the same time, an aspect linked to the circulation of commodities and another aspect independent of it. The problem of how a surplus value is created in the M–C–M' cycle is resolved and the presupposition that M–C and C'–M' are exchanges of equivalents is maintained. What had formerly seemed to be incoherence is resolved by projecting it onto two planes of a new opposition, this time between the sphere of circulation and that of commodity production. As is widely acknowledged, the solution lies in the specific commodity that articulates this opposition and defines the surplus value. In *Capital*, Marx explains the surplus value as being a change in the magnitude of value:

> The change must therefore take place in the commodity which is bought in the first act of circulation, M–C, but not in its value, for it is equivalents which are being exchanged, and the commodity is paid for at its full value. The change can therefore originate only in the actual use-value of the commodity, i.e. in its consumption. In order to extract value out of the consumption of a commodity, our friend the money-owner must be lucky enough to find within the sphere of circulation, on the market, a commodity whose use-value possesses the peculiar property of being source of value, whose actual consumption is therefore itself an objectification of labour, hence a creation of value. The possessor

9 Marx 1976b, 505 [1980, p. 91]. Regarding the insufficiency of the 'deduction' in the categorial presentation Reichelt says that '… in no way does Marx present the historical sequence of the categories as that which "they have in modern bourgeois society". This last is undoubtedly an interpenetration of capitalism, which is only susceptible to theoretical dialectical exhibition when it is fully developed.' (Reichelt 1971, p. 227). Also, Berger states that: '… the historical constitution of the object is the presupposition for the possibility of its systematic investigation'. (Berger 1975, p. 79). My translations.

> of money does find such a special commodity on the market: the capacity for labour, in other words labour power.[10]

It is necessary to recapitulate the reasoning that leads to the concept of labour power here. If the creation of surplus value does not occur in the circulation itself, then it must occur through the mediation of the commodity purchased in the first moment, M–C, so that the value may have increased in the second moment, C–M'. Therefore, the respective commodity must have 'the peculiar property of being a source of value' – a quality that is specific to labour, but not the labour of the money owner himself. As was seen, the money owner 'can create value by his labour, but he cannot create values which can valorise themselves'. For this he has to purchase the labour of others, that is, 'capacity for labour ... labour power' converted into a commodity 'whose actual consumption is therefore itself an objectification of labour, hence a creation of value'.

The existence 'within the sphere of circulation' of labour power as a commodity is the historically determined presupposition integrated by Marx into the presentation to complete the passage of money to capital and define the latter's concept. Referring specifically to capital, he says:

> The historical conditions of its existence are by no means given with the mere circulation of money and commodities. It arises only when the owner of the means of production and subsistence finds the free worker available, on the market, as the seller of his own labour power. And this one historical pre-condition comprises a world's history. Capital, therefore, announces from the outset a new epoch in the process of social production.[11]

The meaning of this 'freedom' of the worker who presents himself 'available, on the market, as the seller of his own labour power' and the way in which the surplus value 'can therefore originate only in the actual use-value of the commodity, i.e. in its consumption', are crucial themes that must be examined in greater detail.

1.2 *The Concept of Surplus Value*

If it is properly understood, the impasse in the definition of surplus value in chapter 5 of *Capital* is not a rhetorical resource Marx made use of to indicate

10 Marx 1976a, p. 270 [1962, p. 181].
11 Marx 1976a, p. 274 [1962, p. 184].

the need to include new historical presuppositions in his analysis. Rather, he exposed the ambivalence of the relations between simple circulation conditions and those of capitalist production. The ambivalence lies in the fact that the conditions of simple circulation are, on the one hand, indispensable and, on the other, insufficient for defining capital. Simple circulation is an indispensable condition because it is the sphere in which the owner of money purchases labour power, the source of value, as a commodity. That situation, however, deranges the set of circumstances characteristic of simple circulation, as will be seen below. According to Marx:

> For the transformation of money into capital, therefore, the owner of money must find the free worker available on the commodity-market; and this worker must be free in the double sense that as a free individual he can dispose of his labour power as his own commodity, and that, on the other hand, he has no other commodity for sale, i.e. he is rid of them, he is free of all the objects needed for the realization of his labour power.[12]

Above all, the meaning of 'freedom' for the worker is that 'he can dispose of his labour power as his own commodity'. He appears as a 'free individual' insofar as he owns a commodity, is legally qualified to sell it, and, at least in principle, to choose to whom and in what conditions he wishes to do so. At the same time, this freedom implies that he is dispossessed 'of all the objects needed for the realization of his labour power', that is, it implies that the worker should not own the means of production he works with, a condition that obliges him to sell 'his labour power' to obtain money and be able to purchase the means of subsistence he needs to consume. He must present himself as the owner of 'his labour power' alone and not of the 'objects needed for the realization' of the production process. Thus:

> in the further development of exchange value this [freedom and equality – JG] will be transformed, and it will ultimately be shown that private

12 Marx 1976a, pp. 272–3 [1962, p. 183]. In chapter 26 *Capital* Volume I, Marx describes as 'primitive accumulation' – or, in an alternative translation of *ursprünglich*, as 'original accumulation' – the historical process whereby the worker appears 'bereft of all the necessary conditions' to work autonomously. It is symptomatic that the historical origin of capitalism is explained by Marx only at the end of the entire systematic presentation of the unfolding of capitalist social forms in Volume I, just as he will proceed with commercial capital, interest-bearing capital and land ownership in Volume III. Marx makes it clear that although history constitutes the object of the presentation, it does not constitute its forms and stages.

> property in the product of one's own labour is identical with the separation of labour and property, so that labour will create alien property and property will command alien labour.[13]

In the conditions of simple circulation, the producer's ownership of the means of production endows him with ownership of his product and, accordingly, with the right to sell this product as a commodity. However, with the 'separation of labour and property' the worker, non-owner of the means of production, is no longer the proprietor of the product. On selling the right to the use of his labour power to the owner of the means of production, the worker concedes the proprietorship of the product to the owner of the means of production. Therefore, his 'labour will create alien property'. At the same time, the ownership of the means of production guarantees the position of labour contractor for the proprietor. His 'property will command alien labour'. Marx explains:

> ... money is converted into capital only: 1) if *commodity production*, i.e., the production of products in the form of commodities, becomes the general mode of production; 2) if the commodity (money) is exchanged against labour power (that is, actually against labour) as a commodity, and consequently if labour is wage-labour; 3) this is the case however only when the objective conditions, that is (considering the productive process as a whole), the products confront labour as independent forces, not as the property of labour but as the property of someone else, and thus in the form of *capital*.[14]

The definition of capital is thus developed and enriched. Capital is no longer restricted to the money that purchases labour power as a commodity to use it and increase its own value; it is also defines itself as the money that purchases the means of production. Money actually purchases: 'the objective conditions that ... confront labour as independent forces ... not as the property of labour but as the property of someone else ... thus in the form of capital'. This expropriation alone ensures that the worker has 'no other commodity for sale' because, insofar as he is no longer the owner of what he produces, the worker is reduced to the proprietorship of his labour power alone. By conceding the ownership of the final product to the capitalist, he 'confronts' the products of his own labour

---

13 Marx 1976b, p. 238 [1983, p. 164].

14 Marx 1969c, pp. 490–1 [1968, pp. 111, 481].

and the means of production – 'objective conditions' in the broadest sense – 'as the property of someone else', that is to say, of the one who employs him and pays him a wage.

In the Draft to the *Contribution to the Critique of Political Economy*, the opposition between the 'objective conditions' alien to the worker and the capitalist's use of labour power enables Marx to determine the circumstances of this use in philosophical terms:

> The only opposite of *reified* [*vergegenständlichte*] labour is *unreified* [*ungegenständliche*] labour, and the opposite to the *objectified* [*objektivierten*] labour, subjective labour. Or, the opposite of past labour, which exists in space, is living labour, which exists in time. As the presently existing unreified [*ungegenständliche*] (and so also not yet objectified) labour, it can be present only as the *power* [*Vermögen*], potentiality [*Möglichkeit*], ability, as the *labour capacity* [*Arbeitsvermögen*] of the living subject.[15]

If the means of production result from the already 'objectified past labour', what opposes them is the 'presently existing', 'not yet objectified', and in this sense 'subjective labour'. It is the 'living labour' opposed to the dead, to labour power defined as the 'capacity' that the wage-earner sells to the capitalist, to the exclusive proprietor of the means with which the 'living subject' can produce.

Yet 'the process of the consumption of labour power is at the same time the production process of commodities and of surplus value'.[16] To understand the formation of surplus value it is necessary to perceive how the process whereby labour power is 'consumed' constitutes the immediate 'production process', the major theme of *Capital* Volume I. Before entering into this theme, the distinction between the spheres of circulation and production is decisive: in the sphere of circulation, the capitalist purchases labour power, a commodity which, just like any other, has value; in the sphere of production he consumes the use-value of the labour power by combining it with the means of production. Marx explains that:

> one consequence of the peculiar nature of labour power as a commodity is this, that it does not in reality pass straight away into the hands of the buyer on the conclusion of the contract between buyer and seller … its use-value consists in the subsequent exercise of that power.[17]

15 Marx 1976b, p. 502 [1980, p. 86].
16 Marx 1976a, p. 279 [1962, p. 189].
17 Marx 1976a, p. 277 [1962, p. 188]. See also 1976b, p. 506 [1980, pp. 90–1].

Like any other commodity, the labour power has its own use-value, which is to produce commodities for the capitalist who purchased it, commodities with their own value, independent of the value of the labour power that produced them.

On discovering that labour power is also constituted by the opposition between value and use-value, Marx proffers a revealing solution for the problem of the origin of surplus value, one that explains the exploitation of labour within the equivalents exchange system. The value of labour power, like that of the other commodities, is determined by the socially necessary time required to produce it; in this case, the time needed to produce the means of living the worker needs to continue performing his activity during the working day.[18] In turn, the use-value of labour power, when consumed, produces new commodities with values higher than the value of the labour power:

> But the past labour embodied in the labour power and the living labour it can perform, and the daily cost of maintaining labour power and its daily expenditure in work, are two totally different things. The former determines the exchange value of the labour power, the latter is its use-value. The fact that half a day's labour is necessary to keep the worker alive during 24 hours does not in any way prevent him from working a whole day. Therefore the value of labour power, and the value which that labour power valorises in the labour process, are two entirely different magnitudes.[19]

For that reason, if the value formation process:

> is not carried beyond the point where the value paid by the capitalist for the labour power is replaced by an exact equivalent, it is simply a process of creating value; but if it is continued beyond that point, it becomes a process of valorisation.[20]

18 The worker's sustenance is not restricted to the replenishment of his physical energy: 'His natural needs, such as food, clothing, fuel and housing vary according to the climatic and other physical peculiarities of his country. On the other hand, the number and extent of his so-called requirements, as also the manner in which they are satisfied, are themselves products of history, and depend therefore to a great extent on the level of civilization attained by a country; in particular they depend on the conditions in which, and consequently on the habits and expectations with which, the class of free workers has been formed'. (Marx 1976a, p. 275 [1962, p. 185]).

19 Marx 1976a, p. 300 [1962, pp. 207–8].

20 Marx 1976a, p. 302 [1962, p. 209].

Thus, for the purchaser of labour power, the mechanism creating surplus value in this fundamental form consists of obliging the worker to undergo a longer working day than is necessary to create the value corresponding to the means of living that replenish his labour power. This is only possible because, bereft of the 'objective conditions' for working, the wage-earner has to accept the terms imposed by the proprietor of those conditions. In this way, the value of the commodities produced comes to be greater than the amount the capitalist disbursed – equivalent to the means of production and the labour power – and the work process becomes converted into a way of valorising the initial value, subordinating itself to the valorisation process. Marx defines as capital this value which valorises itself by means of the production process; or, to be more precise, as 'industrial' capital, quite distinct from commercial capital or interest-bearing capital, which existed long before industrial capital and whose valorisation takes place outside the production sphere.

In this production sphere, surplus value is created during the labour time that exceeds the time required to pay the value of the labour power. Marx warns us that:

> It is just as important for a correct understanding of surplus value to conceive it as merely a congealed quantity of surplus labour time, as nothing but an objectified surplus value, as it is for a proper comprehension of value in general to conceive it as merely a congealed quantity of so many hours of labour, as nothing but objectified labour.[21]

Surplus value corresponds, therefore, to the value of the commodities produced in that part of the working day which exceeds the time needed to produce the equivalent of the worker's subsistence needs. Marx calls that form of surplus value, determined by prolonging the working day and which effectively configures the exploitation of the worker, 'absolute surplus value', even under the assumption that the worker receives the equivalent of his labour power. Throughout *Capital*, Marx maintains this supposition, particularly because he wishes to emphasise that the creation of surplus value does not depend on a form of exploitation in which wages are lower than the value of labour power.

Nevertheless, the development of the central concepts of his critique of political economy were to introduce difficulties to this initial form of resolving the conflict between labour exploitation and the exchange of equivalents. New

21 Marx 1976a, p. 325 [1962, p. 231].

problems would arise related to the effectiveness of the law of value in capitalism leading in the end to the real inversion of its ethical-legal presuppositions of equality and liberty as the bases of bourgeois individuality.

1.3 *The Inversion of the Bourgeois Law of Appropriation*

Marx's ingenious presentation of the passage from the concept of value to the concept of capital is in fact only possible on the basis of his perspective regarding the relation between simple circulation of commodities and capitalist production. In this perspective the concept of capital must be defined and developed by its formal dimension and not by its substance. As Marx himself put it in the *Grundrisse*:

> To develop the concept of capital it is necessary to begin not with labour but with value, and, precisely, with exchange value in an already developed movement of circulation. It is just as impossible to make the transition directly from labour to capital as it is to go from the different human races directly to the banker, or from nature to the steam engine.[22]

Even though the substance of capital is labour, which produces both the surplus value and the means of production, the concept of capital should be obtained based on the value-forms that appear in the sphere of the simple circulation of commodities. First of all, capital must be understood in the form of the money that is paid to the worker as a wage and which defines the capitalist as a purchaser of labour power, and labour must be viewed in the form it takes on in capitalism, that of a commodity, a form capable of producing value and surplus value.

Adopting value and money as the starting points for the presentation of capital has the advantage of not defining capital simply by its material embodiment, that is, by the means of production in which past labour has been accumulated and objectified. The means of production are nothing more than one of the forms in which capital is determined – the form that the worker faces – and which therefore does not completely define capital. On the contrary, it is the social relation in the form of money that shows itself to be most suitable for developing 'the concept of capital'. On the face of it, labour power appears as a commodity and capital as the value that purchases the source of value and creates the conditions for the generation of surplus value. Capital thus constitutes itself through the intermediation of the social relation between the owner

22 Marx 1974, p. 259 [1983, p. 184].

of the means of production and the worker who is deprived of them, and not through the technical relation of labour with the instruments and raw materials used by it.

However, defining labour power as a commodity presupposes an explanation of the social conditions in which commodities circulate, that is, the situation of the economic agents as commodity owners and everything that stems from this situation such as the development of money and the principle of exchange of equivalents. Only then would it be possible to understand the special case in which the commodity being sold is labour power. In this case:

> the exchange between the worker and the capitalist is a simple exchange; each obtains an equivalent; the one obtains money, the other a commodity whose *price* is exactly equal to the money paid for it.[23]

In this initial moment of Marx's analysis, capitalist's purchase of labour power is grounded on the principle of the exchange of equivalents. The value of the labour power 'is exactly equal to the money paid for it', a supposition already mentioned at the end of the preceding subchapter. Although the presentation of *Capital* will later invert this principle, it is fundamental that the inversion appears as a development of the determinations of the exchange of equivalents, or, rather, it is fundamental that the principle itself should be inverted and twisted so that the true role of simple circulation in the entirety of the production of surplus value and capital becomes perfectly clear.

It is undoubtedly paradoxical to state that the equality that marks the relations between commodity owners should be the presupposition for a social relation marked by inequality between the owners and non-owners of the means of production. Marx seems either to have described two different societies or to consider capitalism to be a specific form, historically derived from a more general type of mercantile society. These two alternatives gave rise to a long polemic between those who see in the paradox an insoluble contradiction of Marx's theory and those who see in it a constitutive element of the categorial presentation.[24] Although my own position is closer to the latter alternative, it is

---

23 Marx 1974, pp. 281–2 [1983, p. 204].

24 Rosdolsky sums up well the position of those who criticize Marx's formulation on this point: 'The object of the attack is the close connection between Marx's theory of value and Marx's theory of capital – the fact that, in order to arrive at the laws of the capitalist mode of production, Marx proceeds from the analysis of the simple commodity production, which presupposes the social equality of the participants in exchange, and therefore disregards the inequality which characterize capitalist production' (1977, p. 168); and he

important to stress the systemic aspect of the relationship between simple circulation and capitalist production, beyond any possible historical relationship. This is what I try to explain in the following pages.

The concepts associated with simple circulation serve as fundaments for the deduction of the concepts associated with capitalist production. However, the latter also serve as fundaments for confirming the concepts of simple circulation. In the *Theories of Surplus value*, Marx explained that:

> On the other hand, the product wholly assumes the form of a commodity only – as a result of the fact that the entire product has to be transformed into exchange value and that also all the ingredients necessary for its production enter it as commodities – in other words it wholly becomes a commodity only with the development and on the basis of capitalist production.[25]

The social form typical of simple circulation, that is, the commodity-form, fully develops and is generalised to all the products and all their 'ingredients', such as labour power and the means of production, 'only ... on the basis of capitalist production'. This affirmation, however, should not be understood as a historical explanation because the mercantile society described by Marx in the initial

---

cites Tugan-Baranovsky as the first to present the objection and Schlesinger (1950, pp. 96–7) as one of his most important continuators. He then proposes his own answer to the problem, which generally coincides with Reichelt's (1973, pp. 227–43): the determinations of simple circulation would not be annulled by those of capital, but overcome by the latter, in the sense of the Hegelian *Aufhebung*. Therefore, simple circulation would be denied as an autonomous process, but preserved as part of the wider process of capitalist production. In spite of Rosdolsky and Reichelt, the objection was reformulated by Benetti and Cartelier (1980), for whom commodity production and capital production would correspond to distinct historical stages, so that it was a mistake of Marx to begin *Capital* with the concept of commodity. However, this position commits the error of situating the two levels of Marx's analysis in two distinct historical moments, disregarding the complex relationship of both within the specifically capitalist moment, namely the fact that labour power initially appears as a commodity sold and purchased. Even Postone (1993), while recognising the systemic dimension of categorial presentation and claiming that 'commodity circulation is only a moment of a more complex totality' of capitalist production, also states that 'Marx accords it real social and historical importance' and associate it with 'the great bourgeois revolutions' of the Modern Era (1993, p. 274). It is evident here that Postone confuses the simple circulation of commodities with the commercial capital predominant in the European economy before the eighteenth century: this predominance was indeed a historical fact and brought the bourgeoisie to power, but the formula of commercial capital is not C–M–C, but M–C–M'.

25 Marx 1969c, p. 74 [1968, p. 69].

Part of *Capital* Volume I – a society made up of autonomous producers, all of them proprietors of their own means of production and linked to one another by the exchange of their products – never really existed in a pure state. Mercantile relations were always inserted in far broader range of social conditions in which the economic surplus was extracted by physical coercion, as was the case with slavery, feudalism, and other variants.

In the text cited above Marx is not concerned with the history and prehistory of capitalism, but with the presentation and unfolding of its concepts. In that sense, he adds that:

> The simple circulation is, rather, an abstract sphere of the bourgeois process of production as a whole, which through its own determinations shows itself to be a moment, a mere form of appearance of some deeper process lying behind it, even resulting from it and producing it – industrial capital.[26]

Capital is value, it is the social nexus among private autonomous proprietors who connect through the exchanges of their commodities, but it is a value that valorises. Obviously, on the one hand, this valorisation involves circulation, because the capitalist has to purchase means of production and labour power, and he has to sell the commodity produced. On the other hand, the valorisation of value involves and goes beyond circulation, connecting it to the labour process in which the surplus value is produced, given that the objective of the process of production as a whole is to increase value and not merely to conserve it. Production depends on circulation 'resulting from it'; but it is also a 'whole' that encompasses circulation within the overall objective of valorisation. This objective is what determines the function performed by circulation, 'producing it', and making it 'show itself to be a moment, a mere form of appearance' or a necessary stage that the valorisation must pass through, but nothing more than a stage.

Thus, capital does not absolutely negate the determinations of simple circulation, but it also does not maintain them, as if nothing fundamental were added to them, nothing that would endow them with a new foundation. What is overcome is merely the content of simple circulation, that is, the objective of selling in order to buy use-values, products that satisfy the necessities of final consumption. With its transformation into a mere 'moment' in a greater process, circulation receives the role of executing the stages of movement to

26 Marx 1976b, p. 482 [1980, pp. 68–9].

purchase in order to sell dearer.[27] Furthermore, again in Marx's words, simple circulation 'is, rather, an abstract sphere of the bourgeois process of production as a whole'. It is 'abstract' in the sense that a mercantile society corresponding to the conditions of simple circulation described at the beginning of *Capital*, a world in which all the commodity producers would be the proprietors of their means of production and for that reason, equal to one another and free to dispose of their assets and persons at will, never existed. It is also 'abstract' in the sense of being 'a mere form of appearance of some deeper process' that endows it with different content. In spite of all that, the presentation of simple circulation is crucial to Marx's critical project. Its function is to establish a common starting point with political economy whose presuppositions of justice and equality Marx intended to invert and subvert by taking them to their ultimate consequences.

Indeed, the principle of the exchange of equivalents continues to rule the acts of buying and selling the commodities that enter the production of capital, including the buying and selling of the 'labour power', a commodity which Marx proposes is paid for at its value:

> The owner of the money has paid the value of a day's labour power; he therefore has the use of it for a day, a day's labour belongs to him. On the one hand the daily sustenance of labour power costs only half a day's labour, while on the other hand the very same labour power can remain effective, can work, during a whole day, and consequently the value which its use during one day creates is double what the capitalist pays for that use; this circumstance is a piece of good luck for the buyer, but by no means an injustice towards the seller.[28]

Marx insists that the production of surplus value does not depend on the remuneration of labour power below its value, it does not depend on a moral decision made by the employer of labour power. A 'piece of good luck' for the capitalist does not require 'an injustice' as regards the worker. Beyond the

27 It should not be forgotten that the simple circulation of commodities, with its formula C–M–C, is an effective dimension of capitalist society, since it corresponds, for example, to the movement executed by labour power: the worker sells the only commodity he possesses to the capitalist, C–M, and with the wages obtained buys the means of living, M–C, which he needs to reproduce his physical and mental labour power. Therefore, simple circulation is not historically overcome and replaced by the production and circulation of capital, M–C–M', but is inscribed in the latter and subordinated to its logic, continuing to exist only within it.

28 Marx 1976a, p. 301 [1962, p. 208].

sphere of individuals' wills and consciences, surplus value is created by the functioning of the system and is based on the 'circumstance' that the maintenance of labour power costs less than the value it produces in the whole day's work. The exploitation of the worker does not necessarily consist in his under-remuneration but in forcing him to work for a longer time than would be needed to recompose his labour power.

That, however, is only one aspect of the problem. Although, juridically, capitalists and workers may be equal as proprietors of commodities, and workers are free to sell their labour power, such relations are only established in the sphere of circulation which is 'a mere form of appearance of a deeper process lying behind it'. In the same vein Marx adds:

> In present bourgeois society as a whole, this positing of prices and their circulation etc. appears as the surface process, beneath which, however, in the depths, entirely different processes go on, in which this apparent equality and liberty disappear.[29]

Liberty and equality show themselves to be something 'apparent' that disappears when one passes from 'surface processes' to other 'entirely different processes', that is, when one passes from circulation to 'bourgeois society as a whole'. The meaning of the term 'entirely different' here is that circulation takes place in a capitalist society divided between owners and non-owners of the means of production. In other words, the equality among the agents is established on the basis of their inequality, otherwise surplus value and capital would not be produced. Thus:

> Similarly, because the worker receives the equivalent in the form of money, the form of general wealth, he is in this exchange an equal vis-à-vis the capitalist, like every other party in exchange; at least, so he *seems*. In fact this equality is already disturbed because the worker's relation to the capitalist as a use value, in the form specifically distinct from exchange value, in opposition to value posited as value, is a presupposition of this seemingly simple exchange; because, thus, he already stands in an economically different relation – outside that of exchange ... This semblance exists, nevertheless, as an illusion on his part and to a certain degree on the other side, and thus essentially modifies his relation by comparison to that of workers in other social modes of production.[30]

29 Marx 1974, p. 247 [1983, p. 173].
30 Marx 1974, pp. 283–4 [1983, p. 209].

The worker, therefore only 'seems' to be 'in this exchange, an equal vis-à-vis the capitalist' while 'in fact', 'this equality is disturbed', because the relationship is established between the direct producer bereft of the means to work and the proprietor of those means, the representative of capital – 'value posited as value' – who places himself 'in opposition' to the worker. But equality is not the mere illusory appearance of what is truly inequality, it is the form in which the latter appears.

In the sphere of circulation, the agents of exchange find themselves already in different situations even though they are the owners of equivalent commodities. Their equality and inequality are the two poles of an opposition between a 'surface process' and a process 'in the depths'. Those poles do not annul one another, quite the contrary; they mutually condition one another and maintain themselves, configuring a contradiction that is at the heart of the Marxian analysis of bourgeois society.

To understand this contradiction and decipher the appearance of equality, it is necessary to bear in mind that circulation is part of a global process, and that equality is therefore a moment of inequality 'in the depths'. Marx does not reject the existence of freedom and equality; he just places them in a much broader context of social inequality which nevertheless requires that 'surface process', because the worker needs to be free so that capital can hire him or fire him according to its need for valorisation. Marx's text states that 'this semblance exists, nevertheless, as an illusion', but not because an aspect of liberty and equality does not really exist. The illusion consists in only seeing the liberty and equality and not the inequality that exists and determines the liberty and equality. When the capitalist buys labour power and means of production in just the same way as when he sells the commodity produced in the work process, he is exchanging equivalents. Yet the global process is not reduced to those moments. Its fundamental objective is valorisation, which only occurs based on the inequality of social and economic conditions between capitalists and wage-earning workers. This objective comes to determine the stages of circulation and include them in the totality that involves them and imbues them with new meaning. Founded on inequality, capitalist production, 'by comparison to … other social modes of production', has the distinguishing feature that the relationship between unequal social classes takes place in the sphere of the circulation of commodities based on the equality of market agents.

Interpreting bourgeois social relations only or mainly as being egalitarian and free is the equivalent of extrapolating the principle in force in its non-essential moment to explain the whole. Marx considered liberty and equality to be decisive for distinguishing capitalism from modes of production in which the economic surplus is obtained through violent coercion, but he does not consider them to be constitutive of the foundation of capitalism. His criticism consists in the fact that identifying equality and freedom as the most important characteristics of the system implies reducing the relationship between capitalist and worker to the relationship between buyer and seller of labour power, a relationship which only actually exists because the worker is dispossessed of the means of production. It is this dispossession, this inequality, that creates the situation whereby worker and capitalist appear to be equals, insofar as the worker sells his commodity in exchange for a sum of money corresponding to its value.

After thus identifying the nexus between circulation and capitalist production as a whole, Marx goes on to unmask the egalitarian presuppositions which bourgeois society pretends it is based on. To this end he puts forward the concept of the *reproduction* of the conditions for capital's existence. This is the power capital acquires to reproduce the social situation from which it originated, renewing, at each repetition of the cycle of production and circulation of commodities, the capitalist's concentration of ownership of the means of production and the wage-earner's dispossession of the same. This power of capital constantly increases as most of the surplus value created in a production cycle is reinvested to form the initial capital of a new cycle.

A detailed examination of reproduction will be made in the third chapter of this book. At this point, what is important is to understand how it affects the nexus between the equality and inequality of workers and capitalists, inverting the principle of appropriation of the product through labour, based on which bourgeois society declares its legitimacy.

Considering that the cycle of production and valorisation is constantly repeated, Marx states:

> The exchange of equivalents, the original operation with which we started, is now turned round in such a way that there is only an apparent exchange, since, firstly, the capital which is exchanged for labour power is itself merely a portion of the product of the labour of others which has been appropriated without an equivalent; and, secondly, this capital must not only be replaced by its producer, the worker, but replaced together with an added surplus.[31]

In a hypothetical initial moment, the capitalist presents himself as the owner of a certain sum of money with which he intends to hire and remunerate work-

31 Marx 1976a, p. 729 [1962, p. 609].

ers. However, right after the first cycle in which he produces and sells commodities, this capitalist appropriates to himself the value already produced by the workers, alleging that to be a right conferred on him by his ownership of the means of production. So, in the following cycle, 'the capital which is exchanged for labour power' will be 'a portion of the product of the labour of others which has been appropriated without an equivalent'. From then on labour power comes to be paid with a value that it has produced itself and which the capitalist has appropriated. In that light the above text continues with these words:

> The relation of exchange between capitalist and worker becomes a mere semblance belonging only to the process of circulation, it becomes a mere form, which is alien to the content of the transaction itself, and merely mystifies it. The constant sale and purchase of labour power is the form; the content is the constant appropriation by the capitalist, without equivalent, of a portion of the labour of others which has already been objectified, and his repeated exchange of this labour for a greater quantity of the living labour of others.[32]

Considering each moment in which the labour contract is established in isolation, labour power is always remunerated by a value that belongs to capital. Nevertheless, the sequence of these moments reveals how this is 'a mere form, which is alien to the content of the transaction itself, and merely mystifies it'. The aspect of a 'mere form' refers to the legal formality whereby the capitalist is the owner of the money that is converted into wages, as opposed to the 'content' according to which the value of this money is created by labour power.

As a 'mere form, which is alien to the content', the payment of the worker with the product of his own work implies that the principle of exchange of equivalents 'is now turned round'. From the 'content' point of view, it no longer occurs, indeed has been abolished. Thus, the text continues:

> Originally the rights of property seemed to us to be grounded in a man's own labour. Some such assumption was at least necessary, since only commodity-owners with equal rights confronted each other, and the sole means of appropriating the commodities of others was the alienation of a man's own commodities, commodities which, however, could only be

32 Marx 1976a, pp. 729–30 [Ibid.].

> produced by labour. Now, however, property turns out to be the right, on the part of the capitalist, to appropriate the unpaid labour of others or its product, and the impossibility, on the part of the worker, of appropriating his own product. The separation of property from labour thus becomes the necessary consequence of a law that apparently originated in their identity.[33]

It is no longer labour that confers the right of ownership of the product, as was the case in the rules of simple circulation; it is ownership (of the means of production) that gives the capitalist the right to appropriate the product of the wage labour.

From the point of view of form, however, the situation of exchanging equivalents is preserved, maintaining the agents' freedom and equality. It is a decisive form for enabling the market to establish the mediations between capitalists and wage-earners, compelling the latter to work for essentially economic reasons. With this, the workers are free to be unemployed or to be transferred from one occupation to another according to the interests of capital. In this sense, the 'alienation' mentioned in the text cited above means that the form of appropriation by labour and of the exchange of equivalents must persist, even though its content is other. Consequently, the 'mystification' lies in the fact that the form seems to reflect the content, characterising capitalist production by its agents' freedom and equality insofar as they are defined, in general, as mere buyers and sellers.

Therefore, the affirmation of the formal principles of simple circulation does not imply that, for Marx, a society established on them alone exists, ever existed, or will ever exist. On the contrary, the development of the determinations of simple circulation in the exchange between capital and labour power necessarily leads to a situation in which these principles are 'turned around'. Their permanence in the sphere of circulation and their negation by valorisation are two moments that are distinct but equally valid in the Marxian reconstruction of capitalist production. Taken as a whole, this production involves the determinations of the circulation of commodities just as much as those that turn them around.

In the final analysis, the result of this turning around is to unmask the 'mystifying illusion' that capital also constitutes a factor of production and of value creation which adds to labour in the process of valorisation and is exchanged in the market as an equivalent of labour power. In this way, Marx uncovers how

33 Marx 1976a, p. 730 [1962, pp. 609–10].

the separation of labour from the means of production makes it possible for an external force to dominate labour and impose its own principles for the creation, expansion, and circulation of value. It is by means of this force that capital acquires life and power. Thus, a new configuration of fetishism emerges whose mysteries must now be investigated and clarified.

2 The Subjectivity of Capital

2.1 *The Fetishism of Capital*

To understand how Marx defines the power of capital in both its real and mystifying aspects, it is necessary to understand how he conceives the logic that articulates the relationship between capital and labour. The initial and most visible face of this relationship is that of the exchange between capitalist and worker within which they appear only as buyer and seller, that is, as if labour power were no more than a commodity like any other that money can buy. In this case, in the same way as happens with simple circulation, the money of the capitalist is situated in opposition to the commodities in general, while the commodities, including labour power, are situated in regard to one another in a mere diversity determined by the multiple use-values. In its other face, however, the relationship between capital and labour is marked by inequality regarding the ownership of the means of production. Labour power appears as a special commodity which, on opposing itself to the money in circulation, transforms the latter into money-capital. In this determination, therefore, money is no longer simply opposed to the commodities in general but rather to the labour power commodity. In the words of the *Grundrisse*:

> Capital is by definition money, but not merely money in the simple form of gold and silver, nor merely as money in opposition to circulation, but in the form of all substances – commodities. To that degree, therefore, it does not, as capital, stand in opposition to use value, but exists apart from money precisely only in use values ... In this regard, the opposite of capital cannot itself be a particular commodity, for as such it would form no opposition to capital, since the substance of capital is itself use value; it is not this commodity or that commodity, but all commodities ... The only thing distinct from *objectified* labour is *non-objectified* labour, labour that is still objectifying itself, *labour* as subjectivity. Or, *objectified* labour, i.e. labour that is *present in space*, can also be opposed, as *past labour*, to labour that is *present in time*. If it is to be present in time, alive, then it

> can be present only as the *living subject*, in which it exists as capacity, as possibility; hence as *worker*. The only *use value*, therefore, which can form the opposite pole to capital is *labour*.[34]

In the immediate production and valorisation process, capital acquires and employs any commodity whose use value it needs so that 'it does not, as capital, stand in opposition to use value' as money does in circulation, 'but exists ... only in [the] use values' that it consumes to valorise itself. For this reason, 'the opposite of capital cannot itself be a particular commodity, for as such it would form no opposition to capital'. The opposition of commodity and money is not sufficient in itself to determine money as capital. However, although capital as 'objectified labour' can take the form of any commodity, it is only actually in opposition to 'labour as subjectivity', that is to say, to the labour power that produces the commodities and which is, itself, a commodity. 'The only use value, therefore, which can form the opposite pole to capital is labour', the use value whose consumption creates product and value.

Thus the 'opposition', even though it already appears in the sphere of the sale and purchase of labour power, has its foundations in the conditions of the immediate production of commodities. A more detailed analysis of the relationship between capital and labour in the sphere of immediate production is then necessary to begin to grasp why this relationship takes on the logical figure of an 'opposition'.

Still in the *Grundrisse*, Marx explains that in production, 'Labour is not only the *use-value* which confronts capital, but, rather, it is *the use-value* of capital itself'.[35] On purchasing labour power, capital includes it as part of its own self and acquires the right to put it into action, thereby consuming its use-value which has thus now become part of capital itself. The text continues:

> Through the exchange with the worker, capital has appropriated labour itself; labour has become one of its moments, which now acts as a fructifying vitality upon its merely existent and hence dead objectivity.[36]

By including in itself the value-creating activity as 'one of its moments', capital gives it a specific function in the valorisation process by which capital itself is constituted. As Marx makes it clear in *Capital*:

34 Marx 1974, p. 271 [1983, pp. 197–8].

35 Marx 1974, p. 297 [1983, p. 219].

36 Marx 1974, p. 298 [Ibid.]

> The part of capital, therefore, which is turned into means of production, i.e. the raw material, the auxiliary material and the instruments of labour, does not undergo any quantitative alteration of value in the process of production. For this reason, I call it the constant part of capital, or more briefly, constant capital. On the other hand, the part of capital which is turned into labour power does undergo an alteration of value in the process of production. It both reproduces the equivalent of its own value and produces an excess, a surplus value, which may itself vary, and be more or less according to circumstances. This part of capital is continually being transformed from a constant into a variable magnitude. I therefore call it the variable part of capital, or more briefly, variable capital.[37]

On the one hand, labour power is that part of capital which 'acts as a fructifying vitality upon [the] merely existent and hence dead objectivity' of the means of production. It is the 'vitality' that resuscitates the value contained in the 'dead objectivity' of those means and transfers it to the product without altering its magnitude, and in such a way as to define them as 'constant capital'. On the other hand, labour power is also that part of capital which 'undergoes an alteration of value in the process of production', creating a surplus value beyond the value of labour power and for that reason, it is 'variable capital'. Even the value of the 'constant part of capital' is only transferred to the product through the action of living labour, which simultaneously 'reproduces the equivalent of its own value' in the value of the product and, beyond that, 'produces an excess, a surplus value'. As 'variable capital' labour power becomes part of capital; more than this, it is the part which on undergoing 'an alteration of value' transforms value into capital.

Yet labour power only has this capability because the situation of being deprived of the means of production, which defines it as a commodity, persists in the labour process. Throughout this process, the worker remains a non-owner of the means of production, a situation that obliges him to work under the conditions imposed by capital and for a longer time than needed to replenish his labour power. The compulsion to surplus labour which creates surplus value stems from the fact that the means of production are in opposition to the worker, not only prior to but during the labour process. This is the fundamental 'opposition' which develops into that other, that of the 'vitality' of variable capital and the 'dead objectivity' of constant capital, and

37 Marx 1976a, p. 317 [1962, pp. 223–4].

which underlies the creation of both surplus value and capital. It is regarding this point that Marx formulated his famous metaphor:

> But capital has one sole driving force, the drive to valorise itself, to create surplus value, to make its constant part, the means of production, absorb the greatest possible amount of surplus labour. Capital is dead labour which, vampire-like, is vivified only by sucking living labour, and lives the more, the more labour it sucks.[38]

If the means of production on the one hand appear as a 'part of capital' just like labour power, on the other hand they embody the autonomous power of capital in the face of labour. Through their intermediation, capital presents itself simultaneously as a part and as the whole of its constitutive process. Firstly, capital must always redetermine labour as the opposite that confronts the means of production as an alien objective condition because it is only through the renewed reproduction of the historical situation of expropriation of the means of production that labour power becomes defined as a commodity, the producer of value and surplus value. Secondly, the 'dead objectivity' of the means of production is not something merely passive whose value is transferred to the product. According to Marx's 'vampire' metaphor, the life of capital is not originally its own but that of a 'dead' body only 'vivified by sucking living labour'. It steals the 'fructifying vitality' that belongs to the other, taking from this other the very life on which it, capital, however, depends.

Furthermore, insofar as it includes the source of life within itself, capital establishes a new foundation also for the relationship between commodity and money, between sale and purchase:

> The simple circulation of commodities – selling in order to buy – is a means to a final goal which lies outside circulation, namely the appropriation of use-values, the satisfaction of needs. As against this, the circulation of money as capital is an end in itself [*Selbstzweck*], for the valorisation of value takes place only within this constantly renewed movement.[39]

In the sphere of simple circulation, the purpose of exchange is the individual consumption of the producer, a 'final goal which lies outside circulation' but

38 Marx 1976a, p. 342 [1962, p. 247]. I will analyse this metaphor further in chapter 2, section 3.1.

39 Marx 1976a, p. 253 [1962, p. 167].

which is transformed when circulation comes to be determined by capitalist production. Now the purpose is 'valorisation of value', the formation of capital, 'an end in itself' whose means of achievement are the value-forms of circulation, namely, commodity and money. In simple circulation, sales and purchases occur for a purpose external to the movement of value itself; they are social forms set in motion only by the need for the 'appropriation of use-values' and not for value as such. This indifference between value-forms and value itself, which appear respectively as an external figure and an interior substrate, is overcome by capital. In it, value is the internal content which being the purpose of the movement, externalises itself in each of the forms determined to be a necessary stage of valorisation.

The distance between the internal ambit of value and the external ambit of value-forms is eliminated as the very 'substance' of value adopts a value-form, namely that of labour power, the commodity that is the source of value. In this form, value commands the passage of the commodity-form to the money-form, especially in the case of the passage of the labour power commodity to the wage-money form. Transformed into an end in itself, value has now become the internal content that fully manifests itself in the external form, that is, the content that determines its forms of existence as necessary forms. Value becomes the true meaning of its own movement, defined as a self-constitution process. Not only do forms suppose value as their internal substrate; value also supposes its external forms and reproduces itself through the movement from one form to another. With this the concept of 'process' refers to the coming-to-be of capital by means of the necessary passage through the stages or forms in which it becomes explicit and exteriorises itself in its aspect as content.[40]

Based on these results, Marx proposes an expansion of the meaning of the concept of capital:

> Capital, as self-valorising value, does not just comprise class relations, a definite social character that depends on the existence of labour as wage-

40 Once again Marx's reasoning on this point resonates with Hegel's *Science of Logic* specifically in the relation it establishes between 'internal' and 'external': essence is the internal side before which the forms of existence are initially indifferent, that is, they are not determined as forms of this essence. Getting back to the passage from 'diversity' to 'opposition', in a second moment essence and existence determine themselves as opposites so that the external form becomes the necessary manifestation of essence which then becomes its content. See Hegel 2010, pp. 389–97. The resonance of this reasoning is quite clear in Marx's text on the determination of value-forms in which capital is defined as their content, in particular the second point of the summary of the results concerning the absorption of labour by capital. See Marx 1974, pp. 301–2 [1983, 221–3].

> labour. It is a movement, a circulatory process through different stages … Hence it can only be grasped as a movement, and not as a static thing. … Here value passes through different forms, different movements in which it is both preserved and increases, is valorised.[41]

Capital cannot 'be grasped as … a static thing', as a simple material means of production, as a factor disassociated from any 'definite social character'; it acquires mastery of its valorisation conditions, the power to adopt the form that is most convenient at any moment, unfolding a 'movement … through different stages' that defines it as a 'circulatory process'.

What is being addressed here, however, is not only a movement of self-valorisation, of being 'an end in itself'. For, being the 'content' that presides over the circuit of the forms assumed to valorise itself, 'instead of simply presenting the relations of commodities, it now enters into a private relationship with itself'.[42] In other words:

> In the circulation M–C–M both the money and the commodity function only as different modes of existence of value itself, the money as its general mode of existence, the commodity as its particular or, so to speak, disguised mode. It is constantly changing from one form into the other, without becoming lost in this movement; it thus becomes transformed into an automatic subject.[43]

In the situation of the simple exchange of two commodities analysed in chapter 1, section 2.1, the commodity in relative-form plays an 'active' role towards the commodity in equivalent-form because it relates to its own self through its relationship with the other. This self-relation mediated by the relation with the opposed term is the meaning Marx attributes to the term 'subject' in the text cited above, clearly inspired by Hegelian terminology.[44] 'Subject' is

41 Marx 1978, p. 185 [1963, p. 109].

42 Marx 1976a, p. 256 [1962, p. 169].

43 Marx 1976a, p. 255 [1962, pp. 169 and 168–9].

44 In Hegel's words: 'As a spirit, man does not have an immediate existence, but is essentially turned in upon himself. This function of mediation is an essential moment of the spirit. Its activity consists in transcending and negating its immediate existence so as to turn in again upon itself; it has therefore made itself what it is by means of its activity. Only if it is turned in upon itself can a subject have true reality' (Hegel 1975, p. 50). Since the translation obscures the point that seems to me the most important here, namely the definition of 'subject', I propose another translation: 'As spirit, the human being is not an immediate, but something that had essentially returned to itself. This movement of mediation

the one who reflects on itself, who returns to itself after passing through the other 'without becoming lost in this movement'; it is the one who enters into a 'private relationship with itself' and determines its forms of existence as the moments of that self-relationship.

In simple circulation, the purpose of exchanging two commodities is to consume their use-values and so the value is only present as an inert substrate that enables the exchange but does not determine the passage from one value-form to another. Under these conditions, then, exchange still represents an incomplete figure of the value as 'subject'. In the case of capital, however, the purpose presiding over the movement between the value-forms is value, which confers content on the forms joining them to the material or 'substance' of value and presenting itself as the complete figure of 'subjectivity'. Therefore, the valorisation of the value which constitutes capital is not only valorisation of itself but also by itself; it is self-valorisation. That which in simple circulation is a 'substance' whose movement does not determine by itself its forms becomes a 'a self-moving substance',[45] that is, a movement which occurs exclusively by its own force and which has in itself its own purpose. In other words, it is a 'subject' in the sense described above.

On purchasing the commodity labour power and integrating it into itself as 'variable capital', capital seeks to raise its own status from 'substance' to that of 'subject'. To a certain extent, in fact, it does succeed in this claim insofar as it dominates the conditions of immediate production and the forms of circulation. An analysis of the impasses that the pretension leads to will be presented in chapter 2, section 3.1. What matters here is to indicate that the propensity of capital for becoming the 'subject' of valorisation is at the basis of its character-

---

is an essential moment of the spirit. Its activity consists in transcending and negating its immediacy so as to return to itself; it is thus made itself what it is by means of its activity. Only that which has returned to itself is subject, real effectivity'. Despite the coincidence in terminology, it should be noted that unlike the Hegelian concept of 'subject', which implies a conscious movement of the spirit returning to itself, the concept here employed by Marx to define the power of capital dispenses with consciousness and is characterised, rather, by 'automatism'. Thus, while Hegel calls 'subject' the substance that takes control of its destiny in a movement of reflection, Marx calls 'subject' the power that, through the formal subsumption of the substance of value, labour, steals this substance of the possibility of self-determination. Marx can only think of the 'subjectivity' of capital, therefore, as a formal power that usurps the place of the real substance and prevents it from rising to the condition of self-determination.

45 Marx 1976a, p. 256 [1962, p. 169]. This definition is central to Marx's theory. Lange points out how, already in the form of relative value in simple circulation, it is possible to discern the figure of a 'quasi-subject' preparing the posterior determination of capital as the full subject of its own existence. See Lange 1978, pp. 13–14.

istic fetishism. It consists not only of the illusion that capital is an autonomous source of value production but also, and especially, of capital's effective power to subordinate labour and command its own self-valorisation, growing and expanding its dominion to various spheres of economic life.

Once again, social relations are hidden behind relations among things like commodities, money and means of production, and this time in a more defined and complete way. Capital's 'subjectivity' means that, in addition to being a means to satisfy human needs, this relation among things is the way to increase the value and number of things produced because it meets the needs of capital, to which human needs are submitted and sacrificed. By becoming the purpose of production in general, capital seeks to appropriate all social and material means to achieve it, and as it succeeds in doing so, it presents itself as being the organiser of the relations among people, as a power beyond the reach of their individual wills and consciences. That is why Marx calls capital an 'automatic subject' that imposes itself as an overriding objective on all people and whose authority derives from the transcendental character with which it bedecks itself before them. This fetishism is characterised by the semblance of life it confers on inanimate things and also the power it has over real human lives, insofar as it turns itself into their overriding goal and a force created by the transfiguration of social relations themselves. Capital thus configures a 'vampire-like' idol to which all sacrifices will always be insufficient.

2.2 *The Infinitude of Accumulation*

The Marxian conception of capital as a 'subject' corresponds to the new meaning that self-valorisation confers on circulation and the immediate production of commodities. In this way the strictly quantitative aspect of self-valorisation, inherent to the definition of 'surplus value' and of capital itself, is revealed. Marx explains:

> In truth, however, value is here the subject of a process in which, while constantly assuming the form in turn of money and commodities, it changes its own magnitude, repels itself as surplus value from itself as original value, and thus valorises itself. For the movement in the course of which it adds surplus value is its own movement, its valorisation is therefore self-valorisation. By virtue of being value, it has acquired the occult ability to add value to itself.[46]

46 Marx 1976a, p. 255 [1962, p. 169].

To understand the reasoning set out in this text it is important to remember the general formula for capital, M–C–M': first, the passage from money-form to commodity-form and vice versa has the function of producing M', that is, a final value greater than the initial one; second, the two extremes are qualitatively identical so that the objective of the movement can only be the production of a quantitative difference. What defines capital is that this movement 'is its own movement'; in other words, the quantitative difference is the work of capital, the value that 'repels itself as surplus value from itself as original value'. The 'original value' is already capital because with it the means of production and the labour power needed for the creation of surplus value will be bought. However, precisely in the act of creating a value different from the initial value, it 'repels itself … from itself'. That 'self-repulsion' movement of capital, which constitutes the self-valorisation as a process, stems, on the one hand, from the fact that the employment of the 'original value' has the power to create a distinct value, a surplus; on the other hand, through that creation of a distinct value, the 'original value' defines and confirms itself as capital. Thus, it relates to its own self by means of the negative relation to the other which it potentially contains within itself. The self-repulsion consists in the negative moment of this self-relation. Therefore, the quoted text goes on to state that capital:

> … now enters into a private relationship with itself. It differentiates itself as original value from itself as surplus value, just as God the Father differentiates himself from himself as God the Son, although both are of the same age and form, in fact, one single person; for only by the surplus value of £10 does the £100 originally advanced become capital, and as soon as this has happened, as soon as the son has been created and, through the son, the father, their difference vanishes again, and both become one, £110.[47]

In this well-known reference by Marx to the Christian Trinity, the negative moment of the repulsion of surplus value by the original value due to their quantitative difference reappears. Yet the repulsion is self-repulsion of capital, 'for only by the surplus value of £10 does the £100 originally advanced become capital'. The original value is defined as capital through the relationship with the surplus value, which is produced by capital precisely because it is capital.

In turn, the moment of the return to itself after the self-repulsion indicates the unity of capital in its movement. This unity manifests itself in the qual-

47 Marx 1976a, p. 256 [1962, pp. 169–70].

itative identity of the value-form at the two extremes of the M–C–M' circuit whereby the two values go back to forming a single homogeneous quantity. So 'their difference vanishes again, and both become one, £110', just as the father and the son 'are of the same age and form, in fact, one single person'. Here the very heart of Marx's reasoning is achieved: 'only by the surplus value of £10 does the £100 originally advanced become capital, and as soon as this has happened ... their difference vanishes again, and both become one, £110'. Thus, 'as soon as' the original value becomes determined as capital and does so in a prospective manner 'only by the surplus value', it suppresses its difference from the surplus value and adds the latter to itself to form a greater value that will be capitalised at the beginning of a new production cycle. Or rather, because the surplus value resulting from the use of the original value retroactively determines this original value as capital, it too becomes capital and prepares the renovation and amplification of the M–C–M' circuit. The negative moment of self-repulsion is completed and becomes the affirmative moment of capitalisation. At the beginning, the quantitative difference overlaps the qualitative identity, then the qualitative identity suppresses the quantitative difference and finally stands out at the starting point of a new circuit.

In this way, the movement of self-repulsion leads capital to renew itself with a greater value which corresponds to the addition of the surplus value and enables the reproduction and accumulation of capital. Marx had previously identified this value drive which renews its own circuit so as to always increase its magnitude in the case of hoarding.

> The hoarding drive is measureless [*maßlos*] in its nature. Qualitatively or formally considered, money is limitless, that is, it is the universal representative of material wealth because it is directly convertible into any other commodity. But at the same time every actual sum of money is limited in amount, and therefore has only a limited efficacy as a means of purchase. This contradiction between the quantitative limits and the qualitative lack of limit keeps driving the hoarder back to his Sisyphean task: accumulation. He is in the same situation as the world conqueror, who discovers a new boundary with each country he annexes.[48]

Once more, the incomplete figure in the sphere of simple circulation is fully developed in the transition to the sphere of capitalist production. Due to its qualitative homogeneity, 'money is limitless'; the capacity to accumulate *ad*

48 Marx 1976a, pp. 230–1 [1962, p. 147].

infinitum is part of its very nature. However, 'every actual sum of money' that compose the initial and the final value of the movement made up by both the 'hoarder' and the capitalist 'is limited in amount' and represents a finite quantity. Thus, the double dimension, qualitative and quantitative, which underpins the self-repulsion and accumulation of capital appears to be a 'contradiction between the quantitative limits and the qualitative lack of limit'. With the suppression of the difference between the former magnitudes of value in the identity of the new, united, capitalised value, a tendency towards a 'limitless' accumulation of money emerges, that is, towards the infinitude associated to its qualitative homogeneity.

Nevertheless, the new value transformed into the starting point for the following cycle of production is also an 'actual sum … limited in amount' which seeks to overcome its limit and achieve its potential infinitude and which 'repels itself as surplus value from itself as original value'. That is why accumulation, as well as 'hoarding', is a continual 'drive', and money's double dimension appears to be a 'contradiction' between the finite present and the never-achieved infinite. It is also why Marx was able to elegantly characterise that 'drive' as a 'Sisyphean task', evoking the mythical figure whose punishment was to suffer like a human and be tireless like an immortal; or like the torment experienced by a 'world conqueror' whose pretension to achieve universal dominion always comes up against some 'new boundary'.

There is however a difference between the hoarder's drive and the capitalist's drive, and it resides in the fact that the former is still inscribed in the ambit of simple circulation, while the latter is already in the orbit of capital. Thus:

> The repetition or renewal of the act of selling in order to buy finds its *measure* [*maß*] and goal (as does the process itself) in a final purpose which lies outside it, namely consumption, the satisfaction of definite needs. But in buying in order to sell, on the contrary, the end and the beginning are the same, money or exchange value and this very fact makes the movement an endless one … The simple circulation of commodities – selling in order to buy – is a means to a final goal which lies outside circulation … As against this, the circulation of money as capital is an end in itself [*Selbstzweck*], for the valorisation of value takes place only within this constantly renewed movement. The movement of capital is therefore *measureless* [*maßlos*].[49]

49 Marx 1976a, pp. 252–3 [1962, pp. 166–7].

While the hoarder has to take money out of circulation and renounce its 'measure and goal' of purchase and consumption, the capitalist transforms the circulation into a means to achieve a new end, 'the valorisation of value [which] takes place only within this constantly renewed movement'. As we have seen, the value-forms of circulation are the means available to capital for 'renewing the movement' of its own constitution on an ever-increasing scale. Unlike the hoarder he has no need to refuse circulation but instead to subordinate it to a much broader accumulation process. The purchase of labour power distinguishes the capitalist's 'Sisyphean task' from that of the hoarder, but their tasks are similar in the aspect of being 'measureless'. In any case, it is merely a similarity. The 'measure' of the movement of selling in order to buy is once more to be found in 'consumption, satisfaction of definite needs' so that the interruption of circulation by hoarding loses this reference only during the moment in which it suspends the purchase and consumption of commodities.

The quantity of what the hoarder sells ceases to be directly regulated by the quantity of what he wishes to buy, ceases to have its measurement in consumption, but the 'movement of capital is ... measureless' because in it 'the end and the beginning are the same' and the end becomes a new beginning. Capital shows itself to be identical to itself and encounters no permanent limit outside of itself, no external element that could indefinitely curb its expansion.

Therefore, the primary meaning of the adjective 'measureless' which qualifies the accumulation of capital, stems from the infinitude of this accumulation, that is, from the qualitative identity between its beginning and its end and the constant suppression and replenishment of its quantitative difference. In principle there is no reference external to capital that delimits the magnitude of its accumulation. Capital finds its measure essentially within itself, in the magnitude of value which it attains at the end of each cycle and from which it can depart by acquiring a certain quantity of labour power and means of production for the following cycle. Obviously, Marx takes into account the obstacles and existent conditions for accumulation but his interest up to this point of the categorial presentation is to emphasise that the drive to overcome obstacles stems from capital's contradictory nature. In the process of effectuating this drive, however, the dynamics of capital takes on a more complex feature insofar as it develops new ways of creating surplus value that enrich the content of self-valorisation. The next subchapter will succinctly examine this development so that it becomes feasible to conduct a very precise analysis of a second meaning for 'measureless' in regard to capital, this time in reference to crisis.

2.3 *Relative Surplus Value*

In the realisation of its immanent tendency to valorisation, capital can compensate for a small or null increase of its variable portion, corresponding to the outlay on labour power, by intensifying the exploitation of this power, that is, by increasing the surplus labour-time beyond the necessary labour-time. In this case however, an important obstacle arises, namely, the natural limitation to the working day. If the necessary work period is a fixed quantity because the labour power value is also fixed, then the only way to increase the exploitation of the worker is to obtain an absolute increase in the surplus time, that is to say, by extending the working day. This, however, can only be done up to the point where physical and natural barriers arise. To overcome the obstacle and increase the degree of labour power exploitation – the rate of surplus value – without further lengthening the working day, the solution for capital is to reduce the necessary labour-time because this will provide a proportional increase in the surplus part of the labour-time within a working day of fixed magnitude. In that regard Marx defines a new way of obtaining surplus value:

> I call that surplus value which is produced by the lengthening of the working day, absolute surplus value. In contrast to this, I call that surplus value which arises from the curtailment of the necessary labour-time, and from the corresponding alteration in the respective lengths of the two components of the working day, relative surplus value.[50]

The definition of surplus value presented in chapter 2, section 1.2 was that of 'absolute' surplus value, the fundamental form which exposes the relationship between capital and labour at the origin of valorisation. The development of this relationship, however, results in the 'relative' form of surplus value. This development should be now examined in some detail.

Shortening the necessary labour-time in which the worker produces the equivalent of the replenishment of his labour power means reducing the value of the goods he consumes, because the assumption that labour power is not underpaid must be maintained to preserve the systemic determination of surplus value. Thus, reducing the value of labour power means cheapening the means of subsistence that regulate this value which, in turn, presumes an increase in labour productivity in those branches of the economy that produce the said means of subsistence. In Marx's words:

---

50 Marx 1976a, p. 432 [1962, p. 334].

> Hitherto, in dealing with the production of surplus value in the above form, we have assumed that the mode of production is given and invariable. But when surplus value has to be produced by the conversion of necessary labour into surplus labour, it by no means suffices for capital to take over the labour process in its given or historically transmitted shape, and simply to prolong its duration. The technical and social conditions of the process and consequently the mode of production itself must be revolutionised before the productivity of labour can be increased. Then, with the increase in the productivity of labour, the value of labour power will fall, and the portion of the working day necessary for the reproduction of that value will be shortened.[51]

In other words, insofar as it depends on increasing the productive power of labour to produce relative surplus value, 'the mode of production itself must be revolutionised' in its 'technical and social conditions', and no longer restrict itself to 'taking over the labour process in its given or historically transmitted shape'. As we know, in *Capital* this 'revolution' is described as a process that passes through three basic moments. First, the 'co-operation', in which workers are brought together by capital to carry out the same task, creating a new, social productive power. Second, the 'division of labour' in manufacture, in which capital divides and coordinates tasks among different workers and thus boosts their productivity through the benefits accruing from individual specialisation, in alignment with Adam Smith's well-known analysis in the first chapter of *The Wealth of Nations*. Lastly, the 'large-scale industry' which transforms the workers' tools into machines, thereby removing the natural limitations formerly imposed on production by the worker's body with which the tools were associated.

Marx makes a long and detailed presentation of these three moments, seeking to show how the more complex of them develop from the simpler ones and providing important historical examples of each one. Here, however, what is more important than these details is to analyse how they derive from the relationship between capital and labour already expressed in the form of absolute surplus value. Marx explains that:

> The production of absolute surplus value turns exclusively on the length of the working day, whereas the production of relative surplus value completely revolutionises the technical processes of labour and the groupings

51 Marx 1976a, pp. 431–2 [1962, pp. 333–4].

> into which society is divided. It therefore requires a specifically capitalist mode of production, a mode of production which, along with its methods means and conditions, arises and develops spontaneously on the basis of the formal subsumption of labour under capital. This formal subsumption is then replaced by a real subsumption.[52]

The 'formal subsumption', which already makes the production of absolute surplus value feasible, is based on capital's exclusive ownership of the means of production and the consequent alienation of the wage-earner who has to work under the conditions imposed by capital, while at the same time being converted into an integral part of it. For this exact reason, the 'revolution' in the mode of production, defined as the set of social and technical conditions of production, 'arises … on the basis of the formal subsumption of labour under capital': the proprietorship of these conditions endows the capitalist with the power to organise labour in such a way as to increase its productivity. If subordination occurs 'formally' via the legal relationship of sale and purchase of labour power, it 'really' establishes itself in the sphere of immediate production, where the wage earner is in opposition to the means of production as an alien force that dominates his living activity.

It is in this way that, in the 'co-operation', capital brings together the workers and boosts their productive power; or that it distributes the individual operations of the labour process among the members of the 'manufacture', reserving for itself the sense of the whole that the individual specialist no longer possesses. Finally, it is in this way that capital completes the technical divorce between the worker and the means of production, first when it replaces the worker's manual dexterity by the operation of the tool-machine and later when it replaces human vigour by the traction of a motor mechanism. A system is thus created which is self-driven with a certain degree of independence in relation to the worker, namely, the factory described by Marx as an 'automaton' and a 'monster'.[53] At this moment, production presents itself as a science, completely differentiates itself from the knowledge of the artisan and develops in the service of capital and under its aegis.

On the one hand this process reinforces the fetishism of capital:

> Hence the productive power developed by the worker socially is the productive power of capital. The socially productive power of labour deve-

52 Marx 1976a, p. 645 [1962, pp. 532–3].

53 Marx 1976a, p. 503 [1962, p. 402]. The actual words 'automaton' and 'monster' do not appear in the English version, but they correspond to the words *Automaten* and *Ungeheur* in the original.

> lops as a free gift to capital whenever the workers are placed under certain conditions, and it is capital which places them under these conditions. Because this power costs capital nothing, while on the other hand it is not developed by the worker until its labour itself belongs to capital, it appears as a power which capital possesses by its nature – a productive power inherent to capital.[54]

Capital appears as an autonomous factor of production that would create part of the product value, and also as directly responsible for the increase in labour productivity and technical progress.

On the other hand, with the factory system the 'real subsumption' of labour to capital is accomplished. Marx states that:

> In handicrafts and manufacture, the worker makes use of a tool; in the factory, the machine makes use of him. There the movements of the instruments of labour proceed from him, here it is the movements of the machine that he must follow. In manufacture the workers are the parts of a living mechanism. In the factory we have a lifeless mechanism which is independent of the workers, who are incorporated into it as its living appendages.

And he completes his statement with a quotation from Engels:

> The wearisome routine of endless drudgery in which the same mechanical process is ever repeated, is like the torture of Sisyphus; the burden of toil, like the rock, is ever falling back upon the worn-out drudge.[55]

Capital's dominion becomes effective through the inversion in the control of the labour process now exercised by the means of production in which capital embodies itself to subjugate labour. Therefore, capital not only obtains sur-

---

54 Marx 1976a, p. 451 [1962, p. 353]. This productive force of capital, however, develops independently of the wills and consciences of individual capitalists who only desire, each in his own branch, to reduce the unit cost of their product in order to obtain an extraordinary profit at the expense of their competitors by raising the productivity of labour. Only when, first, the productivity increase is generalised among the competitors and, second, has reached those branches that produce the workers' means of subsistence, are the conditions for the production of relative surplus value achieved.

55 Marx 1976a, p. 548 [1962, p. 445]. The quotation of Engels is from *Condition of the Working Class in England in 1844*. By contrasting the 'living mechanism' of the manufacture, in which the worker has an important technical role, to the 'lifeless mechanism' of the

plus value, but it also commands the labour process, raises its productivity, and reduces the cost of producing commodities. When these commodities consist of the workers' means of subsistence then capital reduces the value of labour power and obtains relative surplus value.

It is worth noting that at the end of Engels' text quoted by Marx the figure of 'Sisyphus' appears, submitted this time to a 'lifeless mechanism' and an 'endless drudgery'. While this is a direct reference to the monotony of working in the factory, it should not be forgotten that the factory emerges from capital's need to boost the labour yield to the maximum in order to obtain more and more surplus value; a surplus which in turn will be invested in expanding the factory and in technical improvements, thereby perpetually re-fuelling the entire process. Through the reciprocal determination between the investment of surplus value and the expansion of the material conditions to produce relative surplus value, the 'endless' accumulation of capital acquires its real basis. It is no longer a simple accumulation of value but of value objectified in the technical base of capital, in a movement which is potentially progressive and unlimited.

Capital's 'torture of Sisyphus' consists of the conflict installed by its double nature, both human and immortal, so to say. Formerly, this conflict was generically defined by the dialectic of the finite and the infinite that is present in the accumulation of money. Now, more clearly than ever, it is determined by the subordination of labour to an alien process and the subordination of the worker to a transcendent and infinite power which seems to him to be immortal. That is the fetishism of capital which attributes to itself the productivity of labour and presents it as its own achievement; one which goes beyond the source of value and therefore grows infinitely, far beyond any form of limitation. 'Hence the great civilizing influence of capital'.[56]

3 The Measureless Nature of Crisis

3.1 *Contradiction and Crisis of Capital*

Throughout his analysis of how capitalism functions, Marx never leaves aside his concern for the study of the system's ever recurring crises, whose concept progresses concomitantly with the stages of capital's categorial presentation. He issued a warning:

---

factory, Marx evokes the image of the 'vampire' as the full realisation of dead labour's dominion over living labour, accomplished by the advent of the 'real subsumption' of labour under capital.

56 Marx 1974, p. 409 [1983, p. 323].

> But now the further development of the potential crisis has to be traced … in so far as crisis arises out of the special aspects of capital which are *peculiar* to it as capital, and not merely comprised in its existence as commodity and money.[57]

Complementing the definition of crisis examined in the first chapter above which was restricted to the determinations of value as commodity and money, it is now necessary to obtain a definition that is 'peculiar to [capital] as capital'. In other words, it is incumbent to go beyond the relationship among the value-forms associated with circulation, even if they are modes of 'existence' [*Dasein*] of capital, to arrive at what commands the movement of these forms, namely, the value that valorises itself in the sphere of the immediate production of commodities.

Up until this point, the self-valorisation movement that constitutes capital has been presented as an infinite progress of accumulation and overcoming of obstacles. Marx, however, goes beyond this in his definition:

> … capital is the limitless [*schrankenlos*] and measureless [*maßlos*] drive to go beyond its limiting barriers [*Schranke*]. Every boundary [*Grenze*] is and has to be a barrier for it. Else it would cease to be capital … If ever it perceived a certain boundary not as a barrier, but became comfortable within it as a boundary, it would itself have declined from exchange value to use-value, from the general form of wealth to a specific, substantial mode of the same. Capital as such creates a specific surplus value because it cannot create an infinite one at once; but it is the constant movement to create more of the same. The quantitative boundary of the surplus value appears to it as a mere natural barrier, as a necessity which it constantly tries to violate and beyond which it constantly seeks to go.[58]

Marx establishes the distinction between 'boundary' and 'barrier' based on the relation of capital to itself, that is, based on its self-valorisation, and he makes the mechanism of that movement quite clear. The 'boundary' is a value magnitude which merely differentiates the value produced from the value previously advanced, presenting the advanced value as something external to the

57 Marx 1969b, pp. 512–13 [1967, p. 513].

58 Marx 1974, pp. 334–5 [1983, pp. 252–3]. The distinction between 'boundary' and 'barrier' also harks back to Hegel's *Science of Logic* (2010, p. 104. The words: 'boundary' and 'barrier' appear in this translation as 'limit' and 'restriction'). Berger also made the same observation (1975, p. 167, footnote 28), and so did Rosdolsky (1978, pp. 187–8, footnote 21).

produced one. The 'barrier' in turn, is the 'quantitative boundary' that 'appears' to capital as 'a mere natural barrier ... which it constantly tries to violate'; it is the 'boundary' as a quantity determined by the 'limitless and measureless drive to go beyond its limiting barriers'; in short, it is the 'boundary' set for capital by capital itself as the magnitude that it must overcome in order to increase its value and thus constitute itself as capital. If this 'boundary' were not a 'barrier' for it, 'it would cease to be capital', because it would not be exercising its potential power to valorise itself *ad infinitum*. And this potential power is realised as a surplus value of a certain magnitude because capital 'cannot create an infinite one at once' but is driven to surpass it and to determine a new 'boundary' as being its next 'barrier', thereby configuring a process of accumulation. Here Marx warns:

> But the whole process of accumulation in the first place resolves itself into *production on an expanding scale*, which on the one hand corresponds to the natural growth of the population, and on the other hand, forms an inherent basis for the phenomena which appear during *crisis*. The measure of this expansion of production is *capital* itself, the existing level of the conditions of production and the measureless impulse of the capitalists to enrich themselves and to enlarge their capital, but by no means *consumption* ...[59]

In simple circulation, the 'measure' of the magnitude of the value to be created lies in the social needs for consumption; in the specifically capitalist production that must create a surplus value, this 'measure ... is capital itself'. Capital defines itself as an 'end in itself' capable of dominating the 'conditions of production' and determining them as the means for achieving this end. Even though it does temporarily curb its 'impulse' to 'create an infinite value', capital also establishes the 'boundary' as a 'barrier' to be surpassed, that is to say, it establishes a quantum that serves as a measure for each cycle of its self-valorisation.

The measure for the value to be created in each cycle indicates the 'boundary' established by capital for itself. For this reason, it does not result from the social needs of consumption or from any other element external to the valorisation process, but instead, from the 'measureless impulse ... to enlarge capital'. From this point of view, measure is determined on the basis of the 'measureless' configuration of capital, taking up here, once more, what was examined

59 Marx 1969b, p. 493 [1967, p. 492].

in chapter 2, section 2.2: its first meaning is the capacity to convert the exterior 'boundaries' into 'barriers' established by the internal conditions of self-valorisation; the second meaning is the 'boundlessness' that is characteristic of basically quantitative alterations. Given that the quantity to be delimited is that of 'production on an expanding scale' in which the entire accumulation process 'resolves itself', its measure can only be determined by capital, which establishes the 'boundary' of this quantity and following that, makes it into a 'barrier' to be overcome. Thus, capital seeks to convert the surplus value into the basis for a new stage of accumulation.

Nevertheless, this 'production on an expanding scale' also 'forms an inherent basis for the phenomena which appear during crisis'. It occurs when not all of the surplus value is invested in new capital, that is, when overcoming the barrier for accumulation does not mean imposing a new and even higher 'boundary' for the following stage; or when the 'measureless' accumulation of capital eventually fails to establish a 'measure' for new capital. Thus:

> It is enough here to demonstrate that capital contains a *particular* restriction of production – which contradicts its general tendency to drive beyond every barrier to production – in order to have uncovered the foundation of *overproduction*, the fundamental contradiction of developed capital.[60]

By indicating that capital contains 'a particular restriction of production' that contradicts its 'tendency to drive beyond every barrier', Marx suggests that the 'boundary' does not always present itself as a 'barrier' and that there would be a 'boundary' that capital fails to transform into the next 'barrier'. While the first meaning of the 'measureless' that qualifies the infinite progress of accumulation indicates unlimited self-valorisation, a second meaning now emerges indicating that the valorisation process can no longer be measured by the value produced under capitalist conditions. This is what appears in the text cited above as being 'the foundation of overproduction, the fundamental contradiction of developed capital', formerly designated as the 'inherent basis for … crisis'.

So, what exactly is this second meaning attributed to 'measureless' and how is it related to 'overproduction'? Again, how is it possible to determine the 'boundary' that crises are linked to? To answer these questions, it is necessary to take up, once more, the conditions of capital's self-valorisation and self-

60 Marx 1974, p. 415 [1983, p. 328].

measurement, its constitutive relation with living labour, the source of value. It was seen above that precisely this relation configures the fetishism of capital: as variable capital, labour composes a totality that reduces it to a mere portion of a whole, but a decisive portion that renders the whole as capital. In this process, value appears as the 'subject' of its own valorisation, absorbing life and power from labour. In Marx's words, cited earlier, 'capital is dead labour which, vampire-like, is vivified only by sucking living labour, and lives the more, the more labour it sucks'.

It is now necessary to examine this metaphor more closely. Capital 'sucks living labour' as a right it acquires through purchasing and submitting the labour power commodity. This is the 'formal subsumption' described in chapter 2, section 2.3, the situation in which the 'free' worker is obliged to sell his labour power to the capitalist and to produce under the conditions imposed on him by the capitalist. Therefore, once labour has become one of its moments, capital can present itself as a formally established totality and it is because of this formal subsumption of labour that capital, as a 'subject', dominates the conditions of its own valorisation. This 'vampire-like' power of capital, however, also reveals its dependence on the vitality of labour whose objectivation constitutes the 'substance' of the value of commodities, for it is only by 'sucking living labour' that the 'dead labour' returns to life and stays alive.

Furthermore, according to a remarkable paragraph of the *Grundrisse*,[61] the non-objectified living labour is included as one of capital's 'moments' for being

---

61 The full quoted text is this: 'Labour posited as *not-capital* as such is: (1) *not-objectified labour, conceived negatively* (itself still objective; the not-objective itself in objective form). As such it is not-raw-material, not-instrument of labour, not-raw-product: labour separated from all means and objects of labour, from its entire objectivity. This living labour, existing as an *abstraction* from these moments of its actual reality (also, not-value); this complete denudation, purely subjective existence of labour, stripped of all objectivity. Labour as *absolute poverty*: poverty not as shortage but as total exclusion of objective wealth. Or also as the existing *not-value*, and hence purely objective use-value, existing without mediation, this objectivity can only be an objectivity not separated from the person: only an objectivity coinciding with his immediate bodily existence. Since the objectivity is purely immediate, it is just as much direct not-objectivity. In other words, not an objectivity which falls outside the immediate presence [Dasein] of the individual himself. (2) *Not-objectified labour, not-value*, conceived *positively*, or as a negativity in relation to itself, is the not-*objectified*, hence non-objective, i.e. subjective existence of labour itself. Labour not as an object, but as activity; not as itself *value*, but as the *living source* of value. [Namely, it is] general wealth (in contrast to capital in which it exists objectively, as reality) as the general possibility of the same, which proves itself as such in action. Thus, it is not at all contradictory, or, rather, the in-every-way mutually contradictory statements that labour is *absolute poverty as object*, on one side, and is, on the other side the *general possibility* of wealth as subject and as activity, are reciprocally determined and follow

'conceived negatively', that is, conceived as the 'total exclusion of objective wealth', for this is the condition that leads it to submit to capital. In turn, this 'negative' condition prevents labour from including capital and reducing it to a 'moment', thus also composing a totality. The means of domination, the 'objective wealth', belongs to capital alone. Thus, once it is 'conceived positively', the non-objectified labour appears '… as activity, … as the *living source* of value … general wealth … as the *general possibility* of the same, which proves itself as such in action'. As the value-forming vitality, labour constitutes the 'substance' of wealth in the capitalist world and has a 'subjective existence' defined as 'negativity in relation to itself'; that is, it is a relationship with its own self mediated by the relationship with the other, the object – tool or raw material – which it works on and transforms.

In this way, labour, being formally included in the totality of capital in order to valorise it, produces the entire 'substance' of value and wealth of which capital itself is made up. For this very reason, however, labour ends up also composing a totality, not from a formal point of view but, instead, from a substantial one. As an activity, as 'negativity in relation to itself' that produces value, it also has a 'subjective existence'. Even so, because of its formal subsumption to capital, the substantial totality composed by labour does not show itself as something determinant whose 'subjective existence' could manifest itself as an imposing force. The 'substance' of value does not convert itself into 'subject', into self-referencing totality on the labour side, only on the side of capital, which formally subordinates labour. Hence the fetishist character of 'subject' assumed by capital, taking the place of the true substance of value, labour. Hence, again, the reason why capital must exclude any possibility of labour's composing a whole on the substantial side of value creation.

Capital includes labour as a 'moment' but excludes it as a potential totality, that is, as the possibility that the 'substance' of value might become a 'subject' in its own right. Otherwise, capital would not be the 'subject'; would not determine the conditions of its self-valorisation and would not establish the fetishism whereby 'substance' is expropriated and, with this, acquires the capacity to reproduce itself immeasurably.

When it includes labour as a 'moment' and excludes it as a potential totality, capital completes the figure of the opposition to labour and reveals its contra-

from the essence of labour, such as it is *presupposed* by capital as its contradiction and as its contradictory being, and such as it, in turn, presupposes capital'. (Marx 1974, pp. 295–6; [1983, pp. 216–17]).

dictory nature, as was shown by the analysis that was begun in chapter 2, section 2.1.[62] On the one hand, capital depends on labour for its self-valorisation and includes labour in itself lowering its status to that of variable capital. On the other hand, capital excludes any possibility that labour might become a whole in its substantial side, an exclusion that implies negating precisely that substantial aspect of labour and only conceiving it 'positively' as a '*living source* of value'. The relationship between capital and labour only occurs if capital includes labour as a moment but excludes it as a potential totality, denying it any pretension to elevate itself from 'substance' to 'subject'. This is why, 'vampire-like', capital lives by stealing the life of labour; it needs this life to revive itself and yet it suppresses it: dead in itself, it only comes back to life by killing what is alive. In its positive aspect as value-creating activity, labour cannot constitute a whole of which capital would be a moment.

The contradictory nature of capital is therefore expressed in the simultaneous affirmation and negation of living labour by the dead one. In the sphere of immediate production, the contradiction appears developed within the framework of the processes characterising the gradual 'real subsumption' of labour to capital analysed in chapter 2, section 2.3. In it, the production of relative surplus value leads to the tendential and generalised growth of the productivity of labour through the use of methods that increase the volume and value of the means of production in proportion to the volume and value of the labour power used. Marx, however, warns that:

> Now, however much the use of machinery may increase surplus labour at the expense of necessary labour by raising the productive power of labour, it is clear that it attains this result only by diminishing the number of workers employed by a given amount of capital. It converts a portion of capital which was previously variable, i.e. had been turned into living labour, into machinery, i.e. into constant capital which does not produce surplus value.[63]

---

62 As I said in the Introduction, my argument on this point is largely based on Theunissen 1974. For him the difference of Marx's definition of 'contradiction' and that of Hegel must be based on an 'inversion' of an idealist dialectic into a materialist one. More than that, however, according to Theunissen the materialist inversion does not simply refer to the inverted object, but also to its form: identity and difference swap positions in Marx's dialectic in relation to Hegel's, so that instead of an external difference hiding a deep identity as by Hegel, in Marx an apparent (juridical) equality conceals an essential (social) inequality.

63 Marx 1976a, p. 531 [1962, p. 429].

Due to capital's position as the 'subject' that subsumes labour in a real way, the increase in the productivity of labour and in the production of relative surplus value generates a crucial tendency in capitalist dynamics, namely, the negation of living labour by dead labour, expressed in the replacement of the worker by the machine, either in terms of value or in physical terms. With this, however, little by little the source of surplus value and value in general is eliminated because as the above text explains, constant capital 'does not produce surplus value'.[64] This happens to be a serious problem in the very ambit of the valorisation that actually constitutes capital. It refers directly to that second meaning of 'measureless' examined above, which can now be examined in greater detail.

Being the 'subject' of valorisation, capital must also provide for itself the adequate measure of growth. It is a complex measurement made up of two others. Marx explains it this way:

> ... we saw that the amount of surplus value depends on two factors, namely the rate of surplus value and the number of workers simultaneously employed. Given the length of the working day, the rate of surplus value is determined by the relative duration of the necessary labour and the surplus labour performed in the course of a working day. The number of workers simultaneously employed depends, for its part, on the ratio of the variable to the constant capital.[65]

Based on the conditions of its self-valorisation capital defines the conditions of its self-measurement, that is, the limits capital sets for itself in each cycle of its accumulation process. In this process, the new value created depends on two previous measurements that combine to form a new measure of valorisation: the number of workers employed by a given capital, multiplied by the rate of surplus value. The first measurement results from the proportion between the magnitudes of the constant and the variable capitals while the second is defined by the proportion between the necessary labour and the surplus labour.

At first glance it might seem that these two different magnitudes emerge independently of one another so that their combination would be fixed by chance. However, the two measurements that combine in the measurement

64 See also: 'surplus value does not arise from the labour power that has been replaced by the machinery, but from the labour power actually employed in working with the machinery. Surplus value arises only from the variable part of capital ...' (Marx 1976a, p. 530 [Ibid.]).

65 Marx 1976a, pp. 530–1 [Ibid.].

of valorisation – the rate of surplus value and the ratio of constant to variable capital – are determined by one and the same process of capital production and they change according to its tendencies:

> Hence there is an immanent contradiction in the application of machinery to the production of surplus value, since, of the two factors of the surplus value created by a given amount of capital, one, the rate of surplus value, cannot be increased except by diminishing the other, the number of workers.[66]

The reduction of the necessary labour time performed to obtain relative surplus value occurs by increasing the constant part of capital in relation to the variable part. In order to increase the rate of surplus value, the base on which it operates is reduced. Thus, the same production tendency on the part of capital leads to inverse movements in the two kinds of measurement that combine to form the measurement of valorisation. There is an 'immanent contradiction' in this tendency in the sense that the same movement runs in opposite directions.

If the concept of 'contradiction' seems here to be less precise than the one previously presented, it should be remembered that it corresponds to the manifestation of the previous one. Because it needs to subordinate living labour and transform it into the moment of value creation, but at the same time deny it as a totalising 'substance', capital replaces the workers with means of production and, in so doing, limits the base of its valorisation. This observation enables Marx to state that:

> capital itself is the moving [*prozessierend*] contradiction, in that it presses to reduce labour time to a minimum, while it posits labour time, on the other side, as sole measure and source of wealth.[67]

This text highlights the root of 'measureless' in its second meaning. Capital configures a formal whole in its relationship with wage-earning labour, appearing as the 'subject' that determines the conditions of its own valorisation and its self-measurement but, as the totality composed in this way is merely formal, it still 'posits labour time, on the other side, as sole measure and source of wealth'. If labour is considered part of capital, it would seem that the measure established by it is determined by capital itself, that is, it would seem that capital

66 Marx 1976a, p. 531 [Ibid.].
67 Marx 1974, p. [1983, p. 601].

as a 'subject' measures itself. However, also as a 'subject', capital raises the productivity of labour and 'presses to reduce labour time to a minimum' so that in fact it restricts its own base of valorisation. The measure resulting from joining the two previous measures that express the two aspects of the contradictory relation of capital seems to lose validity precisely because of this contradiction:

> as soon as labour in the direct form has ceased to be the great well-spring of wealth, labour-time ceases and must cease to be its measure, and hence exchange value [must cease to be] of use-value.[68]

The two measures clash with one another and instead of combining to form a resultant measure, they lead to mismeasure.

Given that the two measures are not independent, their union is neither fortuitous or nor external; on the contrary, they contradict one another because they are different expressions, eventually in opposition, of the same contradictory whole, that is, the moving contradiction that configures capital. Thus, the self-reference that enables capital to measure itself is inverted into a loss of reference of the valorisation process. Capital itself intends to measure and determine its self-valorisation through the subordination of the source of value measurement, labour, but insofar as it reduces the value of the labour power employed by it, it suppresses the object to be measured. The resulting mismeasure represents the contrary of capital's tendency 'to drive beyond every barrier to production' quoted above; it indicates that 'capital contains a *particular* restriction of production – which contradicts' this tendency. In this meaning of a limit that is not necessarily transformed into boundary or mere obstacle to be overcome, mismeasurement consists in the inverse of the initially attributed meaning of infinite progress and unbridled accumulation.

---

68 Marx 1974, p. 705 [1983, p. 601]. In this passage from 'measure' to 'measureless', Marx's inspiration in Hegel is again apparent. In the *Science of Logic*, Hegel defines 'measure' as the qualitative determination of quantity by means of which it is possible to fix a limit for quantity escaping from the 'bad infinity' and to explain the qualitative changes of beings through the quantitative alterations in their combined measures (as in chemical procedures). When attempting to develop these concepts, however, he concluded that a reconciliation between quality and quantity, an explanation of 'qualitative leap' in the ambit of the Doctrine of Being is impossible, precisely because measures oppose and contradict one another. The result of this contradiction is the 'measureless' [*maßlos*] (See Hegel 2010, pp. 323–5). As will be seen in Chapters 3 and 4 below, one of the main ideas of this book is that the Marxian concept of crisis also takes up critically the logic of the measureless, which derives from the contradictions that prevent capital from fully performing the measuring function it usurps from labour.

Again, harking back to the text of the *Grundrisse* quoted above, when it refers to a 'particular restriction of production', it uncovers 'the foundation of overproduction, the fundamental contradiction of developed capital'. It is precisely this loss of reference for self-valorisation that leads to 'overproduction', production in excess. While in the case of simple circulation the possibility of this excess refers to social consumption, now the 'excess' refers to the growth of capital itself which characterises the excess as being the fruit of its mismeasurement.

Therefore, when Marx declares that 'labour time ceases and must cease to be [the] measure' of value, what he has in mind is the labour time defined by capital, that is, the labour capitalised as variable capital. This measure is affected by the two opposing tendencies that arise from capital's pretension to become the 'subject' of valorisation and of measurement. With this, it becomes measureless, for capital:

> ... wants to use labour time as the measuring rod for the giant social forces thereby created, and to confine them within the limits required to maintain the already created value as value. Forces of production and social relations – two different sides of the development of the social individual – appear to capital as mere means and are merely means for it to produce on its limited foundation. In fact, however, they are the material conditions to blow this foundation sky-high.[69]

In other words, the 'giant social forces' capital creates have to be measured by the time of an increasingly reduced work period in relation to these forces, thereby imposing on labour the double imperative of 'maintaining the already created value as value' and of 'producing on its limited foundation'. In this way the parameters of the excess that characterise 'overproduction' are defined: the need to produce new value and, at the same time, conserve the 'already created value' embodied in constant capital.

This question will be further developed in the fourth chapter of this book, which will examine the meaning attributed to 'overproduction' in a more advanced stage of the presentation in *Capital* as well as its relationship with the corresponding concept of crisis. For the moment it is sufficient to emphasise that 'overproduction' and its excesses exist in the various contexts in which capital appears as though it were referring to itself. Whenever capital distinguishes itself from itself, separating itself into its multiple aspects only to

---

69 Marx 1974, p. 706 [1983, p. 602].

seek, immediately afterwards, to reunite with itself by harmonising this multiplicity, then the measureless emerges, showing that, in the end, harmony is impossible.

3.2 *Crisis as a Potential Power*

By its contradictory character, capital engenders opposing tendencies that come into conflict when they compete for realisation. The opposition of these tendencies, therefore, is present from the simplest forms in which the concept of capital is defined in Marx's analysis. In fact, already in the *Grundrisse* he stated that:

> The simple concept of capital has to contain its civilizing tendencies etc. *in themselves*; they must not, as in the economics books until now, appear merely as external consequences. Likewise, the contradictions which are later released, demonstrated as already latent within it.[70]

Thus, both the progressive side of capital's accumulation and the side of its crises must be 'demonstrated as already latent within it', that is, they must already be contained 'in themselves' in the 'simple concept of capital', without there being any need to wait for posterior developments of the categorial presentation in order to understand them. What stands out in this 'simple concept' is the 'latency' of the two sides, the interiority of the tendencies as opposed to the 'merely external consequences'. In the case of crises, this conception of 'latency' or immanence many times reiterated by Marx needs, therefore, to be reconstituted in some detail.

The main task here is to understand to what extent and in what sense Marx's explanation of crises advances with the introduction of the determinations stemming from the 'simple concept of capital' in regard to the threshold achieved in the sphere of the simple circulation of commodities. Harking back briefly to chapter 1, section 2.4, it was seen that the concept of crisis already appears in simple circulation but merely as a possibility whose effective realisation at that point is not yet well explained. Marx conceded that:

> it cannot be said that the *abstract form of crisis* is the *cause of crisis*. If one asks what its cause is, one wants to know why *its abstract form*, the form of its possibility, turns from possibility into *actuality*.[71]

---

70 Marx 1974, p. 414 [1983, p. 327].

71 Marx 1969b, p. 515 [1967, p. 515].

What was lacking before was a demonstration of the 'cause of crisis' that would allow one to explain its occurrence as the fulfilment of its possibility. It was this lack which led Marx to describe the 'form of crisis' brought about by the metamorphosis of commodities as 'abstract', that is, separated from the conditions of its passage to effective existence.

His use of the adjective 'abstract' also indicates how Marx defines the meaning of this possibility: 'the general, abstract possibility of crisis denotes no more than the *most abstract form* of crisis, without content, without a compelling motivating factor'.[72] The crisis is formal because of its contraposition to the 'content' which the form still lacks. Marx identifies this 'content' with the 'cause of crisis', with the 'motivating factor' that makes 'its possibility turn into actuality'. However, the simple metamorphosis of commodities already has a content, namely, the purpose of selling in order to purchase, to obtain money to acquire the goods necessary for consumption. If the simple metamorphosis is not a pure form without content, then why does the above text apparently affirm the opposite?

In that regard, Marx proffers an important clarification:

> No crisis can exist unless sale and purchase are separated from one another and come into contradiction, or the contradictions contained in money as a means of payment actually come into play; crisis, therefore, cannot exist without manifesting itself at the same time in its simple form, as the contradiction between sale and purchase and the contradiction of money as a means of payment. But these are merely *forms*, general possibilities of crisis, and hence also forms, abstract forms, of actual crisis. In them, the mode of existence [*Dasein*] of crisis appears in its simplest forms, and in so far as this form is itself the simplest content of crisis, in its simplest content. But the content is not yet *grounded* [*begründet*].[73]

The purpose of selling in order to buy does indeed represent 'content' but it is the 'simplest content' that 'is not yet grounded'. Thus, according to the text, the crisis appears in the metamorphosis of the commodities as something that simply occurs, as a mere observable 'mode of existence' whereas, when it is the result of the 'grounded content' of capitalist production, it endows itself with an 'actual' existence determined by its grounding.

---

72 Marx 1969b, p. 509 [1967, p. 510].

73 Marx 1969b, p. 512 [1967, pp. 512–13].

The difference becomes clear by recalling an important point discussed in chapter 2, section 2.1: capital's 'subjectivity' means that it impresses a value-form on the 'substance' of value and commands the movement of this form to achieve its own valorisation. This finality is the content that 'grounds' the metamorphoses of the value-forms as something essentially determined by the 'private relationship [of capital] with itself', that is, as something 'contained' in capital and as a manifestation of its interiority. Given that the said interiority is contradictory, its negative aspect determines not only the normal sequence of metamorphoses but also the tendency to crisis that 'grounds' some kind of abnormality in that sequence. The text continues as follows:

> The contradictions developed in the circulation of commodities, which are further developed in the circulation of money – and thus, also, the possibilities of crisis – reproduce themselves, automatically in capital, since developed circulation of commodities and of money, in fact, only takes place on the basis of capital.[74]

While the finality of simple circulation – individual consumption and 'selling in order to buy' – is defined outside the sphere of value reproduction, the content of capitalist production defines itself within this sphere and even expands it, because the self-valorisation implies the metamorphosis of value. Therefore, as a 'subject' which has in itself its end and the power to adapt its forms of existence to the achievement of this end, capital can be considered 'grounded content'. Marx conceives capital as an interiority based on which certain contradictory determinations, including that of crisis, are exteriorised. In other words, it is impossible to explain the occurrence of crises in the categorial framework of simple circulation which merely describes their general form but not the 'cause' that makes them break out. Crises remain there as a 'formal possibility'.

Differently, when the 'content' is no longer defined from the exterior but instead from the interior of valorisation, it becomes 'grounded content', that is to say, grounded in the 'subjectivity' of capital, which in turn 'grounds' the manifestation of the opposite tendencies that result from it. When, moreover, the determinations of simple circulation are inscribed in those of capital and receive from the latter a foundation, the crisis acquires a new significance. In addition to endangering the satisfaction of individual consumption needs, the difficulty to carry out exchanges endangers the very valorisation of the capital.

---

74 Marx 1969b, p. 512 [1967, p. 513].

Since capital is defined as self-valorisation, the danger takes the form of the negation of capital by the tendencies that capital itself has developed; it consists in capital's self-negation in opposition to its self-affirmation.

The negative side of the contradiction that constitutes capital is always present alongside the affirmative side, but the two combine in opposite ways. In one case negation functions as the 'boundary' that measures and limits valorisation while at the same time establishing a 'barrier', a milestone to be always overcome in the 'measureless' movement of accumulation. In the other case, the negation presents itself as a 'boundary' that does not convert itself into a 'barrier', and mismeasurement appears as a tendency to crisis. According to Marx, political economy perceived this manifestation of capital's contradictory character in a one-sided manner:

> Those economists who, like Ricardo, conceived production as directly identical with the self-realization of capital … have therefore grasped the positive essence of capital more correctly and deeply than those who, like Sismondi, emphasized the barriers of consumption and of the available circle of counter-values, although the latter has better grasped the limited nature of production based on capital, its negative one-sidedness.[75]

The analysis of the relationship between production and realization or of the eventual 'barriers of consumption' mentioned in the text will be left to the fourth chapter of this book. What is more important to examine at this point is how each school of economic theory has grasped only one side of the contradiction of capital: David Ricardo includes the negative side in the positive one with the latter prevailing; Sismonde de Sismondi, on the contrary, includes the positive side in the negative one, with the negative one prevailing. Both schools are simultaneously correct and incorrect in Marx's view insofar as he conceives the two sides united in the contradiction that implies capital's force and failure as a formal 'subject'.

However, even those who see the possibility of crisis as being intrinsic to capital and grasp 'the limited nature of production based on capital, its negative one-sidedness', are incapable of identifying the 'grounded content' of the crisis. Marx proceeds with his critique:

> This shows how insipid the economists are who, when they are no longer able to explain away the phenomenon of overproduction and crisis, are

75 Marx 1974, p. 410 [1983, p. 324].

> content to say that these forms contain the possibility of *crisis*, that it is therefore *accidental* [*zufällig*] whether or not crises occur and consequently their occurrence is itself a mere *accident* [*Zufall*].[76]

Marx does not consider crises to be chance events resulting from the realisation of a possibility that could just as easily not have happened. Crises are no 'mere accident' because they are based on one of the opposite 'latent' dispositions of capital. Thus, it is not enough merely to register the fact that they may or may not occur; it is not enough to understand crises as a possibility without penetrating the 'ground' or 'cause' of their actualisation. It must be explained how crises 'turn from possibility into actuality', making themselves a 'possibility' in the sense of a potency, a capability to create an effect. The 'possibility' has a real dimension which corresponds, in crisis, to the prevalence of the negative side over the positive one. Leaving aside the external conditions that may eventually associate themselves with this potency to either reinforce or weaken it, the potency tends to 'turn into actuality' based on its own self. This is the meaning of 'latency' of crisis already at the level of the 'simple concept' of capital. It is expressed in capital's recurrent failure to provide the measure for its valorisation process and transform the 'boundaries' into 'barriers' in order to continue accumulating.

What emerges very clearly from all this is the problem of the modalities of crisis, already examined in chapter 1, section 2.4 in relation to the simple circulation of commodities. It is interesting to observe how many texts cited in that subchapter frequently refer, not only to the contraposition of the 'abstract form' and the 'content' of the crisis, but also to the contraposition of the 'possibility' of crisis and its 'actuality'. In fact, even if the simple circulation were limited to the 'general possibilities of crisis' without presenting its 'grounded content', it must be remembered that 'crisis cannot exist without manifesting itself at the same time in its simple form, as the contradiction between sale and purchase and the contradiction of money as a means of payment'.[77] The crises appear as an interruption or diminishment in the rhythm of the metamorphoses of commodities and money. The crises determined by the 'grounded content' of capital devaluation also appear in the same way. It is not possible to advance any further in this initial stage of presentation of the 'simple concept' of capital corresponding to the immediate production of commodities. According to Marx:

76 Marx 1969b, p. 512 [1967, p. 513]. *Zufall* and *zufällig* can also be translated as 'by chance' and 'at random'.

77 See footnote 73.

> The mere (direct) *production process* of capital in itself, cannot add anything new here. In order to exist at all, its conditions are presupposed. The first section dealing with capital – the *direct* process of production – does not contribute any new element of crisis. *In itself* it does contain such an element, because the production process implies appropriation and hence production of surplus value. But this cannot be shown when dealing with the production process itself, for the latter is not concerned with the *realization* either of the reproduced value or of the surplus value. This can only emerge in the *circulation process* which is in itself and for itself also a *process of reproduction*.[78]

Although the sphere of immediate or 'direct' production of commodities by capital already presents the determination of crisis 'contained in itself', this determination 'cannot be shown', because the production 'is not concerned with the realization' of the commodities.

Undoubtedly, surplus value is embodied in these commodities; they are forms of capital and accordingly, circulation is merely the moment in which the 'content' determined in the sphere of production by capital appears. However, the point at issue is no longer just the circulation of value, in whose framework crisis is defined as a 'general possibility', but the circulation of capital. In it, crisis is by no means a 'mere accident' as some of the economists Marx criticises would have it. Even so, it is still not possible here to explain how the production of surplus value is the 'element' that leads to a situation beyond that of crisis's being a simple possibility. 'Content' and 'form' still present themselves in isolation, as if they were mutually independent. They will only really be brought together as production process and realisation process when they are included in the broader context 'which is in itself and for itself also a process of reproduction'. Thus, the truly dialectical relationship between 'content' and 'form' that confers on crisis its richest and most complex significance must be sought for in the reproduction of capital.

78 Marx 1969b, p. 513 [1967, p. 513].

CHAPTER 3

The Figures of Reproduction

1 The Circuits of Capital

1.1 *The Meaning of Capital's Circulation*

One of the outstanding aspects in Marx's analysis of the passage from the simple circulation to immediate production of commodities by capital is that in its own valorisation capital becomes the fundament of the metamorphosis of value. According to the conclusions of chapter 2, section 2.1, the movement of the value-forms is determined by capital as an 'an end in itself', that is, it is determined by the 'private relationship' capital establishes with itself, constituting the stages of self-valorisation.

Nevertheless, Marx is careful to point out that in *Capital* Volume I, the purchase of the means of production and labour power and the sale of the commodities produced:

> were discussed only in so far as this was necessary for the understanding of the second stage, the capitalist production process. Thus, the different forms with which capital clothes itself in its different stages, alternatively assuming them and casting them aside, remained uninvestigated. These will now be the immediate object of our inquiry.[1]

In other words, while *Capital* Volume I is basically dedicated to presenting the immediate production of commodities by capital, and only considers the other stages of the circuit as presuppositions for this presentation, in *Capital* Volume II, what was presupposed before becomes the theme of investigation, namely the specific determinations of the circulation of capital. Now it is no longer sufficient merely to be aware that capital is the content that presides over the circuit of its forms. It is necessary to understand how the circuit itself introduces new aspects in the determination of content, for, as Marx himself put it, 'we have to explain, not only how capital produces, but also how capital is produced'.[2]

At this moment in the presentation of the concepts, what is being addressed is 'how capital is produced' by its own self, that is, capital's reproduction.

1 Marx 1978, p. 109 [1963, p. 31].
2 Marx 1969b, p. 513 [1967, p. 513].

 | DOI:10.1163/9789004690721_005

Moreover, given that the historical origin and the social conditions for the emergence and constant replenishment of capital are also studied in *Capital* Volume I, the focus now is not just on the reproduction in general but, instead, on how reproduction comes about through the circulation of capital. 'Circulation', however, has a double meaning in this new ambit of Marxian investigation.

On the one hand, it refers to a sphere that is distinct from the immediate production by capital, but which has this production as its presupposition. The elements that constitute constant capital and variable capital are commodities and so is the result of capitalist production in which the surplus value to be achieved is already included: 'Commodities become commodity capital as the functional form of existence of the already valorised capital that has arisen directly from the production process itself'.[3] Commodities circulate as a product of capital, which needs to sell them to adopt the money-form and be able, once more, to purchase labour power and the means of production, thereby resuming the valorisation process.

On the other hand, circulation has a broader meaning associated with the movement of one form of capital to the other, a process that goes through the various stages of self-valorisation and embraces the production stage. *Capital* Volume II explains that:

> The circuit of capital is thus a unified process of circulation and production, it includes both. Insofar as the two phases M–C and C'–M' are processes of circulation, the circulation of capital forms part of the general circulation of commodities. But by taking part in functionally determined sections or stages in the circuit of capital, which do not just pertain to the sphere of circulation, but also to that of production, capital performs its own circuit within the general circulation of commodities.[4]

In the narrow sense, capital's sale and purchase of commodities is inscribed in the framework of circulation in general which defines the form of the self-valorisation process. In the broader sense, however, the movement of capital circulation encompasses production and, once it is inserted in the overall goal of capital reproduction, it transforms the specific characteristics of the circulation of commodities. Circulation depends on immediate production, but

3 Marx 1978, p. 121 [1963, p. 43].
4 Marx 1978, p. 139 [1963, pp. 64–5].

immediate production also depends on circulation because in order to attain the production stage, capital needs to go through the stages of selling and buying.

Nevertheless, even though production and circulation each present themselves as the means to obtaining the other, they are constituted by independent determinations. As has already been shown (see chapter 2, section 1.2), the determinations of immediate production are formed by the relation between the labour process and the valorisation process, while those of circulation refer to the conditions of commodity metamorphosis.

> Capital as the unity of circulation and production is at the same time the division [*Unterschied*] between them, and a division whose aspects are separated in space and time, at that. In each moment it has an indifferent form towards the other. For the individual capital, the transition from the one into the other appears as chance [*Zufall*], as dependent on external, uncontrollable circumstances.[5]

Circulation and production do not define themselves by one another. Their 'unity' is still that of 'aspects separated in space and time'; their difference is that of two 'indifferent moments'. In other words, their unity and difference are still separate, so that the unity joins the 'different' two without placing them in a mutually constitutive relationship capable of defining a new and inclusive process.

Already in the *Theories of Surplus Value*, Marx anticipated this distinction between the level of analysis of his future *Capital* Volume I and II, stating that: '… it is necessary to describe the circulation or reproduction process *before* dealing with the already existing capital – *capital and profit*'.[6] Thus, presenting the reproduction process through the intermediation of the circulation process before presenting 'the already existing capital', as Marx does in Volume II, means apprehending the circulation of capital through the abstraction of the tendencies inherent to the production sphere. More than that, it means that 'it is necessary' to perform this abstraction and hence conceive the primary and most general determinations of reproduction. Later, *Capital* would explain that:

> In order to grasp these forms in their pure state, we must first of all abstract from all aspects that have nothing to do with the change and

5 Marx 1974, p. 508 [1983, p. 522].
6 Marx 1969b, p. 513 [1967, p. 513].

> constitution of the forms as such. We shall therefore assume here, both that commodities are sold at their values, and that the circumstances in which this takes place do not change.[7]

Considering only the 'change of the forms' – the metamorphosis of value that occurs in sale and purchase – 'grasped in their pure state', implies restricting the analysis to the 'assumption that commodities are sold at their values'; implies, therefore, leaving aside from the analysis the determinations of the 'existing capital – capital and profit', because the level of analysis of the 'existing capital' will be that in which the determination of prices is given by the competition among capitals. The assumption that the law of value is in force without the deviations of the price-form indicates that the global tendencies of capitalist production, executed by the competition among capitals, are not yet taken into account in the examination, and indicates that circulation is still being conceived as a sphere that is independent of these tendencies.

Capital Volume II presents circulation and reproduction on a level of analysis prior to the 'already existing capital – *capital and profit*'. Accordingly, it is not possible to demand that it should take into consideration aspects developed later within the framework of competition and the affirmation of capitalism's global tendencies. It is of great importance to understand this point for the explanation of crises. On the one hand, since immediate production is a necessary stage in the circuit of capital, crisis cannot simply cloak itself with the same characteristics as in the general circulation of commodities, from which the circulation of capital is distinguished at the moment it joins production. On the other hand, production and circulation in the strict sense present themselves just as much separated as unified, that is to say, their unity and their difference constitute 'an indifferent form' of each 'towards the other'. Hence not only does 'the transition from the one into the other appear as chance', but also its interruption, the crisis, is accidental and defines itself precisely in the context of this accidental difference. In *Capital* Volume II crisis no longer simply results from the separation of the buying and selling of commodities but rather from the difference between production and circulation of capital. This difference, however, is established in a level of analysis on which circulation and production are 'indifferent towards [each] other'. Thus, crisis appears as a mere formal possibility.

7 Marx 1978, p. 109 [1963, p. 32].

1.2 *The Forms of the Circuit*

Before analysing the continuous movement of reproduction, Marx presents the metamorphosis or transition of one value form to another that capital successively adopts to complete its self-valorisation. At the beginning, it is a movement that already exists within the circuit of an individual capital and the strategy of the categorial presentation consists in departing from this movement to develop the concept of reproduction as a resumption or repetition of the circuit. Metamorphosis is the inevitable means to self-valorisation and thus carries out the 'subjectivity' of capital as the domination of the conditions of its own existence and as the power to convert them into moments of its relations with itself; that is, the power to differentiate itself from itself in each one of its forms and to always recover itself in the unity of the fluid process from one form to another. In Marx's words:

> It lies in the nature of the case, however, that the circuit itself determines that capital is tied up for certain intervals in the particular sections of the cycle. In each of its phases industrial capital is tied to a specific form, as money capital, productive capital or commodity capital. Only after it has fulfilled the function corresponding to the particular form it is in does it receive the form in which it can enter a new phase of transformation.[8]

In its circuit, capital temporarily fixes itself in one of the three mentioned forms, each of which corresponds to a specific function in the overall process: 1) money capital, which is different from money in general because, to achieve its goal of valorisation, it cannot purchase just any commodity, but must purchase labour power and the means of production; 2) productive capital, the form in which variable capital is combined with constant capital in immediate production; 3) and the commodity capital resulting from this production, that is, the commodities produced by capital in which there must be a value greater than the value of the commodities purchased by money capital and which have to be sold for this value to realise itself and reappear in its universal form of money.

In the first Part of *Capital* Volume II, Marx makes a detailed presentation of the movements of these forms. To this end he formulates three different circuit configurations, according to which of the forms is taken as the starting and finishing point: 1) the circuit of money capital [M–C ... P ... C'–M'];[9] 2) the cir-

8 Marx 1978, p. 133 [1963, pp. 58–9].

9 In this formula and those of the other two circuits, the dots indicate an interruption of the circulation by the production process and the apostrophe on the two final-value forms represent the greater value they contain compared to the initial forms, after the production valorised the value.

cuit of productive capital [P ... C'–M'–C ... P], in which reproduction already appears intermediated by circulation; 3) the circuit of commodity capital [C'–M'–C ... P ... M'], in which the intermediary C is different from the initial C' because it consists of labour power and the means of production. Based on the analyses of each of these three circuits and of the three of them together, Marx draws important conclusions which will be examined below, albeit not in great detail.

Before that, however, it is important to stress that the circuit of individual capital presents itself as a succession of transitions from one functional form of value to another, forms in which capital distributes itself and fixes itself according to its self-valorisation needs. It is in this division that the possibility of crisis arises:

> The circuit of capital proceeds normally only as long as its various phases pass into each other without delay. If capital comes to a standstill in the first phase, M–C, money capital forms into a hoard; if this happens in the production phase, the means of production cease to function, and labour power remains unoccupied; if in the last phase, C'–M', unsalable stocks of commodities obstruct the flow of circulation.[10]

According to its function, each of capital's value forms defines a type of crisis. Outstanding among them are: the second type, associated to productive capital and characterised by unemployment of labour power and underutilisation of the means of production; and the third type, associated to commodity capital, in which it is not possible to sell the commodities produced.

On the one hand, if the circuit's normal occurrence corresponds to an uninterrupted sequence of metamorphoses, on the other, the very unity represented by the fluid sequence presupposes a difference among the forms and thus the possibility of their autonomisation. In the words of an already quoted text, 'capital is tied up for certain intervals in the particular sections of the cycle' and can eventually lose control of its successive circuit, becoming immobilised in a 'particular section'. While it may be similar to the crises of simple circulation, this loss of control is distinguished from them because the interruption of metamorphoses now implies a paralysis of the production and valorisation processes. The division into three circuit phases can be redefined as a division into two: the phases of circulation in the strict sense and the phase of production. Marx concludes that:

10 Marx 1978, p. 133 [1963, p. 56].

> the circulation process as a whole or the reproduction process of capital is the unity of its production phase and its circulation phase, so that it comprises both these processes or phases. Therein lies a further developed possibility or abstract form of crisis.[11]

In the separation of the circulation phase from the production phase 'lies a … possibility or abstract form of crisis', because, as one of texts cited above states, 'in each moment it has an indifferent form towards the other. For the individual capital, the transition from the one into the other appears as accident'. The mutual indifference of the two phases, each one determined by itself without considering the other, makes both their unity and their separation appear to be something entirely casual. This is an 'abstract form of crisis' because it does not reveal the determinant ground for the realisation of either one of the alternatives, the cause that would make the effectuation of one of the possibilities feasible. However, it is also a 'further developed … form of crisis' in relation to the form of crisis in simple circulation because the split does not occur simply between the phases of circulation – buying and selling – but between circulation itself and production. This allows a glimpse of the foundation of crisis as based on the global process that synthesises the two moments.

This definition of crisis acquires even richer and more complex meaning with the development determinations proper to the circuit of capital. When the three circuit configurations described above are considered together:

> In a constantly rotating orbit, every point is simultaneously a starting-point and a point of return. If we interrupt the rotation, then not every starting point is a point of return. Thus we have seen that not only does every particular circuit (implicitly) presuppose the others, but also that the repetition of the circuit in one form includes the motions which have to take place in the other forms of the circuit. Thus the entire distinction presents itself as merely one of form, a merely subjective distinction that exists only for the observer.[12]

The difference among the three circuits is 'merely one of form, merely subjective', for it results from the analytical division of 'a constantly rotating orbit' in which each value form of capital is at the beginning of a circuit and simultan-

11 Marx 1969b, p. 513 [1967, p. 514]. The analysis of this text will be taken up again at the end of this chapter.

12 Marx 1978, pp. 180–1 [1963, p. 105].

eously at the end and in the middle of the other two, depending on how the analysis reconstitutes the circuits to highlight some particular aspect.

As a set 'every particular circuit (implicitly) presuppose the others', because each value-form, M, C and P, performs three functions at the same time, depending on whether it is considered in one or other of the circuits. Thus, 'the repetition of the circuit in one form includes the motions which have to take place in the other forms', so that the three forms of the circuit occur together. Therefore, in addition to the idea of a succession of phases in which capital distributes itself, Marx introduces the idea of their simultaneity. In his own words:

> All portions of the capital go through the circuit in succession, and, at any one time, they find themselves in various stages of it. Thus industrial capital in the continuity of its circuit is simultaneously in all of its stages, and in the various functional forms corresponding to them ... The real circuit of industrial capital in its continuity is therefore not only a unified process of circulation and production, but also a unit of all of its three circuits ... The succession of its various parts is there determined by their coexistence, i.e. by the way capital is divided ... The coexistence, which determines the continuity of production, however, exists only through the movement in which the portions of capital successively describe the various stages. The coexistence is itself only the result of the succession.[13]

In its effective movement, individual capital divides its total value among the three forms presenting itself as money capital, productive capital and commodity capital. This simultaneity is verifiable not only by the fact that in each type of circuit capital appears in all three value forms but also because capital exists in each one of these forms at the same time in all three circuits. Hence, in a given circuit the three value-forms overlap one another and also each one of them performs a different function in the three circuits. Each one is the starting point, the middle and the arrival point; each one is always in movement.

That is why the above text states that 'the succession of its various parts is there determined by their coexistence', for the function of each form is to enable the transition to the following form so that the division of the total value of capital into the three concomitant parts imposes continuous transformation on them. When a form passes to the following form, the latter must do the same thing: money capital becomes productive capital and productive capital becomes commodity capital which finally becomes money capital. Oth-

13 Marx 1978, pp. 182–3 [1963, pp. 106–7].

erwise, two parts of capital would have the same form, or rather, instead of splitting into three parts, capital would divide into two or even concentrate itself entirely in just one. Thus, 'the coexistence is itself only the result of the succession'. The 'coexistence' of the three forms can only be maintained if the normal sequence of metamorphoses is undisturbed.

In contrast to this normality, crisis acquires the more complex meaning already referred to:

> If C'–M' comes to a halt in the case of one portion, for example, if the commodity is unsalable, then the circuit of this part is interrupted and its replacement by its means of production is not accomplished; the successive parts that emerge from the production process as C' find their change of function barred by their predecessors. If this continues for some time, production is restricted and the whole process brought to a standstill. Every delay in the succession brings the coexistence into disarray, every delay in one stage causes a greater or lesser delay in the entire circuit, not only that of the portion of the capital that is delayed, but also that of the entire individual capital.[14]

Should there be any interruption of the passage from one value-form of capital to another, then, according to the initial definition of crisis, that 'brings the coexistence into disarray', implying 'delay ... not only that of the portion of the capital that is delayed, but also that of the entire individual capital'.

Considering that the juxtaposition of the three parts results from the division of capital according to a precise measure of the magnitude of value of each part, the 'disarray' provoked by the interruption at one stage of the process leads to an unmeasured division of value. Conversely, since 'the succession of its various parts is there determined by their coexistence', it can be safely inferred that the paralysis of the sequence is also provoked by a problem in the juxtaposition, that is, by a distribution of the total value among the parts that does not conform to the magnitudes required by each one of them as determined by the need for self-valorisation. In this way, the crisis can no longer be defined as a simple paralysis in the movements of the value-forms but rather by what is its underlying cause, namely, the possible measureless distribution of value on the part of the capital itself. In turn, a disproportional distribution of that kind could stem from the delay or the difficulty in realising one or another of the metamorphoses of capital that leads to the concentration of value in one of its specific forms.

14 Marx 1978, p. 183 [1963, p. 107].

Thus, the dialectic between measure and the measureless examined in chapter 2, section 3.1 reappears, this time in the context of the proper sharing of the value amounts among the three forms and against the background of its always possible inadequacy or disproportionality. Even so, however, it still is little more than 'a further developed possibility or abstract form of crisis', as defined above. Although the crisis already arises from the measureless relationship of capital with itself, the foundation of this lack of measure has yet to be presented. Essentially it is determined by the contradiction that constitutes capital in the sphere of immediate production and that will only be completed in the global process of capitalist production. However, if the measureless fundament is not exhibited, mismeasurement itself is visible, because the fundament appears in the retroactive movement of the categorial presentation, in which the more concrete forms of capital are at the base of the simpler forms presented prior to them. The reconstitution of the circulation of capital in *Capital* Volume II presupposes the complete global process and exposes its measureless side without yet revealing its cause.

The concomitant manifestation and occultation of this measureless aspect in the definition of crisis is recurrent at all moments of *Capital* Volume II precisely for the reasons set out here. It will be necessary to take up this conflict again and develop it, gradually clarifying it in accordance with the context in which it appears.

1.3 *The Turnover of Capital*

The determinations examined above acquire a different character when the movement of capital circulation becomes more complex. According to Marx's definition:

> when the entire capital value that the individual capitalist invests in one branch of production or other has described its cyclical movement, it exists once again in its original form and can then repeat the same process. It has to repeat it, if the value is to be perpetuated and valorised as capital value. In the life of the capital, the particular [*einzelne*] circuit forms only a section that is constantly repeated, i.e. a period ... The circuit of capital, when this is taken not as an isolated act but as a periodic process, is called its turnover.[15]

15 Marx 1978, p. 235 [1963, pp. 156–7]. In the quoted text, it was necessary to alter the translation of the German adjective *einzeln*, from 'individual' to 'particular'. Although, in principle, 'individual' is a correct translation, in chapter 3, section 2.1 we will see that Marx

After examining the circuits of capital, Marx perceives that the interpenetration of the circuits introduces the conditions in which each value-form of capital marks the beginning of another circuit leading capital to 'repeat the same process ... as a periodic process'. This interpretation makes it possible to surpass the analysis of the 'circuit ... taken ... as an isolated act' and go on to the analysis of its periodicity, which 'is called its turnover'.

The last stage of Marx's presentation of the circuits of capital leads to the next stage which develops the 'subjectivity' of capital as its power of 'repeating the same process' and repeating it as a necessity 'if the value is to be perpetuated and valorised as capital value'. Just as the forms of the circuit of individual capital, the forms belonging to the turnover are moments in capital's relationship with itself, except that they are determined by the specific nature of this movement. It means that here the reciprocal mediation of the phases of production and circulation takes place within the ambit of their periodic sequence. Basically, it is about productive capital in the forms it adopts in the course of its circulation, and the functions of money capital and commodity capital in the context of the reproduction of productive capital. Hence, circulation depends on the production process, or, rather, on the different ways in which the value of the elements of productive capital is transferred to commodity capital in immediate production.

It is these different modes of transfer that define the types of turnover and also the new parts into which capital is divided. With that, Marx is now able to address the classical distinction political economy makes between *fixed capital* and *circulating capital*. Fixed capital:

> does not circulate in its use form. It is rather its value that circulates, and does so gradually, bit by bit, in the degree to which it is transferred to the product that circulates as a commodity. A part of its value always remains fixed in it as long as it continues to function and remains distinct from the commodities that it helps to produce. This peculiarity is what gives this part of the constant capital the form of *fixed capital*. All other material components of the capital advanced in the production process, on the other hand, form, by contrast to it, *circulating* or *fluid capital*.[16]

makes an important terminological distinction between the words *einzeln* and *individuell*, but it appears in the above text because the circuit is 'particular' [*einzeln*], when it 'forms only a section' of the 'life of the capital' as a whole.

16 Marx 1978, p. 238 [1963, p. 159]. Marx takes up the distinction between fixed and circulating capital once more from political economy, although for Marx this distinction presupposes the anterior one between 'constant' and 'variable' capital, which did not occur in the works

Fixed capital is the 'part of the constant capital' whose materiality does not transform itself into that of the product; it 'does not circulate in its use form', unlike circulating capital which is transformed by the labour process into the materiality of the product, as in the case of auxiliary and raw materials.

Taking up, once again, the characteristics of the capitalist production process, it is possible to understand this double dimension of labour: on the one hand it transforms the materiality of the means of production into the materiality of the product; on the other, as a valorisation process in itself, it transfers the value of the means of production to the value of the product. Even though it does not convert itself into the use-value of the product, fixed capital has its value transferred to the commodity produced insofar as, with the wear and deterioration caused by its functioning and the passage of time on the machines and installations, for example, this fixed capital is inevitably consumed. It is in the measure of this faster or slower wear that the value is transferred to the product, circulating 'gradually, bit by bit', while a symmetrical measure conserves 'part of its value ... fixed ... distinct from the commodities', bound to the part of the use-value of the means of production that are still intact and have suffered no wear.

The circulating capital is defined in a very different way:

> The fluid capital entering the production process transfers its whole value to the product and must therefore be constantly replaced in kind by the sale of the product if the production process is to continue without interruption.

The counterposition is clear:

> The fixed capital entering the production process transfers only a part of its value (the wear and tear) to the product and continues to function in the production process despite this wear and tear; hence it only needs to be replaced in kind at shorter or longer intervals, in any case not as often as the fluid capital.[17]

---

of the economists. For this reason, their confusion of the two distinctions made Smith attribute the origin of value to the form of its transference in circulation and Ricardo to only include the workers' means of subsistence in circulating capital, excluding the raw and accessory materials as he was unable to define them as creators of value. Marx considered that Ricardo's mistake consisted in establishing a distinction based on a natural quality of the means of production, namely their durability for successive work periods, instead of basing it on capital's historical-social determination.

17 Marx 1978, p. 262 [1963, p. 183].

The form of transfer of value determines the form of reproduction of each of the parts into which productive capital divides itself and, with it, the time-frame for its replenishment. The replenishment of circulating capital, which is entirely transformed into product, must occur whenever a new production stage is to be initiated, that is, at each turnover of capital. The replenishment of fixed capital, however, does not occur at each turnover because on each occasion it only transfers a part of its value, and it is only after a certain length of time that its value will be completely transferred and will have to be replaced.

Generally speaking, the reproduction of fixed capital involves large sums that need to be disbursed over considerable periods, covering several turnovers of the circulating capital. Therefore, the moments in which it takes place are strategical for the reproduction of capital as a whole and for the continuation of capitalist production. Marx associates such moments to the crises:

> The result is that the cycle of related turnovers, extending over a number of years, within which the capital is confined by its fixed component, is one of the material foundations for the periodical crisis in which business passes through successive periods of stagnation, moderate activity, over-excitement and crisis. The periods for which capital is invested certainly differ greatly, and do not coincide in time. But a crisis is always the starting point of a large volume of new investment. It is also, therefore, if we consider the society as a whole, more or less a new material basis for the next turnover cycle.[18]

The fact that crises are here related to the replenishment of fixed capital does not necessarily mean that the latter is the determinant factor of their eruption, otherwise there would be a crisis every time there was a need to replenish fixed capital. The text makes it clear that this is just 'one of the material foundations' of crisis in its periodicity. Certainly, 'a crisis is always the starting-point of a large volume of new investment', that is, investment in more productive and more profitable equipment, with superior technology to that which was worn out and must be replaced; but the replacement of worn-out fixed capital material by new material at the same technological level, is not absolutely associated with crises. One could even think the opposite, that it is crises that anticipate the obsolescence of the old equipment and demand investments in more profitable means of production.

---

18 Marx 1978, p. 264 [1963, pp. 185–6].

In any case, the text leaves no doubt that the 'successive periods' which 'business passes through' are intimately related to the productivity of the installed fixed capital and are determined by the rate of the valorisation provided by this part of capital. Whenever this rate drops to a very low a level, a crisis supervenes, and it is necessary to replace the old equipment with new, more productive equipment. Although only *Capital* Volume III will properly analyse this problem, which refers to capitalist reproduction as a whole, *Capital* Volume II allows us to advance a little further and conclude that the relationship between crisis and the replenishment of fixed capital does not occur solely because the said replenishment constitutes a 'material foundation' for the periodic crises.

According to one of the previously cited texts, the reproduction of circulating capital, which is totally consumed in a single turnover, must be carried out 'constantly in kind by the sale of the product'. Given that its use-value disappeared in the labour process, the elements of circulating capital must be acquired again so that a new labour process can be started. This, in turn, is only possible using the money obtained from the sale of the commodities produced in the previous labour process. The case of fixed capital is different for Marx:

> The peculiar circulation of fixed capital gives rise to a peculiar turnover ... Its value thus acquires a dual existence. A part of it remains tied to its use form or natural form, which pertains to the production process, while another part separates off from this form as money. In the course of its function, the part of the value of the means of labour that exists in the natural form steadily declines, while the part of its value converted into the money form steadily increases, until the means of labour eventually expires, and its entire value has separated off from its dead body and been transformed into money.[19]

While part of the value remains tied to the fixed capital until it is completely worn out, the part corresponding to the wear and tear in each turnover is transferred to the commodity and with the sale of the latter is converted into money. This sum of money has to be put aside for the future purchase of the elements of fixed capital when this capital becomes completely worn out. Thus, in each turnover, 'the part of its value converted into the money form steadily increases' until it is the equivalent of the worn-out elements and the value of the new elements that need to be purchased to replace them. The text con-

19 Marx 1978, pp. 242–3 [1963, pp. 163–4].

cludes that 'Until this reproduction time arrives, its value is accumulated gradually, in the first instance in the form of a money reserve fund'.[20] Forming this fund, however, through which the reproduction of fixed capital 'in kind' takes place, depends on the sale of the commodities produced during the previous turnovers, something that can always be difficult and uncertain under capitalist conditions. Realisation crises can delay the formation of such a reserve fund and may mean that at the end of the 'reproduction time' of fixed capital, it is not equivalent to the value of the new equipment that needs to be purchased.

Money capital plays an analogous role and is equally crucial in the case of circulating capital. Firstly, because the replenishment of circulating capital must always be done 'constantly in kind' at each turnover depending on the sale of the product, that is, on the passage of capital into its money-form. Secondly, because even this situation is not so simple: during the sale of the commodity capital and the purchase of the elements of the productive capital, for technical and economic reasons, the production process must carry on. To ensure its continuity, the capitalist needs to form a reserve fund of money sufficient for him to continue purchasing the means of production and keeping labour employed without having to wait for the sale of the product. In a critical tone, Marx observes that:

> The economists, who have never produced a clear account of the turnover mechanism, constantly overlook this basic aspect, i.e. the fact that only a part of the industrial capital can be actually engaged in the production process, if production is to proceed without interruption. In other words, one part can function as productive capital only on condition that another part is withdrawn from production proper in the form of commodity or money capital. Since this is overlooked, so also is the importance and role of money capital in general.[21]

The continuity of the turnovers requires that capital be divided into a part allocated to the production process and another part to the circulation process, adopting in the first part the form of productive capital and in the second part the form of commodity capital and money capital. The division into these three value-forms of the individual capital circuit is established by the sequence of

20 Marx 1978, p. 243 [1963, p. 164].

21 Marx 1978, p. 342 [1963, p. 269]. In the English translation, between the phrases 'without interruption' and 'In other words' the following sentence, present in the original, has been omitted: 'While one part finds itself in the production period, another part must always find itself in the circulation period'. My translation.

circuits, that is, by the turnover. It is the turnover that confers a specific function in the self-valorisation process to each of those forms and retroactively founds them. The different modes of value transfer determine the division of capital into fixed and circulating capital and institute a true chronological temporality in each transfer process whose synchronisation entails that the division of value into three parts be conserved.

Money, which already in simple circulation is the value-form that establishes the unity through differentiation – the social division of labour – plays a similar role here: it enables capital to divide into parts and the parts to coexist in a continuous movement of passing from one form to another. Thus, the permanent distinction of these parts makes the unity necessary for self-valorisation to become possible. The formation of reserve funds of money, constantly subtracted from both the sphere of circulation and of production, is indispensable for the periodic replenishment of fixed capital and to ensure that the replenishment of the circulating capital does not imply any interruption of the production process.

However, the formation of these funds requires that the division of capital should be in suitable proportions for the due performance of the functions of each part in regard to one another and to the whole. The difficulty of accomplishing this task in the capitalist economy lies in the unplanned nature of that division, something that Marx illustrates by means of a counterposition:

> If we were to consider a communist society in place of a capitalist one, then money capital would immediately be done away with, and so too the disguises that transactions acquire through it. The matter would be simply reduced to the fact that the society must reckon in advance how much labour, means of production and means of subsistence it can spend, without dislocation, on branches of industry which, like the building of railways, for instance, supply neither means of production nor means of subsistence, nor any kind of useful effect, for a long period, a year or more, though they certainly do withdraw labour, means of production and means of subsistence from the total annual product. In capitalist society, on the other hand, where social understanding asserts itself only *post festum*, major disturbances can and must occur constantly.[22]

Since in capitalism there is only 'social understanding ... *post festum*', the proportionality of the division of capital is not ensured. Hence the supervention of

22 Marx 1978, p. 390 [1963, pp. 316–17]. The text sequence is enlightening regarding how far an explanation of crises based on the elements developed so far can go, beyond an

crises characterised by 'major disturbances' in the turnover movements, that is, by interruptions in the turnover and in the passages among the parts into which capital is divided. The juxtaposition of the parts then appears as immobility and reciprocal indifference. It is also important to observe that Marx draws a comparison of the function of planning in a 'communist society' with that of money capital in capitalism. In both cases what is involved is the organisation of the different temporalities that exist among the various branches of production. The economic resources invested in each part of capital produce results in different rhythms whose harmonisation is complex, so the crises express the possible disorganisation of the temporalities and of the system of interdependence among these branches. The movement of each individual capital is paralysed and so is the circulation between the various socially divided capitals.

Therefore, the analysis of the crisis now requires a more comprehensive definition of the social distribution of value that involves not only the differentiation of the parts of the individual capital but also that of the major departments of social production in their reciprocal dependence. Better stated, it is necessary to consider the internal division of individual capital as the result of external divisions commanded by the division of the total social capital. The differences between the simultaneous movements and the possible conciliation of the diverse temporalities of the various individual capitals is subordinated to this division. Social capital thus constitutes the most complex form of Marxian analysis of capitalist circulation, and it is with its concept that *Capital* Volume II is completed.

2 The Reproduction of Social Capital

2.1 *Simple and Expanded Reproduction*

According to the Marxian project of presentation, the concept of social capital cannot immediately correspond to the wealth of determinations that it has in actual reality, and far less to the form of existence that it possesses in the minds of the economic agents. Instead, Marx defines it by means of an abstract relationship among individual capitals:

> But each particular [*einzelne*] capital forms only a fraction of the social capital, a fraction that has acquired independence and been endowed

embryonic price inflation theory based on the difficulty of conciliating the different temporalities of each branch of the economy.

> with individual life, so to speak, just as each particular [*einzelne*] capitalist is no more than an element of the capitalist class. The movement of the social capital is made up of the totality of movements of these autonomous fractions, the turnover of the individual [individuellen] capitals.[23]

Similar to the individual producers in the division of labour that occurs in the context of simple circulation examined in chapter 1, section 1.2, here the whole of social capital does not derive from the aggregation of individual capitals that are independent of it. On the contrary, it expresses the set of the relations among individual capitals or the 'totality of movements … the turnover of the individual capitals' that determines each one's specific position in accord to the needs of the overall set.

In the text cited above, Marx establishes the difference between a mere aggregation and the overall set of social relations among capitals by the difference between capital's 'individual' character and its 'particular' character. Insofar as it is a 'fraction of the social capital', each of the various capitals presents itself as the result of the segmentation of the social capital, as an instance of its universality, as a particularisation of social capital's 'totality'. However, after having 'acquired independence', particular capital is 'endowed with individual life, so to speak'; that is, it seems to exist for itself alone as an independent individual, only submitted to its immediate dispositions.

To begin with, it is important to perceive that the difference between the two determinations of capital is not the fruit of the will of the researcher anxious to compose a subjectively abstract universality based on given individual capitals, and then define singular capital as a mere case of social capital. Quite the contrary, by describing social capital as a 'totality', Marx characterises it as the set of relations that differentiates its 'fractions' – particular capitals – while at the same time defining itself on the basis of this difference and conferring autonomy on its fractions – 'individual capitals'. This double movement of the relationship, which institutes difference and is also determined by it, corresponds to the effective realisation of the social capital. In Marx's view, the categorial presentation must mirror and reconstitute the real movement. What is thus mirrored, nevertheless, is an aspect of reality in which the relation among individual capitals is apprehended unilaterally under the aspect of complementarity.

---

23 Marx 1978, p. 427 [1963, pp. 351–2]. In the two cases stated in the above text the English translation of *einzelne* has been changed from 'individual' to 'particular' for the reasons stated in footnote 15 above.

> However, the circuits of individual capitals are interlinked, they presuppose one another and condition one another, and it is precisely by being interlinked in this way that they constitute the movement of the total social capital.[24]

If, on the one hand, social capital is constituted because individual capitals are 'interlinked', that is, because they 'presuppose one another and condition one another', on the other hand, the mutual conditionings among them also 'presuppose' the relationship that differentiates them and reunites them in a 'totality'. Marx does not conceive social capital as a homogenising universality in which the individuality dissolves into a mere particular case. Instead, he conceives it as the 'totality' that institutes the difference and, parting from it, constitutes itself as a relationship that needs the difference as such. This is how social capital confers 'individual life' on particular capitals.

Furthermore, the same text makes it quite clear that individual capitals relate to one another 'by being interlinked' and 'conditioning one another', that is, that social capital is defined by the complementarity of individual capitals. At this level of the presentation, the more complex determination of competition is excluded. For that reason, the movement that institutes the difference between particular capitals is still unilaterally addressed and their relation is 'abstract', as stated above. The connection of particular capitals in the sphere of circulation are essentially affirmative: the social capital divides itself according to its reproduction needs and also according to them 'interlinks' its parts. The negative aspect of the linking of particular capitals does not appear in the form of competition or opposition among them as it does in *Capital* Volume III but rather as a mere 'independence' of each one of them.

In this context, it must be stressed that the autonomisation of the parts of the social capital, not yet being determined by competition, does not coincide with the division of the society's total capital among individual capitalists or companies. Even considering social capital still on an abstract plane, as social capital in its generality, the need for reproduction imposes on social capital a division different from that observed in a mere particular capital taken as an example.

This issue is clarified in the following passage which, in spite of its length deserves to be quoted in full:

24 Marx 1978, p. 429 [1963, pp. 353–4]. See also Marx 1969b, pp. 510–11 [1967, p. 511].

> As long as we were dealing with capital's value production and the value of its product individually, the natural form of the commodity product was a matter of complete indifference for the analysis, whether it was machines or corn or mirrors. This was always simply an example, and any branch of production whatever could equally serve as illustration. What we were dealing with then was the actual immediate process of production, which presented itself at each turn as the process of an individual capital. In so far as the reproduction came into consideration, it was sufficient to assume that the opportunity arose within the circulation sphere for the part of the product that represented capital value to be transformed back into its elements of production, and therefore into its shape as productive capital, just as we could assume that worker and capitalist found on the market the commodities on which they spent their wages and surplus value. But this purely formal manner of presentation is no longer sufficient once we consider the total social capital and the value of its product. The transformation of one portion of the product's value back into capital, the entry of another part into the individual consumption of the capitalist and working classes, forms a movement within the value of the product in which the total capital has resulted; and this movement is not only a replacement of values, but a replacement of materials, and is therefore conditioned not just by the mutual relations of the value components of the social product but equally by their use-values, their material shape.[25]

Up until the last Part of *Capital* Volume II, the purpose of the categorial presentation is to insist on the basic determination of capital as self-valorising value and the presentation concentrates on value and surplus value, leaving aside the specific use-value produced by a given particular capital. Marx said that:

> Use-values is certainly not *la chose qu'on aime pour lui-même* in the production of commodities. Use-values are produced by capitalists only because and in so far as they form the material substratum of exchange value, are the bearers of exchange value.[26]

It is precisely this indifference in regard to use-value that defines capital as 'an end in itself' and thus as 'subject', and so the first two Parts of *Capital* Volume II

25 Marx 1978, p. 470 [1963, p. 393].
26 Marx 1976a, p. 293 [1962, p. 201].

still focus on particular capital. The 'formality' of this procedure consists in 'assuming that worker and capitalist found on the market the commodities' for the productive and the individual consumption that are essential to reproduction, an assumption that is no longer possible or 'sufficient once we consider the total social capital'.

On examining the theme of the reproduction of 'total social capital' Marx must take into account the way in which the products required for the replacement in kind of each part of this capital are 'found on the market'. The movement of replacement then consists of 'not only a replacement of values, but a replacement of materials, and is therefore conditioned not just by the mutual relations of the value components' – the proportions between the value magnitudes of the segments of social capital – 'but equally by their use-values, their material shape', which conciliate the need for the specific product of the various segments with the production of each of them. When he considers the production of a society as a whole, Marx has to explain how whatever is necessary is produced in the necessary amounts. The greater complexity in the level of presentation requires the return of use-value. This does not mean that the use-value comes to define the purpose of production, thereby depriving capital of its character as a value that valorises itself. On the contrary, the determination of the use-value is always subordinated to the determination of self-valorisation, so that the more complex 'subjectivity' of social capital consists precisely of a quantitative and qualitative division of its component parts which ensures reproduction.

Marx continues by stating that:

> The immediate form in which the problem presents itself is this. How is the *capital* consumed in production replaced in its value out of the annual product, and how is the movement of this replacement intertwined with the consumption of surplus value by the capitalist and of wages by the workers?[27]

The question is, how does social capital divide itself? Part of the answer has already appeared in the preceding text citations. First, the '*capital* consumed in production [is] replaced in its value out of the annual product', and 'the transformation of one portion of the product's value back into capital' occurs. Second 'the entry of another part into the individual consumption of the ... working classes' occurs and third, 'the entry of another part into the individual

27 Marx 1978, p. 469 [1963, p. 392].

consumption of the capitalist ... class' takes place because 'the movement of this replacement [is] intertwined with the consumption of surplus value by the capitalist and of wages by the workers'. Thus, each segment of the social capital is divided into three portions: the portion that replaces the used up constant capital; the portion that meets the consumption needs of the workers when they spend their wages, and which corresponds to the replacement of the variable capital; and the portion equivalent to the capitalists' consumption of the surplus value.

The other part of the response can be deduced from the following text:

> This overall process involves both productive consumption (the immediate production process) together with the changes of form that mediate it (which considered in their material aspect are exchanges), and individual consumption, with the changes of form or exchanges which mediate this ... The circuits of individual capitals, therefore, when considered as combined into the social capital, i.e. considered in their totality, do not encompass just the circulation of capital, but also commodity circulation in general. In its fundamentals, the latter can consist of only two components: (1) the specific circuit of capital, and (2) the circuit of those commodities that go into individual consumption, i.e. the commodities on which the workers spend their wages and the capitalist their surplus value (or part of it).[28]

If the 'overall process involves both productive consumption ... and individual consumption', then the social capital must be divided into 'two components: (1) the specific circuit of capital, and (2) the circuit of those commodities that go into individual consumption' of workers and capitalists, something discernible in the previous divisions within each component part.

Consequently, there must be a Department[29] producing the means of production to replace the constant capital spent by all Departments, and another Department producing the means of final consumption for workers and capitalists. Hence these means of consumption would appear to be simple commodities rather than capital on adopting the form of the C–M–C circuit. Workers' consumption, however, is different from capitalists' consumption because, while for workers it seems to be simply the consumption of commodities, for

28 Marx 1978, p. 428 [1963, p. 352].

29 'Department' is the widely accepted translation, in these texts, for the term *Abteilung*, which Marx uses to denote each of the sectors into which social capital divides itself in the process of its reproduction.

social capital it represents reproduction of labour power and thus reproduction of variable capital. In each Department, the value of the product is internally divided into the three portions already mentioned and so Marx was able to construct his famous reproduction schemes with the following form:

Department I: $C_1 + V_1 + SV_1 = P_1$
Department II: $C_2 + V_2 + SV_2 = P_2$

Here, I is the Department of means of production and P_1 is its product; II is the Department of means of consumption and P_2 is its product; C is the constant capital; V is the variable capital and SV is the surplus value.

In the relation between these two major Departments, Marx synthesises the multiple relations by means of which the various branches or individual capitals produce for one another. Independently of one another, they determine the magnitude of the value to be allocated to each one of their own parts, but at the same time they are the purchasers of one another's products. It can be seen from the above system of equations that Department I must produce as its product, P_1, the total means of production needed to replace its own constant capital, C_1, and that of Department II, C_2, whose values were transferred to the respective products at the end of the labour period under consideration. Furthermore, Department II must produce as its product, P_2, the total means of final consumption purchased by the workers and capitalists of both Departments, corresponding to each Department's variable capitals, V_1 and V_2, and to the surplus values of both, SV_1 and SV_2, because, for now, capitalists are supposed to use surplus value only for their individual consumption. That is, expressing the reasoning again in the form of equations:

$$P_1 = C_1 + C_2$$
$$P_2 = V_1 + SV_1 + V_2 + SV_2$$

In fact, with the help of some numerical examples, Marx makes a detailed examination of how the magnitudes of each component part of the product of value of the two Departments and also their respective organic compositions (C/V) and their surplus value rates (SV/V) should be combined in such a way as to ensure their reproduction.

For the purposes of this book however, the interest lies in the general lines along which all this unfolds. Taking into account that P_1 already has an adequate 'material shape' for the replacement of C_1, achieved simply by exchanges made among the capitalists of Department I itself, it is important to note that the remainder of its product, equivalent to C2, is purchased by the capitalists of Department II with the money obtained from the sale of the means of consumption to the workers and capitalists in Department I. By means of that same purchase, Department I not only supply the resources for Department II to purchase the remainder of its product, C2, but also replaces its labour power, V1, and allows its capitalists to spend the surplus value that they have appropriated to themselves.

Thus, what is more outstanding than the internal exchanges among the capitalists of each Department, which absorbs part of its own products, is the exchange between the two Departments by means of which the general condition of reproduction is established. It is effectuated through the purchasing of C2 with the equivalent of the purchases of the means of consumption by workers and capitalists of Department I, namely, V1 + SV1. In other words, the basic condition for reproduction is the equivalence between the constant capital replaced by Department II and the sum of the variable capital and the surplus value of Department I; or,

$$C2 = V1 + SV1$$

It is the exact proportion between the two magnitudes that guarantees the normality of the reproduction movement of the social capital, for if one side of the equation were larger, there would be an excess in one of the Departments and a lack in the other, preventing them from producing again to the same extent they did before.

After completing this general examination, Marx introduces the key element that endows the reproduction with its specifically capitalist nature: the accumulation of capital, the increase in the magnitudes of value of both constant and variable capital brought about by investment of part of the surplus value obtained in a given period to expand the production base in the following period. In regard to the precise manner with which this investment takes place and the motives that lead to it, Marx points out:

> ... the idea that accumulation is achieved at the expense of consumption – considered in this general way – is an illusion that contradicts the essence of capitalist production, in as much as it assumes that the purpose and driving motive of this is consumption, and not the grabbing of surplus value and its capitalization, i.e. accumulation.[30]

30 Marx 1978, p. 579 [1963, pp. 498–9].

Capitalists do not invest in the expansion of production to enjoy the consumption provided by the surplus value and so they do not feel that the capitalisation of part of it is in any way a sacrifice. They are merely compelled by the 'driving motive' of capital, given that it had been converted into the true 'subject' of the process of continuous valorisation of the value.

If capitalists were to consume the entire amount of the surplus value, the portions into which the capital of the two Departments is divided would conserve their former values and reproduction would be on a 'simple' scale. With the investment of part of the surplus value in increasing the value of variable capital and constant capital, however, reproduction occurs on an 'expanded scale'. In this case the portion of the product of Department I equivalent to the surplus value to be capitalised in the increasing of C1, will not be used by its capitalists to purchase means of subsistence equivalent to C2 but to increase C1 through exchanges internal to Department I. The equilibrium equation for simple reproduction now becomes:

$$C2 < V1 + SV1$$[31]

Of course, the growth in C1 means that more variable capital will also be employed in Department I according to its organic composition of capital; in turn, the increase in V1 is what enables the workers of that Department to purchase more means of subsistence from Department II, thereby providing the money for that Department to increase its constant capital beyond what it draws from its own surplus value to be invested.

All the numerical examples and the explanations proffered by Marx about the equilibrium of reproduction 'on expanded scale' are basically intended to show how reproduction with accumulation is possible provided that the relat-

31 Despite his explanations and numerical examples, Marx never formulated the equilibrium of reproduction on expanded scale in a neat equation as he did with simple reproduction. That led to various discussions and attempts to find the formula, ranging from Bukharin's equation in 1924 and other attempts by Paul Sweezy 1942, Roman Rosdolsky 1968, and Shigeto Tsuru 1993 to, more recently, Mario Robles and Roberto Escorcia 2015. These discussions cannot be carried on independently of the sophisticated mathematics used in some of the models, and so it is sufficient to mention them without reproducing them in full. In any case, I agree with Moseley's observation that 'the anarchic nature of capitalist production makes it extremely unlikely that the necessary balance can be achieved between the quantity of fixed capital goods that need to be replaced in any given year and the quantity of those goods that are produced each year' (2015, p. 233 n.16). In my opinion, it was not part of Marx's plans to find the formula for reproduction on an expanded scale.

ive magnitudes value in the two Departments keep an exact proportion. The exact proportion is the central problem here, according to Marx's comment:

> reproduction on an expanded scale (which is conceived here simply as production pursued with a greater investment of capital) has nothing to do with the absolute size of the product, that for a given volume of commodities it simply assumes a different arrangement or a different determination of the functions of the various elements of the given product and is this in the first instance only simple reproduction as far as its value goes. It is not the quantity, but the qualitative character of the given elements of simple reproduction that is changed, and this change is the material precondition for the ensuing reproduction on an expanded scale.[32]

The difference between 'simple' and 'expanded' reproduction or between the mere general concept of reproduction and the concept that corresponds to the capitalist demand for accumulation solely depends on an 'arrangement or a different determination of the functions of the various elements of the given product'. Once again, Marx discards the mere quantitative dimension of the 'absolute size of the product' and formulates the problem of reproduction as one also of qualitatively determined quantities. It is a question of the proportion between the component parts of value distributed according to their 'functions' and the interest in continuing the accumulation of capital. With the qualitative determination of quantity reappears the Marxian concept of 'measure' examined in the second chapter above. Now 'measure' is defined as the need of social capital to divide its global value according to the 'functions' of the different use-values in expanded reproduction.

Social capital must always find the exact measure for qualitative and quantitative distribution, so that the exchanges between the different Departments may occur without leading to relative excesses or scarcities of products that would jeopardise the accumulation and even the absolute magnitude of the reproduced product. Anticipating eventual objections that the figures presented in his examples were devices to make his model plausible and to demonstrate the possibility of the system finding the accurate proportions it needs, Marx explains that:

> What is arbitrarily chosen here, for both Departments I and II, is the ratio of variable capital to constant capital; arbitrary also is the identity of this ratio between the Departments and their subdivisions. This identity is

32 Marx 1978, p. 582 [1963, p. 501]

> assumed here only for the sake of simplification, and the assumption of different ratios would not change anything at all in the conditions of the problem or its solution.[33]

The 'arbitrary' element in Marx's examples does not concern the exact figures alone but also the proportions among the figures. What is fundamental, however, is that such proportion should exist.

Achieving the exact proportion of values is not a problem that the author can solve in an artificial manner with numerical equations and illustrations but, rather, it is an effective process that social capital must execute, and it is precisely this process which constitutes its 'social' character. The accurate measure of its distribution results from this process in which capital appears as a 'subject' with its own life, formulates the 'conditions of the problem' and internalises them as its moments. It is under this determination that capital presides over the 'arrangement' of the relative amounts of value in each one of its portions and provides itself with the means to reproduce itself in general and on an expanded scale. Nevertheless, it was already observed that in this form of 'subjectivity' there also reside elements that impede the full achievement of its immanent tendencies to unrestrictedly dominate the reality. In the case considered here, the exact measure to ensure the increasing and constant reproduction of social capital is not to be found. Such difficulty constitutes a new modality of crisis, or rather, a richer and more complex apprehension of the phenomenon of crises.

2.2 *Crisis as Interdepartmental Disproportion*

In the general terms in which the problem is being analysed here, the successful reproduction of social capital depends on the occurrence of an exact distribution of values that makes the full exchanges of the two large production Departments possible. Marx observes that:

> The real balance, however, as far as the actual commodity exchange is concerned, i.e. the reconversion of the various parts of the annual product, requires that equal values of commodities are reciprocally exchanged.[34]

Essentially it is a case of achieving the system's 'balance'. Harmony is ensured only if each Department sells to the other whatever is necessary for it to pur-

33 Marx 1978, p. 483 [1963, p. 406].
34 Marx 1978, p. 570 [1963, p. 490].

chase, from the Department it sells to, the amount of value adequate for its own reproduction. In other words, there must be correspondence between what each one needs to sell and the other to buy. The proportion or measure thus present in the division of value among the 'various parts of the annual product' of both Departments must be expressed in the amount of the 'equal values of commodities reciprocally exchanged', that is, in the measure of the consumption needs of each Department. The qualitatively determined quantities refer not only to the constant capital, variable capital and surplus value of each Department but also to the means of production and consumption 'reciprocally exchanged' and combined.

However, for the measure expressed in the equilibrium equation of simple reproduction, the situation of expanded reproduction represents a mismeasurement that reflects the Sisyphean nature of the task of accumulation. It momentarily disorganises the system and leads it always to find a new point of balance, a new temporary measure that conciliates the Departments' mutual supply and demand. In addition to that positive aspect of the mismeasure inherent to accumulation, there is another, insofar as:

> The existence of capitalist accumulation excludes the possibility that C2 may be equal to (V+SV)1. Yet even with capitalist accumulation, the case could arise in which, as a result of the accumulation achieved in the previous run of production periods, C2 was not only equal to (V+SV)1, but in fact even greater. This would mean over-production in Department II and could only be balanced out by a major crash, as a result of which capital would be transferred from Department II to Department I.[35]

In other words, if C2 is not smaller than (V+SV)1 in exactly the right measure, then a mass of means of consumption corresponding to the excess of value generated by Department II will not be sold to the workers and capitalists of Department I. In turn the consumption of the latter will be lower than it should be, thereby creating a situation of 'over-production in Department II' and making this Department unable to expand and possibly even reproduce itself on a simple scale. In the end such a situation will create difficulties for the replacement of Department I's variable capital and, in the medium- to long-term, for the reproduction of the system as a whole. This is what Marx refers to when he speaks of the case 'in which, as a result of the accumulation achieved in

35 Marx 1978, p. 596 [1963, pp. 515–16]. I have replaced 'IIc' and I (v+sv) of the English translation with C2 and (V+SV)1 according to the original Portuguese of my book.

the previous run of production periods, C2 was not … equal to (V+SV)1', that is, when he indicates the divergence in the Departments' exchanges as the expression of the loss of measure of the production of each one in the demand of the other. A divergence that 'could only be balanced out by a major crash', a crisis. The crisis therefore mirrors a disproportion in the division of the value of social capital resulting from the loss of the reciprocal reference or measure of the two Departments.

Given that the crisis consists in the mismatch between interdepartmental supply and demand, between their reciprocal sales and purchases, it is only natural that it should appear as an irregularity in the movement of the money that intermediates the circulation of commodities. For Marx:

> the fact that the production of commodities is the general form of capitalist production already implies that money plays a role, not just as means of circulation, but also as money capital within the circulation sphere, and gives rise to certain conditions for normal exchange that are peculiar to this mode of production, i.e. conditions for the normal course of reproduction, whether simple or on an expanded scale, which turn to an equal number of conditions for an abnormal course, possibilities of crisis, since, on the basis of the spontaneous pattern of this production, this balance is itself an accident.[36]

On the one hand, as the relation between the Departments basically occurs through the circulation of commodities, the specific determinations of the commodity-form prevail, and the crisis is defined as the possibility of an 'abnormal course' as an alternative to the 'conditions for normal exchange … i.e. conditions for the normal course of reproduction'. On the other hand, the fact that 'money plays a role … as money capital' means that the form of the individual capital circuit also prevail in the sense that each Department is autonomous in regard to the other.

Thus, money capital represents the connecting element between the two spheres – immediate production and the interdepartment circulation. The distinction between the two spheres is projected in the exchanges between the Departments in such a way that they remain independent in their investment decisions regarding how much each one will produce in each period and how much they can increase production in the following period, capitalising part of their surplus value. Yet the Departments are dependent on one another

36 Marx 1978, pp. 570–1 [1963, pp. 490–1].

to put their decisions into effect and these decisions will only be effective if there is equilibrium in the value magnitudes of the commodities that circulate between them. The function of money capital becomes that of uniting, in the sphere of circulation, that which in the sphere of production is autonomous, so as to guarantee that the unity of the two spheres implies the harmonisation of the interests of both Departments, at the same time dependent and independent.

Marx concludes that:

> … these necessary preconditions all mutually require one another, but they are mediated by a very complicated process which involves … processes of circulation that proceed independently, even if they are intertwined with one another. The very complexity of the process provides many occasions for it to take an abnormal course.[37]

The dissociation and the unity of the two spheres, production and circulation, appear in their complex form. Insofar as they are determined by the production of Department, the 'processes of circulation … proceed independently' of one another; but insofar as they are determined by mutual needs, 'they are intertwined with one another'. By assuming the restriction that the two Departments are connected exclusively through the circulation of the commodities they produce, Marx indicates the possibility of an eventual 'abnormal course', which would occur on 'many occasions'.

In addition to an indetermination as to the outcome of the process, Marx also refers to the complexity of the modal status of crisis at this moment of its definition:

> this intertwining and coalescence of the processes of reproduction or circulation of different capitals is on the one hand necessary [*notwendig*] to the division of labour, on the other hand is accidental; and thus the definition of the content of crisis is already fuller.[38]

The 'necessity', the inevitability of the relation between the two Departments appears as an 'intertwining', that is, it takes place in the sphere of circulation

---

37 Marx 1978, p. 571 [1963, p. 491].

38 Marx 1969b, p. 511 [1967, p. 511]. The 'necessity' mentioned in this text should not be identified with the reciprocal needs or demands of the two Departments, otherwise Marx would have used the word *Bedürfnis* and not *Notwendigkeit* as he did. The latter has an exclusively modal meaning.

within which each Department has to sell to the other and buy from the other the commodities that ensure its reproduction. The 'necessity' also appears as 'coalescence', that is, in the fact that both Departments are obliged to grow together so that the accumulation of each one can be possible in the course of the production periods. This mercantile form of the process, however, means that purchase and sale remain at the base of the 'division of labour' executed by capital, preserving the general form of the sociability of concrete labour, immediately characterised as private labour. For that reason, exchange is the essential form of connection between Departments that are not entirely determined by one another, always leaving room for a certain degree of reciprocal independence and indifference.

That is why Marx considers the occurrence of 'intertwining and coalescence' in the precise proportions that are needed to ensure the reproduction of each Department and hence the social capital as a whole to be 'accidental'. Although the connection between both Departments in the sphere of circulation is a 'necessity', their relative autonomy in the sphere of production makes the realisation of that connection something merely 'accidental'. The division of labour presided over by capital – indeed, the division of social labour according to the functions its parts must perform for successful expanded reproduction – implies the simultaneous 'necessity' of unity and the 'possibility' of separation. In other words, it implies that the unity is established through the mediation of difference, as a result that may or may not occur.

The 'very complexity' of the modal status of the crisis defined in the framework of the reproduction of social capital is analogous to that examined at the level of simple circulation of commodities (see chapter 1, section 2.4) because it, too, is rooted in the tendency towards external autonomisation of the interiorly unified moments. On that basis Marx defines a new concept of crisis:

> ... the independence of the two correlated aspects can only *show itself* forcibly, as a destructive process. It is just the *crisis* in which they assert their unity, the unity of the different aspects. The independence which these two linked and complimentary phases assume in relation to each other is forcibly destroyed. Thus the crisis manifests the unity of the two phases that have become independent to each other. There would be no crisis without this inner unity of factors that are apparently indifferent to each other.[39]

39 Marx 1969b, p. 500 [1967, p. 501].

Just as in the selling and purchasing relationship, and precisely because this is the form the 'intertwining' of the two Departments takes, the crisis is not reduced to the separation of the buying and selling phases, that is, to the mere disproportion between the Departments. Instead, the crisis lies in the fact that the separation of sale and purchase, that is, the Departments' independence is 'forcibly destroyed' in the 'inner unity of factors that are apparently indifferent to each other'. This point needs to be examined in more detail.

The two Departments of social production are distinguished from one another by the different use-value of their products, but this difference does not precede the relation in which they 'intertwine' and 'coalesce'. Marx states that the Departments 'have *become* independent to each other', that is, their independence is the result of the very relation through which the reproduction of social capital takes place. The specialisation of the product of each Department is a consequence of the division of labour carried out by capital, and if their difference gets to the point where it seems to be an 'indifference', this is due to the diversity of the use-values produced by each one. The 'inner unity' of the Departments is present even in the 'apparent indifference' with which they each define their own rates of accumulation. Hence, the 'independence of the two correlated aspects can only *show itself* forcibly, as a destructive process', that is, 'destructive' of the 'inner unity' represented by the need that the two Departments sell to one another an appropriate quantity of commodities and rapidly reproduce themselves.

Achieving the exact proportions of the qualitatively determined quantities required by the reproduction, that is, the measures that social capital determines for itself as the 'subject' of its own reproduction, is a result of the highest 'complexity' because, also as a 'subject', social capital divides itself into Departments which become autonomous insofar as they independently define their own rates of accumulation. It is only by means of *post festum* exchanges, and even then, only possibly, that the measures of accumulation match to establish the necessary social measure. This measure thus appears as if it were 'accidental'. For social capital, not only the unity of the Departments is a necessity but also their differentiation and autonomisation, since unity must result from the mediating action of difference, that is, from the unifying process. It follows that the precise combination of measures, defined, in principle, independently in each Department, is an 'accident' determined by social capital's complex 'necessity'. Once again, the possibility of an 'abnormal course' in the reproduction – crisis as a mere possibility – is based on the capital's characteristic 'necessity'. It is indeed an 'accident'; only not an 'accident' external to 'necessity' but defined by it.

The crisis exposes the impossibility that the opposing aspects of the capital relation appear as merely 'independent'. It represents the disproportion that highlights the need for proportion in the exchanges between the Departments, or the emergence of the 'inner unity' that reveals their mutual indifference as a mere appearance. In the crisis the Departments are no longer 'diverse', each external to the other; they are differentiated by the very process that unifies them, that is, they are 'opposites'. Thus, the fixing of measures, originally established autonomously within each Department, presents itself in the crisis as a fixing of opposing measures: crisis is defined as the moment when the autonomous measures oppose one another; as the contradiction of measures, and hence as mismeasurement. Insofar as it exposes the possible opposition of the accumulation rates and the Departments' reciprocal demands, the crisis makes explicit the inverse of this possibility, namely, the need for these rates, these measures, to harmonise. This is the sense in which mismeasurement cannot be a simple contingency, external to the system of capital but, instead, the result of the latent necessity that emerges when capital intends to constitute itself as a totality and fulfil its aspirations to the condition of 'subject'.

Nevertheless, even though at this point of his presentation Marx achieves a more precise definition of the modality of crises and manages to avoid an interpretation that sees them as a mere chance occurrence, it is important to stress that he still only manages to explain mismeasurement in its general form. The presentation of the reproduction of social capital does not provide an exposition of the fundaments of mismeasurement and its necessary irruption in the sphere of circulation. This fundament, established in the framework of capital's constitutive determinations in the sphere of immediate production, remains hidden, given that production and circulation are considered as separate processes, reunited as complementary moments but independent of one another in the movement of social reproduction.

However, the independence of the two processes, characteristic of the analysis of social capital, makes it possible to delimit the extent to which the modal determination of crisis advances:

> The circulation process as a whole or the reproduction process of capital is the unity of its production phase and its circulation phase, so that it comprises both these processes or phases. Therein lies a further developed possibility or abstract form of crisis.[40]

40 Marx 1969b, p. 513 [1967, p. 514].

Although it is more than just an 'accident', crisis here is not something inevitable. The mediation of the unity of the 'production phase and its circulation phase' by their difference means that both the occurrence of a crisis and its non-occurrence are only possibilities. Of course, they are possibilities determined by the necessity immanent to the constitution of capital and each of them is a 'further developed possibility' compared to the mere possibility of crisis that is associated with the ambit of simple circulation. Yet they remain an 'abstract form' because they are inserted in a moment of the presentation in which production and circulation appear externally united based on their immediate difference. The possibility that the measures established separately by each Department may come into opposition defines only the form, not the cause of mismeasurement.

Therefore, the effort both to deduce from the 'abstract' moment of their determination an explanation for the complex way in which crises effectively occur, and to reach definitive conclusions regarding the historical viability of capitalism, with optimistic or pessimistic forecasts about its future, constitutes, above all, a methodological mistake. Part of the Marxist literature made this mistake, disregarding the plan Marx elaborated for the presentation of his work whereby the concepts were to be only gradually deduced.[41] The introduction

41 The discussion of the reproduction schemes of social capital in *Capital* Volume II began in the latter years of the nineteenth century and was taken up again on many occasions in the course of the twentieth century as the foundation for a broader, more ambitious discussion of the viability or unviability of capitalism itself. In the early days the debate was led by the Russian 'legal Marxists' – Tugan-Baranovsky, Bulgákov, Struve – who were inspired by the reproduction schemes of social capital in *Capital* Volume II to attack their rivals, the 'Narodniki', and defend the viability of Russian capitalism. Their formulations, however, went so far as to attempt to demonstrate the potential immortality of the capitalist system in general and accordingly they were contested by a group of German Marxists, most notably by Rosa Luxemburg (1976), who based herself on the flaws in the Marxian formulation of the reproduction schemes to negate the viability of reproduction in the long-run, considering capitalism as chronically condemned to the impasse between the value of labour power and the value it creates for capital. In Luxemburg's view, this difference would lead to a fatal tendency to under-consumption and consequent systemic crisis, only to be put off by imperialist expansion into territories and social spheres that were not yet capitalist. These interpretations generated the *Zusammenbruchstheorie* – the theory of capitalism's economic collapse reformulated in 1929 by Grossman (1992), still making use of the expanded reproduction schemes introduced in *Capital* Volume II. Later, in 1968, in a study of *Grundrisse*, Rosdolsky published a critique and a synthesis of a considerable part of the discussion, indicating that the basic mistake of all the participants had been their failure to understand the methodology and architecture of *Capital*. The defenders of capitalism's viability and those of its unviability alike had expected a proximity to reality in Volume II that would only exist in Volume III, where the relationship between individual

of the concept of crisis in the framework of the schemes of the reproduction of social capital could not offer more than an initial characterisation of mismeasurement, that is, as capital's loss of reference to its own self during the self-valorisation process. The very gaps in this characterisation point to the more complex determinations by means of which the fundament of mismeasurement can be revealed: the moment in which crisis can finally acquire the status of something necessary and inevitable. To what extent, however, did Marx really intend to define the concept of crisis as necessary and inevitable? This is one of the fundamental themes in Marxist debates to this day, renewed with impetus at every irruption of a real economic crisis.

---

capitals and branches of production would no longer be one of mere complementarity but of competition. More recently, authors who investigate the crisis unleashed in 2008 are inclined to consider the disproportion between the departments of social production as a real ground for crisis that must be combined with some of those presented in *Capital* Volume III. This is the case, for example, with Harvey, who rejects the fall of the rate of profit as a 'solid law' and as a convincing explanation for crisis and prefers to use the concept of inter-departmental disproportionality combined with a variant of the underconsumption thesis (2010, p. 94).

CHAPTER 4

Capital as a Totality

1 Competition and Profit

1.1 *Competition as a Process of Realisation*

The more capital develops as the 'subject' of its movement of self-determination, the more its constitutive dispositions present themselves as immanent tendencies whose realisation does not depend on external conditions. It would therefore be reasonable to expect that at the end of this movement the conditions for the full actualisation of capital's tendencies would only depend on its internal determinations. If, however, this occurs, it is in a hardly perceptible, highly complex manner, in which the phenomena frequently manifest the internal determinations in an inverse and obfuscating manner. The realisation of these immanent tendencies takes on special significance when they are tendencies that lead to crisis, for in this case what is in play is a richer and more concrete explanation for the actual crises.

Up until now, crisis has appeared as a mere possibility that tendencies may come to be realised, corresponding to the still abstract level of the presentation of *Capital* Volume II. In it the reproduction of social capital is still marked by an external unity of the production and circulation processes, neither of which impresses its fundamental characteristics on the other. This mutual determination is precisely what constitutes the level of presentation that *Capital* Volume III, our theme from this point on, strives to attain. In surpassing the study of reproduction conducted only from the standpoint of circulation, Volume III proposes to explain the 'process as a whole',[1] describing the profound imbrication between production and circulation and thereby revealing that the mode of effectuation of crises is a necessary consequence of the specific form of capital. In Marx's own words:

> In Volume II, of course, we had to present this sphere of circulation only in relation to the determinations of form it produces to demonstrate the

1 In his editing of *Capital* Volume III, Engels modified the subtitle given by Marx for the *1863–5 Manuscript*. In the English translation Engels' modification does not seem to be substantial, from 'Forms of the process as a whole' (Marx 2016, p. 47) to 'The Process of capitalist Production as a Whole' (Marx 1981, p. 5). In the original, however, it is considerable, from 'Die Gestaltungen des Gesamtprocesses' (Marx 1992, p. 5) to 'Der Gesamtprozeß der kapitalistischen Produktion' (Marx 1964, p. 5).

 | DOI:10.1163/9789004690721_006

> further development of the forms of capital that takes place in it. In actual fact, however, this sphere is the sphere of competition, which is subject to accident in each individual case; i.e. where the inner law that prevails through the accidents and governs them is visible only when these accidents are combined in large numbers, so that it remains invisible and incomprehensible to the individual agents of production themselves. Furthermore, however, the actual production process, as the unity of the immediate production process and the process of circulation, produces new configurations in which the threads of the inner connection get more and more lost, the relations of production becoming independent of one another and the components of value ossifying into independent forms.[2]

Given the richness of its various aspects, this text can serve to guide our analysis in this subchapter. It will now be analysed gradually and in detail.

At the start of the text, Marx recalls that the approach adopted to capitalist reproduction in *Capital* Volume II was limited to the 'determinations of form' characteristic of the sphere of circulation, that is, the relations of sale and purchase between the two Departments into which social capital divides itself. In this case, as Marx explained in the *Grundrisse*: 'In so far as one capitalist *buys* from others, buys commodities, or sells, they are within the simple exchange relation and do not relate to one another as capital'.[3] Although the agents that face one another are capitalists, they appear to each other as mere buyers or sellers of commodities. In other words, their capitals 'do not relate to one another as capital', but as commodities and money, 'determinations of form' of the 'the simple exchange relation'. Nevertheless, if 'in actual fact' the capitals must 'relate to one another as capital', their relations must not only include the buying and selling of commodities but also go beyond that and present themselves as a 'sphere of' inter-capitalist competition. Only in its competition with others does capital have before it another capital and not a mere exchange value.

Thus, all the individual capitals define themselves as capital pursuing the identical objective of self-valorisation. This is already why they clash over the relatively scarce opportunities to achieve their common goal. This conflict, competition, stems from the opposition between that which is common to all capital and the necessarily determined existence of capital as individual capital: each individual capital must achieve the common goal as if it were its own

2 Marx 1981, pp. 966–7 [1964, p. 836].
3 Marx 1974, p. 421 [1983, p. 336].

alone and to the detriment of the others. Marx continues by stating that: '... the essence of capital, which, as will be developed more closely in connection with competition, *is* something which repels itself ...'; and, furthermore:

> Since value forms the foundations of capital, and since capital therefore necessarily exists only through exchange for *counter-value*, capital thus necessarily repels itself from itself. A *universal capital*, one without alien capitals confronting it, with which it exchanges ... is therefore a non-thing. The reciprocal repulsion between capitals is already contained in capital as realized exchange value.[4]

Competition, as 'reciprocal repulsion between capitals', has its origin in the 'essence of capital, ... which repels itself', that is, in capital's self-repulsion. This movement of self-repulsion already identified in the context of the accumulation of capital (see chapter 2, section 2.2) appears here with the meaning that capital's form of existence is the multiplicity of capitals that repel one another, that reciprocally differentiate and negate one another, because, for each capital, the common purpose affirms itself as if one capital alone should achieve it and, accordingly, should impede all the others from doing the same. Considered in its essential determination as a value that self-valorises, individual capital 'necessarily repels itself from itself' because each individual capital strives to achieve its determination by itself for itself alone, repelling itself from the others and repelling them precisely because they have the very same intention.

Capital Volume III adds that:

> Here the individual has an effect only as part of a social power, as an atom in the mass, and it is in this form that competition brings into play the social character of production and consumption. The side that is temporarily weaker in competition is also that in which the individual operates independently of the mass of his competitors, and often directly against them, illustrating precisely in this way the dependence of one on the other, whereas the stronger side always acts towards its opponent as a more or less united whole.[5]

In the text Marx distinguishes between two 'sides' of the relationship between universality and individuality. First there is the aspect of 'competition' among

4 Marx 1974, p. 421, footnotes [1983, p. 336].
5 Marx 1981, p. 295 [1964, pp. 203–4].

the multiple capitals, 'that in which the individual operates independently of the mass of his competitors, and often directly against them'; a side, therefore, in which each individual capital performs as an autonomous individual and in opposition to the others. Second, the universality present as a determination common to all capital which manifests itself in the 'mass' of singular capitals as the 'social power' they wield.

Each of these sides of the individual capital appears as if it has no relation to the other, so that the universal side defines itself as an abstract generality and the competition side as pure conflict among free, autonomous individuals; it is not by chance that freedom is the unilateral form in which capitalism is viewed. It is, however, competition that establishes the relation between the two sides, by highlighting the 'dependence of one on the other' of the various capitals, that is, the dependence instituted in the interior of the external independence of individual capitals. The opposition between internal dependence and external independence expresses the self-repulsion that is constitutive of the 'essence of capital' as a reciprocal repulsion among individual capitals.

The 'side of competition' is thus not restricted to a mere struggle among independent individuals because it is presided over by the internal movement that represents the universal aspect of capital. This last, in turn, is not reduced to an abstract generality: the 'mass' of which individual capital is but an 'atom' does not consist of a sum of individuals but, instead, of a 'mass of competitors' because, in it, the individual capital is already determined by the competition, by the 'universal' which repels itself from itself. Although competition expresses the self-repulsion inherent to capital, it also endows the constitutive dispositions of capital with the necessary form of manifestation that 'brings into play the social character of production and consumption' in a society of free proprietors of the commodities.

How then does the 'social power' of competition perform and why is competition the necessary form of capital's functioning? Going back to the *Grundrisse*:

> Conceptually, *competition* is nothing other than the inner *nature of capital*, its essential determination, appearing in and realized as the reciprocal interaction of many capitals with one another, the inner tendency as external necessity. (Capital exists and can only exist as many capitals, and its self-determination therefore appears as their reciprocal interaction with one another).[6]

6 Marx 1974, p. 414 [1983, p. 327].

Marx begins by taking up, once more, the idea that capital takes the form of existence of 'many capitals', in such a way that the repulsion that characterises its 'inner nature' appears as the singular capitals' repulsion of one another. Marx adds, however, that the repulsion of the 'many capitals' is also a 'reciprocal interaction' that they perform. By means of this 'reciprocal interaction', they impose on one another conformity to the 'essential determination' of capital, delimiting each one's space on the market and creating a permanent conflict around the redistribution of this space. Any individual capital that fails to obey the 'essential determination' – for example, by not adapting its own valorisation rate to the measure of the total social capital total – will lose space to the others and may even come to be excluded from the market altogether. Considering that such a possibility is a capitalist's nightmare, it obliges them to at least accompany the average efficiency standards or even endeavour to surpass them and obtain extraordinary gains, expanding, in that way, their niche in the general space.

Therefore, the individual capitals' 'dependence on one another' mentioned above, does not refer to the complementarity of the buying and selling but to the imposition of capital's 'essential determination' by means of the conflict among individual capitals who fight one another for self-valorisation opportunities. Because each capitalist wants to realise for himself the 'inner tendency' constitutive of capital, he tries to prevent the others from doing so, but, in the attempt, he obliges them to act in the same way. Hence the 'inner tendency' affirms itself through the constitutive negativity of the competition and takes on the aspect of an 'external necessity' for each individual capital, that is, a necessity imposed by the other individual capitals.

That's why the 'inner tendency' does not manifest itself directly in the performances of individual capitals, quite the contrary, it imposes on them from outside, not from inside; it imposes itself in an indirect and negative manner through the competitive struggle. The 'essential determinations' of capital are always in the nature of a 'tendency' that depends on external conditions to be realised and is only realised in a manner that seems to be the inverse of a 'self-determination', namely, as an 'external necessity', as a contingency.

It is now possible to understand another aspect of the first text cited in this subchapter:

> the sphere of competition, which is subject to accident in each individual case; i.e. where the inner law that prevails through the accidents and governs them is visible only when these accidents are combined in large numbers.

In other words, 'in each individual case' the 'inner law' presents itself as the pressure exercised by the other capitals; an 'external', insofar as they appear to one another to be independent, and a pressure 'subject to accident', because in their independence they seem to escape from any kind of reciprocal control and do not show any notable regularity that might indicate the existence of a 'law'. The law 'is visible only' as that which 'prevails through the accidents', when they 'are combined in large numbers', so that they do not fail to appear to be accidents to each individual and in this way fulfil the 'inner law'. The accident does not subordinate itself to the law by annulling itself, but by converting itself into the means for the realisation of the law.

Again, in the *Grundrisse*, Marx explains that point in the following way:

> Competition generally, this essential locomotive force of the bourgeois economy, does not establish its laws, but is rather their executor. Unlimited competition is therefore not the presupposition for the truth of the economic laws, but rather the consequence – the form of appearance in which their necessity realizes itself ... Competition therefore does not *explain* these laws; rather, it lets them be *seen*, but does not produce them.[7]

Competition is the 'locomotive force' because it is the 'executor' of the laws but the laws themselves are situated at the fundamental level of the relationship between capital and living labour. At this fundamental level, instead of manifesting itself as an explicit contradiction – that is, as an opposition to living labour – capital's self-negation appears as opposition among the 'many capitals'. It is only through this opposition, through this negation and the conflict of individual capitals and their eventual reciprocal elimination, that the necessity of the 'inner law' manifests and 'realises itself'.

Here Marx's formulation is very similar to Hegel's famous 'cunning of reason' whereby to attain its realisation, the 'universal' uses the conflict of particular individuals and preserves itself not only despite these individuals' mutual destruction but also because of it.[8] In Marx, the equivalent of the Hegelian 'universal' is social capital, which affirms itself through the competitive negation among numerous capitals. This is yet another aspect of capital's 'subjectivity', which repels itself from itself, engendering multiplicity and external conflict as the expression of its own internal conflict, in order to resolve it momentarily only to replace it immediately afterwards, but this time in a more complex

7 Marx 1974, p. 552 [1983, p. 457].
8 See Hegel 1975, p. 89 [1955, p. 105].

manner. The immediate subjects of the economy are unaware of this 'subjectivity' because, as the following stretch of the first text cited in this item declared, 'inner law ... remains invisible and incomprehensible to the individual agents of production themselves'. The agents see the occurrences as mere chance events and not as 'the form of appearance in which their necessity realizes itself'. This is why their conscious actions only lead indirectly to the realisation of the 'inner tendencies', insofar as the 'subjective' universality of their capitals serves as the *sine qua non* condition for its effectuation.

In turn, the 'external necessity' with which the agents impose the 'inner tendencies' on one another makes the competition recuperate and realise all the constitutive dispositions of the industrial capital that were presented in *Capital* Volume I and II. In these volumes, however, the dispositions were considered in a formal manner, that is, as if they were merely juxtaposed because of their associations with the autonomous spheres of circulation and immediate production, which were not considered as mutually determining one another. In *Capital* Volume III, however, taking up once more the first text in this item, we find that 'the actual production process, as the unity of the immediate production process and the process of circulation, produces new configurations', configurations resulting from the imbrication of two processes in an internal unity that implies an 'actual production process' and no longer a simple tendency. Competition performs this role because, in repulsion of one another by the 'many capitals', it realises and condenses the various moments of capital's self-negation. It is itself a richer and fuller form of the development of self-negation; it is the form in which capital's 'inner tendency' to self-affirmation and self-negation becomes effective as an 'external necessity' for mutual determination and mutual negation of the singular capitals.

Thus, even within the dimension in which capital gradually dominates the conditions of its own constitution and reproduction, Marx considers that 'competition is the mode generally in which capital enforces its mode of production'.[9] In the opposed dimension, however, the one in which the 'inner tendencies' also lead to capital's self-negation, it is the competition that effectuates the potential crisis, acting through the same means of reciprocal coercion of the individual capitals. The tendency to crisis finds the conditions for its realisation in an 'external necessity', not less necessary for being external. This is the point at which it should be possible to explain crisis as an absolutely necessary consequence of the structure of capitalism, as stemming from the fact that this system inevitably leads to crisis.

---

9 Marx 1974, p. 730 [1983, p. 625].

Turning back for the last time to the first text cited in this item, however, a difficulty arises here insofar as, in the 'new configurations' that the 'actual production process' assumes, 'the threads of the inner connection get more and more lost'. In other words, the form of the competition autonomises itself from the 'inner tendencies' that lead to crisis, thereby making it very difficult to precisely define the modal status of crisis, that is, the necessity for its effectuation. Accordingly, this chapter sets itself the tasks of examining the development of the determinations of crisis in the sphere of competition – especially the tendency for the fall of the rate of profit and for the cyclical overaccumulation of capital – and then of conducting a preliminary discussion of the problems intrinsic to Marx's formulation regarding the modal status of crisis at this advanced stage of the categorial presentation. Only from there will it be possible to finally make a rigorous assessment of what I consider to be the fundament of Marx's critique of capitalism and of political economy.

1.2 *The Formation of the Rate of Profit*

To describe the capitalist production process as a whole and the way in which its immanent determinations impose themselves, it is of central importance that the economic surplus should present itself in the form of profit. It is the form in which the calculation of the valorisation of capital can reveal the tendencies and movements of the valorisation itself. While up until now, especially when taking the categories of circulation as the starting point, it has been possible to define profit as the mere expression of surplus value in the form of money, once the fact that capitalist production is realised through competition is taken into consideration, the relationship between surplus value and profit becomes complicated and, with that, so does the definition of profit. Establishing this relationship requires the introduction of some new concepts, and they will be the study object of the present subchapter.

First of all, Marx defines the sum of the constant and variable capital values (expressed as money) employed in the production of a commodity, that is, the total capital used in this production, as 'cost price'. He explains that:

> As this represented derivative of the total capital advanced, the surplus value takes on the transformed form of *profit* … Profit, as we are originally faced with it, is thus the same thing as surplus value, save in a mystified form, though one that necessarily arises from the capitalist mode of production. Because no distinction between constant and variable capital can be recognized in the apparent formation of the cost price, the origin of the change in value that occurs in the course of the production process is shifted from the variable capital to the capital as a whole. Because

> the price of labour power appears at one pole in the transformed form of wages, surplus value appears at the other pole in the transformed form of profit.[10]

If surplus is to be taken as 'derivative' only of the living labour incorporated to capital – an assumption that corresponds to the fundamental reality of capitalism according to Marx – then it persists as surplus value. However, surplus value itself only exists because labour power operates in conditions imposed by capital, becoming integrated to capital as its variable part and entering into the composition of capital just as much as constant capital does. Given that 'no distinction between constant and variable capital can be recognized in the apparent formation of the cost price', then it is possible for the explanation of the origin of the surplus to be 'shifted' from variable capital to total capital, and it is also possible that surplus comes to be viewed as a 'derivative' of the latter. The condition in which surplus value is created gives it the appearance of profit precisely because 'the price of labour power appears at one pole in the transformed form of wages', as the labour power has become part of the capital.

Living labour, however, continues to be the only source of surplus value, so that considering surplus value as being 'a represented derivative of the total capital advanced' actually means concealing its true origin. In turn, this concealment derives from capital's aspiration to constitute a totality that the labour power is a part of, and in this way become the 'subject' of its self-valorisation. In its aspect as total capital, capital presents itself as if it were the source of surplus value, its 'derivative', which takes the form of profit. By means of this fetishistic process, profit appears as a 'transformed form' of surplus value and furthermore, as a 'mystified form ... that necessarily arises from the capitalist mode of production', that is, 'from the' conditions that include labour power in capital. This mystification is a 'necessity' because the conditions for the creation of surplus value cloak it with the form of profit.

Therefore, the question that arises is, how is profit determined? According to Marx's formulation, 'it is the transformation of surplus value into profit that is derived from the transformation of the rate of surplus value into the profit rate, not the other way round'.[11] Marx defines the rate of surplus value previously mentioned in chapter 2, section 2.3 as the ratio of the surplus labour time and the actually necessary time, corresponding to the surplus value and the variable capital that produced it. In turn, the profit rate is the ratio between the surplus

10 Marx 1981, pp. 126–7 [1964, p. 46].

11 Marx 1981, p. 134 [1964, p. 53].

value and the total capital used in its production and it essentially depends on two factors: first the rate of surplus value, for, given the magnitude of the labour power, it is what determines how much surplus will be produced; and second, the ratio between variable capital and constant capital, which together make up total capital. Marx refers to this composition as the 'organic' composition when the relation of the values of variable capital and constant capital mirrors the technical relation between labour power and the means of production used. Given the variable capital, the volume of constant capital to be added to it to compose total capital will depend on the ratio between the two parts of total capital.

So, according to the variation in the organic composition of different capitals, the same rate of surplus value may correspond to several different rates of profit. In the same way, the rates of profit of different capitals may be the same but correspond to different rates of surplus value due to the differences in the organic compositions of these capitals or even due to the ratio of surplus value to profit. However, saying that the transformation of surplus value into profit must be 'derived' from the transformation of the rate of surplus value into the rate of profit, implies identifying a difference between profit and surplus value; implies stating that the same profit can express various different surplus values and vice versa. This is considerably more problematical than affirming the same thing about the respective rates. So how does Marx propose to get around this difficulty?

What intervenes here is the competition among the capitals invested in different branches of social production and with different organic compositions due to different technical requirements, specific to the product of each branch. Even supposing that all their surplus value rates were identical, the diversity of their organic compositions would mean that each one had a different profit rate. Thus, capitals in the less profitable branches would emigrate to those with higher profit rates, increasing the latter's product supply and making the profit rate to fall. At the same time, in the abandoned branches, the profit rate would go up because of the reduction in product supply. The overall tendency of these movements is to level off the rates of profit and different amounts of profit would be attributed to each individual capital according to the application of the average rate of profit to the sum of each individual's constant and variable capitals. A specific amount of profit determined by the average rate of profit multiplied by the amount of the total capital in question is added to the cost price of each capital, defining what Marx calls the 'price of production'.

The transformation of surplus value into profit 'derived' from the transformation of the surplus value rate into profit rate, that is to say, into average rate of profit, configures the determination of the price of production. This price is different from the value because it is equal to the cost price plus the profit calculated on the basis of the average rate of profit of the various branches and not on the surplus value. The resulting discrepancy between the profit and the surplus value of individual capitals has some significant implications that must be mentioned. The first is that, in Marx's words:

> if *profits* as a percentage of capital are equal over a period, say a year, so that capitals of equal size yield equal profits in the same period of time, then the *prices* of the commodities must be different from their *values*.[12]

The difference between values and prices of production gave rise to a complex question referred to in the Marxist literature as the 'transformation problem'. Its importance for the definition of 'crisis' will become apparent a little farther on. A second implication concerns the distribution of profit amounts among the different individual capitals:

> In this way there prevails, and necessarily so, a tendency to make production prices into mere transformed forms of value, or to transform profits into mere portions of surplus value that are distributed not in proportion to the surplus value that is created in each particular sphere of production, but rather in proportion to the amount of capital applied in each of

12 Marx 1969b, p. 190 [1967, p. 187]. The problem of the transformation of values into prices was based on an observation made by Marx himself (Marx 1981, pp. 264–5 [1964, p. 174]) about the need to calculate the price of production based on the cost prices and not the values. The Marx-Engels Gesamtausgabe's recent publication of manuscripts Marx wrote in the late 1870s shows that he was aware of the conceptual and mathematical difficulty and was seeking a solution but that apparently he had not yet arrived at a satisfactory one (Marx 2012). In the Marxist tradition, the debate begins with the answer given by Hilferding (1910) to Böhm-Bawerk (1896) and Bortkiewicz (1907). For a critical summary of the problem and its solutions, see Napoleoni 1981 and, more recently, Moseley 2015. If we consider that values can already be expressed monetarily from the outset, and that they only assert themselves as social averages together with averages derived from them – the prices of production – it is possible to reach the conclusion that market prices hold directly, indirectly, and also contradictorily, a whole system of averages and deviations related to each other, imposing themselves by negating the others and negating themselves by imposing them. On all these levels, values and prices present themselves as different measures, albeit functional to the system of valorisation of capital. The classical formulation of the problem fails to realise that the various forms always coexist when it requires a 'transformation', that is, an event which suppose a passage between two different and independent situations.

> these spheres, so that equal amounts of capital, no matter how they are composed, receive equal shares (aliquot parts) of the totality of surplus value produced by the total social capital.[13]

The amount of profit attributed to the singular capitals does not correspond 'to the surplus value that is created in each particular sphere of production' that those capitals belong to, but instead is distributed according to 'the amount of capital applied' in these spheres. It is no longer only the magnitude of variable capital that produces the surplus value that counts, but instead, the magnitude of total capital. Therefore, even if the magnitude of the variable capital employed in a certain branch is low, if it is compensated by a high magnitude of constant capital, the individual capitals in this branch of activity will receive a mass of profit equal to that of the individual capitals in another branch of equal magnitude and different organic composition.

That being so, however, the fundamental principles of the distribution 'of surplus value produced by the total social capital' take on a new aspect. In regard to this important point, it is worth citing a longer passage:

> Surplus value in the form of profit is no longer related to the portion of capital laid out on labour, which is where it derives from, but rather to the total capital. The profit rate is governed by its own laws, which permit to it to vary while the rate of surplus value remains the same, and even require this variation. All this conceals the true nature of surplus value more and more, concealing therefore the real mechanism of capital. This happens still more with the transformation of profit into average profit and of values into prices of production, the governing averages of market price. A complex social process intervenes here, the equalization of capitals, which cuts the relative average prices of commodities loose from their values, and the average profits in the various spheres of production from the actual exploitation of labour by the particular capitals involved (quite apart from the individual capital investments in each particular sphere of production). The average prices of commodities not only seem to differ from their value, i.e. from the labour realized in them, but actually do differ, and the average profit of a particular capital differs from the surplus value this capital has extracted from the workers employed by it. The value of commodities appears directly only in the influence of the changing productivity of labour on the rise and fall of prices of produc-

13 Marx 1981, pp. 173–4 [1964, p. 183].

> tion; on their movement, not on their final limits. Profit now appears as determined only secondarily by the direct exploitation of labour, in so far as, given market prices that are seemingly independent of this exploitation, it permits the capitalist to realize a profit departing from the average. Normal average profits as such seem immanent in capital independently of exploitation.[14]

This text enables us to gain a better understanding as to why Marx characterises profit as a 'mystified form', a transformed form of surplus value. Surplus value is 'concealed' in profit because the reference of profit is total capital and not just its variable part, that is to say, not just living labour. Thus, the 'true nature of surplus value' lies in remaining 'concealed', because 'profit now appears as determined only secondarily by the direct exploitation of labour' insofar as it directly depends on the distribution of the global surplus according to the average rate of profit applied to each individual capital. The 'actual exploitation of labour by the particular capitals involved' becomes invisible to the economic agents. On the one hand, this fact obscures 'the real mechanism of capital' and its definition as a value that self-valorises through the appropriation and accumulation of the surplus value. On the other hand, in a complementary manner, 'normal average profits as such seem immanent in capital independently of exploitation', as if it were capital that produced them.

To Marx, this movement of transfiguration designed to conceal is 'necessarily' determined by the fundamental conditions of capitalist production, so that surplus value can only exist in the guise of profit. Capital's characteristic 'subjectivity' creates a fetish whereby the source of profit appears to be total capital and not living labour. This fetish of capital's, however, is not a mere illusion; it is based on the real movement that equalises the profit rates of the various branches of production by means of the competition. This is why, in the *Grundrisse*, Marx observes that: 'So as to impose the inherent laws of capital upon it as external necessity, competition seemingly turns all of them over. *Inverts them*'.[15] Even the 'inherent law' by means of which capital takes the place of labour as a source of profit, is 'inverted' in 'external necessity': the replacement of the living labour by the means of production takes place when an individual capitalist discerns the possibility of obtaining extraordinary, above-average profits by introducing technical innovations; in turn, his rivals will also be obliged to adopt them as an 'external necessity' for survival.

14 Marx 1981, pp. 967–8 [1964, pp. 836–7]. Translation slightly modified by me.
15 Marx 1974, p. 761 [1983, p. 654].

There can be no doubt that real competition does not limit itself to this apparently passive role of realising capital's internal determinations and performing as a mechanism to 'transform', 'conceal' or 'invert' them. It performs this role in a specific way and creates its own configurations as well. It must be borne in mind that the respective argument in *Capital* Volume III is based on the restrictive hypothesis of 'unlimited competition', which Marx adopted with two main intentions. The first is to initially accept the point of view whereby all the economic variables could be considered to define themselves based on market conditions and then go on to criticise it for failing to consider 'the true nature of surplus value … concealing therefore the real mechanism of capital' in the words of the text cited earlier. The second purpose is to establish the 'social process of equalisation of capitals' which tends towards the average rate of profit with which capital presents a new way of calculating and measuring the magnitude of its valorisation.

Indeed, it seems that Marx's main interest here is to reveal how capital engenders a form of self-measurement that is itself a result of its own fetish:

> Since the capitalist can exploit labour only by advancing constant capital, and since he can valorise the constant capital only by advancing the variable, these are both one and the same in his representation, and this is all the more so in that the actual degree of his profit is determined in relation not to his variable capital but to his total capital; not by the rate of surplus value but by the rate of profit, which as we shall see, may remain the same while expressing different rates of surplus value.[16]

On the one hand, constant capital is not just activated by variable capital, but it too is a condition for variable capital to be brought into play; which means that both forms of capital in their aspect as production factors are 'the same' in the capitalist's 'representation'. On the other hand, constant capital also implies a cost for the capitalist, a cost that needs to be discounted so that he can measure 'the actual degree of his profit' which is the only thing he is really interested in.

Nevertheless, the resultant measurement of this fetishism is not arbitrary or illusory. In addition to having its origin in the real movement of capital's 'subjectivity', it establishes a new measure for the valorisation of social capital and for that of individual capitals in their specific branches, namely, the rate of

16 Marx 1981, p. 133 [1964, p. 52]. Translation slightly modified by me.

profit. This rate does not replace the former measure, the rate of surplus value, as the means to evaluate the degree of exploitation of labour power. It presents itself as a different measure, based on the rate of surplus value and mirroring, in a more complex manner, capitalist production's fundamental determinations, such as the variations in labour productivity, while at the same time it does so through the intermediation of competition.

As a form of measurement, the rate of profit is especially important in Marx's theory of crises, which, to explain them, refers to the opposition and conflict among the various measures specific to each one of the different aspects that constitute the process of capital's effectuation. The relationship between the rate of surplus value and the rate of profit develops in various moments that must be the object of more detailed analysis. So, it is this development that must be revisited next, analysing how the tendencies of the global process of capital production influence it and how crises are determined in their actuality by it.

2 The Tendential Fall in the Rate of Profit

2.1 *The Fall of the Rate of Profit as Mismeasurement*

In the first two Parts of *Capital* Volume III, Marx describes the relation between the rate of surplus value and the average rate of profit by means of mathematical exercises combining variations of their determinant factors in isolation or together. In the third Part, however, he does not limit himself to presupposing the difference between the two rates but seeks for a relationship between them in the dispositions that constitute capital. Marx obtains the rate of profit from the rate of surplus value and the organic composition, variables that depend on the specifically capitalist way that the increase in labour productivity occurs. Therefore, at this stage of Marx's presentation of the capitalist production process, it is necessary to turn back to those characteristics of the sphere of immediate production that concern the increase in productivity, and which are the foundation for the essential relationship among the component variables of the average rate of profit.

The first determination concerns the organic composition of capital:

> ... it has been shown to be a law of the capitalist mode of production that its development does in fact involve a relative decline in the relation of variable capital to constant and hence also to the total capital set in motion ... This progressive decline in the variable capital in relation to the constant capital, and hence in relation to the total capital

> as well, is identical with the progressively rising organic composition, on average, of the social capital as a whole.[17]

Actually, Marx is reiterating here an important result of *Capital* Volume I when he explains how 'this progressive decline in the variable capital in relation to the constant capital' expresses a disposition to the negation of the living labour by the dead labour, the 'vampirism' of capital and its contradictory relation with labour power. Now he adds that the disposition translates into 'progressively rising organic composition', that is, in the diminishing measure of variable capital in relation to the constant capital 'and hence in relation to the total capital as well'.

These propositions complete themselves with the definition of the rate of profit which also refers to the sum of variable capital and constant capital. In the *Grundrisse* Marx had already come to the following conclusion:

> Thus, in the same proportion as capital takes up a larger place as capital in the production process relative to immediate labour, i.e. the more the relative surplus value grows – the value-creating power of capital – the more *does the rate of profit fall*.[18]

So, the tendency of the average rate of profit to fall, one of Marx's most famous and most controverted enunciations,[19] he derives from the tendency whereby 'capital takes up a larger place as capital in the production process relative to immediate labour'. In other words, he derives the fall in the average rate of profit from the tendency to a progressive increase in the technical composition of capital – the mass of means of production used in relation to the mass of living labour – which should be reflected in the composition of value between constant capital and variable capital.

Leaving aside, for the moment, the discussion on the nature of the 'tendency' Marx attributes to these movements, it is already possible to address these points that provoked the controversy which I have just alluded to. Basing themselves on the numerical example used by Marx to begin his presentation of the profit rate's tendency to fall in chapter 13 of *Capital* Volume III, some authors objected that the Marxist theorem could only be demonstrated if the rate of surplus value remained unaltered, thereby isolating the effect on the profit of

17 Marx 1981, p. 222 [1964, p. 318].
18 Marx 1974, p. 747 [1983, p. 655].
19 Among the authors who recently explain economic crises mainly by the fall in the average rate of profit are mainly Kliman 2011, Carchedi 2011, and Roberts 2016.

the increase in the organic composition – a supposition that would indeed be highly restrictive and questionable. The objection was that the probable growth in the rate of surplus value could annul the growth of the organic composition and even raise the rate of profit instead of lowering it, provided that the increase in the magnitude of the surplus, brought about by the increase in the rate of surplus value, were equal to or surpassed the increase in the magnitude of constant capital in relation to variable capital. In this case, the simultaneous, indeterminate alteration of the two variables would impede Marx's intended verification of any tendency, that is, the possible predominance of the effect of one on the other.[20]

However, the numerical example at the beginning of chapter 13 can be considered a simple teaching device to facilitate an understanding of the problem and never its final version or the expression of a rigid postulate that Marx was necessarily bound to adhere to. Further on in that chapter Marx removes this constant surplus value rate restriction in passages such as this:

> The tendential fall in the rate of profit is linked with a tendential rise in the rate of surplus value, i.e. in the level of exploitation of labour … The profit rate does not fall because labour becomes less productive but rather because it becomes more productive. The rise in the rate of surplus value and the fall in the rate of profit are simply particular forms that express the growing productivity of labour in capitalist terms.[21]

Thus, contrary to the objection formulated by those critics, Marx is not obliged to fix a certain surplus value rate in order to prove his theorem and to even propose that the rate increases at the same time that the profit rate falls.

So then, how to explain that the increase in the rate of surplus value does not annul or surpass the elevation in the organic composition of capital? It is a complicated question. Marx, however, thought of getting over that difficulty by defining a nexus between the two variables in the 'capitalist terms' in

20 The two most important classical formulators of this objection were Sweezy 1942 and Robinson 1949. Both stated that Marx postulates the constancy of the surplus value rate, which would lead to an increase in wages with the growth of labour productivity, thereby contradicting the law of the negation of the living labour by the dead labour. As already noted by Rosdolsky 1978, both were wrong. Indeed, nowhere at all does Marx suppose the constancy of the surplus value rate. On the other hand, when Rosdolsky states that even with the growth of that rate, the organic composition would increase, his arguments are not very convincing, because he merely repeats Marx's words, without paying attention to the problem I will seek to point out and clarify.

21 Marx 1981, p. 347 [1964, p. 250].

which the productivity of labour increases, or in other words in terms of 'the value-creating power of capital', or of the 'capital ... as capital' in the words of a text cited above. Obviously, the rate referred to here is the rate of relative surplus value because the rate of absolute surplus value is not determined by the increasing productivity neither is it related to the increase in the organic composition. In the case of the relative surplus value, capital's permanent impulse to adopt technical innovations in the labour process leads to the elevation of productivity. On the one hand, when it affects the Department where the means of subsistence are produced, the elevation reduces their unit value and, consequently, the time needed to reproduce the value of the labour power, thereby increasing the rate of surplus value. On the other hand, this elevation of productivity is obtained by employing a greater volume of the means of production in relation to the living labour – the main way to make the labour more productive in 'capitalist terms' – increasing the organic composition of capital.

From this point on, Marx's explanation for the rate of surplus value increasing less than the organic composition is as follows:

> The law of the falling rate of profit, as expressing the same or even a rising rate of surplus value, means in other words: taking any particular quantity of average social capital, e.g. a capital of 100, an ever greater portion of this is presented in means of labour and an ever lesser portion in living labour. Since the total mass of living labour added to the means of production falls in relation to the value of these means of production, so too does the unpaid labour, and the portion of value that it presents, in relation to the value of the total capital advanced. Alternatively, an ever smaller aliquot part of the total capital laid out is converted into living labour, and hence the total capital absorbs ever less surplus labour in relation to its size, even though the ratio between the unpaid and paid parts of the labour applied may at the same time be growing.[22]

Marx's reasoning is that the basis for the appropriation of more unpaid labour – the mass of labour power acquired by the variable part of the capital – shrinks in comparison to the total capital, that is, it gradually diminishes in relative terms, even when there is growth of the rate of surplus value. The expansion of the unpaid part of labour achieved by restricting the paid part takes place on an increasingly smaller base in proportion to the total capital, meaning that it

22 Marx 1981, p. 322 [1964, pp. 225–6].

cannot increase as much as this proportion, which is the organic composition. This does not imply, obviously, an absolute decline in variable capital. On the contrary, with the increase in the total capital used it will probably be necessary to employ a larger contingent of workers to put this capital to work, thereby increasing variable capital despite the drop in the value of labour power.

In this case, the elevation of the technical composition of capital is not compensated for by an alteration in the two parts of capital that would reduce the value of constant capital more than the value of variable capital because, otherwise, the increasing technical composition would not express a growing organic composition. Marx is well aware of this when he reformulates his earlier argument:

> With the exception of isolated cases (e.g. when the productivity of labour cheapens all the elements of both constant and variable capital to the same extent), the rate of profit will fall, despite the higher rate of surplus value: (1) because even a greater unpaid portion of the smaller total sum of newly added labour is less than a smaller aliquot unpaid portion of the greater total sum was, and (2) because the higher composition of capital is expressed, in the case of the individual commodity, in the fact that the whole portion of the commodity's value in which the newly added labour presents itself falls in comparison with the portion of value that presents itself in raw materials, ancillary materials and wear and tear of the fixed capital.[23]

If the increase in productivity in general is neutral, reducing the value of the means of production and the workers' means of subsistence in equal measures and maintaining the same proportion between them as before, then the organic composition of capital increases just as much as the technical composition does. If the increase in productivity makes the means of subsistence cheaper to a greater extent than the means of production, in spite of its being able to reduce the value of the latter, the elevation of the technical composition will be boosted in an even greater growth of constant capital in proportion to variable capital. Lastly, if we suppose that the technical progress does not reduce labour costs, but instead reduces the value of the means of production more than that of the means of subsistence, the organic composition will only not go up if this reduction is just as intense or more intense than the elevation of the technical composition, thereby annulling or surpassing its effect. If

23 Marx 1981, p. 333 [1964, pp. 236–7].

the reduction of the value of the means of production compared to the means of subsistence is not as strong as the elevation of the technical composition, then this elevation will be mirrored in the elevation of the organic composition, albeit in an attenuated manner.

In these three situations, which cover most of the possible cases, the organic composition grows more than the rate of relative surplus value leading to a drop in the average rate of profit. In the final analysis, the base for obtaining the surplus cannot grow as much as the total capital, that is, variable capital must increase to a lesser proportion than constant capital does. Marx emphasises that as follows:

> But the same laws of production and accumulation mean that the value of the constant capital increases along with its mass, and progressively more quickly than that of the variable portion of capital which is converted into living labour. The same laws, therefore, produce both a growing absolute mass of profit for the social capital, and a falling rate of profit.[24]

The 'laws' Marx refers to explain that the increase in labour productivity reflects capital's propensity to subordinate living labour, the propensity to 'vampirism' and fetishism inherent to it. It is symptomatic, however, that 'the same laws of production and accumulation' of capital produce opposite effects, causing an increase in 'the value of the constant capital ... progressively more quickly than that of the variable portion of capital'. Consequently, the organic composition must grow with a greater intensity than the rate of surplus value and the average rate of profit must fall at the same time as the rate of surplus value goes up. However, Marx's demonstration of the tendential fall of the rate of profit is not free from problems and they will be discussed in the next item. What is important to underscore for now, is that the variation in the rate of profit in the opposite direction to that of the rate of surplus value is determined by the same fundament, by the same 'law of production and accumulation'.

In the preceding item, we saw that the two rates are different ways in which capital measures its valorisation and accordingly, regulates its production rhythm. However, if in this process capital determines two inverse movements for these two forms of measurement, then they are not just different, they are opposites in the strictest sense of the term: mutually negative expressions of the same contradictory fundament. Measured by the rate of surplus value, the valorisation of capital grows whereas, measured by the rate of profit,

24 Marx 1981, p. 325 [1964, p. 229].

it decreases. It is precisely this opposition between the two measures that defines mismeasurement. It is the inability of capital itself to unequivocally assess its own process of constitution, reproduction, and accumulation or, in other terms, it is capital's loss of self-reference in the course of its self-determination.

As was explained in chapter 2, section 3.1, mismeasurement expresses the inherent contradiction in capital's insistence on lowering living labour to be merely part a whole that capital itself forms, and impeding labour from forming a whole of which it, capital, would be but a part. According to one side of the relationship, capital measures its valorisation by the rate of profit, as if it were the creator of surplus value; according to the other side, however, this pretension clashes with the reality that living labour alone creates surplus value, so that the measurement based on the rate of surplus value sets itself in opposition to the rate of profit. Up to this point the problem of mismeasurement associated to the increase in the organic composition and of the consequent relative reduction in the quantity of living labour employed has been merely sketched out but from here on mismeasurement acquires a new content because these tendencies express themselves in the opposition of the two measures of self-valorisation. Combined with the elevation of the organic composition, the increasing rate of surplus value expresses itself in a decreasing rate of profit.

Even though the rate of profit is a fetishist form of self-measurement, it is, nevertheless, real. The fetish now defines itself as an intrinsic contradiction to the self-measurement process. In their opposition, the two forms by means of which capital achieves its measure delimit its competence to calculate its own parameters and determine itself as a reality. However, the loss of reference resulting from that fetishist measurement can only be resolved by its constantly self-replacing in the fall of the rate of profit. Capital only gets back its hidden reference, the rate of surplus value, in the form of the declining rate of profit which expresses inversely the rate of surplus value. This tendency indicates the limit that gradually appears on the horizon: the more capital valorises from one point of view, the more it de-valorises from the other. Whether there is an ultimate limit to valorisation and whether the process that determines such a limit is a 'law' and a predominant and inexorable 'tendency' will be the theme of discussion that follows. In Marx's own words: 'We shall show later on why this fall does not present itself in such an absolute form, but rather more in the tendency to a progressive fall'.[25]

25 Marx 1981, p. 319 [1964, p. 223].

2.2 *Tendencies as Necessary 'Laws'*

One of the main sources of the misunderstanding regarding how capital's immanent tendencies realise is the fact that Marx often refers to them as 'laws', as for example the 'law' of the fall in the rate of profit. To evaluate the term in the general context of the critique of political economy and, more specifically, in the context of a theory of crises, it is necessary to put aside the traditional notion of a 'law' as the enunciation of a constant, non-contradictory relation between phenomena, for this is the notion that creates an expectation that the rate of profit is continually falling.

In the preceding subchapter we saw that 'the same laws of production and accumulation' lead to opposite pressures on the rate of profit, resulting from simultaneous increases in the organic composition of capital and the rate of surplus value. Marx is referring to this when he states that: 'These two movements not only go hand in hand; they mutually condition one another, and are phenomena that express the same law'.[26] In other words, these two determinants of the profit rate 'mutually condition one another' because they are 'phenomena that express the same law', that is, because they have a common base that expresses itself in opposite movements, or rather, in the opposition of phases of the same movement. Hence the criticism of Marx:

> Yet these two aspects[27] involved in the accumulation process cannot just be considered as existing quietly side by side, which is how Ricardo treats them; they contain a contradiction, and this is announced by the appearance of contradictory tendencies and phenomena. The contending agencies function simultaneously in opposition to one another.[28]

Here Marx's objection to Ricardo has an eminently methodological meaning, namely, he feels that Ricardo saw the opposing moments 'quietly side by side' corresponding to 'going hand in hand' in the preceding text. To Marx, on the contrary, 'they contain a contradiction', in the sense that the fundament of these movements, considering their status of opposition and not of mere indifference, presents itself as a single determination and is therefore, contradictory.

Thus, Marx conceives the tendencies of the organic composition to increase and the rate of profit to fall as: '… this law – I mean this inner and necessary

26 Marx 1981, p. 355 [1964, p. 257].

27 In the original, Marx uses a term with strong Hegelian echoes: 'moments', closer to the Hegelian terminology than 'aspects'.

28 Marx 1981, p. 357 [1964, p. 259].

connection between two apparently contradictory phenomena'.[29] Generally speaking, this is the form of Marx's understanding of the 'laws' in capitalism: the logical necessity characteristic of a law stems from the very contradiction in which its terms are defined. Instead of being a non-contradictory nexus among phenomena or between phenomena and their causes, a relationship is a 'law' precisely when its terms present contradictory aspects of a common fundament, which defines them in opposition to one another. The contradiction is 'apparent', if it is taken to be a casual inversion of indifferent factors, exterior to one another but placed 'side by side'. This 'appearance' reveals something real, however, if it is taken to be an expression of the contradiction intrinsic to the fundament of these factors. This is why Marx refers to them as 'moments' determined by a contradictory relationship whose activity is quite the contrary of 'quiet side by side', passive, dead and unproductive – incapable of creating.

It is precisely this Marxian concept of 'law' that makes it possible to understand why a 'law' presents itself as a 'tendency': it is the passage of the structural variables of the rate of profit – organic composition and surplus value – to those that oppose the fall in the rate of profit, namely, the so-called 'counteracting factors' described in chapter 14 of *Capital* Volume III. In that chapter Marx affirms that: 'We see here once again how the same factors that produce the tendency for the rate of profit to fall also moderate the realization of this tendency'.[30] The effective fall in the rate of profit, resulting from the 'realization of this tendency', is then 'moderated' by the set of conditions Marx enumerated in chapter 14 ranging from the increase in the intensive and extensive exploitation of labour in large-scale industry, through the reduction in the value of constant capital brought about by the enhanced productivity in the Department that produces the means of production, to the formation of a 'surplus population' by those sectors that dismiss labour to be made use of by other sectors of lower organic composition and therefore with higher rates of profit.

Marx gives a detailed explanation of how these forces act on the rate of surplus value and the organic composition in the inverse direction to the one leading to a fall in the rate of profit. Before analysing his explanation, however, it is important to underscore that these forces stem from the 'same factors that produce the tendency for the rate of profit to fall' because they too are expressions of capitalism's inherent need to obtain relative surplus value, continually

29 Marx 1981, p. 331 [1964, p. 235].
30 Marx 1981, p. 343 [1964, p. 246].

elevating the productivity of labour. The fundament appears here, once more, as 'a contradiction … announced by the appearance of contradictory tendencies and phenomena', as stated in an above-cited text, indicating the complex nature of the 'law'. Therefore, referring to one of these forces, namely, the increase of the rate of surplus value through the greater extension and intensity of the daily work, Marx says:

> It does not annul the general law, but it has the effect that this law operates more as a tendency, i.e. as a general law whose absolute realization is held up, delayed and weakened by counteracting factors.[31]

The main meaning of 'tendency' for Marx is therefore that of a 'general law whose absolute realization is held up, delayed, and weakened by counteracting factors' created by the same fundamental relation that determines the law. The necessary character of 'tendency' does not imply in its 'absolute realisation' in the sense that its effects will always be manifest, that is, it does not require that the drop in the rate of profit should be empirically observable. It is a 'law' that has been 'weakened' and 'delayed', but not 'annulled'; it is just temporarily 'held up'. Continuing that line of argument, Marx says:

> We have shown in general, therefore, how the same causes that bring about a fall in the general rate of profit provoke counter effects that inhibit this fall, delay it and in part even paralyse it. These do not annul the law, but they weaken its effect. If this were not the case, it would not be the fall in the general rate of profit that was incomprehensible, but rather the relative slowness of this fall. The law operates therefore, simply as a tendency, whose effect is decisive only under certain circumstances and over long periods.[32]

---

31 Marx 1981, pp. 341–2 [1964, p. 244]. It is interesting to compare this affirmation in the form it appears in the edition of *Capital* Volume III edited by Engels with that of the *Manuscripts from 1863–1867* published by the Marx-Engels Gesamtausgabe (Marx 2016, pp. 342–3 [1992, p. 308]). In his edition, Engels maintains the verbs *aufgehalten* ('held up'), *verlangsamt* ('delayed') and *abgeschwächt* ('weakened'), from Marx's manuscripts but cuts out 'paralysirt', far more emphatic an indication than 'counteracting'.

32 Marx 1981, p. 346 [1964, p. 249]. Here Engels remains faithful to the original manuscripts and only replaces Marx's phrase 'relatively weak proportion of that fall' with the phrase 'the relative slowness of this fall'. Thus, he transforms the idea of a weakness that could impede the realisation of a tendency with a temporal idea that does not threaten the sure realisation of the tendency.

Marx attributes the character of 'tendency' to the 'law' because he observes that the effective fall in the rate of profit does not always impose itself and also because he believes that it only predominates 'over long periods'. It is quite plausible, however, to conclude that Marx makes a distinction between the conditions determining the fall in the rate of profit and the conditions counteracting it, for he considers the former to be closer to the constitutive determinations of capital and therefore better able to impose themselves. This would be the reason why he states that even though it is 'weakened' or 'delayed', the law is not 'annulled'. The fall in the average rate of profit would be derived from the self-negation inherent to capital whereas the 'circumstances' that attenuate it would consist precisely of just 'circumstances', that is, factors that aggregate themselves to the system's movements but that do not proceed directly from its internal structure – factors like the elevation of the rate of absolute surplus value, the payment of wages lower than the level of labour power value, and overseas trade.

Nevertheless, in his enumeration of the counteracting conditions Marx places on the same plane these factors which have nothing to do with the alterations in productivity and a condition strictly related to it, namely, the decrease in the value of the elements of constant capital. Unlike the other factors, this last one is of special importance: the general increase in productivity, insofar as it affects the Department that produces the means of production, lowers the unit value of its products and it may even neutralise the effect of the rise in the technical composition of capital. In this case, the organic composition does not grow, at least not in the proportion that it would if the unit value of the means of production remained unaltered. Furthermore, if the reduction in the value of these means is so great that the organic composition goes up less than the rate of surplus value, then the rate of profit may not fall after all and the tendency is 'held up'.

Marx foresees this possibility when he warns that:

> the *total price* of the commodity would fall in the same proportion as the productivity of labour increases, while the *proportions* between the different components of the price of the commodity may remain *the same* (constant), *fall*, as previously investigated, or rise, if the increase in the rate of surplus value was associated with a significant depreciation in the components of the constant capital.[33]

---

33 Marx 2016, 354 [1992, p. 319]. Engels' edition of *Capital* Volume III presents an important variation when, immediately after this excerpt, it introduces the sentence: 'In practice,

Contrary to the earlier conclusion mentioned above whereby Marx sees a structural difference among the conditions that lead to a fall in the average rate of profit and those that attenuate them, here he considers that an increase in labour productivity could just as easily result in the organic composition staying the same, as it could result in its increasing or decreasing. A 'significant depreciation in the components of the constant capital' could occur and annul the tendency for the rate of profit to fall.

Certainly, the technical composition of capital rises as a consequence of its propensity to create more relative surplus value which, in turn, expresses capital's constitutive disposition to replace living labour with dead labour. This, however, does not imply that the growing volume of the means of production in relation to the volume of labour power expresses the proportions between their respective values with the same intensity. Marx makes this point clearer:

> … the value of the constant capital does not increase in the same proportion as its material volume … In other words, the same development that raises the mass of constant capital in comparison with variable reduces the value of its elements, as a result of the higher productivity of labour, and hence prevents the value of the constant capital, even though this grows steadily, from growing in the same degree as its material volume, i.e. the material volume of the means of production that are set in motion by the same amount of labour power. In certain cases, the mass of the constant capital elements may increase while their total value remains the same or even falls.[34]

The organic composition only mirrors the proportion between the volume of means of production and labour power expressed by the technical composition, if an alteration of the values of constant capital and variable capital corresponds exactly to the alterations in those volumes. If an increase in productivity intensely affects the Department that produces the elements of constant capital, the organic composition may not go up as much as the technical composition. It may even not go up enough to compensate for the increase in the rate of relative surplus value resulting from an increase in

however, the rate of profit will fall in the long run' (Marx 1981, p. 337 [1964, p. 240]). With this, Engels suggests that the tendency for the rate of profit to fall predominates over the counter tendencies and makes it plausible to interpret Marx as having affirmed that the fall in the rate of profit would be closer to the profound determination of capitalist production than the counteracting tendencies.

34 Marx 1981, p. 343 [1964, pp. 245–6].

productivity in the Department that produces the workers' means of livelihood, because as *Capital* Volume I already explains:

> In order to make the value of labour power go down, the rise in the productivity of labour must seize upon those branches of industry whose products determine the value of labour power, and consequently either belong to the category of normal means of subsistence, or are capable of replacing them … But an increase in the productivity of labour in those branches of industry which supply neither the necessary means of subsistence nor the means by which they are produced leaves the value of labour power undisturbed.[35]

Thus, if the growing productivity of capitalist production in general reduces the average value of the means of production more than the average value of the means of livelihood, growth in the organic composition may be less intense than that of the rate of surplus value and fail to be expressed as a fall in the rate of profit. The conclusion that the tendency of the rate of profit to fall predominates over the specific counter tendency of the reduction in the value of constant capital depends on the supposition that the forces in play combine in adequate proportions and follow very clear trajectories in determined directions. Only a precise combination of all these variables can configure a contradiction of measures that define the mismeasurement of capital, that is, the loss of reference that puts capital's self-valorisation at risk and imposes limits that are difficult to transpose.

The problem is that the definition of these variables does not arise from the system's internal objective to replace living labour with dead labour but, instead, from the objectives imposed on individual capitalists in their day to day competition. As has been shown previously, each capitalist is obliged to adopt technical innovations to produce at a value lower than the average social costs and obtain extraordinary profits. When most of them do this, then the respective technology becomes generalised, and the extraordinary profits disappear. This is how Marx explains the constantly renewed search for new techniques and the continual repetition of the process, according to the dialectic of universalisation and particularisation. However, still in *Capital* Volume I he makes the proviso that:

> This augmentation of surplus value is pocketed by the capitalist himself, whether or not his commodities belong to the class of necessary

35 Marx 1976a, p. 432 [1962, p. 334].

> means, and therefore participate in determining the general value of labour power. Hence, quite independently of this, there is a motive for each individual capitalist to cheapen his commodities by increasing the productivity of labour.[36]

Or again:

> When an individual capitalist cheapens shirts, for instance, by increasing the productivity of labour, he by no means necessarily aims to reduce the value of labour power and shorten necessary labour-time in proportion to this. But he contributes towards increasing the general rate of surplus value only in so far as he ultimately contributes to this result. The general and necessary tendencies of capital must be distinguished from their forms of appearance.[37]

To the capitalists seeking to increase labour productivity, it does not matter which sector of the economy that increase occurs in. Their immediate motives are indifferent to the system's overall finality of making the means of subsistence ever cheaper and in this way obtaining relative surplus value and realising capital's inherent and essential propensity to achieve the real subsumption of living labour.

---

36 Marx 1976a, pp. 434–5 [1962, p. 336].

37 Marx 1976a, p. 433 [1962, p. 335]. For the debate on this topic, see Okishio 1961 and 1977. In them Okishio criticises Marx's 'Law of tendency', stating that for the individual capitalist it is indifferent whether he invests in a labour-saving technology, or in means of production. He joined in the debate on the predominance of the profit rate's tendency to fall started by Dobb 1937 and Paul Sweezy 1942. Dobb concluded that Marx had left the decision open as to which tendency would predominate (1937, pp. 86–7), and Sweezy thinks that if both the organic composition of capital and the rate of surplus value are variable, then the direction in which the rate of profit varies is indeterminate (1942, pp. 102–4). Later in *Political Economy and Capitalism: Notes on Dobb's Theory of Crisis* (1978), Anwar Shaikh replied to Okishio, taking up Marx's own arguments, but the author did not actually prove that a decision in favour of a labour-saving technology was anything more than a possibility. However that may be, I do not think that Okishio's theorem necessarily contradicts the tendency that Marx observed but, rather, that it establishes an important mediation in its realisation. This is roughly the view of Kliman, for whom Okishio has been wrongly interpreted as a denier of Marx's law of the tendential fall of the rate of profit (2011, pp. 105–8). Despite Okishio and these different interpretations of Okishio, Kliman takes this fall as the profound cause of crises and seeks to demonstrate empirically the permanent tendency to diminishing profits in the capitalist economy, only offset at times by the physical destruction of capital, in wars, and by the fall in its price. Roberts 2016 takes the same direction, without developing the same kind of theoretical preoccupation.

From this argument it follows that, taking into account only the various ways in which capital's constitutive determinations manifest themselves through the laws of competition, it is not possible to affirm that a decrease in the value of the elements of constant capital should be necessarily more intense than the reduction in the value of labour power, at least, not to the extent of reverting the fall in the rate of profit. However, the same can be said of the inverse situation. Neither of the two opposing tendencies has all the necessary conditions for its realisation so that the complex combination of the variables leading the average rate of profit to fall or not fall is an uncertain result, not an absolute necessity. This is why the above text concluded that: 'The general and necessary tendencies of capital must be distinguished from their forms of appearance'. Despite their being 'necessary', the tendencies must be 'distinguished' from their 'forms of appearance' because, in the dispute with the opposing tendency, it is possible that the link between the internal determination and its effective realisation is lost. So, what is the point in saying that the tendencies are 'necessary'? If in the words of *Capital* Volume III,

> … it is a self-evident necessity, deriving from the essence of the capitalist mode of production itself, that as it advances the general average rate of surplus value must be expressed in a falling general rate of profit …[38]

then the question needs to be re-phrased: why is it that the rate of surplus value 'must be expressed' as a fall in the rate of profit? Why does Marx talk about a 'self-evident necessity' stemming from the 'essence' of capitalism? If this 'essence' does not contain all the conditions of its 'appearance', and if these conditions do not inevitably lead to the final predominance of the 'essence', then what does 'necessity' mean here?

Marx's association of the terms 'law' and 'tendency' can just as easily lead to the conclusion that the tendency imposes itself inexorably, as a law, that is, as an absolute necessity that excludes any possibility of realising its opposite, as it can lead to the conclusion that the law is not always realised and so it takes on the nature of a tendency. Actually, even if it is not absolute, to Marx, the necessity for the fall in the rate of profit must predominate over the counter-conditions. It is a 'necessity', but a relative one; a necessity that admits the possibility of its opposite and one whose realisation depends on external conditions that it must subordinate as contingencies. What the ambivalence of the association of 'law' and 'tendency' reveals is that the character of tendency is

38 Marx 1981, p. 319 [1964, p. 223].

equivalent to the modal status of a necessity that only prevails when it imposes itself on contingencies that it manages to dominate, but not annul.

However, the problem is even more complex. If, as a text quoted above declares, the countertendencies arise from the 'same causes that bring about a fall in the general rate of profit' then the same modal status should be attributed to them that is attributed to the tendency. More specifically, the decrease in the value of constant capital is also determined by the constitutive tendency of capital to increase productivity in general; it too dons the guise of relative necessity in the sense that its occurrence realises one of capital's basic propensities and not a mere accidental circumstance. So, given that is not an accident, this countertendency can never be completely inscribed in the opposite necessity, namely, the tendency of the rate of profit to fall. In turn, as it cannot be inscribed, this tendential fall of the rate of profit can never completely transform itself into an absolute necessity, insofar as it will never reach the point of entirely excluding the opposite necessity. Even if the rate of profit does fall 'over long periods' it will always be possible that the cheapening of the elements of constant capital will drive it up again and impede it from arriving at a final limit.

Marx does not present these conclusions explicitly, but they are perfectly coherent with his sinuous, complex, and unfinished text. Sometimes he seems to support the idea that, even as a relative necessity, the fall in the average rate of profit must predominate in the long run. At other times, as we have just seen, he proffers an argument in the opposite direction. Regarding this situation, it is fairly evident that in spite of all Engels' editorial efforts, the third part of *Capital* Volume III would have been the object of a thorough revision and elaboration on the part of Marx himself. In any case, based on the available text, one cannot categorically state that the tendential fall of the average rate of profit predominates to the extent of definitively making the continuation of the valorisation process unfeasible, that is to say, of taking capital to an insuperable limit, to a collapse brought about by purely economic causes. The definition of crisis calls for further development beyond the concepts of collapse or chronic paralysis of the capitalist system.

3 Periodical Overaccumulation

3.1 *Overaccumulation as Mismeasurement*

The valorisation process's loss of reference, which creates an impasse in the form of the tendential fall in the average rate of profit, acquires new significance with the 'Developments of the law's internal contradictions', the title given by Engels to chapter 15 of his edition of *Capital* Volume III. The 'development' of the tendency consists, more specifically, of the opposition between the valorisation and the devaluation of capital, simultaneous moments of the tendency that will present themselves at separate moments in different phases of the accumulation process, that is, as distinct phases of the relation between the production and the valorisation processes.

Thus, it is on the horizon of accumulation that the conflict now takes place expressed by the mutual loss of reference between accumulation and production, or better put, by the recurrent difficulty of valorisation to serve as a measure for production. At this point of the categorial presentation of *Capital*, the concept of overproduction, already relevant in the *Grundrisse*, emerged as the basic form of expression of mismeasurement:

> (This nonsense about the impossibility of overproduction; in other words, the assertion of the immediate identity of capital's process of production and its process of realization ... Overproduction takes place in connection with realization, not otherwise).[39]

In the criticism Marx makes here of political economy, he denies the 'immediate identity' of production and valorisation as a basis for affirming the 'impossibility of overproduction'. In his view, the two processes are mediated by one another and for this reason they present themselves as a relationship based on their difference; a unity that can always conceal itself in the autonomisation and incompatibility of their moments. Hence the possibility of 'overproduction'.

In *Capital*, Marx completes this statement with the following:

> Even under the most extreme assumption that might be made, absolute overproduction of capital is not overproduction in general, not absolute overproduction of the means of production. It is an overproduction of means of production only in so far as *these function as capital*.[40]

Therefore, the excess of means of production is not simply equivalent to the excess of some kind of commodity but, instead, to the excess of the means of production as form of capital. It is an excess because the means of production should be associated with a certain volume of labour power exploited

39 Marx 1974, pp. 423–4 [1983, p. 338].
40 Marx 1981, p. 364 [1964, pp. 265–6].

under a certain level of productivity and through a positive rate of valorisation. From this follows the more precise and encompassing definition proposed by Marx:

> Overproduction of capital and not of individual commodities – though this overproduction of capital always involves overproduction of commodities – is nothing more than over-accumulation of capital.[41]

The meaning of 'over-accumulation' here is that the production of the means of production surpasses the needs of capital valorisation. In other words, in an even clearer formulation, 'over-accumulation' means that 'periodically … too much is produced in the way of means of labour and means of subsistence, too much to function as means for exploiting the workers at a given rate of profit'.[42]

The key element for characterising overproduction, for evaluating production and deciding when it is excessive in relation to the valorisation, is the rate of profit. Even supposing a constant rhythm of accumulation – a continuous increment in the production of the means of production – an excess of accumulation could occur, due to the variations in the rate of profit, originating, in turn, from the increase in the organic composition of capital that accompanies accumulation. In this case, the higher organic composition would mean that new investments would result in ever lower rates of profit until a point where it would no longer be feasible for the system to carry on expanding because the gains obtained by employing more capital would not compensate for the costs of the investments, making this use of capital superfluous or excessive in relation to the reduced rate of profit.

Marx presented another motive for the fall in the rate of profit, the progressive depletion of the labour available for employment:

> Thus as soon as capital has grown in such proportion to the working population that neither the absolute labour-time that this working population supplies nor its relative surplus labour-time can be extended … where, therefore, the expanded capital produces only the same mass of surplus value as before, there will be an absolute overproduction of capital; i.e. the expanded C + ΔC will not produce any more profit, or will even produce less profit, than capital C did before its increase by ΔC. In both cases there would even be a sharper and more sudden fall in the general rate

41 Marx 1981, p. 359 [1964, p. 261].

42 Marx 1981, p. 376 [1964, p. 268].

> of profit, but this time on account of a change in the composition of capital which would not be due to a development in productivity, but rather to a rise in the money value of the variable capital on account of higher wages and to a corresponding decline in the proportion of surplus labour to necessary labour.[43]

Marx's entire reasoning is obviously based on the presupposition that technology and productivity of labour remain unaltered during a given period of time. First, the economic expansion would increase variable capital along with constant capital and would make it possible to employ a greater number of currently unemployed workers. Then, the progressive depletion of the industrial reserve army would increasingly restrict the room for manoeuvre within which capital, by firing veteran workers and hiring new ones, can manage to keep wage levels sufficiently low to maintain a given rate of profit. In the end there would be 'a rise in the money value of the variable capital on account of higher wages' and stemming from this, a 'decline in the proportion of surplus labour to necessary labour', that is, in the exploitation or surplus value rate. Furthermore, 'the expanded $C + \Delta C$ will not produce any more profit ... than capital C did before its increase by ΔC', thereby making itself excessive and leading to a crisis characterised by a general rate of profit that is too low or even non-existent.

Marx continues describing this process in the following terms:

> The chief disruption, and the one possessing the sharpest character, would occur in connection with capital in so far as it possesses the property of value ... Part of the commodities on the market can complete their process of circulation and reproduction only by an immense reduction in their prices, i.e. by a devaluation in the capital they represent. The elements of fixed capital are more or less devalued in the same way. Added to this is the fact that since certain price relationships are assumed in the reproduction process, and govern it, this process is thrown into stagnation and confusion by the general fall of prices. This disturbance and stagnation paralyses the function of money as a means of payment, which is given along with the development of capital and depends on those presupposed price relationships. The chain of payment obligations at specific dates is broken in a hundred places, and this is still further intensified by an accompanying breakdown of the credit system, which

43 Marx 1981, p. 360 [1964, pp. 261–2].

> had developed alongside capital. All this therefore leads to violent and acute crisis, sudden forcible devaluations, an actual stagnation and disruption in the reproduction process, and hence to an actual decline in reproduction.[44]

It is important to start by observing how the forms of crisis, previously described in a more abstract moment of the categorial presentation, converge in this text. The first form is the difficulty found to sell the commodities produced by capital, which 'can complete their process of circulation and reproduction only by an immense reduction in their prices', that is to say, with prices below the correspondent value because of the reduction in the rate of profit. This situation disorganises the buying and selling process among capitalists and consequently, 'paralyses the function of money as a means of payment ... The chain of payment obligations at specific dates is broken in a hundred places'. Hence a second form of crisis is defined, namely, the 'stagnation and disruption in the reproduction process' of social capital which depends on the existence of correct proportions among the values and quantities of commodities being exchanged among the various branches of production, a situation that was examined in the third chapter of this book. The crisis here means an 'actual decline in reproduction' or, in other words, an 'stagnation and confusion' that come to reign.

Nevertheless, the context in which the previous definitions of crisis converge is the devaluation of capital. It is the fall of the rate of profit, characteristic of over-accumulation, that now presents itself as the foundation of social capital's reproduction problems and in the forms under which it appears in the circulation of money and commodities. The 'immense reduction in their prices' indicates that the market value of the commodity capital has dropped significantly and that the 'elements of fixed capital are more or less devalued in the same way' to the extent that Marx actually uses the word 'disruption' to qualify this devaluation. At this moment, the expanded reproduction, losing its reference measure, provokes a 'sharper and more sudden fall in the general rate of profit'. It becomes unfeasible to continue expanding production and even just to simply produce, that is, to conserve the levels of simple reproduction, because of the reduction in the rate of profit of social capital, although the various sectors may be affected to different extents.

Devaluation counters the need for the continuous self-valorisation of existing capital and thus for its expanded reproduction. According to Marx:

44 Marx 1981, pp. 362–3 [1964, pp. 264–5].

> To express the contradiction in the most general terms, it consists in the fact that the capitalist mode of production tends towards an absolute development of the productive forces irrespective of value and the surplus value this contains, and even irrespective of the social relations within which capitalist production takes place; while on the other hand its purpose is to maintain the existing capital value and to valorise it to the utmost extent possible (i.e. an ever accelerated increase in this value). In its specific character it is directed towards using the existing capital value as a means for the greatest possible valorisation of this value. The methods through which it attains this end involve a decline in the profit rate, the devaluation of the existing capital and the development of the productive forces of labour at the cost of the productive forces already produced.[45]

Once more the contradiction described by Marx results from the opposition between capital's ends and its means but, in this case, it is restricted to a specific situation. The contradiction does not manifest itself during normal reproduction because the finality of the system, accumulation, coincides with the conservation of the value of the existing capital which is the means of accumulation. In the crisis, however, the accumulation brings with it devaluation of the existing capital, thereby putting ends and means in opposition. The 'purpose' of the accumulation is 'to maintain the existing capital value' but, also, it 'is directed towards using the existing capital value as a means for the greatest possible valorisation of this value', so that, actually, it is the conservation of the existing capital as the 'purpose' that sets itself in opposition to its own self as the 'means'. Considering that accumulation is the creation of new value departing from the value of the existing capital, the two moments contained in it enter into opposition in over-accumulation. However, the act of conserving in order to create and the act of creating to conserve, reciprocally mediated by the accumulation, become incompatible when the accumulation is excessive. The creation of new value leads to the devaluation of the old capital and in this devaluation lie the means for its continuing to occur.

It is possible to understand then why Marx concluded the above text saying that the 'development of the productive forces of labour at the cost of the productive forces already produced' was necessary. Even though it is an end in itself, the conservation of the existing capital has a quantitative limit that corresponds to the value of this capital, and it cannot always be maintained in

45 Marx 1981, pp. 357–8 [1964, p. 259].

view of the tendency to 'absolute development of the productive forces', which impels capital to grow without limits. At certain moments, the destruction of the existing base for accumulation becomes necessary in order to maintain the valorisation, capital's basic objective.

This contradiction was explained in the *Grundrisse*, in a similar way:

> hence it is evident that ... all conditions of wealth, that the greatest conditions for the reproduction of wealth, i.e. the abundant development of the social individual – that the development of the productive forces brought about by the historical development of capital itself, when it reaches a certain point, suspends [*aufhebt*] the self-valorisation of capital, instead of positing it.[46]

In this case, the text continues, the 'violent destruction of capital' becomes 'a condition of its self-preservation',[47] configuring a complete inversion of the terms that constitute the accumulation. As a result:

> ... the highest development of productive power together with the greatest expansion of existing wealth will coincide with depreciation of capital, degradation of the labourer, and a most straitened exhaustion of its vital powers. These contradictions lead to explosions, cataclysms, crisis, in which by momentaneous suspension and annihilation of a great portion of capital the latter is violently reduced to the point where it can go on. These contradictions ... lead it back to the point where it is enabled [to go on] fully employing its productive powers without committing suicide.[48]

At the end of the text Marx indicates that the violent destruction of the existing capital does not necessarily lead to a definitive collapse of accumulation but may 'lead it back to the point where it is enabled [to go on] fully employing its productive powers' and resume the accumulation.

The reason is explained in *Capital* Volume III:

> Stagnation in production makes part of the working class idle and hence places the employed workers in conditions where they have to accept a fall in wages, even beneath the average; an operation that has exactly

46 Marx 1974, p. 749 [1983, p. 641].
47 Marx 1974, p. 749 [1983, p. 642].
48 Marx 1974, p. 750 [1983, pp. 642–3]. Original in English.

> the same effect for capital as if relative or absolute surplus value had been increased while wages remained at the average ... The fall in prices and the competitive struggle, on the other hand, impel each capitalist to reduce the individual value of his total product below its general value by employing new machinery, new and improved methods of labour and new forms of combination. That is, they impel him to raise the productivity of a given quantity of labour, to reduce the proportion of variable capital to constant and thereby to dismiss workers, in short to create an artificial surplus population. The devaluation of the elements of constant capital, moreover, itself involves a rise in the profit rate. The mass of constant capital applied grows as against the variable, but the value of this mass may have fallen. The stagnation in production that has intervened prepares the ground for a later expansion of production – within the capitalist limits.[49]

The text gives a clear explanation of the conditions whereby, in the crisis, 'stagnation in production' inverts the situation that originally led to a fall in the rate of profit. Firstly, the idleness of part of the constant capital will also make part of the variable capital idle, leading to the dismissal of workers who will join the reserve of available labour power. Capitalists will then be in a position to force the workers still in employment 'to accept a fall in wages', thus raising both the rate of surplus value and the rate of profit. Secondly, the effect of this situation would be merely temporary if it were not accompanied by capitalists' investments in 'new machinery, new and improved methods of labour and new forms of combination' that increase labour productivity and enable them, not only 'to dismiss workers' and in this way, 'create an artificial surplus population', but also to reduce the value of the means of subsistence and raise the rate of relative surplus value in a more lasting manner.

Nevertheless, the 'devaluation of the elements of constant capital ... involves a rise in the profit rate' that comes from the 'devaluation of the existing capital' brought about by the crisis itself and also the 'devaluation' resulting from the employment of 'new machinery, new and improved methods' that make the former material base obsolete and save some of the costs associated to the circulating part of the constant capital. Marx takes care to deny that the new investment can diminish the organic composition of capital by reducing the value of constant capital more than that of variable capital stating, instead, that what is reduced is 'the proportion of variable capital to constant'. However,

49 Marx 1981, pp. 363–4 [1964, p. 265].

he then leaves the final result of the change in organic composition undefined when he states that the 'mass of constant capital applied grows as against the variable, but the value of this mass may have fallen'. In other words, the increase in technical composition may not translate into value, that is, into organic composition. It is also possible that due to the reduction in the organic composition, profit will start to rise again after the crisis is over.[50]

In any event, the most important point is that the rate of profit rises again, making it possible to resume accumulation, that is, to alter the situation in which 'C + ΔC will not produce any more profit, or will even produce less profit, than capital C did before its increase by ΔC', as one of the texts cited earlier put it. Nevertheless, the process is not harmonious. It is only brought about by the obsolescence of part of the old capital that has become antiquated, and its violent replacement by new capital ΔC. In Marx's own words:

> In actual fact [*Wirklichkeit*], the situation would take the form that one portion of the capital would lie completely or partially idle (since it would first have to expel the capital already functioning from its position, to be valorised at all), while the other portion would be valorised at a lower rate of profit, owing to the pressure of the unoccupied or semi-occupied capital. The fact that a portion of the additional capital might take the place of the old, and that the old capital might thus take up a position within the additional capital, would be a matter of indifference here, as the old capital sum would be on one side of the account, the additional capital on the other.[51]

The 'indifference' the text refers to concerns the mass of obsolete means of production that remain in the already established capitalist's hands and also to the new improved means of production that they incorporate, in counter-position to the new capital of the capitalists that establish themselves in the wake of the crisis. However, the process of dividing gains and losses is conflict-ridden: 'As to which section is particularly to be affected by this idling, this is decided in the course of the competitive struggle'.[52] Competition reappears here to clarify the

50 This is exactly one of Kliman's main arguments in his critique of those who reject the fall in the rate of profit as the profound cause of crises (2011, p. 129). It was also an objection made by Harman, when discussing the decrease in the value of constant capital as a countertendency to the fall in the average rate of profit (2009, p. 72).

51 Marx 1981, p. 360 [1964, p. 262].

52 Marx 1981, p. 361 [1964, p. 263]. The advent of competition and crisis creates a tendency for capital to become centralised and concentrated in the hands of an ever-diminishing number of capitalists.

way in which the immanent tendency of social capital to share losses among capitalists and replace the old technology with a more productive one, in order to then generalise the innovations and lead the overcoming of crisis, becomes 'actual' [*Wirklich*]. Each individual capitalist strives to develop techniques that ensure for himself a rate of profit higher than the average rate reduced in the crisis, and that leads them together at the end of the process to a higher rate of profit and the ousting of the crisis.

This reasoning was anticipated in *Capital* Volume II:

> The means of labour are for the most part revolutionised by the progress of industry. Hence they are not replaced in their original form, but in the revolutionised form. On the one hand, the volume of fixed capital that is invested in a particular natural form, and has to last out for a definite average lifespan within this, is a reason why new machines, etc. are introduced only gradually, and hence forms an obstacle to the rapid general introduction of improved means of labour. On the other hand, competition forces the replacement of old means of labour by new ones before they natural demise, particularly when decisive revolutions have taken place. Catastrophes, crises, etc. are the principal causes that compel such premature renewals of equipment on a broad social scale.[53]

Even though there may be resistance to replacing 'the volume of fixed capital that is invested in a particular natural form' with 'improved means of labour' before the expiry of the 'average lifespan' of the fixed capital, crises 'compel such premature renewals' by means of the only possible way to resume accumulation, namely the competition among capitalists.

It must be stated at once that behind this argument there is the idea that crises and resumptions repeat themselves cyclically, periodically. This idea is present in *Capital* Volume I and II in passages such as:

> Just as the heavenly bodies always repeat a certain movement once they have been flung into it, so also does social production, once it has been flung into this movement of alternate expansion and contraction. Effects become causes in their turn, and the various vicissitudes of the whole process, which always reproduces its own conditions, take on the form of periodicity.[54]

53 Marx 1978, p. 250 [1963, p. 171].

54 Marx 1976a, p. 786 [1962, p. 662].

Indeed, once the circumstances which led to the lowering of the rate of profit have been overcome, it is plausible to expect that they will reappear in the following moment when the rate of profit has gone up again, because they do not come about through the action of chance factors external to industrial capital, but instead through the effectuation of its own immanent tendencies. This was the meaning of the final part of the above text: 'The stagnation in production that has intervened prepares the ground for a later expansion of production – within the capitalist limits'. Even if they do 'prepare the ground' for a new phase of accumulation, the conditions of crisis remain there as their 'capitalist limits', that is, as the constitutive contradiction that will reappear with all its consequences, not eliminated by the new accumulation. So even when it is in expansion, the system continues to be contradictory and the crisis subsists in a latent state as the symmetric of the conditions that effectuate expansion, and vice versa when crisis occurs, when it is the conditions for expansion that remain latent. Each moment conserves, within it, its opposite and cannot avoid coexisting with it.

Although it represents the end of a phase of economic expansion, the crisis may reveal itself as the means of producing the conditions for overcoming itself and defining a new phase of expansion which will be followed by a new crisis, and so on, successively. This is why 'effects become causes in their turn'. The rigidity with which each moment is characterised as a cause or as an effect, or as an end or a means, is lost, configuring a dialectic in which capital finds itself condemned to the 'Sisyphean task' whereby it always repeats the 'whole process, … always reproduces its own conditions' and adopts 'the form of periodicity'. Each new moment of the cycle is experienced as if it were the preceding one; each new crisis seems to tread the same path as the preceding expansion, because in these phases the essential contradiction is reproduced that impedes them from freeing themselves from one another.

Obviously, the present is not a mere repetition of the past and here the second aspect of Marx's reasoning is appropriate: 'Capitalist production constantly strives to overcome these immanent barriers, but it overcomes them only by means that set up the barriers afresh and on a more powerful scale'.[55] These 'immanent barriers' are not just simply reset, they are 'on a more powerful scale'. The formulation in the *Grundrisse* went even farther: 'Yet, these regularly recurring catastrophes lead to their repetition on a higher scale, and finally to its violent overthrow'.[56]

55 Marx 1981, p. 358 [1964, p. 260].
56 Marx 1974, p. 750 [1983, p. 643]. Original in English.

Marx indicates that the cycles are distinguished, from the purely quantitative point of view, by the fact that the phases of valorisation and devaluation succeed one another 'on a higher scale' because each cycle takes the preceding cycle as the base for its own development. He foresees that more value is produced in each expansion, but the devaluation is also greater in each succeeding crisis. However, stating that the process will eventually lead to the 'violent overthrow' of the capitalist system, as the text cited from the *Grundrisse* does, is very different from merely affirming that the successive crises will become more intense.[57] In the *Grundrisse*, the complex problem of capitalism's economic collapse is configured as 'violent' and above all, inevitable. The extent to which Marx avoided the theme in *Capital* will be a question that I will return to later in the Conclusions.

From the qualitative point of view, Marx also points out a distinction between the cycles, this time according to the change in the material base or in the type of technology, as a result of the competition among capitalists and the system's constant need to reduce its costs in general. From the fact that the means of production 'are not replaced in their original form, but in the revolutionised form', Marx explained the duration of cycles by the periodic need to replace fixed capital; in doing so he obtained parameters for the determination of the phases of capitalist production. Taking into account more profound alterations in the material base and its associated social and political institutions, some Marxist authors describe even longer cycles encompassing various shorter ones and characterised by alterations destined to overcome crises of long periods of stagnation.[58] Although it is interesting for its explanations of

57 Capitalism's inevitable collapse has been a recurrent theme of debate in the Marxist field since the beginning of the twentieth century. Outstanding figures include Karl Kautsky with his 'chronic stagnation' concept and after him, Henrik Grossmann with the book *The Law of Accumulation and Breakdown of the Capitalist System* (1929). In recent times, the most important author to defend the idea that the capitalist system will collapse seems to me to have been Robert Kurz, in works such as *Der Kollaps der Modernisierung. Vom Zusammenbruch des Kasernensozialismus zur Krise der Weltökonomie* (1991), to *The Substance of Capital* (2016). Despite his sharp and radical critique of capitalism, I do not agree with the point of view that seems to remove from social and political agents the ability to destroy capitalism and create another social system.

58 Even if these 50-year 'long waves' had already been the theme of discussions at the beginning of the twentieth century and designated by the name of their statistical formulator Kondratiev, they became especially important in the debates of the 1970s, as an explanation for the economic stagnation of the time. On this subject, it is impossible not to mention Mandel's classic *Long waves of capitalist development* (1978), for whom technological innovations by themselves do not have the capacity to take the capitalist system from a phase of long depression to a phase of long ascension. If the passage from a long

historical aspects of capitalism, the long cycles theory has even greater problems associated to it than the theory of cycles in general, as we shall see in the next subchapter.

In any case, the main aspect of the concept of economic cycles consists of explaining the valorisation and devaluation, not as simultaneous tendencies, but rather as being distinct and alternating phases of the development of capital's constitutive contradiction. Defining crisis as a cycle introduces a more complex meaning than that of its definition as a conflict between concomitant forces:

> These various influences sometimes tend to exhibit themselves side by side, spatially; at other times one after the other temporally; and at certain points the conflict of contending agencies breaks through in crisis. Crisis are never more than momentary, violent solutions for the existing contradictions, violent eruptions that re-establish the disturbed balance for the time being.[59]

As we have seen, in addition to being viewed as the end of a phase of expansion, crisis can also be considered as a means for preparing a new expansion; in this sense it is the 'solution for the existing contradictions' and not just the form of manifestation of these contradictions; it then 're-establishes the disturbed balance for the time being' rather than just exposing the unbalance.

However, defining crisis as a 'solution' for the contradictions of the capitalist system at a certain stage of its development introduces the risk that crisis will be viewed as a positive, functional, domesticated phenomenon. Perhaps this explains Marx's emphasis on the expansive nature of the scale on which production and crisis succeed one another: this would help to minimise a more optimistic interpretation of the crisis as a growth crisis. A more rigorous understanding of the concept of cycle should also curb the danger

---

expansion to that of a long depression occurs due to the increase of organic composition and the consequent reduction of the rate of profit, the reverse passage depends on counteracting conditions that cannot be perfectly predictable. At the time of Mandel's work, other authors developed the theme, such as Gordon (1978) and Kotz (1987), who develops a good summary and problematisation of the theme. The debate was resumed by Robert Brenner (2002), for whom the end of the twentieth century had witnessed two shorter Kondratiev cycles: the first between the end of the World War II and the mid-1980's (40 years), and the second would have started in the mid-1980's, with the end of its ascending phase foreseen for 2010. As for the causes of the cycle, Brenner approximately agrees with Mandel.

59 Marx 1981, p. 357 [1964, p. 259].

of such optimism, for the crisis and the expansion are one another's means of realisation; 'effects [that] become causes in their turn', otherwise it would not be feasible to think in terms of periodicity. However, once more, a complete understanding of the cycle means having recourse to modal categories to determine to what extent the moment of crisis and the expansion of capital are necessarily determined by one another. This will be the theme of the next subchapters.

3.2 *The 'Bad Infinity' of the Cycle*

What the concept of cyclic crisis endeavours to explain is more than just the predominance of a tendency over a counter tendency, that is, of capital's valorisation impulse over the forces that lead to its devaluation in the moments of expansion, or of devaluation over valorisation in the moments of open crisis. The difficulties inherent to the explanation of that simple predominance have been identified earlier in this chapter. Now, however, it is necessary to explain the alternations of the cycle phases according to which each phase remains latent while the other is manifesting itself and then the latent phase expresses itself and the other phase passes into a condition of mere latency.

Marx describes this alternation, or rather, this resumption of expansion after crisis in the following words:

> How then is this conflict resolved? How are the relations corresponding to a 'healthy' movement of capitalist production to be restored? The method of resolution is already implicit in the way in which the conflict is stated.[60]

Just as the determinants of crisis are present as contradictions in the expansive phase of the cycle, in a similar way, the solution of the contradictions that make a new phase of accumulation feasible, the 'method of resolution ... of the conflict' followed by the devaluation of the capital, is also 'already implicit' in the crisis. Therefore, if each of the opposing and successive stages, namely '*healthy* movement' and crisis is 'already implicit' in the essential conditions of the preceding stage, then it must necessarily derive from the other and not exist as a mere possibility. In each phase of the cycle, the passage to the following stage would not only be possible but would be a necessary development of the 'already implicit' potentialities in the preceding phase.

Thus, the endeavour is actually to do more than just explain the alternation of the inverse phases of the cycle; it is necessary to understand the modality

60 Marx 1981, p. 191 [1964, p. 263]. My italics.

of the passage from one phase to another, that is, how the predominant elements in a given phase make way for those of the following phase, or in other words, how each phase determines the following phase and is itself determined by what took place previously. In this passage, the decisive aspect is the way in which the phases are 'implicit' in one another, that is, whether their reciprocal determination occurs in a necessary or only possible way. If this passage is a mere possibility, then maybe sometimes one phase does not follow the other and there is no foreseeable economic cycle.

However, given that the cyclical periodicity is based precisely on the inclusion of the essential elements of each phase in those of the opposite phase, then it corresponds satisfactorily with the contradictory nature of capital. It consists in a form of movement that expresses the contradiction more faithfully than the previously examined forms do insofar as they were characterised by the pure domination of one tendency over the other, as in the case of economic collapse, or the eternalisation of the system. In the cyclic form, neither of the phases can become absolute and deny the other the possibility of expressing itself, as is the case, at the outside, with the theories that forecast a final destiny for capitalism. The two phases must not only admit the possibility of one another but actually require the existence of the other as something necessary, because each one would be determined by the other and would have in the other the means of its own determination.

Undoubtedly each phase excludes the possibility of the other phase constituting a whole that would relegate the first phase to the condition of a mere middle term. At the same time however, it intends to include the other as the middle term to compose, on its side, a whole. This relationship between the two phases corresponds to the form of contradiction 'as such' that characterises capital itself, as was explained in the second chapter: on the one hand the two phases reciprocally exclude one another in the sense that each one predominates in its time over the other and relegates the other to mere latency, encompassing it to compose its own totality; on the other hand, they include one another in such a way that in the valorisation phase, the conditions for devaluation are prepared and vice versa. This last aspect is what determines the end of the predominance of one of the phases over the other and their alternation.

The very definition of cycle means that the transition from one phase to another is necessary, but it is important to examine how this necessity comes into being, and accordingly examine the arguments Marx proposed to explain it. Then it is necessary to verify whether, according to his arguments, each of the phases does indeed contain the component elements of the other and to what extent it does so. In this way it will be possible to evaluate the extent to which they are mutually conditioned, that is, assess whether the passage from one phase to the following one occurs based on the conditions of the preceding phase or whether these conditions would also allow for a different result which albeit foreseeable was not the only possibility and for this reason not obligatory.

An initial and rudimentary explanation for the necessary transition among the phases of the cycle is that, under capitalist conditions, production tends to grow faster than the capacity for social consumption, making it difficult to sell the commodities already produced and thus leading to a drop in their prices and the devaluation of the capital that produced them. In fact, Marx sometimes exposes a kind of reasoning in texts like this one:

> Since capital's purpose is not the satisfaction of needs but the production of profit, and since it attains this purpose only by methods that determine the mass of production by reference exclusively to the yardstick of production, and not the reverse, there must be a constant tension between the restricted dimensions of consumption on the capitalist basis, and a production that is constantly striving to overcome these immanent barriers.[61]

If on the one hand, these 'restricted dimensions of consumption' create an 'immanent barrier' to capitalism, on the other, in this system, 'production ... is constantly striving to overcome' this barrier so that the 'barrier' does not end up making the system definitively unviable or leading it to collapse. Furthermore, in none of the texts in which he puts forward the idea of a 'tension' between production and consumption does Marx go so far as to offer an explanation for the possible or necessary periodicity of the transition from a phase in which this 'tension' predominates to a phase in which it is latent, or vice versa. While it is undeniable that 'there must be a constant tension' between production and consumption, it is difficult to construe this as the origin of a cycle; and even if production 'is constantly striving to overcome' its barrier, it is impossible to guarantee that such overcoming will always be repeated and adopt a cyclical form. Maybe this is why the discrepancy between production and consumption is an explanation adopted much more by theories of collapse or chronic paralysis of the system than by theories of economic cycle. In any event, there are various texts of Marx that dis-

61 Marx 1981, p. 365 [1964, p. 267].

approve of the sub-consumption critique of capitalism, making it necessary to relativise the importance of his own mentions of the theme, which certainly do not represent the most interesting and original aspect of his critique.[62]

A second explanation refers to the already examined alterations in the organic composition of capital. The ratio between constant capital and variable capital would tend to increase with accumulation, leading the rate of profit to fall to the point where it would no longer be feasible to continue operating with the same technological standard. The consequent devaluation of the capital in use would then impose a complete change in the type of technology, reducing the organic composition of capital, raising the rate of profit once more and making accumulation feasible. Such an oscillation in the organic composition, however, requires that its effect should be analysed separately from any other factor affecting the rate of profit. Even so, when endeavouring to explain the increase in the organic composition during the expansive phase of the cycle, it is necessary to take into account the earlier remarks regarding the profit rate's

62 As early as the beginning of the nineteenth century authors like Hodgskin, Sismondi and Rodbertus developed critical theories of capitalism according to which the system would suffer from a chronic insufficiency of consumption. Although he was sympathetic with their intention to identify a structural flaw in capitalism, Marx criticised their narrow sub-consumption vision: 'It is a pure tautology to say that crises are provoked by a lack of effective demand or effective consumption. ... If the attempt is made to give this tautology the semblance of greater profundity, by the statement that the working class receives too small a portion of its own product, and that the evil would be remedied if it received a bigger share, i.e. if its wages rose, we need only note that crises are always prepared by a period in which wages generally rise, and the working class actually does receive a greater share in the part of the annual product destined for consumption' (Marx 1978, pp. 486–7 [1963, p. 409]). It is symptomatic that Marx made this criticism when he presented the equations of reproduction in *Capital* Volume II, which demonstrate the possibility that the part of the commodities not consumed by workers and capitalists consist of means of production. It is also symptomatic that the main advocate in the early twentieth century of underconsumption as the correct explanation for crises, Rosa Luxemburg (1976), tried to demonstrate the inconsistency of Marx's equations. From that moment on, the theory that crises stem from underconsumption was adopted by various Marxist authors, particularly by Sweezy (1942), who thus tried to bring Marx closer to Keynes. More recent authors do not consider underconsumption as the main cause of crises but combine it with some other element, generally with the disproportionality of the departments of social capital reproduction, as is the case of Stanley Bober (2008), David Harvey (2011), and John Bellamy Foster and Robert McChesney (2012). As should be evident to the reader of this book, I do not regard underconsumption as an explanation for crisis suited to the properly Marxian concept of capital, although there are some passages in *Capital* Volume III which may give rise to such an interpretation.

tendency to fall, namely, that a sharp increase in the technical composition of capital may not be reflected in the same proportion by an increase in the value composition of constant capital and variable capital. In turn, when explaining the reduction of the organic composition resulting from a crisis and the devaluation of the existing capital, it must be remembered that, for such a reduction to take place, the value of the elements of constant capital must decrease more than those of variable capital.

In the same way, the conditions of crisis do not necessarily imply the resumption of capital accumulation. As we have seen, individual capitalists invest with the immediate aim of reducing costs and not of achieving any specific change in the organic composition of social capital. They may invest in diminishing the value of constant capital and of variable capital at the same time and only the final disposition of the whole can decide the final direction of the investment for the organic composition. The original tendency would be to reuse the means of production that had been lying idle and the rate of adoption of technical innovation could be low. Lastly, the re-hiring of workers dismissed during the crisis increases the value of variable capital and increases the rate of surplus value, but at the same time it involves an increase in the overall mass of wages that could annul the effect of the reduction in the organic composition on the rate of profit.

The solution for this undefinition is to admit that the objective of the changes in the technical composition of capital is to face up to adverse situations in regard to the availability of labour power. With this, a third kind of explanation emerges in Marx's texts for the existence of economic cycles.

Initially, the accumulation would lead to the depletion of the industrial reserve army, the consequent increase in wages and the reduction of the rates of surplus value and profit to the point where a crisis occurs. The devaluation of the existing capital and the technological revolution would come as a response to the crisis, recomposing the labour reserve, lowering wages, and increasing the rates of surplus value and profit. Therefore, the cycles could always be explained by those periodic movements of depletion and re-composition of the labour reserve which would cause the respective increases and decreases in individual wages and, inversely, reductions and increases in the profits.

Ever since *Capital* Volume I, the presupposition for this explanation has been the constancy of the technical and organic compositions:

> If we assume that, while all other circumstances remain the same, the composition of capital also remains constant (i.e. a definite mass of the means of production continues to need the same mass of labour power to set it in motion), then the demand for labour, and the fund for the sub-

> sistence of the workers, both clearly increase in the same proportion as the capital, and with the same rapidity.[63]

In other words, the growth in the 'demand for labour', which progressively reduces the reserve of workers and pushes up wages is proportional to the growth of capital, to the accumulation, only if 'the composition of capital also remains constant'. Otherwise, the gradual increase in the technical composition would mean that the number of workers employed might not be as high as the mass of means of production incorporated to capital. The employment of labour power would increase but not in proportion to the rhythm of accumulation.

In *Capital* Volume III Marx adds that:

> given the link between production prices and commodity values and leaving aside the oscillating movements of market prices, experience ought always, on the face of it, to confirm that when wages rise the rate of profit falls, and vice versa. But we have seen how the profit rate may be affected independently of wage movements, by movements in the value of constant capital; so that wages and rate of profit may rise or fall in the same direction, instead of in opposite ones, both can rise and fall together.[64]

Thus, the problem goes beyond one of mere proportion; the continual alteration of the organic composition, not just the technical composition, can significantly modify the other elements cited in the third type of explanation. If the value composition alters together with the technical composition, the expansion of the demand for labour will tend to be just as intense as the accumulation of capital. If, however, the organic composition does not increase at the same rate as the technical composition due to a fall in the value of the elements of the constant capital, then the rate of profit may either fall or remain unaltered, in spite of the wage increases stemming from the depletion of the labour power reserve. This is why the same quoted text states that 'wages and rate of profit may rise or fall in the same direction, instead of in opposite ones, both can rise and fall together', thereby annulling the rule that 'when wages rise the profit rate falls, and vice versa' and contradicting the presuppositions of the third explanation.

---

63 Marx 1976a, p. 763 [1962, p. 641].

64 Marx 1981, p. 1008 [1964, p. 876].

The supposition that the organic composition of capital remains constant is decisive for explaining the cycle on the basis of the movements of the labour demand, but it is not a merely theoretical supposition. Marx considers it as a real possibility:

> Growth of capital, i.e. accumulation of capital, involves a reduction in the rate of profit only in so far as this growth brings with it those changes in the ratio between the organic components of capital that were considered above. Yet despite the constant and daily transformations in the mode of production, a greater or smaller part of this total capital, now this, now that, continues to accumulate for a certain period of time on the basis of a given average ratio of these components, so that its growth does not involve any organic change and is thus no cause for a fall in the rate of profit.[65]

Here two distinct patterns of accumulation within the society's total capital can be distinguished. In the first of them a part of the individual capitals grows 'on the basis of a given average ratio of these components', variable capital and constant capital, 'so that its growth does not involve any organic change' in its composition; in the second, the 'transformations in the mode of production' brought about by the other part of the individual capitals implies technological change and a reorganisation of social relations within capitalism which do, in fact, modify the organic composition. Marx considers that the first case only exists 'for a certain period of time', that is, precisely when 'the demand for labour ... increases in the same proportion as the capital', in the words of one of the texts cited above; that is, when the rate of profit goes down purely as a consequence of the increase in wages because, in practice, the composition of capital remains unaltered. The second case corresponds to a radical change in the kind of technology which would raise the organic composition and lead to the dismissal of workers and a fall in wages in the context of a crisis and the devaluation of the existing capital.

The impasse that prevented a precise configuration of the economic cycle seems to have been overcome by combining the explanation based on changes in the rate of profit resulting from alterations in the organic composition, and the explanation that attributes these changes to the variations in wages associated to the greater or lesser demand for labour. However, it is possible to repair this combination as well. First of all, it is important to remember that,

65 Marx 1981, p. 372 [1964, p. 273].

for Marx, the immediate determinant of innovations is competition among capitalists and each one's need to obtain extraordinary profits, producing their commodities with an individual value lower than the average. In the proposed combination, however, the direction of innovations is essentially a reduction in wages via dismissal of workers, that is, the adoption of a technology that uses less labour power. This might well be the final result of the process according to Marx but, in general, it is not the individual capitalist's immediate motivation or conscious intention when he invests in expanding his base of production.

Secondly, in addition to the above, it must be pointed out that the relationship between the demand for labour and the organic composition of capital varies according to the conditions of the specific branch of production the capitalist is engaged in. In Marx's words:

> If we consider the total social capital, we can say that the movement of its accumulation sometimes causes periodic changes, and at other times distributes various phases simultaneously over the different spheres of production. In some spheres a change in the composition of capital occurs without any increase in its absolute magnitude, as a consequence of simple concentration; in others the absolute growth of capital is connected with an absolute diminution in its variable component, or in other words, in the labour power absorbed by it; in others again, capital continues to grow for a time on its existing technical basis, and attracts additional labour power in proportion to its increase, while at other times it undergoes organic change and reduces its variable component.[66]

This text describes the situation in three different types of production sphere. In the first type there is a 'concentration' or centralisation of capital in the hands of a few, a process that accompanies the increase in the organic composition; in the other two situations, the organic composition varies as a function of the growth in the magnitude of capital. In any one of the three situations, however, the capitalist invests without giving any immediate thought to the increase in organic composition that may or may not occur even with the growth of the capital 'on its existing technical basis'. In the 'spheres of production' that find themselves in the third situation, the growth in the mass of capital implies that there will be a greater demand for labour and a probable reduction in wages whereas in the second situation, this effect will be attenuated or even annulled by the increase in the technical and organic composition.

66 Marx 1976a, p. 782 [1962, pp. 658–9].

In any event, what is important in all three situations is that the changes in the composition of capital are 'sometimes … periodic, and at other times distribute various phases simultaneously over the different spheres of production'. That is, although the moments when the organic composition remains the same and those when it grows may alternate, it is also possible that these moments should coincide in time and only be distinguishable from one another by their occurrence in the various coexisting spheres. In the latter case, the situation in one sphere may compensate that in another or, rather, the sphere in which the technical composition goes up may free workers for a second sphere in which the composition remains constant. This second sphere therefore 'attracts additional labour power' from the first sphere and raises its workers' wages while the first sphere lowers the wages of its workers. The overall effect on the economy as a whole may be an increase in wages insufficient to bring about a drop in the rate of profit, impeding any prediction that cyclical phases must necessarily occur brought about by movements affecting all spheres at the same time and with the same intensity.

Furthermore, even if there were periodicity of the phases of increase and constancy of the organic composition in each one of the 'spheres of production', the combination of their different rhythms could result in an absence of periodicity for the overall set of social capital. Again, even if their combination did result in a periodic movement, it is in no way certain that it would obey the necessary uniform rhythm. Marx even goes so far as to foresee a kind of regularity that would suppress the cycle instead of reproducing it:

> With the growth of the total capital, its variable constituent, the labour incorporated in it, does admittedly increase, but in a constantly diminishing proportion. The intermediate pauses in which accumulation works as a simple extension of production on a given technical basis are shortened. It is not merely that an accelerated accumulation of the total capital, accelerated in a constantly growing progression, is needed to absorb an additional number of workers, or even, on account of the constant metamorphosis of old capital, to keep employed those already performing their functions.[67]

If the accumulation in the spheres where the technical composition remains constant is not sufficiently intense to employ the 'additional number of workers' its growth demands, and also to absorb those being liberated by the spheres

67 Marx 1976a, pp. 781–2 [1962, p. 658].

in which the 'constant metamorphosis of old capital' occurs, then the industrial reserve army will increase. This increase occurs because social capital accumulates but in such a way that its variable part grows proportionally less than its constant part, creating a result that is equivalent to an increase in the organic composition. The combination of the different rhythms of the various production spheres leads to the predominance of the tendency for the organic composition to increase and it gradually attains all spheres of production. This means it shortens the 'intermediate pauses in which accumulation works as a simple extension of production on a given technical basis', first in the individual spheres and consequently, in the economy as a whole.

This result was already foreseen in *Capital* Volume I:

> Until now the duration of these cycles has been ten or eleven years, but there is no reason to consider this duration as constant. On the contrary, we ought to conclude, on the basis of the laws of capitalist production as we have just expounded them, that the duration is variable, and that the length of the cycles will gradually diminish.[68]

The shortening of the cycles predicted by Marx would be the fruit of the gradual predominance of the increase in the organic composition, probably associated to the gradual tendency of the rate of profit to fall as a continuous and persistent movement. However, as we shall see in the next item, neither the predominance of tendencies or counter tendencies nor the prolongation of the cycles can be calculated or foreseen with precision. Furthermore, often despite his intention to unequivocally identify a determined direction, Marx's arguments actually reveal the opposite, namely that the clash of the opposing tendencies leads to an indeterminacy as to the result and final form of the movement of capital. This is, however, the correct consequence of his project of dialectically presenting the critique of political economy.

3.3 *Necessity in the Cycle*

Lastly some considerations are needed about the modal aspect of the cyclic over-accumulation problem. The three explanations for the periodicity of crisis examined in the preceding item in this attempt at a more complete definition have proved to be insufficient in providing evidence that the valorisation and devaluation of capital succeed one another cyclically or at least that the cycle

68 Marx 1976a, p. 786 footnote [1962, p. 662]. This passage appears in the French edition of 1872 and was only inserted a s a footnote in the fourth German edition of 1890.

is regular and uniform. According to the last two explanations, each phase of the cycle must contain the elements of its own negation which would have developed during the period of predominance of the respective phase and ended up manifesting themselves. Given that the elements of this negation would be precisely the elements characteristic of the opposite phase, the transition from one phase to another would be contained in each phase as its necessary result and the expectation that the development of the specific conditions of both cases will occur in approximately uniform time intervals determines the necessity, not the mere possibility, that such development will be cyclic and regular.

The problem is that each phase is not just a negation of the other: to itself it is a positive reality, with singular characteristics of its own. Therefore, the self-negation of one phase does not imply the inevitable passage to the other because, even though it is inherent and necessary to the conditions of that other posterior phase, it does not define it regarding its positive aspects. In other words, it is not just because the valorisation goes down to a minimum that the devaluation of the existing capital, characterised by the idleness or physical destruction of constant capital, worker unemployment and a drop in social consumption levels, will determine the emergence of specific technical innovations and a reorganisation of labour relations capable of creating a base for a new period of accumulation on a greater scale.

It would be a serious mistake to suppose an identity between the negation of one phase and the emergence of the following phase in the cycle. To explain why the passage from one phase to another is a necessary phenomenon, much more is needed than the negative reference one phase has in another; there needs to be an indication of a positive reference in the sense that the conditions of each phase need to be contained in the anterior phase and in turn contain those of the posterior phase. This type of inclusion is what frees the sequence of cycle phases from the condition of being a mere possibility or an accident brought about by factors completely external to the constitutive elements of each phase. If these last were the case, then the devaluation would simply be a chance event, interrupting the valorisation, and in turn the valorisation would be a chance occurrence putting an end to the permanent devaluation crisis. Each phase includes the conditions of the other, however, for both the valorisation and the devaluation are determined by the constitutive dispositions of capital; their sequence is necessary.

Even so, the necessity that the two phases should take place cannot be an absolute one precisely because the constitutive elements of each must contain those of the other as a condition that cannot be dissolved in the other and that must necessarily take place at some later moment. The two phases in opposition are reciprocally determined so that the necessity of one implies the necessity of the other but the said necessity is a relative one defined by the relations of one phase with the other. What does this mean then for the explanation of the regular passage from one phase to the other?

Firstly, even if one accepts the idea that the self-negation of one phase is identical to the determination of the other, none of the analysed explanations demonstrates that the self-negation of one phase inevitably leads to its end, and far less, that it defines the exact moment when this end would be attained. Alongside the tendencies that express such self-negation such as the increase in organic composition or the depletion of the labour reserve, countertendencies also develop, impeding the necessities of both from becoming absolute and susceptible to being precisely predicted. The devaluation of the existing capital also implies this necessarily, but not absolutely necessarily; there will be a reduction in the value of the means of production and a replenishment of the labour reserve.

Secondly, considering that the self-negation of a phase does not entirely determine the following phase in its positive particularities, the three explanations that have been examined also fail to demonstrate that the conditions of each phase stem from one another in an absolutely necessary way. Why is that? One of the texts cited above in chapter 4, section 3.1 provides the answer to this question: 'various influences sometimes tend to exhibit themselves side by side, spatially; at other times one after the other temporally'. The validity of the 'influences' that cause valorisation and devaluation is successive but at the same time they are juxtaposed in space in the sense that at each stage of succession the conditions that explain the transition from one to the other are simultaneously present. It is necessary, however, that the temporal aspect of the succession should predominate over the 'spatial' aspect of coexistence for the succession to constitute a cycle. Thus, the inclusion of the conditions of one phase among the conditions of the other means that the conditions that include must subordinate those that are included, manifesting themselves and keeping the others in a state of latency until such moment as their development weakens this predominance and inverts it, becoming latent what was in effect and entering into effect what was merely latent.

However, if both phases are equally necessary why does that inversion occur at all? Or put another way, if they effectively express themselves 'side by side', or 'one after the other' why must the temporal dimension prevail over the spatial one in determining the effective reality? As we have observed in various texts cited, Marx often emphasises the simultaneous occurrence of effects contradicting what he calls the 'laws of capitalist production' so that the question raised above cannot be addressed with the argument that a contradiction only manifests one of its moments at a time so as to keep its contradictory nature concealed. Actually, this kind of solution merely conceals the dialectic between succession and simultaneousness, one that Marx clearly never fully explains.

Therefore, the necessary presence of the conditions of one phase in those of another does not mean that they succeed one another in an absolutely necessary manner, far less does it mean that such succession occurs at regular time intervals.[69] The necessity of the succession is relative because it depends on the way that the tendencies and countertendencies combine 'side by side, spatially'. This is why the cycle is unpredictable in regard to the circumstances and duration of its phases and cannot be considered the most complete manifestation of the contradictory nature of capital. This is also why crises cannot be considered to be mere phases of a cycle, that is, a moment when accumulation re-structures itself to embark on a new stage. In principle, crises do not perform a positive functional role in capitalist reproduction; on the contrary, they indicate the negative side present in capital.

This conclusion does not mean, however, that the cycles will necessarily get shorter and shorter until they disappear altogether, when they would be replaced by the tendency to permanent accumulation or, on the contrary, by the tendency to paralysis and definitive stagnation of accumulation. The conditions that determine the non-definition of the cycle are precisely those that impede the prediction of its lengthening or shortening, in the same way that the predominance of the expansive phase, making accumulation perennial, or the gradual predominance of the capital devaluation phase, shrinking accumulation, cannot be predicted. Although these moments can be detected at various times and create the appearance of a cycle, the conditions of each

69 Most of the authors who have studied the cycles have perceived the need to define their occurrence and alternation as something necessary and inevitable and some have even gone so far as to confer this status on the 50-year cycles. Among them, perhaps the oldest is Grossmann 1992 [1929], who seeks purely economic elements, and even more so from the sphere of industrial capital to prove the necessity of the cycle's occurrence. After him, the attempt was made by Itoh 1978 and Weisskopf 1996. They were duly criticised by Kotz 1987 and by Mandel 1984, whose criticism can also be extended to the studies of shorter cycles including 10-year cycles, for these studies endeavour to obtain an *absolutely* necessary determination for such movements as the only alternative to their being a mere possibility. The same critical perspective was adopted by Brenner 2002 in his proposition that a shorter 'long wave' cycle would have occurred in the second half of the twentieth century. In regard to the modality of the economic cycle, my own proposition is to consider this figure of capitalist dynamics also as being a *relative* necessity, thereby escaping not only from the appeal of casual external elements, but also from the alternative between the mere possibility of the occurrence of a cyclical movement and a rigid absolute determination of the cycle that excludes extra-economic factors and human action.

phase are not entirely contained in the preceding phase, and they do not contain the entirety of those of the following one; their following of one another is only relatively necessary. Nothing can ensure that a tendency predominant at a given moment will continue to affirm itself, far less that the movement of the system is directed towards an end determined by this tendency, because the opposing tendency also acts with the same necessity and may invert or annul the determination of the former one.

A crisis may just as readily perform the function of re-establishing the conditions for a resumption of accumulation as it may extrapolate this positive role and, even though it is performing a therapeutic function, create worse conditions than the former ones. This situation configures a certain degree of undefinition regarding the general form of movement capital necessarily takes on, albeit it must necessarily always be in movement. Assessing to what extent and to what depth all of this compromises Marx's project of critique of capitalism calls for a specific reflection which will be developed in the final considerations that follow, by means of an examination of the different temporalities the system presents itself in and the modality of each one, especially those that refer directly to the question of crisis.

Conclusions

1 The Time of Crisis

The reconstitution of the concept of crisis performed in the course of the presentation of *Capital* makes it possible to define the richer and fuller content it receives in Marxian theory and indicate how its determinations come into effect. For it must not be forgotten that, as Marx said in the preface to *Capital* Volume I:

> … it is the ultimate aim of this work to reveal the economic law of motion of modern society … My standpoint, from which the development of the economic formation of society is viewed as a process of natural history …[1]

Paradoxically, conceiving capital as a historically circumscribed social relation implies exposing its 'development … as a process of natural history', that is, understanding that its history is the result of a 'law of motion' immanent to it and by means of which its richest determinations express themselves. This is, indeed, the 'ultimate aim' of the categorial presentation and the criterion to be used to assess to what extent Marx was successful in his critical analysis of capitalism.

Thus, once again, the problem of the nexus between the categorial development and the effective development of capitalism comes to the fore. In the Introduction, we saw that although the categorial development undertaken by Marx often had to have recourse to historical presuppositions, the order of both these developments is essentially distinct. Now it is necessary to consider that even in their distinction, they are related. By means of a progressive enrichment, the categorial presentation develops the content of the concepts of crisis and capital to the fullest and this exposes the 'subjectivity' of capital in the most 'concrete' form, that is, the one that configures capital's capacity to dominate the necessary conditions for its self-realisation and the subordination of all the other social relations, thereby constituting a totality. Categorial presentation is therefore an indispensable requirement for grasping the law of motion of the capital that presides over its effective development. The effective development, in turn, not only constitutes the presentation's presupposition but also the most 'concrete' content it can achieve, its goal and objective.

1 Marx 1976a, p. 92 [1962, pp. 15–16].

 | DOI:10.1163/9789004690721_007

Therefore, rather than a set of historical conditions independent from the capitalist 'law of motion', the 'process of natural history' mentioned by Marx refers to the conditions determined by this 'law'. In this sense, the history in question is the history resulting from the development over time of capital's totalising power. This question was quite clear to Marx ever since the *Grundrisse*:

> While in the completed bourgeois system every economic relation presupposes every other in its bourgeois economic form, and everything posited is thus also a presupposition, this is the case with every organic system. This organic system itself, as a totality, has its presuppositions, and its development to its totality consists precisely in subordinating all elements of society to itself, or in creating out of it the organs which it still lacks. This is historically how it becomes a totality. The process of becoming this totality forms a moment of its process, of its development.[2]

Marx endeavours to present the concept of capital in its multiple and contradictory determinations in order to characterise its object as a force capable of 'subordinating all elements of society to itself'. When these elements already exist, they are imbued with new meaning, and can be used by capital to create 'the organs which it still lacks'. Capital is defined, first of all, as a subordinating force and secondly as a creating force, capable of creating 'organs' because it forms an 'organic system'. What it creates are the 'organs which it still lacks' because capital is the 'process of becoming' an organic, articulated totality capable, in its aspect as a totality, of creating 'organs' that are members of a whole. This is 'historically how it becomes a totality': its conversion into a totality, the act of creating social relations as 'organs', is what defines a 'history' in the more precise meaning of the realisation of a process and not in the meaning of the context in which an event finds itself passively inserted.

This is how the well-known passage in *Capital* Volume I that explains the transition from 'Co-operation' to 'Manufacture' and then to 'Large-Scale Industry' should be understood. Far from being a simple description of the Industrial Revolution as it unfolded in England, it is a demonstration of how the effective conditions of labour's 'formal subsumption' have the inner capability of developing to become the conditions of 'real subsumption' because they express capital's dominance of the work process and the fetishist representation that

2 Marx 1974, p. 278 [1983, p. 203].

capital, too, is a production factor. Thus, the transition corresponds to the realisation of the process by which capital 'subordinates all elements of society to itself'.

The same occurs with the submission capital imposes on economic relations that are prior and external to it, in parallel with the domination of the labour process and the consequent improvement of the technical and institutional conditions that compose the material base for capitalist accumulation. We must undoubtedly take into account the proviso made in *Capital* Volume III:

> In theory, we assume that the laws of the capitalist mode of production develop in their pure form. In reality, this is only an approximation; but the approximation is all the more exact, the more the capitalist mode of production is developed and the less it is adulterated by survivals of earlier economic conditions with which it is amalgamated.[3]

Capital 'is amalgamated' with 'survivals of earlier economic conditions', reducing them to mere moments of its own valorisation process and integrating them to the pursuit of its own finalities. Capital destroys them or radically modifies them, should they change from being means to being obstacles to achieving its ends.

Industrial capital's domination of the technical and social conditions of labour and its subordination 'of earlier economic conditions' are both processes, because they occur in a way that is not immediate but that instead develops through the mediation of various forms that capital effectively adopts in its totalising movement. In the strict sense of history defined above, it is the sequence of these forms that defines the history of capitalism, that is, according to the time inherent to the effectuation of capital's fundamental determinations. Nothing could be more mistaken than to imagine that it imposes itself immediately or that it rushes ahead to swallow up the preceding forms, since in fact its processual nature implies that it realises its tendencies in its own time. So then, the problem is to understand how this time inherent to capitalism is determined, and whether it is cyclical or linear.

What gives the impression, at first sight, that capital can immediately realise its disposition to 'subordinate all elements of society to itself', is accumulation's seemingly continual aspect; it appears to proceed undeterred and indefinitely. The apparent absence of punctuations in accumulation's continuity obscures

3 Marx 1981, p. 275 [1964, p. 184].

its actual temporal demarcations and accordingly obscures the very perception of the process and the time that it requires to unfold as well.

Actually, accumulation takes on this appearance due to the qualitative homogeneity of capital in its money-form, the most convenient form in which to express the quantitative alterations that characterise accumulation. Nevertheless, it is important to bear in mind that the 'contradiction between the quantitative limits and the qualitative lack of limit keeps driving the hoarder back to his Sisyphean task'.[4] On the one hand, as we saw in chapter 2, section 2.2, in spite of always being limited, any quantity of money is qualitatively indistinguishable from any other and the opposition of quantity and quality determines the dialectic of the finite and the infinite that causes accumulation to always be taken up again, confirming its nature as a 'Sisyphean task'. On the other hand, a limited amount of money always represents the end of one stage of accumulation and the beginning of another, differentiating them and marking the arrival and departure platforms in a process with pretensions to infinitude. With this, the illusion of indistinct value accumulation dissipates, and in its place emerges a first form of temporality in capital's movement, a form in which it achieves linear infinitude via a succession of determined points, each one surpassed in turn, due to its finite nature, by a succeeding point in time.

Thus, the continuous expansion of accumulation, instead of taking place within an undefined homogeneous time span, occurs in a punctuated time span. The imperious command to accumulate defines the order in which capital dominates the material bases for its valorisation and integrates the 'survivals of earlier economic conditions'. In both cases, the processes are marked by a sequence of points at which specific amounts of accumulated value determine the transformation of reality to a gradually increasing extent, according to capital's possibilities, needs and objectives.

Furthermore, this punctuated form of time also constitutes the cyclical infinitude of capital's movement because each finite amount of accumulated value corresponds to the final point of a stage or phase and the initial point of another one, which is to say that, at this point, both an end and a beginning present themselves. Consequently, even though the simple circulation of commodities (C–M–C) also takes on a cyclical form, it is the capital-money circuit (M–C–M') that expresses more adequately the unity of cyclic movement and capital's tendency to progress to the infinite: the value-form that appears at the beginning and the end of the formula is money, whose qualitative homogen-

4 Marx 1976a, pp. 230–1 [1962, p. 147].

eity as universal representative of value identifies the departure point with the arrival point and makes the arrival point M' become the departure point for a new stage of accumulation, thereby configuring a sequence of cycles. Capital carries out this process because it is capable of reproducing itself with its own forces, that is, because it dominates and interiorises the means of its own valorisation. It no longer knows of any limits or measurement outside of its own sphere, so it has arrived at a situation of self-measurement that leads to a measureless accumulation.

However, the punctuated form of time also configures the previously examined second meaning of 'measureless', namely, the opposition of measurements that constitute the fundament for devaluation and crises. With this, the problem emerges of the effective realisation of the crisis, the main point of interest of this book. Stemming, as it does, from capital's contradictory nature and its loss of reference to its own self, crisis expresses the negative aspect of the totalising movement of the reproduction of capital; it implies its paralysis. In a preliminary approach, the crisis marks the point in which the movement will be detained. Even if the movement is resumed at a later moment, the crisis interrupted it and was the arrival point of a stage of linear development.

In a more detailed approach, subchapters chapter 3, section 1.2 and chapter 3, section 1.3 concluded that the different forms of value turnover and transfer from the fixed part and the circulating part of the individual capital require that it should divide itself synchronically into money capital, commodity capital and productive capital. Any eventual tardiness or lack of synchronisation between the production and circulation stages can lead to either excess or lack of one or other of those three forms of capital, making it difficult for the turnover to continue. Lack of synchrony between the production and the circulation phases, however, is not a merely casual event. The fluidity of the passage from one form to another depends on the capital's dividing itself in exactly the right proportions for each one of them. Should there be an excess of capital in one of the three, there will be a lack of it in at least one of the others, so then the stages of production and circulation will have different rhythms and not all of the value realised or produced in one of the stages will be transferred to the other. They will no longer occur simultaneously at the same pace and the movement as a whole will suffer delays or even paralysis. This would be an example of capital's inability to always distribute itself in the right measure to meet the needs of constant turnover; it would be a case in which a measurement will interrupt the movement of capital at a given point.

Subchapters chapter 3, section 2.1 and chapter 3, section 2.2 came to a similar conclusion, namely, that the measured quantity of commodities sold by each Department that the social capital is divided into is, generally speaking, established by the consumption needs of the other Department. Measureless here is the disproportion between what one Department produces and the other needs to consume. Each Department's production must be calibrated by the other's lacks, but nothing can guarantee that the measure will be implemented, because the Departments decide on their production volumes prior to putting them on the market and do so conditioned by their own investment capacities. The two measurements, that of the production capacity of one Department and the consumption necessities of the other, are not only different from one another, they are opposed to one another. For it is social capital, as the totalising 'subject' of the economic relations, which determines not only the complementarity of the mutual necessities but also the autonomisation of the Departments in relation to one another. This opposition between the unity and the autonomy of the two Departments derives from capital's constitutive contradiction, which presents itself in the opposition of the two measurements, that is, as the measureless. The consequence of this failure on the part of social capital in its self-measurement is the reduction in sales and purchases between the Departments and even the possible interruption of that exchange.

Thus, the second meaning of 'measureless' concerning capital corresponds to a paralysis in its movement by the demarcation of the point at which the supposedly constant and infinite accumulation and circulation processes find their limits.

This simple punctuated organisation of time does not disappear but instead it is encompassed by a more complex temporal form whereby the spheres of immediate production and capital circulation are considered as parts of a broader whole. In the examination of this question in Chapter 4, it was shown that in capitalist production as a whole, capital is defined as measureless by the tendential fall in the average rate of profit and the periodic devaluation of the existing capital. Here mismeasurement manifests itself as a process, as a systematic transformation that effectuates the self-negating determination of capital. In other words, the limit points become markers of the stages of a descending movement or the passing from an expansion stage to a retraction stage and vice versa, and no longer just the end of an expansive impulse.

The conception of crisis as a process and not just the end point of another process to which it is opposed is initially delineated in the theorem of the tendential fall in the average rate of profit, according to which the same 'law of motion' that leads capital to expand and form a totality also increases its organic composition in the bid to increase labour productivity and obtain an increase in the relative surplus value. As chapter 4, section 2.1 explains, these effects complement one another and bring about a drop in the average rate of profit in such a way that total capital valorises less and less in proportion to the increase in its volume and may arrive at a situation in which this increase is actually prejudicial, that is to say, a situation of absolute devaluation.

The more the system endeavours to avoid relative or absolute devaluation of capital by raising the rate of surplus value, the more it has to raise labour productivity. This means it tends to also raise the organic composition of capital, but then the average rate of profit drops even more, initiating a vicious circle. The crisis is then defined as a process because its two constitutive moments complement one another in delimiting successive stages in which the devaluation is ever greater. This negative process also derives from capital's 'law of motion' which determines its 'natural history', but now it becomes a history of the system's gradual contraction, its failure to affirm itself as a totality that gathers to itself the entire set of existing social relations. Considered in this way, albeit still in simple and immediate terms, the 'law' of decrease in the average rate of profit implies that history must be conceived as a constant, linear movement on the part of capital towards its own end, that is, conceived as a kind of self-destruction.

The simplicity of this linear conception of the history of capitalism as self-negation can be overcome by a change of approach to the relationship between valorisation and devaluation. Marx states that:

> These various influences sometimes tend to exhibit themselves side by side, spatially; at other times one after the other temporally; and at certain points the conflict of contending agencies breaks through in crisis. Crisis are never more than momentary, violent solutions for the existing contradictions, violent eruptions that re-establish the disturbed balance for the time being.[5]

Instead of only considering the aspect of simultaneity – the 'side by side' condition – of the rise in the rate of surplus value and the fall in the rate of profit, Marx proposes that these 'various influences' also occur 'one after the other temporally' as tendencies and countertendencies manifesting themselves alternately.

Crisis is characterised by the devaluation of the existing capital when the accumulation reaches the point where factors such as the elevation of the organic composition or the depletion of the labour reserve reduce the rate of profit to a level from which it can only be recuperated if part of the installed capital is idle. The more the system endeavours to curb this devaluation by

5 Marx 1981, p. 357 [1964, p. 259].

investing in constant capital but with the same technology as before, the more it provokes it, creating a negative process once more. Marx predicts that the way out of this vicious circle is the adoption of a new technology that re-establishes the rate of profit and capital valorisation conditions, allowing for the resumption of accumulation's expansive moment.

A broader concept of 'process' is present in this transition and it no longer refers solely to the periods of expansion or retraction in themselves but also to the cyclic passage from one period to the other. Already in *Capital* Volume I, Marx warns that: 'The expansion by fits and starts of the scale of production is the precondition for its equally sudden contraction; the latter again evokes the former'.[6] Each period of expansion or retraction must contain within it the conditions for the next period which in turn will contain the conditions for the following one, thereby configuring a cyclic process defined as being the unity of opposing phases that complete one another.

It does not follow from this, however, that the 'law of motion' can endow the history of capitalism with the form of a pure cycle, that is, a succession of highs and lows of the same amplitude. Quite the contrary, we have seen that Marx emphasises the tendency for accumulation to be parting from the broader base established after the preceding crisis, which in turn potentiates the destructive effects of the crises to come. Instead of a simple circle, what is delineated is the figure of a spiral whose point of inflection would be precisely the crisis, after which the circle would be repeated on a higher level.

Therefore, the idea re-emerges of a tendency determined by capitalism's inherently contradictory structure. In this case however, it is not a tendency that expresses itself in a constant, linear manner, as a direct interpretation of the theorem of the falling average rate of profit might suggest; it is a tendency that manifests itself as a series of economic cycles. Both the cyclical processes of expansion and crisis and the passage from one to the other define the moments of a longer-term realisation of this tendency, now presented as a more complex and far-reaching form of the processual nature typical of capital's movement. An economic expansion, a crisis, and the passage from one to the other, all represent stages in capitalism's specific history, demarcation points along the trajectory to a supposedly defined destination.

According to this conception, it is not possible to talk about the history of crises as if it were apart from the history of capitalism, as if they were independent and as if the latter could be reconstituted with reference only to capital's expansive and totalising aspect. Instead, insofar as a crisis reveals the

6 Marx 1976a, p. 785 [1962, p. 662].

self-negating aspect that is also constitutively inscribed in capital, it becomes decisive for any determination of the complete form of the process whereby capital effectuates its contradictory dispositions. It is crises that fully configure the history of capitalism as being one of movements marked by advances, paralysis, regressions, and profound revolutions in the technical and institutional bases that are particular to this mode of production. They are what define the temporality specific to the social regime presided over by capital. What remains to be discussed, in a detailed and conclusive manner, is whether a crisis is just as inevitable as the expansive and totalising impulse that stems from capital's 'subjectivity', that is, it remains to decide whether crisis, in its aspect as a constitutive element of capital, must necessarily occur. Only then will it be possible to determine its importance in the history of capital.

2 The Effective Crisis

Marx defines capital, by the very form of its constitution, as being necessarily processual, that is, a contradictory social relation that must always expand its dominion but also always deny this expansive disposition. What then would be the form of movement necessarily assumed for this double-sided process? Or, better put, how does the history of this process correspond to the necessary effectuation of its opposing determinations? The answer to these questions depends on the mode of realisation of capital's inherent potentialities; depends on how the passage of capital's constitutive determinations from potency to act takes place. Thus, we get back to the problem of the modalities, whose general structure was presented in the Introduction and has always been in sight throughout the reconstitution carried out in the four chapters that followed. Now the task is to recuperate the main results of that reconstitution to complete the analysis of the forms that capital confers on its history.

Countering capital's reproduction and accumulation movement, crisis first appears as a possible paralysis which punctuates this movement and configures it as a series of interruptions and resumptions on an increasingly higher scale. In the sphere of the circulation of the value forms of capital, this paralysis presents itself as a mere possibility, and expressions that Marx himself used such as 'formal possibility' or 'simple possibility' could give the false impression that it is a sphere that does not contemplate any necessary determination of crisis. However, in his reasoning Marx always stressed that the possibility of separating the phases of circulation results from the necessity that the process itself has to separate them. This implies that the phases are not indifferent to one another, as would be the case if their difference were established by an external force, but rather opposed, autonomised by the unity that both embraces and differentiates them. The fluidity of the passage from one phase to the other is just as necessary as its interruption, because both the unity and the autonomation of the two opposing phases are determined by the circulation's objectives, namely, selling in order to buy, in the case of simple circulation, and buying in order to sell (at a higher price) in the case of capital circulation. In the logic of the division of labour, economic agents must sell and later buy or buy and later sell, and it is equally necessary that these two acts should alternate without interruption, so that the objective of the system can be achieved.

Given that the separation of the opposite phases and their unity are both equally necessary, neither one can exclude the other and become absolute; on the contrary, the two necessities mutually condition one another, as Marx proposed in the manuscript written at the beginning of the 1860s: 'the crisis manifests the unity of the two phases that have become independent of each other'.[7] Thus the crisis reflects the separation of the two phases, buying and selling, but it also reveals that the separation is contrary to their necessary unity, and Marx's text goes on to say that if the two phases:

> ... were only separate, without being a unity, then their unity could not be established by force and there could be no crisis. If they were only a unity without being separate, then no violent separation would be possible, implying a crisis.[8]

The very definition of crisis requires that the unity and the separation of the two phases should both be necessary. In the same way as with the continuity of the circulation of capital, the crisis shows that the separation of the phases is only necessary if their unity is also necessary because, if one of them were merely a possibility, then the other would become absolute. In this last case, however, the unity of the two phases would not be 'established by force'. The necessity for each phase is relative because it defines itself as a necessity that affirms itself by means of its relationship with the other.

Nevertheless, during the period when one of the alternatives, crisis or continuous movement, is in evidence, this relation remains concealed, because the alternative that is in evidence necessarily predominates over the other as if it

7 Marx 1969b, p. 500 [1967, p. 501].
8 Marx 1969b, p. 513 [1967, p. 514].

were the only, absolute one before which the other would be reduced to the condition of a mere possibility. This is why Marx's texts mark the presence of these two modalities in the sphere of circulation in general, ranging from the simple circulation of commodities and the circuit of individual capital to the reproduction of social capital itself.

In a situation where the measurements of the various forms and parts of capital are all appropriate, sales and purchases succeed one another in a fluid manner, the turnovers of the individual capitals are harmonised and the Departments into which social capital is divided intertwine, making their reproduction on a larger scale feasible. The success of capital's self-measurement is the actualisation of a necessity that is supposedly absolute and makes crises appear to be random events. When, however, these measurements are not appropriate, sales fail to correspond to purchases, the turnover of the parts of the individual capitals enters into disagreement, and consumption is no longer equivalent to the product of the Departments of social capital. The paralysis of these various movements indicates that capital's incapacity to perform its self-measurement expresses a necessity that now appears to be absolute, downgrading the continuity of circulation to the status of a mere chance occurrence. Beyond these appearances, the concretisation of the opposite alternative to the one in effect will not be the work of any external accident but, instead, the realisation of a power inherent to capital. As a potential power, possibility is a necessity but a necessity that can only be relative, conditioned.[9]

The concealment of this relative and potential nature of the opposing alternatives is therefore due to the predominance of one of them over the other. However, this predominance cannot be explained merely by examining the sphere of circulation as if it were independent of the conditions peculiar to the sphere of production, because all that can be identified in the sphere of circulation is the observance or non-observance of the measures that ensure the normality of these movements of capital. The combination of the determinations of immediate production and those of circulation must be taken into account;

9 I believe it is possible here to transpose to Marx Hegel's argument regarding the 'relative necessity' in the 'Doctrine of Essence' of his *Science of Logic*: when possibility is a potency inherent in the thing and not just a chance occurrence, then it is a necessity in the sense that it should be actualised. However, this necessity derived from possibility cannot exclude other possibilities, it cannot be the only one, absolute; it cannot even present the realisation of the other possibility as if it were a mere accident. It must admit that there are other possibilities, or rather, admit that the possibility of the occurrence of a different event is not a mere accident, but in fact, a distinct potentiality that exists in the thing. See Hegel 2010, pp. 482–5 [1986, pp. 207–13].

a combination in which capital's 'subjectivity' presents itself fully developed and grounds with its contradictions both the tendency to measurement and to mismeasurement.

On this more complex level of categorial presentation, crisis ceases to be characterised as the mere punctual paralysis of a movement and determines itself as a process. Initially, Marx defines it as a fall in the average rate of profit resulting from the complementary increase of two key variables: the rate of relative surplus value and the organic composition of capital. Even though it manages to temporarily curb the fall in the rate of profit, the increase in the rate of relative surplus value also provokes the growth of the organic composition which, in the long run, tends to reduce the rate of profit even more. Thus, what is configured is the opposition between the measures of valorisation that characterises mismeasurement, that is, the increasing difficulty of capital in establishing the parameters for its own valorisation and, therefore, to distribute itself in adequate proportions to reproduce itself, whether it be as individual capital or as social capital.

However, as we saw in chapter 4, section 2.2, it must be acknowledged that the counteracting conditions enumerated by Marx have the same modal status as the tendency to fall of the average rate of profit. This is particularly true of the reduction in the value of the elements of constant capital. Clearly the attempt to compensate for the fall in the average rate of profit takes place through investments that lead to an elevation of the technical composition of capital, but this elevation is not always mirrored with the same intensity in the value composition of the variable and constant parts of capital. If the general increase in productivity reduces the value of the means of production more than it reduces the value of the worker's means of subsistence, then the elevation of the organic composition will be smaller than the elevation of the technical composition and could be compensated by the elevation of the rate of surplus value, leaving the rate of profit unaltered; and the organic composition of capital might even increase less than the rate of surplus value, so then the rate of profit would go up instead of down.

The supposition that the organic composition rises more than the rate of surplus value implies that the increase in productivity lowers the value of the workers' means of subsistence more than the value of the means of production, that is, it implies that the technical progress is labour cost-saving. Indeed, this tendency corresponds to the essential determination of capitalism, according to which dead labour negates living labour. However, the way that determination is carried out does not guarantee that it will be the final result: quite often it is more advantageous for the individual capitalist to obtain an increase in productivity by reducing the value of some elements of the constant capital such as energy or raw materials. Thus, in the weigh off between the tendency to reduction in the rate of profit and the countertendency to reduction in the value of the constant capital, it is difficult to predict with any certainty which of the two will prevail.

It is due to these difficulties that the fall in the average rate of profit is of such a complex nature. Marx calls it a 'law' thereby conferring on it the modal status of a 'necessity', but he also clearly states that the 'law' is only a tendency and, therefore, not always in force, alternating with moments when the counter tendencies prevail. Even if the latter were merely possibilities, the necessity of a falling average rate of profit would not be an absolute one. Marx goes on to add that 'These two movements not only go hand in hand; they mutually condition one another, and are phenomena that express the same law'.[10] With this, Marx indicates that he does not consider the reduction in the elements of constant capital to be merely possible and liable to be absorbed, little by little, by the necessity of the fall in the rate of profit until it is neutralised by this fall. The countertendency is an expression of 'the same law' that commands the tendency; it is a potentiality inherent to the system. Both tendency and countertendency configure themselves as relative necessities that cannot be completely absorbed by one another for 'these two movements … mutually condition one another'.

Thus, a fatal collapse of capitalism brought about by the persistent fall in the rate of profit is a hypothesis discarded by the very way in which Marx defines the system's variables. Nevertheless, the cycle of alternating periods of capital valorisation and devaluation cannot acquire the status of absolute necessity either. Neither of the alternatives, converted into opposite and successive phases of a cycle, contains the complete set of conditions for determining the following phase. Valorisation depends on constantly overcoming the conditions that devaluate the existing capital, just as the moment in which devaluation occurs engenders the new re-valorisation criteria. Certainly, the passage from one phase to another occurs because each of them contains part of the conditions of the next one, but only in part. In general, the element that triggers the passing from one phase to another was not present in the preceding phase and so the cycle cannot be rigorously predicted. The same goes for the case of the conception whereby cycles get shorter and shorter, leading eventually to the predominance of a determined tendency. If so, this tendency would become an absolute necessity, the only possible alternative.

10 Marx 1981, p. 355 [1964, p. 257].

For this reason, both the pure cycle and the longer cycle in which a tendency to economic expansion or stagnation prevails, occur because their occurrence is a necessity, but not an absolute necessity. It is not possible to forecast how long each phase will last or the moment when one phase will be succeeded by the next or even the tendency that will be most notable during a given phase. There is no movement towards a pre-established end, there is no single tendency that can definitively prevail over the opposite tendency. However, this non-definition is not complete: albeit with its exact sequence disfigured, there is a movement determined by the conflict between the opposing potentialities that constitute capital and configure its history as a peculiar and necessary product.

3 The Modalities of Crisis

Based on the results obtained so far, we know that cycles and tendencies are phenomena that necessarily occur in capitalism, that they are perfectly explicable by the set of the social system's constitutive potentialities and the circumstances which at every moment associate themselves with these potentialities, but the two phenomena are not perfectly predictable. Understanding that lack of congruence between explanation and prediction calls for a more detailed examination of the modalities problem implicit in Marx's conception of economic crises and capital accumulation.

Ever since the Introduction to this book, we have seen that Marx could use modal terminology, albeit in a non-systematic form, to analyse the effectuation of the potentialities contained in capital because he defined capital as a 'subject' capable of subjugating and presiding over all the other social and economic relations and composing a totality. Marx explains the way capitalism functions as being that of an effective reality, that is, not an aggregation of social conditions and relations whose existence is only ascertained, but instead, as an organic kind of whole, in which relations exist and interact because they are determined by capital, which establishes the role of each one of them within the process of its self-valorisation. The effective reality of the social relations presents itself as a manifestation of the power of capital, so that within the whole there is nothing indifferent or external to this power. In this sense, capital claims to be something unconditioned, whose expansion knows no limits and whose drive to dominate is inevitable, that is, which could not be otherwise.

Such a claim on the part of capital would correspond to the Hegelian category of an 'absolute necessity' if here too it were a question of an active substance whose fundamental or inner determinations were exteriorised completely and unequivocally, configuring full unity of the essential interior and the appearing exterior. Defined in this way, as active and determinant content, the substance would seem like a 'subject'. However, the substance that actually creates value is labour. Capital transforms it into a commodity and downgrades it to a moment of a totality. It captures the substantiality of labour, taking possession of it, imbuing it (from here on, its own self) with the active and determinant nature that defines a 'subjectivity'. Thus, capital only converts itself into a 'subject' because it acquires the substance of labour, or, putting it another way, the substance does not become 'subject' through its own development, but because it incorporates a power that is strange to it.

As examined in chapter 2, section 3.1, the formation of capital's 'subjectivity' is indissociable from the negation of living labour by dead labour, which configures a contradiction whereby the subject-capital needs to simultaneously affirm and deny the substance-labour: affirm it as being a 'moment' of the whole composed by capital in relation to its own self; and deny any pretension on the part of labour to compose a whole in which capital itself would be downgraded to a simple 'moment'. These are two opposing relations to which that same substance, labour, is submitted to capital's power in its pretension to be the 'subject' of all social and economic life. The first relationship is defined by the affirmation of the substance-labour as part of the totality formed by the subject-capital. With this, capital acquires a content, the valorisation of value that serves as the foundation for the necessary effectuation of all the determinations of immediate production and of the circulation of commodities. The second relationship is defined by the negation of the substance-labour, that is, by the refusal to allow it, too, to raise itself to the status of self-determinant subject. This reveals the merely formal nature of dominance of capital over labour based on the exclusion of the worker from the proprietorship of the means of production and, consequently, the merely formal nature of capital's 'subjectivity', its fetishist side, and its lack of substantial content. The result is the unfeasibility of the self-valorisation of value, an unfeasibility that necessarily forms the basis for the determinations that frustrate expansion and lead to its opposite – capital's devaluation and paralysis.

Therefore, the contradictory imposition of capital on labour leads to two opposing fundaments, one formal and the other real, and they determine, in equally necessary ways, two contrary realities: self-measurement or mismeasurement; self-valorisation or devaluation; expansion or crisis. Both are necessary but neither of them is absolutely necessary because neither one is capable of reducing the other to the status of a mere accident that could be disdained or absorbed. Even though it is just formal, the fundament of capital expansion and accumulation is also real in a way, at least for as long as it sustains its domination of substance and appropriates it as the effective ballast of its valorisation. However, its contradictory nature impedes it from sustaining this situation forever and makes evident the incompatibility between the ballast constituted by productive labour and the valorisation fabricated on this ballast by capital. In turn, the emergence of the real fundament does not imply the unmasking and definitive destruction of capital's domination. If the substance-labour cannot raise itself to the position of subject through its own determinations, capital can submit it once more and create new economic means of ensuring its formal domination.

Internally split because of its essential contradiction, capital never achieves its expansive tendencies in a lasting way, never permanently constitutes an effective reality, in the full meaning of Hegel's term *Wirklichkeit*.[11] Yet equally unenduring is the destruction of the reality that it does come to create so long as some uprising of the substance against the form does not entirely dismantle and destroy the social structures of capital's formal domination. As long as this does not happen, all the events of collapse or stagnation will be reversible, at least in principle.

As long as this does not happen, the effectuation of each one of the opposing fundaments is perfectly explicable as being a manifestation of capital's

---

11 In addition to defining itself by the elevation of the substance to subject, Hegel's *Wirklichkeit* is defined by the full manifestation of all the dispositions present in a fundament or 'ground' (*Grund*), that is, by an essence determining the form of its appearance. This fundament may be merely formal, when the difference between the funding content and the founded content is restricted to the form, to the mere difference between being fundament and being founded. It becomes 'real ground', however, when the funding content is different from the founded content given that the act of being is not merely formal but, instead, a manifestation of part of the content of the fundament; that is, the fundament only brings about a part of its dispositions in the founded content and that is precisely the difference between fundament and founded. In *The Science of Logic* Hegel states that full unity occurs in a third stage, the 'complete' [*vollständig*] fundament, in which fundament and founded are identical as to form and to content. Once more, in Marx's analysis, a passage such as the ones from 'formal' fundament and 'real' fundament to 'complete' fundament would be impossible for capital, which always imposes itself on labour through the social form of its exclusive proprietorship of the means of production. When the substantial content produced by labour emerges and unmasks the formality of the whole composed by capital, it does so in the figure of a crisis which, in itself, fails to establish an effective new reality and, accordingly, is subject to being once more reduced to a 'moment' of capital.

constitutive dispositions, not only in regard to its accumulation but also to its crises. However, each one of these fundaments fails to contain the complete set of conditions for the subsequent manifestation of the opposite fundament. As an example, during the period an economic expansion is in course, all the conditions that determine it seem to derive from capital's expansive fundament because the constitutive potentialities of this fundament incorporate the circumstances that allow for its realisation and so it becomes possible to explain it. Nevertheless, the conditions that determine the end of this phase and the beginning of a phase of capital devaluation – albeit meeting in the expansive fundament as its negation – also depend on circumstances outside the sphere of the fundament, making an accurate prognosis, based only on the preceding phase, difficult to make. The same reasoning applies to the duration of a prolonged crisis.

A cycle can thus be explained as a necessary result but not as an absolute necessity, totally self-determined and foreseeable. A long-term tendency observed during a certain number of cycles can also be considered a relative necessity because the gradual predominance of the conditions of crisis or of expansion equally depend on factors not to be found in the fundamental dispositions of capital. Therefore, whatever does in fact occur, occurs necessarily, but not in a predetermined form or rhythm. The articulation of variables, the order that results from it and, consequently, the way these variables arrange themselves in time are by no means the product of an absolute necessity. In spite of its being a processual social relation, capital does not categorically establish the specific form in which its processes develop. This is why all of its forms are explicable but not one of them is perfectly foreseeable. The flexibility of the forms of movement does not imply that they are indifferent to the internal dispositions of capital; rather, it does imply the existence of a constitutive split between these same dispositions. Parting from the original bifurcation of the opposing fundaments and the posterior ramification of the pathways of their manifestation, a space is opened for the interference of contingent circumstances in the definition of the forms effectively assume by the movements of capital.

According to this interpretation, Marx's own hesitation when using modal categories to describe the realisation of the tendencies and countertendencies arises from the complexity associated to the status of a relative necessity. From it stems, for example, the ambiguity of the terms 'law' and 'tendency'. The word 'law' suggests all the inevitability, the absolute necessity of a strict law, whether of the expansion of capital, or of an irreversible collapse or an irremediable stagnation. The word 'tendency', however, tones down the necessity and characterises the fall in the average rate of profit, among other things, as a long-term phenomenon.[12] In its necessary aspect, 'law' is imperious and makes it possible to foresee an unequivocal destiny for capitalism but in its relative aspect, it indicates that there are always countertendencies dialectically defined by the 'tendency', attenuating, postponing and even inverting its effects.

The complexity of the relative status of capital's 'laws' and 'tendencies' in Marx also allows for the comprehension of varied and divergent interpretations evoked by his conception of economic crises. In general, each of these interpretations clings to a given definition of crisis corresponding to a specific moment in the categorial presentation in *Capital*, and then converts it into the only correct definition, failing to take into account the presentation as a whole and the various definitions it contains. Little attention is usually paid to the modalities of realisation of capital's dispositions and the explanations for the crises oscillate from the affirmation of their absolute necessity to their simply being a possibility, varying from a prognosis of imminent collapse to the eternalisation of capitalism.[13]

---

12 When enunciating the 'law' of the fall in the average rate of profit, Marx emphasizes its inevitability: '... it does prove that it is a self-evident necessity, deriving from the nature [*Wesen*] of the capitalist mode of production itself, that as it advances the general rate of surplus value must be expressed in a *falling general rate of profit*'. (Marx 1981, p. 319 [1964, p. 223]). In this passage, it is important to note not only the use of the word 'necessity', but also, that based on it, the fall in the rate of profit is 'proved' because the rate of surplus value 'must' express itself in the rate of profit. However, a few lines earlier in the same paragraph Marx announces: 'We shall show later on why this fall does not present itself in such an absolute form, but rather more in a tendency to a progressive fall'. (Marx 1981, p. 319 [1962, p. 223]). Even though a 'self-evident necessity ... must' lead to a fall in the rate of profit, it does not do so in an 'absolute form'. Therefore the 'tendency' would indicate a relative form of 'necessity'.

13 Although many of the authors mentioned in the footnotes of this book have not explicitly dealt with crises from the perspective of modal logic, this perspective is implicit in the solutions they present, ranging from necessity conceived as inescapable fatality to possibility conceived as mere accident. A recent author who makes the modal problem explicit is Chris Harman, who, in a similar way to this book, seeks to reconstitute the concept of crisis in *Capital* by assigning to each moment the modality of 'possible' or 'inevitable' (2009, pp. 57–8). However, by remaining in this dichotomy and defining necessity as 'inevitability', he fails to resolve some of the difficulties of the Marxian theory of crises that I have presented throughout these pages. In addition to Harman, another author who seeks to think about crisis from the point of view of modalities is Carchedi. He proposes to think of crisis in terms of what 'can' and what 'must' happen, and suggests a kind of modal category, the 'eventual necessity', but does not develop theoretically the potentiality of this category as a middle term between possibility and necessity. In the end, when analysing the 2008 crisis exclusively in the terms of the inevitable fall of the rate of profit, Carchedi does not grant countertendencies the same modal status he grants to the tendency, repeating the traditional formulas.

It is symptomatic that these debates have produced such disparate conclusions, ranging from the inevitability of the system's collapse to the affirmation of its capacity to regenerate which conceives the crisis as being a stage of growth, destructive at first, but beneficial in the long run. The interpretation that the collapse of capitalism is inexorable rests on the same modal premise as the one for which the crisis is nothing more than an accident along the way, namely, the confusion between relative necessity and absolute necessity. The collapse hypothesis holds that capital's negative fundament imposes itself as absolute whereas for the growth hypothesis, it is the affirmative fundament that always triumphs in the end. In both cases, the difficulty is to explain why a recovery of the economy can occur even after a long period of profound crisis, or, on the contrary, why a serious crisis occurs that threatens the very existence of a system that appeared to be so strong. Also, having recourse to the conception that what are inevitable are the economic cycles because their phases would necessarily lead from one to the other incurs the same confusion when it considers the relative necessity, intrinsically liable to chance occurrences, as if it were absolute, making it possible to concoct 'infallible' predictions.

Lastly there is a group of interpretations that have sought to escape these impasses by expanding the strictly economic variables to aggregate variables related to them but belonging to the political, social and cultural spheres. A whole new field opens up with the incorporation of elements such as the economic policies of governments, social pacts between capitalists and workers, scientific and technological revolutions, and the establishment of institutions dedicated to producing and disseminating ideologies that favour the survival of capitalism. According to these interpretations, capital reproduction depends on extra-economic mechanisms that regulate it and articulate it to broader gears, constituting large institutional landmarks that define distinct historical regimes and periods of capital accumulation.[14]

---

14 These interpretations were presented by the so-called Regulation School in France and by the Social Structures of Accumulation School, mostly composed by authors from USA. Through the Regulation School's concept of 'mode of regulation' and SSA's concept of 'institutional structure', the authors linked to these currents understand crises as a phenomenon that, even in its economic dimension, is broadly determined by the way in which capitalism is socially and politically organised. As it is impossible to detail here the multiple aspects of the conception of capitalism developed by these authors, I want to briefly expose my objections regarding their conception. First, it must be emphasised that, beyond the institutional forms of labour organisation taken into account by these theorists, such as trade unions, I believe that it is the non-institutionalised class struggle that constitutes the key variable of the value of labour power or of the difference between this value and the average and minimum wage. Furthermore, secondly, if

Even though they do offer more complete explanations for the effectuation of tendencies to economic expansion or to crises, these perspectives also need to be viewed with reservations. It is true that considering technological and institutional transformations along with economic policy variables enables a better understanding of how capital's fundamental dispositions manage to articulate a series of circumstances that lead either to the realisation of its expansive tendency or of its negative tendency. These are the circumstances from the spheres of institutional policy, of institutionalised science or institutionalised culture that aggregate themselves to capital's disposition to valorisation and define the long phases of accumulation whose exhaustion in turn aggregates itself to capital's disposition to devaluation and define the phases of a prolonged stagnation. The explanatory power of that type of interpretation derives from its capacity to conjugate capital's constitutive dispositions with external circumstances, putting them both on the same level.

This explanatory power, however, does not imply any power of prediction, because the constitutive dispositions are actually not on the same level as the circumstances; the latter are external and only associate themselves to the internal dispositions fortuitously. The circumstances only play an essential role because they act on the dispositions, but they do not have a modal status of their own that would enable them to add themselves to the relative necessity and raise it to the condition of absolute necessity. To perform effectively, circumstances must either reinforce or oppose the tendency in force, effectuating the passage to the antagonistic tendency. The very process whereby this reinforcement or opposition occurs is *a priori* undefined, impeding any absolutely precise prognosis regarding the resulting form of movement. *A posteriori*, however, in the explanations for the accomplished fact, the process has already taken place, it has already conjugated the circumstances to one of cap-

the market organization is an 'institution', I think it is necessary to distinguish this type of institution from political institutions (such as the state, or NGOs) and social institutions (such as private education, churches, museums and other organs of diffusion of 'culture'). Since they do not make the distinction, the Regulation and the SSA schools consider that these institutions ensure the rate of profit by maintaining long-term expectations; and it is only when these institutions begin to fail that a reversal of profit expectations occurs and hence a fall in profits and, with the fall in profits, a fall in investment. Finally, from the perspective of this book, the most serious problem regarding such theories is that they enlarge the field of social variables only in order to achieve an absolutely necessary explanation of the crises and the 'long waves' that they believe is impossible to obtain by remaining in the economic field alone. They thus end up falling into contradiction.

ital's fundamental dispositions and placed them on the same level of reality. The political or cultural institutional conditions show themselves to be so well integrated to the economic determinations or so contrary to them, that a long phase of capital accumulation or a profound crisis seems inevitable.

Furthermore, the explanations that have recourse to a combination of political, social and cultural conditions with capital's own tendencies and countertendencies are concentrated in the institutional dimension, that is, in the policy institutionalised by the State and by political parties, in society structured in non-governmental organisations, in science and in art produced and diffused via institutional channels. All these forms of life are in a close relationship with economy, considered also in the institutional perspective of the market, the stock exchanges, the banks and so on. This is why it is plausible to compose a totality of conditions that are coherent with one another and capable of explaining bygone events as if they could not have happened in any other way. The decisive circumstances of great historical changes, however, are usually those that have escaped from the sphere of institutional life, whether it was the political sphere or the cultural one. They too exist within a system engendered by the reproduction of capital, but they are not susceptible to domestication and suddenly rebel against the system and may radically transform it.

Just like the interpretations of crisis that only consider the economic point of view, the interpretations that expand their scope to include political and social circumstances end up hypostasising the relative necessity into absolute necessity. They endeavour to widen the scope precisely in order to obtain powers of explanation and prediction which they observe to be lacking in the interpretations that restrict themselves to the economic ambit. However, the difference between explaining and predicting reveals here, once again, the unfeasibility of this aspiration. Political, technological and social changes, despite their relations with the conditions of the historical moment in which they are produced, are not completely determined by these conditions, not completely contained in them, and even some of the leading defenders of their importance acknowledge that.[15] The relative nature of the opposing necessities in the heart of capital itself constitutes the main objection to any kind of economic determinism, all the more so when it is expanded to other spheres of sociability.

---

15 I refer here to Mandel 1978 and Kotz 1987, already commented on in a note on long waves in Chapter 4.

4 The Power of Fetishism

As an effective manifestation of capital's inherent negativity, crisis is also related to the fetishism propagated throughout the entire economic system to hide its exploitation of labour power. In a fetishist manner the constitutive determinations of capital effectuate themselves, taking on an inverted appearance before the consciousness of social agents. Could the same thing be true of crisis? Or rather, could crisis be capable of unmasking the appearances capital adopts and enabling social agents to become aware of the contradictory reality that governs their actions? Could it be that crisis facilitates a critique of capitalism, and if so, to what extent? To answer these questions in regard to their most important developments, it is necessary to re-examine some of the various aspects of the way that fetishist inversion presents itself and then, to understand how it would be possible to invert that inversion.

One of the first aspects of fetishism is a result of the division of labour presided over by capital, which autonomises people to the point where they believe their relations are those of independent individuals and mediated by contracts that preserve and materialise their freedom. In that ambit, people perceive their autonomy as a primitive reality based on which they derive a reciprocal relationship, the fruit of their own free will. Also because of this division of labour, they see their relationship as basically occurring in the sphere of exchanges, that is, the market, which treats all involved equally as the proprietors of commodities, even though, for some of the proprietors, their only commodity is their labour power. For capital, it is decisive that labour power should be a commodity up for sale and for this reason the worker must have the legal status of a free proprietor, just like his employer, and effectuate this condition in the sphere of mercantile circulation which thus becomes considered as being the determinant space for all economic life. It is what appears to establish how much of each commodity should be produced and the proportions in which resources should be allocated to each branch of production.

Thus, by presenting production as being dependent on circulation and not the other way round, fetishism engenders two inversions. Firstly, the legal equality of sellers and purchasers of the labour power in the market inverts and conceals the social inequality between capitalists and wage-earners, an inequality that is the foundation of the legal equality. Secondly, capital's power of self-measurement based on which it distributes its total value among the various branches of production, appears as if it were a self-regulatory capacity of the market in which the divergent interests of free and equal proprietors would be confronted and resolved. For this reason, competition among capitalists themselves and among workers in the labour market is conceived by economic agents as being the most suitable way of harmonising their conflicts and determining prices that allocate resources and products perfectly.

A second aspect of capital's fetishism unfolds from this. If the market is the determining sphere of the distribution of values among the branches of production and thus of production as such, then all the production factors bought by capital in the market look to be of equal importance. Labour power, raw materials, equipment, energy, all are considered to be inputs whose market value will be proportionally incorporated to the value of the final product. Accordingly, the means of production, from whose proprietorship labour power is excluded by capital, would seem to create just as much value as labour. More than this: the role of capital in production is expected to be not only that of creating value in the product but also of coordinating and boosting the work process.

Here arises the real subsumption of labour to capital, whose organising powers of cooperation, division of labour and improvement in production techniques consolidate the impression that capital also creates value. In the three chapters of *Capital* Volume I in which Marx analyses this process,[16] he explains how capital's self-attributed function of increasing labour productivity becomes mistaken for the value creation process itself. Therefore, again in the sphere of its production, value appears as a social relation external to its direct producers and endowed with a natural character that imposes itself on them and commands them – the value that valorises itself.

From this second aspect of fetishism, a third one unfolds which Marx called the 'trinity formula' of capital. He states that, even supposing there was correspondence between values and prices of production and there was stability in the division of value into its component parts:

> … the real movement would necessarily appear in a distorted form: not as the dissolution of a value magnitude given in advance into three parts which assume the mutually independent forms of revenue, but conversely as the formation of this value magnitude from the sum of the component elements of wages, profit and ground-rent, taken as determined independently and separately. The reason why this illusion [*Schein*] would necessarily arise is that in the real movement of individual capitals and their commodity product it is not the value of commodities that

16 See *Capital* Volume I chapter 13 'Co-operation', chapter 14 'Division of Labour and Manufacture' and chapter 15 'Machinery and Modern Industry'.

> appears [*erscheint*] the premise of its own dissolution but, on the contrary, the components into which it can be dissolved functions as the premises for a commodity's value.[17]

The text explains the inversion that occurs between the sphere of value production in capitalist society and the sphere of its distribution as income among the three major classes, namely, workers' wages, capitalists' profits, and the ground-rent of the rural and urban landowners. Although value is only actually produced by living labour, capital, by means of its fetishism, also claims this capacity and extends it to the land, which, in agriculture, appears to join itself to labour in the creation of its product value. Thus, the three parts into which value divides itself and distributes itself as income transfigure themselves into three autonomous sources of value governed by their own rules which will be added together to form the final value of the product. The result of the first division into three sources of income is inverted to become the source of value production and, based on the form of appearance or manifestation [*Erscheinung*] of the internal dispositions of capitalist production, an illusory appearance [*Schein*] is created that gives the social relations an objective and natural character.

In the same way as the inversion of results into fundaments, the relation between appearance as manifestation and appearance as illusion articulates the fourth and last aspect of fetishism to be examined here. It concerns the 'inversion which converts the Property Laws of commodity production into Laws of capitalist appropriation' previously examined in chapter 2, section 1.3. Once again, the reproduction of capital leads to an inversion of one of the system's fundaments, namely, the principle of the exchange of equivalents in the buying and selling of the labour power commodity, into an opposite result: when re-hiring the labour power for a new period of production, the capitalist pays it a wage value that was actually created by the very living labour of the preceding period.

Marx concludes by saying that:

> The relation of exchange between capitalist and worker becomes a mere semblance belonging only to the process of circulation, it becomes a mere form, which is alien to the content of the transaction itself, and merely mystifies it. The constant sale and purchase of labour power is the form; the content is the constant appropriation by the capitalist, without equi-

17 Marx 1981, pp. 1009–10 [1964, p. 877].

> valent, of a portion of the labour of others which has already been objectified, and his repeated exchange of this labour for a greater quantity of the living labour of others.[18]

The 'form' of exchanging equivalents is preserved because, according to the labour contract for each production period, the worker receives an amount that belongs to the capitalist. The repetition of the process, however, negates this form because the 'equivalent' with which the capitalist pays for the labour power was created earlier by the living labour and not by the capitalist. This is the true 'content' of the relationship; it is in opposition to the form and concealed by it. Accordingly, the 'form' is just an illusory appearance that manifests the 'content' in an inverted manner 'and merely mystifies it'.

In other words, the content of the relation of buying and selling of labour power negates the general principle of the exchange of equivalents; it actually negates the condition of seller of commodities as free as, and equal to the capitalist buyer, attributed to the worker in the labour market. The workers' freedom and equality are reduced to mere form, to a 'mystifying' appearance when compared to the real content of the relation of labour power with capital. Nevertheless, it is this very content that determines its own 'mystification' because it reiterates labour power as a commodity that the wage-earner is legally free but economically compelled to sell. Capital stipulates legal conditions of equality in the contract only to negate them afterwards, but it does so in a way that conceals the negation by 'mystifying it' and formally preserving the universal principles of exchange of equivalents, to its own advantage.

While it provides the opportunity for a split between content and form, the reproduction of capital conceals this split and only exposes the 'mystified' content, that is, a content identical to the form. With this, as long as capital is reproducing itself in a smooth flowing manner, the rupture of the principle of exchange of equivalents in the labour market never reveals itself to the individual economic agents; as long as capital exercises its totalising power, all the other forms of fetishism are maintained too, because part of this power is precisely the capacity to conceal itself, to present its fundaments as results, and its results as fundaments, masking its social nature in the guise of an eternal natural law. Fluid reproduction implies, however, agreement between real measure of valorisation, the rate of surplus value and the fetishist measure,

18 Marx 1976a, pp. 729–30 [1962, p. 609].

the average rate of profit. Capital's totalising power also depends on the fetishist inclusion of constant capital in the cost price on which profit calculation is based. When the discrepancy between the real measure and the fetishist measure reaches an extreme degree, a crisis breaks out that reveals the opposition between them.

In the context of all these aspects of capital's fetishism, it is worth remembering that well-known statement of Marx: 'all science would be superfluous if the form of appearance of things directly coincided with their essence'.[19] In Marx's view the task that only 'science' could perform would be the unmasking of the 'essence' of capital which lies behind the 'form of appearance' that gives the deceitful impression of a natural equality when what 'essentially' exists is a socially and historically determined inequality. The 'science' defined by Marx is necessarily critical because through criticism it discovers the forms of inversion adopted by capital, inaccessible to common sense and the understanding of the individuals who suppose its 'form of appearance' to be identical to its content. Nevertheless, when the discrepancy between the real measure of valorisation and the fetishist one becomes exacerbated then gaps appear among the various 'forms of appearance' of capitalist social relations that enable the economic agents to distance themselves from capital's mystifying appearance, that is to say, enables the criticism to no longer be the privilege of those who analyse capitalism 'scientifically'.

In this way, any assessment of the crises' capacity to unmask the forms in which the fundaments of capital are inverted when they manifest themselves in their results, requires an analysis of the effects that crises generally have on the various aspects of fetishism examined above.

In the case of the first aspect of fetishism examined, a crisis must shake confidence in the market's powers of distribution. On the capitalists' side, with the crisis, competition no longer serves as an instrument for sharing out profits and becomes one for sharing out losses, but still in an unequal way, creating conflicts among the 'enemy brothers'.[20] The bankruptcy of some individual capitalists leads to a centralisation of the ownership of capital excluding various capitals and generating new hierarchies. On the workers' side, the crisis results in unemployment for many and a drop in wages for those who manage to keep their jobs. It is likely that there will be deception with the market

19 Marx 1981, p. 956 [1964, p. 825].

20 'For the class as a whole, the loss is unavoidable. But how much each individual member has to bear, the extent to which he has to participate in it, now becomes a question of strength and cunning, and competition now becomes a struggle of enemy brothers'. (Marx 1981, pp. 361–2 [1964, p. 208]).

system, but the problem is, to what extent could this deception make the workers become aware of the profound social inequality behind the legal equality presupposed by the system?[21]

Above all, if a crisis does not imply an abrupt and complete collapse of the capitalist system, whose inevitability I have engaged in refuting in this book, then it means that during the crisis the reproduction of capital still carries on, in spite of all the difficulties and the reduction in its total volume. If these difficulties are not too great, then reproduction could proceed and invert results into presuppositions preserving the illusion of the 'Trinity Formula' and all the other forms of fetishism already examined: profit presents itself as the return correspondent to the part created by capital in the total value of commodities; capital pretends that it employs workers and remunerates them using part of the value that it has produced; and the labour contract always appears to be egalitarian, at least in formal terms. Even if there is discontent because of the unemployment and the reduction of wages, it is unlikely that the employees will perceive that they are being paid with values that they themselves have produced for the capitalist, and the unemployed will hardly stop believing in the formal power of a labour contract by means of which they could reintegrate themselves in the social and economic system.

Without a doubt, a crisis tends to reveal that the market does not perform its role of distributing profits and employment satisfactorily. However, specifically in the case of the second aspect of fetishism examined above, although it reduces the economic agents' confidence in the powers of the market, a crisis will not always prevent them from viewing capital as a tradeable production factor, alongside labour and land, so that the hierarchy between production and circulation of commodities tends to remain inverted in agents' minds. The market continues to be seen as the determinant sphere of economic life and crisis will not be viewed as a phenomenon intrinsic to capitalist production but, instead, as a commercial problem arising from a chance combination of autonomous and external factors. As a market crisis, it will be considered

21 Several of the letters exchanged by Marx with different interlocutors, and especially the final paragraph of the well-known postface to the second German edition of *Capital* dated 24 January 1873, show that Marx expected a repercussion of the crises in the minds of social agents: 'The fact that the movement of capitalist society is full of contradictions impresses itself most strikingly on the practical bourgeois in the changes of the periodic cycle through which modern industry passes, the summit of which is the general crisis. That crisis is once again approaching, although yet it is only in its preliminary stages, and by the universality of its field of action and the intensity of its impact it will drum dialectics even into the heads of the upstarts in charge of the new Holy Prussian-German Empire': (Marx 1976a, p. 103 [1962, p. 28]).

a mere possibility, that is, the random emergence of obstacles to the normal selling or buying of products, exactly as in Stuart Mill's theory of crisis examined in chapter 1, section 2.4.[22]

The modality of a mere chance event will then confirm the most elementary form of commodity fetishism exposed in the first chapter of *Capital* Volume 1, since the inversion of social relations into relations among things endows crisis with the appearance of natural catastrophes like tidal waves, droughts or epidemics that would naturally affect production and the trading of basic products.[23] Still in the external contingency modality, the crisis could also be attributed to the arbitrary actions of government leaders, to errors caused by the interference of institutions external to the economic system or to the immoral conduct of some individuals in their commercial or financial dealings. In this case, instead of shaking people's faith in the market, the crisis might even reinforce it and further mystify this trust in the power of 'normality'. Depending on the specific conditions in which it occurs, a crisis may even create additional illusions of its own.

Furthermore, being a crisis in the market, it would not be considered as a necessary manifestation of the mismeasurement in capital's self-valorisation process resulting from opposing impulses in the production sphere, and, in the final analysis, from the contradiction intrinsic to capital's relationship with wage-earning labour. The crisis would not be associated with the inequality of social classes, constitutive of capital. If the perception that the market is the decisive sphere for the combination of independent factors persists, then not only will the necessity of crisis be concealed and only its possibility admitted, but also social conflict will be reduced to a mere disagreement between buyers and sellers of commodities, perceived as being agents of the market and, in principle, on an equal footing. Only in the case of a profound crisis, undeniably derived from the sphere of production could the high level of unemployment and the cuts in wages lead workers to perceive the extent to which their freedom is merely formal and restricted, and the extent to which their interests are opposed to those of the capitalists. This perception, however, does not depend on the outbreak of a crisis alone, but also on the workers' previous experience

22 See Marx's critique in Marx 1969b, p. 502 [1967, p. 502]. The theme of commercial crises will be resumed in the Postface.

23 This natural appearance of all social relations mediated by a relation among things was already evident in the following words in the section on the commodity fetishism: '… in the midst of the accidental and ever-fluctuating exchange relations between the products, the labour-time socially necessary to produce them asserts itself as a regulative law of nature. In the same way, the law of gravity asserts itself when a person's house collapses on top of him'. (Marx 1976a, p. 168 [1962, p. 89]).

and the level of organisation they have achieved; aspects that the crisis cannot necessarily and unequivocally determine at all.

In regard to the capacity for critical analysis that an economic crisis might arouse in social agents, and especially in the working class, it is perfectly plausible to imagine that capital's characteristic modality of the interplay of tendencies and counter tendencies, namely, the relative necessity, is also determinant here. In a short period of abnormal reproduction of capital, the mechanisms of fetishist inversion will hardly cease to function in their mission to impede any radical criticism of the system. However, the continuation of the crisis or a reproduction far below the minimum levels of valorisation required may lead such mechanisms to fail so that an ever harsher and more incisive criticism on the part of the social agents will be inevitable.

However, just as the necessity of a crisis requires the intervention of conditions that are not contained entirely in the constitutive dispositions of capital to be effectuated, so the necessity that the crisis should determine effective criticism requires social conditions indirectly created by the capitalist system, that is to say, forms of social life and organisation that are only compatible with the reproduction of capital, not functional to it. Once the economic crisis has broken out, these usually non-institutionalised forms turn against the maintenance of the system. Thus, the crisis determines the criticism but in a relative mode, in the sense that the determination has to relate to conditions distinct from those of the crisis itself if it is to develop, deepen and radicalise.

This investigation of the concept of economic crisis in Marx's works cannot go beyond this point in terms of the concept of criticism. Nevertheless, it can be concluded that even allowing for the corrosion of capital's fetishist structures in times of crisis, the absolute necessity that the crisis should lead to a clear perception of these structures and the condemnation of the system that institutes them is just as hard to demonstrate as the absolute necessity that no such thing should occur, and that the system should survive. What will happen will be the effectuation of one of capital's immanent necessities, but this necessity does not predetermine what is going to happen nor the form that it will take for its effectuation in the course of time. There is no way in which to deduce a teleology based on the Marxian critique of political economy. This, however, is not because capital excludes ends and finitude from its constitution or because it is not powerful enough to achieve these ends, but because of the fact that, in containing its ends and finitude, capital is as much the process of creation as of destruction of the totality of social relations; it is the movement of opposite necessities whose contradiction resolves itself and restores itself in equal measure; it is the 'subject' which, reflecting back on its own self, instates and dissolves itself in equal measure.

Postface

Precisely ten years after the publication of *The Negative of Capital* in Brazil the global crisis of 2008 broke out, undermining the declarations of the economists who ever since the 1990s had been denying the risk of its ever happening in what they called the New Economy. Faced with the undeniable fact, they began to describe the crisis as being of a financial nature, the fruit of speculation in government and private bonds. They recommended that clear limits and rules should be established for the banking system to restore to capitalism its supposed healthy and hardworking vocation. However, this attempt to minimise the importance of the crisis and to obscure its authentic nature was just as foreseeable as the earlier attempt to negate its very possibility. I had forearmed myself against both those subterfuges in *The Negative of Capital* by adopting two arguments derived from Karl Marx's works.

Firstly, against the attempt to deny the possibility of crisis, I argued that crises are inherent to capitalism because they stem from the contradictory relation of capital and wage labour. This relation already constitutes the opposition between use-value and value that defines the commodity and, unfolding into all the other capitalist social forms, constitutes the successive oppositions between commodity and money, between variable capital and constant capital, culminating in the way in which the surplus value created by labour power is distributed among the various branches and types of capital, including commercial capital and interest-bearing capital. I stated that all these social forms and phases of the valorisation process also bring with them their opposite, namely, the negative of valorisation. For Marx, in each social form the content of the concept of capital is enriched together with the concept of crisis. Even when it is not cited in any specific passage of Marx's works, crisis is always inseparable from capital and present as the element that makes it possible to criticise not only capitalism itself, but, equally, those theoreticians that see it as a balanced and eternal system.

Secondly, countering the attempt to reduce the crisis to a mere financial disturbance, I stressed how the crises have their origins in the sphere of capitalist production. Relegated to the condition of a financial phenomenon, crisis would not have its basis in the deep contradiction of capital; it would be as if capital produced commodities in a harmonious relation with labour power or as if the measureless creation and circulation of surplus value in the sectors into which capitalist reproduction is divided, resulted from the mismeasurement of one sector only – interest-bearing capital. Emphatically rejecting that kind of solution, in *The Negative of Capital* I concentrated on the forms of crisis that

 | DOI:10.1163/9789004690721_008

correspond to production and reproduction as described in *Capital* Volume I and II as well as on the tendential fall of the average rate of profit addressed in the first three Parts of *Capital* Volume III. The analyses of commercial capital and interest-bearing capital made by Marx in the fourth and fifth Parts of *Capital* Volume III were practically left out. That was a radical refusal, excessive perhaps, but justified by the need to highlight the aspect that still seems to me to be decisive in Marx's explanation for the crises. Being intrinsic to capitalism, they are rooted in the relation between productive capital and labour and not in the relation of capital with its own self. Crises are structural and correspond to the objective aspect of the criticism, that is, a self-criticism of capital's, which, in the crises, reveals its own failure.

However, in 2008 the real estate credit bubble burst and its dissemination to other economic sectors of the United States and Europe seemed to confirm the diagnosis that the nature of the crises was, above all, financial. Even authors associated with Marxist thinking defended that approach, whether it was based on *Capital* Volume III, or on the need to update and complete Marx's analysis, given that, from 1980s on, the financial sphere had supposedly acquired predominance and centrality.[1]

It was no longer possible to ignore the issue. First, it was necessary to show that a careful examination of Marx's texts does not permit the conception that the financial side of the crises are more important than capitalism's profound and decisive determinations. Following this, it was necessary to identify in these texts far richer alternatives for interpreting the financial sphere than those which were derived from a problematic attempt to draw Marx closer to the approaches of later economists like Keynes, Kalecki and Schumpeter. The need to expose the position of finance in relation to production as complementary and not autonomous became very clear. Furthermore, there was a glaring need to expose Marx's plans for the continuation of *Capital* Volume III which, in addition to a chapter on interest-bearing capital, includes a chapter on commercial capital. It was therefore necessary to explain not only the credit crises but also the commercial crises.

This is what I intend to do in this Postface.

The proposed clarification has had to take the form of a Postface because it would not be convenient to add another chapter to *The Negative of Capital*. Even if it were feasible to resume the writing style of twenty-five years ago, the intention and the structure of the book would be drained of its particular character. Moreover, the Postface form reinforces the book's argument because the Parts of Marx's works on commercial capital and interest-bearing capital, albeit

1 See, for example, Brenner 2002, Chesnais 2005, Harman 2009, Foster and McChesney 2012.

enriching the content of the general concept of crisis, do not confer a more solid determination on that concept in regard to the modes of effectuation of the economic tendencies. In other words, addressing the question of crisis in its commercial aspect or its credit aspect does not make it acquire any more inevitability than it has in the spheres of production and circulation of capital. Marx's mentions of a 'credit cycle' do not enable us to rigorously foresee capital's movements throughout the valorisation process. For that reason, too, it was not worth inserting it in the body of the book's text.

However, the current commitment to address the theme of commercial and financial crises effectively added an important dimension to the book. As I will explain farther on, the *relative* aspect of the 'relative necessity' that a crisis should occur, tends to obscure the *necessity* of the crisis in the guise of a mere possibility. Commercial capital and interest-bearing capital play an important role in the general framework of fetishism precisely because, in spite of actually being in an accessory position in relation to the sphere of production, they appear to be central and decisive. They perfect the figure of the real illusion that marks the capitalist system and whose denunciation is a determinant part of Marx's critique of political economy.

Largely for this reason, I perceived that it would be convenient to address the question of commercial capital and not just interest-bearing capital, albeit the debate on the 2008 crisis has tended to preferentially focus on financial themes. It is not by chance that Marx presents commercial capital before presenting interest-bearing capital. He pointedly separates money's mercantile function in the form of the so-called money-dealing capital from the specific function that money takes on in credit. The frequent confusion of the two functions attributes a power to money that it only actually has as capital, retroactively projecting the speculative forms of capitalisation on the forms of crisis in the production and reproduction spheres. Seeking to differentiate forms and functions, Marx studies the concept of money-dealing capital in the last chapter of the Part on commercial capital in *Capital* Volume III. In doing so he prepares the way for the passage to the interest-bearing capital in the subsequent Part of his book. This structure of Marx's work will be respected in the analyses of the commercial and credit crises that I will make in the subchapters that follow.

1 Commercial Capital and Its Crises

1.1 *Commercial Capital*

In appearance, commercial capital in the form of commodities and commercial capital in the form of money cannot be distinguished from commodity capital and money capital. From the beginning Marx is careful to point out that the distinction is due to the mere fact that in those mercantile forms, capital is owned by a special group of capitalists exclusively dedicated to the circulation of commodities and money and in whose hands the producers' commodity capital and the money capital become 'commodity-dealing capital' and 'money-dealing capital'. In Marx's words:

> *Commercial capital*, therefore, is absolutely nothing more than the *commodity capital* of the producer which has to go through the process of transformation into money and has to perform its function as commodity capital on the market; only instead of being an incidental operation carried out by the producer himself, this function now appears as the *exclusive operation* of a particular *set* of capitalists, the merchants, and acquires an autonomous position as the business of a particular capital investment.[2]

Up until this moment of the presentation, Marx takes it as given that the industrialist buys the raw material directly from his producer and sells the commodity produced to the final consumer. From here on, however, he assumes that the commercial function is delegated to a group whose capital does not leave the sphere of circulation, constantly metamorphosing from commodity capital to money capital and vice versa.

The industrialist must still begin the process by selling the commodities he has produced to the trader, C–M; and must also conclude the process by purchasing the raw material for a new production circuit from an intermediary trader, M–C'. Thus, for the industrialist, the complete form of the circuit continues to be that of commodity capital as exhibited in *Capital* Volume II: C–M–C'. The commercial capital circuit, however, obeys the general formula for capital, M–C–M', 'purchase to sell' (at a higher price). The first stage of the circuit, M–C, coincides with the initial stage C–M of the C–M–C' circuit, the sale made by the industrialist to the trader so that the latter can re-sell the commodities to the final consumer or to another industrialist in the next link of the production chain. The operation is thus marked by the connection that unifies and at the same time separates the forms of capital of these two groups, traders and producers. Although the processes of production and circulation are intertwined, the unfolding of the proprietorship and functions of the capital invested in each phase of the total process makes their autonomisation

2 Marx 2016, p. 379 [1993, p. 344].

feasible, with important consequences also for the explanation of the crises as will be seen below.

It is in the interests of the industrial capitalists, now practically circumscribed to production activities, to divide tasks with the traders only to the extent that doing so frees them to dedicate themselves to the production of commodities and the creation of surplus value, avoiding all the uncertainties of the sales process. The industrialists receive in advance from the traders the money capital that will be obtained by the sale and can then use it to purchase inputs that will enable the immediate renewal of the production of commodities. The traders are the ones who are left with the problem of selling and it is in their hands that the *commodity's death leap*[3] is performed or not. Thus, the industrialists interpose this part of the autonomised social capital between them and the final consumer and do not directly experience the pressure of an eventual drop in demand for their product. For them the sphere of creation and accumulation of surplus value seems to rotate *in moto perpetuo*, only interrupted when a prolonged crisis impedes the traders from continuing to purchase the commodities produced.

In general, the advantage of this division of tasks is so great that industrialists are disposed to share with traders part of the profits they would have received if they executed the entire production and sales circuit themselves. If the industrialists did so then the market price of their product would tend to be the same as the price of production, that is, the individual cost plus the average rate of profit. However, it is the trader who charges the market price and lives off the difference between that price and the price of production, recalculated on the basis of a profit rate which now has to take into account the gains of the commercial sector. Given that the trader's profit stems from this difference between the market price and the now lower production price, it seems to represent an increase in the price charged by the industrialist; it appears to result from a sly, sometimes fraudulent mercantile manoeuvre. Marx explains that for the trader:

> … in fact the *excess* of his *sale price* over his *purchase price* – and this difference forms the only source of his profit – must be an excess of its commercial price over its production price, and in the last analysis the merchant sells all commodities *above* their values.[4]

3 'Salto mortale', the expressive image in Marx 1976a, p. 200 [1991, p. 100].

4 Marx 2016, p. 392 [1993, p. 357].

Mercantile profit is yet another form of capital's fetishism this time resulting from the division of tasks between industrial capital and commercial capital. The price established by the trader seems to add excessively to the value the commodity has when it is produced; it appears to be arbitrarily greater than the price of production which, generally speaking, is mistaken for the value. The mechanisms of competition among capitalists and of equalisation of the rate of profit dissimulate the fact that the price of industrial production goes down to accommodate the slice of the profit that goes to the traders.

The system allows for it to be included but at the same time it gives the impression that the price of industrial production is the fair value of the commodity, so that while the industrialist seems to receive an appropriate gain for his activity, the trader appears to be taking advantage, proposing an exaggerated overpricing and living off abusive profits. The operation that enables the industrialist to extract surplus value from the worker is disguised and the profit appears as if it were the exclusive work of the trader with his haggling and sharp practices. Instead of the worker being exploited, it now appears that it is the consumer, in a real fetishist inversion that is at the base of contemporary legal tendencies whereby consumer rights take the place of the former labour rights now viewed as something that has been surpassed.

Indeed, that encounter with history at this stage of Marx's presentation is not by chance. A revealing passage in *Capital* Volume III manuscripts states that:

> In the course of scientific analysis, the formation of the *general rate of profit* appears to proceed from the productive capitals and the competition between them, being only later rectified, supplemented and modified by the intervention of mercantile capital. In the course of historical development, the situation is exactly the reverse.[5]

5 Marx 2016, p. 395 [1993, pp. 360–1]. The importance of form in 'scientific analysis' is explained in the following passage which comments on the order in which the items in the section on commercial capital in Volume III will be presented: '*How* he makes this profit is a question we shall go into only later. Here we want first of all to consider *just the form* [*bloße Form*] of his capital's movement'. (Marx 2016, p. 378 [1993, p. 343]). That means to say, before understanding the insertion of commercial capital in the equalisation of the industrial profit rates, or the way in which the trader 'makes this profit', it is necessary to understand the '*simple form*' of movement of his capital.

As on other occasions,[6] Marx makes it clear that the order in which the categories of the critique of political economy are presented does not have to correspond to the order in which they emerged and developed in the course of history. The presentation reconstitutes the articulations of social forms within a capitalist society sufficiently mature for the thread of such articulation to be apparent. In this case, industrial capital is the dominant form of modern surplus value extraction, and it subordinates the commercial capital form to its circuit and its mode of self-valorisation. Therefore, the creation of surplus value takes place in the production sphere by industrial capital and commercial capital participates in it only insofar as it is delegated the function of ensuring the circulation of commodities in which the surplus value is already contained. Commercial capital receives a part of this surplus value but does not produce it as it is dependent on industrial capital in whose orbit and logic it inscribes itself. As the text cited above states, the distribution of the surplus value seems 'to proceed from the productive capitals and the competition between them', and the competition with the commercial sphere is inserted 'only later' in exactly the same order as Marx planned for the presentation in *Capital* Volume III.

This 'only later', however, refers to the hierarchy of the social forms within the already constituted capitalism. Historically, commercial capital is far anterior to industrial capital: the way that trade creates surplus, buying cheap and selling dearer, is more ancient than the way surplus value is created in production based on paying the worker a wage with a lower value than the value of the commodities he produces. At a certain moment, however, the historical inversion takes place whereby the more ancient form bows to the later one in a turning that occurs in the social reality itself:

> Within the capitalist mode of Production, commercial capital is demoted [*herabgesetzt*] from its earlier separate existence to become a *particular moment* of capital investment in general, and the equalization of profits reduces its profit rate to the general average.[7]

6 For example, in the Introduction of 1857, Marx states that: 'It would therefore be unfeasible and wrong to let the economic categories follow one another in the same sequence as that in which they were historically decisive. Their sequence is determined, rather, by their relation to one another in modern bourgeois society, which is precisely the opposite of that which seems to be their natural order or which corresponds to historical development The point is not the historic position of the economic relations in the succession of different forms of society ... Rather, their order within modern bourgeois society'. (Marx 1974, pp. 107–8 [1976c, p. 42]).

7 Marx 2016, p. 432 [1993, p. 398].

The expression 'demoted ... to a particular moment', with obvious Hegelian resonance enables an understanding of the process described by Marx. Mercantile capital possessed a 'separate existence' prior to the development of industrial capital; afterwards it becomes a 'particular moment' of a far broader whole and it becomes one of the forms that industrial capital must take on in its social reproduction. The specific rate of profit of the mercantile sphere is equalised with the rate of profit of the production sphere by virtue of general competition and should the commercial sphere obtain higher profits the industrial capitalists might consider it more advantageous to sell the commodities they produce themselves and thereby reduce the importance of the group dedicated exclusively to trading. This is how equalisation subordinates commercial capital 'demoted ... to a particular moment' of industrial capital. It is only this logic and hence this form of recent existence of commercial capital that Marx needs to expound, not its historically anterior 'separate existence'. However, the autonomous form does not disappear altogether.

The group of capitalists to which developed capitalism delegates the commercial activity seems to be inheritor, through direct evolution, of the ancient merchant traders. The traders of today seem to be identical to the traders of every age, handling money, buying cheap and selling dear, negotiating, haggling over prices. Therefore, the profits they reap also seem to be identical with the profits that merchants have been reaping for a long time, an over-price considered to be exorbitant, the fruit of their business skills. This illusion arises from the fact that they constitute a special group, even within the reproduction of developed forms of industrial capitalism. Thus, that former 'separate existence' seems to be perpetuated in the present-day form even though their former autonomy was totally different from their current situation. It seems as if history had endured, proceeded without alteration from the former times to the present, hiding the preponderance of industrial capital and, consequently, concealing the fact that it is in the productive sphere that surplus values is obtained, by exploiting wage-earning labour.

In fact, however, the passage from one period to another, the commercial capital's loss of autonomy and the inversion of the importance of the two spheres are historically determined processes. The superiority of the exploitation of wage-earning labour with its corollary of technical progress and capital centralisation ends up imposing itself on the former forms of obtaining an economic surplus. In that regard Marx comments that: 'In the stages that preceded capitalist society, it was trade that prevailed over industry; in modern society it is the reverse'.[8] The difference between the historical periods is fun-

8 Marx 2016, p. 435 [1993, p. 403].

damental, but the way in which industry subordinates trade 'in modern society' still separates commercial profit from the profit of the producer, impeding any perception of the historical difference, that is, any perception that industry has come to 'prevail' over trade and determine the general rate of profit itself.

This movement is even more intense in the case of the second division of tasks which distinguishes a group of traders that is only involved in handling money and no longer commodities in general. Here 'the less developed Production is, the more monetary wealth is concentrated in the hands of merchants and appears in the specific form of mercantile wealth'.[9] In those social formations where the production of commodities has not yet constituted the sphere in which surplus value is generated, it is money 'in the hands of merchants', and not in those of the direct producers, that impels the trade in which economic surplus is created. The resulting 'concentration' confers great importance on money-handling to the point that exclusive functions are generated for it, independent of those it performs in trade as a whole. Marx deems the operations of payment and receipt in currency, accounting and cash compensation, as well as operations involving foreign currency exchange to be eminently 'technical'.[10] Not only does the passage to capitalism not annul the character of money-dealing capital assumed by the money 'concentrated in the hands' of its negotiators, on the contrary, it reinforces it. Although the latter function as mere cashiers for the commercial and industrial capitalists, the special condition that they enjoyed in the past projects itself as autonomy in the present.

In some of the 'stages that preceded capitalist society' as well as in the initial stages of bourgeois society the 'monetary wealth' of the money-dealers symbolised the power to create economic surplus. Once more, the way in which 'monetary wealth' is submitted to industrial capital in 'modern society' keeps up the appearance that nothing has changed and that the respective fortune constitutes capital as such. In addition to the aforementioned confusion regarding the origin of profit, a new mistake arises confusing the 'technical' functions of money-dealing capital with the credit functions of the interest-bearing capital, as I will explain in the second part of this Postface. By performing specific functions of the business with money, money-dealing capital, more than commercial commodities capital, mixes up social forms from different periods.

---

9 Marx 2016, p. 432 [1993, p. 397].

10 Marx 2016, pp. 422–4 [1993, pp. 388–90]. A few lines prior to that, Marx begins this fourth subchapter with the words: 'The purely *technical movements* that money undergoes in the circulation process of *productive capital* ... as the function of a *special* capital, which practices them, and them alone, as its specific operations, transforms this capital into *money-dealing capital*'. (Marx 2016, p. 387 [1993, p. 387]).

This is probably why Marx introduces his remarks on the history of commercial capital when he addresses the question of money-dealing capital. In the *1863–7 Manuscripts* that are the basis of Engels edition of *Capital* Volume III, the examination of commercial capital ends with the topic of money-dealing capital and includes historical references. In his edition, Engels unfolded the final topic to form a new and final chapter dedicated to 'Historical Material on Merchant's Capital'. Engels may have been inspired to do so by the fact that Marx himself had planned to end the chapter on interest-bearing capital with a topic he called *Vorbürgerliches* ('Pre-bourgeois'), that is, on interest in the times of 'Pre-Capitalist Relations'.[11] On creating chapter twenty, however, Engels exhibits the history on one side, separate from the money-dealing capital on the other. In that way he fails to capture the most distinct feature of money-dealing capital whose pre-capitalist autonomy is mistaken for the posterior form of traders' autonomy subordinated to production. Concentrated as 'monetary wealth' and representing capital in its own right, the dealer's money is yet another form in which the effective origin of surplus value in capitalism is kept hidden. The examination of that social form is the appropriate moment for raising some historical considerations because it synthesises and dissimulates the transition from a stage when 'trade prevailed over industry' to a 'modern' stage that inverts the relation between the two spheres. Lastly, money-dealing capital is addressed in the last topic in chapter four[12] of the *1863–7 Manuscripts* as a preamble to the following chapter on interest-bearing capital. It constitutes the most complex form of the fetishism of money prior to money's presenting itself as a commodity.

1.2 *Commercial Crisis*

Economic crises have frequently been called 'commercial crises'.[13] Marx registered various references in the press of his day and the British Parliament debates in which the theme is denominated and discussed under that heading. Sometimes, he even used the term himself,[14] but always in reference to a set of industrial and agricultural phenomena in which he included the acute

11 See in Marx 2016, topic 6 of the long chapter on interest-bearing capital that starts on page 693. The preceding chapter on commercial capital, however, ends with the fourth topic which addresses money-dealing capital, from pages. 421–43 [1993, p. 646 and pp. 387–410].

12 The *1863–7 Manuscripts* are organised in seven chapters which Engels later transformed into seven sections in his edition of *Capital* Volume III.

13 See, for example, two books published in Marx's time: Briaune 1840 and Juglar 1862.

14 See Marx 1976a, pp. 219, 236 (footnote 50), 353 (footnote 31) and 585 [1991, pp. 114, 127, 218 (footnote 64), 438. See also Marx 2016, pp. 610–11 [1993, pp. 572–3].

oscillations of the market. It is not by chance that most of the mentions of such crises appear in *Capital* Volume I in the ambit of commodity production, and that in *Capital* Volume III they only appear in the fifth Part associated to the cycle of credit for production and not in the fourth one, which concerns commercial capital itself. In Marx's view, even a sharp fall in the supply of raw materials that provokes a shortage for industry is never a problem whose origin lies in the trading conditions, but rather in the labour conditions in agriculture or mining.[15]

Nevertheless, the beginning of the fourth Part of *Capital* Volume III suggests just the opposite. Even though Marx does not use the term 'commercial' there to describe the crises, he does address the question of mismeasurement in the ambit of capital's mercantile form and does so without connecting the buying and selling difficulties to any problem in the spheres of production or credit. Indeed, he gives no explanation for the 'stoppage, an interruption in the reproduction' by paralysis of the market;[16] he merely cites examples, as if the supply crisis could occur due to random circumstances such as wars or climate setbacks. It is as if the crisis were a mere possibility of not being able to sell the product despite the intervention of the group of traders. In the explanations proffered in the fourth Part of *Capital* Volume III, the selling conditions seem to be identical to those when the sales are supposed to be effectuated by the direct producer; that is, they seem to be those of the simple circulation of commodities, as described in *Capital* Volume I, or those of the circuit of commodity capital described at the beginning of *Capital* Volume II.[17]

Capital Volume III, however, incorporates a crucial difference. While it does not alter the modal status of the crisis, the intermediation of sales by the trader increases the possibility of not selling. The industrialist distances himself from the problem when he transfers the task of selling the product to the trader,

---

15 This is the case with the analyses of the cotton shortages in the English textiles industry made in the chapter on machinery in *Capital* Volume I (Marx 1976a, pp. 575–88 [1991, pp. 402–413]) and in Volume III, of the effects of changes in prices of raw-materials on the rate of profit. Marx 2016, pp. 229–246 [1993, pp. 191–207].

16 Marx 2016, p. 379 [1993, p. 344]. A few lines before that, Marx says: 'Let us assume that the merchant does not succeed in selling his 30,000 ells in the interval that the linen producer takes before putting a further 30,000 ell on the market, at a value of £3,000'. (Marx 2016, p. 379 [1993, p. 344]). That possibility is maintained in the continuation of the text which adds that 'All this shows precisely that the commodity has not yet been definitely sold when it passes from the hands of the producer into those of the merchant …' (Marx 2016, p. 280 [1993, p. 345]).

17 Marx resumes the development of *Capital* Volume II at the beginning of chapter four of the *1863–7 Manuscripts*. See Marx 2016, pp. 367 and 389 [1993, pp. 341 and 354].

but it is precisely this distance that shatters the necessary unity of the measure of production and the measure of final consumption. Trade works as a shock absorber between market demand and product supply, thereby increasing the chance of crisis. The trader's capital:

> finds no barrier in production itself, or only a very elastic one, given the tremendous elasticity of the reproduction process, which can always be driven beyond any given barrier. Apart from the separation of C–M and M–C, which follows from the nature of the commodity, a *fictitious demand* is therefore created.[18]

First of all, it is interesting to note in the text the occurrence of the term 'fictitious' in the ambit of commercial capital before that of interest-bearing capital in which it is better known. In any event, it characterises the force of the real illusion in both cases. What Marx calls 'fictitious' here is the demand represented by the traders' orders placed with the industrialists according to the former consumers demand, which may have altered or come to be altered before the product is ready at some time in the future. These orders are based on a precarious, transitory measurement, imagined on the basis of a real situation, but one that may be obsolete. Again, the more commercial intermediaries there are between the producer and the final consumer, the more difficult it will be to get that measure right and the more readily a crisis will occur.

This miscalculation, this mismeasurement, to take up one of the central theses of *The Negative of Capital* is a mere possibility stemming from the 'separation of C–M and M–C, which follows from the nature of the commodity' and one that exists ever since the simple circulation described in *Capital* Volume I.[19] Even if the 'fictitious' element of this demand is boosted, as in the case when

---

18 Marx 2016, p. 411 [1993, p. 377]. In his edition of *Capital* Volume III Engels replaces the expression 'fictitious demand', that Marx used in the Manuscripts with 'active demand' (1981, p. 316 [1964, p. 419]). In this way an important meaning is lost, that was possibly present in the factory inspector's report quoted by Marx, which says: 'I fear that consignments of woollen goods often take the place of real demand, and that periods of *apparent prosperity*, i.e. of *full work*, are not always periods of legitimate demand'. (Marx 2016, p. 234 [1993, p. 196]). Instead of a 'real', 'legitimate demand', the sales 'consignments' merely create an 'apparent prosperity'.

19 *Capital* Volume III is explicit on this point: 'Because commercial capital is confined to the circulation sphere, and because its sole function is to mediate the exchange of commodities, no further conditions are needed for its existence ... than are necessary for the simple circulation of commodities and money'. (Marx 2016, p. 430 [1993, p. 396]). It could be said that there lies the reason why commercial capital is the first to appear in history.

traders conduct their sales and purchases using bills of exchange passed from hand to hand, that is, using money as a means of payment and not a means of circulation, the crisis continues to be only a possibility.[20] No doubt the destructive impact of the crisis increases, but the fact that one of the traders in the debt chain cannot manage to honour the bills he issued and originates a succession of defaults continues to be unexplained. Not even the development, by the banks, of the means of payment in the system of commercial credit and costing alters the crisis's modality, that is, makes it pass from being a contingency event to being a necessary one. It appears as if some unforeseen happening can impede a trader from selling and so, from paying his debt to other traders and the banks, unleashing an effect in series and some bankruptcies.

The continuation of the text on 'fictitious demand', however, inverts this initial direction. Marx concludes that 'despite the *autonomy it has acquired*, the movement of commercial capital is never anything more than the movement of productive capital within the sphere of circulation'.[21] In developed capitalism, commercial intermediation takes on the almost exclusive meaning of facilitating the reproduction of social capital, enabling productive capital to concentrate on its basic activity. This is the only reason why the industrialist accepts the idea of dividing the task and passing part of the surplus value to the trader so that the creation of surplus value can be guaranteed as the main objective of production. If that were not so, he would enter the sphere of circulation himself, impose his interests and monopolise the profit. Thus:

> Since commercial capital is nothing at all but the form in which a part of the productive capital functioning in the circulation process *has become autonomous*, all questions relating to it must be resolved in this way: the problem must at the outset be put in the form in which the phenomena peculiar to commercial capital do not yet appear independently but are still in direct connection with productive capital.[22]

20 This is apparent in the way *Capital* Volume III presents the hypothesis of a chain of traders connected by bills of exchange: 'If his money had circulated as means of payment, so that he only had to pay for it say six weeks after the receipt of the linen, then, if he had sold the linen before this time, he could have paid the linen producer without himself having to advance any money capital. If he had not sold the linen, he would have had to advance the £3,000 six weeks after the purchase, instead of immediately'. (Marx 2016, p. 480 [1993, p. 346]).

21 Marx 2016, p. 411 [1993, p. 377].

22 Marx 2016, p. 406 [1993, pp. 372–3].

Just like 'all questions relating' to trade, commercial crises cannot be understood 'independently' from productive capital. Commercial capital's subordinate role in social reproduction on an expanded scale is maintained also in cases of reduced scale of reproduction and crisis. It is the very conditions in which surplus value is generated that create the conditions in which the generation of surplus value suffers a blow; it is the production of commodities that defines how they will lose value, that is, how the valorisation will revert to devaluation of the existing capital. It is a manifestation of mismeasurement that has its foundation in the contradictory character of the relation between capital and wage-earning labour, based on which all the other cases of mismeasurement derive, each in its own particular form.

The same character defines the necessity of a crisis because capitalism's founding contradiction can only be resolved in a provisional manner when the tendency to accumulation, latent during the crisis, manifests itself once more. However, the modal status of commercial crisis, albeit inscribed in the greater range of necessity, persists as the typical possibility of the circulation of commodities. A problem that is merely commercial can only exert influence as it serves to trigger the eruption of profound problems rooted in the mode of production as such.

This does not mean commercial problems should be disdained. For it is Marx himself who highlights 'autonomy' in the penultimate text cited above and 'autonomous' form in the last one. Indeed, 'commercial capital is never anything more than the movement of productive capital within the sphere of circulation', but 'despite the *autonomy it has acquired*'; and 'commercial capital is nothing at all but ... a part of the productive capital functioning in the circulation process', but in an 'autonomous form'. Thus, the preponderance of the productive sphere over that of circulation does not invalidate the fact that the division of tasks among the parts of social capital goes on to the point where interests other than the original one appear and may even oppose to it. This is precisely the main aspect of the crisis at the presentation level of commercial capital. The excluding side of the relation between capital and wage-earning labour projects itself as a mutual exclusion of the forms of capital. Therefore, despite his proviso regarding the 'autonomy' of commercial capital in the penultimate text cited above, Marx continues by saying that:

> This inner dependence in combination with external autonomy drives commercial capital to a point where the *inner connection* is forcibly re-established by way of a crisis. This explains the phenomenon that crises do not first break out and are not first apparent in the retail trade, which

> has to do with immediate consumption, but rather in the sphere of wholesale trade (as well as *banking*) which places the money capital of the entire society at the wholesalers' disposal.[23]

In a concise and clear way, the text explains the complex relations between those two parts of capital. The preceding parts of the text stated that 'commercial capital is never anything more than the movement of productive capital within the sphere of circulation', that is, stated that both capitals are part of the totality of social capital. However, those parts also described commercial capital as being an autonomised form of the 'part of the productive capital' that escapes from the producer's direct control. Thus, on the one hand, industrial capital submits commercial capital to its orbit and its imperatives while on the other, the 'autonomous' commercial capital enables social reproduction to overcome its barriers. These opposing dimensions derive from the relations of commercial capital with industrial capital, depicted in the last of the texts cited above as being simultaneously 'inner dependence' and 'external autonomy'. The unity of those two forms of capital and the submission of the commercial form to the productive form is an internal determination, hidden by the external separation of the two capitals and the autonomy that trade acquires in the face of production.

In this context, crisis is defined as the violent way by which 'the inner connection is forcibly re-established' when the external autonomy gets to the point that it is impossible to carry on. Hence, the term 'external' designates, not the dissimulating appearance of an 'inner' truth but, instead, one of the sides of the opposition between productive and commercial capital. In fact, the circulation of money and commodities acquires independence from production insofar as it is handed over to a special group of capitalists. This independence, however, constitutes an 'external' side because it only exists if it is functional for the process as a whole, allowing the producer to dedicate himself to the creation of surplus value. That is why commercial capital is 'dependent' on a far broader framework that designates its role and takes on the nature of an internal dimension.

There is a remarkable similarity in the reasoning here with that which Marx used to explain the simpler form of a crisis in the metamorphosis of sale and purchase. In the manuscripts published after his death under the title of *Theories of Surplus Value*, he analyses how the 'the unity of two processes' manifests itself in the 'separation of these two phases and their becoming independ-

23 Marx 2016, p. 411 [1993, pp. 377–8].

ent of each other'.[24] In no way can separation and autonomisation progress indefinitely because they are the result of a relationship that unites the two processes, separating them. It is because purchase and sale, or commercial capital and productive capital are each determined by their bond with the opposing term, that their autonomy only exists within the sphere of this relationship. If autonomy goes too far, it ends up making its impossibility explicit and revealing the nexus that establishes it. As Marx says in the *Theories of Surplus Value*, it is 'the *crisis* in which they assert their unity, the unity of the different aspects'.

The argument is all the more forceful in the case of the relation between commercial and industrial capitals because, besides the opposition of the two terms, there is a subordination of one to the other, configuring a contradiction.[25] Insofar as it permits the external autonomy of the sphere of circulation in charge of commercial capitalists and at the same time imposes on that sphere an 'inner dependence' on its own interests, productive capital contradicts itself. Along very general terms: it excludes what it has included; it does not oppose any kind of other but opposes its own self. Purchase and sale have the same status in the sequence of 'selling to purchase' of the simple circulation of commodities and are therefore merely opposed. On the contrary, production and circulation have a different status in the reproduction of social capital: production must subordinate circulation and oppose it within that subordination which means to say, it must oppose its own self, contradict itself. Thus, while in the separation of sale and purchase two equivalent terms are involved, so that their separation is only a possibility, in the case of productive capital and commercial capital the separation mirrors an internal split in productive capital derived from the contradiction that constitutes it and which necessarily manifests itself in a crisis.

---

24 The complete text, cited in the first chapter of this book, is: '... purchase and sale – or the metamorphosis of commodities – present the unity of two processes, or rather the movement of one process through two opposite phases, and thus essentially the unity of the two phases, the movement is essentially just as much the separation of these two phases and their becoming independent of each other. Since, however, they belong together, the independence of the two correlated aspects can only *show itself* forcibly, as a destructive process. It is just the *crisis* in which they assert their unity, the unity of the different aspects. The independence which these two linked and complimentary phases assume in relation to each other is forcibly destroyed. Thus, the crisis manifests the unity of the two phases that have become independent to each other. There would be no crisis without this inner unity of factors that are apparently indifferent to each other'. (Marx 1969b, p. 500 [1982, p. 1123]).

25 Regarding the difference between 'opposition' and 'contradiction' as categories of Hegel's *Science of Logic* critically taken up by Marx, see chapter 2, section 3.1 above.

In other words, the conditions that determine the crisis in productive capital are what determine the violent emergence, not only of the 'inner connection' between commercial capital and productive capital, but also that of the general crisis. For this reason, Marx's text states that the first branch of commerce to be affected is the one closest to the producer, namely the wholesale trade and not 'the retail trade, which has to do with immediate consumption'. To Marx, the long chain of traders who pass the product from hand to hand to the final consumer has its weak point at the beginning, in the wholesaler, the first to buy from the producer and the one who receives the first impact of the fall in production. The retail trade is only affected at the end of the chain.

However, the observable phenomenon is quite the reverse. The crisis seems to begin in the retail market due to some kind of difficulty in sales and only later affects production. This is just one more form of the already examined 'fictitious demand' in which the mismatch between production and consumption increases with the multiplication of the number of intermediaries between the two spheres, but in which the measure that guides production presents itself as coming directly from consumption. Ultimately, it is just one more of those situations in which, as Marx puts it, 'This is how everything appears from the standpoint of competition: *falsely*'.[26] The competition among capitalists creates the fetishism of the market as the element that defines production and trade. Marked, as it is, by the 'fictitious demand', the real illusion implies not only the mismatch of measures but also the inversion of the sequence of the determinant spheres of the economy so that the consumer market, supposedly governed by the law of supply and demand, appears to be the decisive sphere for all the others, including the production sphere.

From the standpoint of modalities, *The Negative of Capital* explains that the main cause of the production crisis, the fall in the average rate of profit, is equivalent to a relative, not an absolute necessity. The same conditions that lead to the fall engender conditions capable of attenuating or even reverting it. Therefore, even within the production sphere, the occurrence of crisis, albeit they are the effectuation of a fundamental tendency, cannot be foreseen with precision in regard to their form and temporality. The autonomy of commercial capital reinforces this uncertainty and the relative character of crisis necessity. Tendencies and countertendencies must now also pass through the autonomised sphere of circulation to manifest themselves in the outbreak or the closure of a crisis period. Just as problems in production may not be reflected immediately in the final consumption, the resumption of production may take some time

26 Marx 2016, p. 845 [1993, p. 799].

before it can be felt in that ambit. More than that, if tendencies or counter-tendencies in production are very strong, they may possibly be alleviated and reversed along the length of the autonomous commercial chain so that crises or resumptions of accumulation may not even manifest themselves clearly.

Nevertheless, since the visible phenomenon is that crisis begins in the final market, the commercial sphere seems to be completely autonomous and decisive. A crisis would not appear to be necessary even in relative terms. Its eventual occurrence would merely be the effectuation of a possibility inherent to mercantile circulation, like the 'separation of C–M and M–C, which follows from the nature of the commodity', in the words of the first text cited in this item. There would be no subordination of commercial capital to productive capital and therefore, no contradiction, only opposition of two equivalent terms – sale and purchase – only the mere possibility of a crisis. Marx registers the social agents' perception of the crises as follows:

> With the regularity of a repetitive phenomenon we periodically experience in each crisis the constant reappearance of the verbiage in the parliamentary discourse, in the entities of the money market, assuring us that production is 'sound' but that suddenly it became 'unsound' by chance and due to commercial adventuring.[27]

The surprise of parliamentarians and 'entities of the money market'; the idea that a crisis emerges 'suddenly' from 'chance and commercial adventuring' without any connection to the ever 'sound' and solid production stems from the very way in which the spheres of production and circulation articulate with one another, with the autonomy of circulation on the external side and its dependence on production on the internal side. Even when the side of circulation's dependence imposes itself in a crisis, it can be negated or perceived in an inverted form as if production depended on circulation and not the other way around. This is certainly helped by the fact that, as explained in the preceding item, the limited autonomy of commercial capital within developed capitalism is mistaken for its former true autonomy in the 'stages that preceded capitalist society'. The way in which the profits of commercial capital are equalised

27 Marx 2008, p. 17. It seems that Engels did not make use of this text in his editing of *Capital* volume II. In the manuscript Marx added a footnote: 'Even Tooke in his *History of Prices*, which, generally speaking has its merits, resembles a war historian whose hero regularly loses battles but who always conducts the war in a "salutary" manner up until the moment he takes a beating. In that text there are allusions to crises that take on a specific form, the commercial crises'. (Marx 2008, p. 17). My translation.

to those of productive capital makes them appear as an addition to the profits of the production sphere and identical to the addition the merchants of old imposed on the costs and values considered to be legitimate.

When the speculation fostered by commercial credit banks are joined to the 'chances and adventures' accused of corrupting 'sound' production, then the 'fictitious demand' scheme is complete. Now, to the complications that the mercantile intermediation brings to the effectuation of the relative necessity of the crisis in the production sphere must be added the byways and deviations of bank-based financing. More than just creating conditions that relativise the necessity of a crisis they will bring about a complete reversal in the relationship between the 'inner dependence' and the 'external autonomy' of the parts into which social capital is divided, that is to say, in the necessity that presents itself as a simple possibility, 'chance event and adventure'. In the terrain of modalities, too, the increasingly complex forms of fetishism generate new determinations.

2 Interest-Bearing Capital and Its Crises

2.1 *Interest-Bearing Capital*

The development of money business associated to trading commodities in general led to the appearance of the most ancient form of interest-bearing capital, usury. The loan form requires, above all, a centralisation of the pecuniary proprietorship accumulated in the economy, placing at the disposal of a specific social group the means to facilitate or impede access to the social power represented by money. For this reason, the same money-dealers who already conducted payment operations in general, discounts of credit notes and foreign currency exchange are those who began to loan to those who needed to pay off debts or pay taxes, honour a promissory note or bill of exchange, or import or export commodities. In Marx's words:

> The development of usurer's capital is bound up with that of *merchant's capital* (and particularly with that of money-dealing capital) … We have already seen how hoard formation necessarily arises along with money. But the professional hoarder only becomes serious when he transforms himself into a usurer.[28]

28 Marx 2016, p. 693 [1993, p. 646]. In addition, Marx identifies an inverse relation between the mercantile social form and money: 'the less developed the character of the product as a commodity, the less exchange value has taken command of production in its whole

For a hoarder to accumulate 'seriously', he must be able to count on not only the money he saves but also the interest paid by third parties as supposed compensation for the hoarders not having spent it himself but loaned it. The emergence of the loan form requires, therefore, more than just the money to be hoarded. Marx explains that: 'with the development of trade, purchase and payment become separate in time',[29] so that money:

> in the form of *means of payment* ... emerges as the absolute form of the commodity. And it is particularly its function as means of payment that develops *interest*, and with it money capital.[30]

Thus, hoarding, the formation of stocks of money in the hands of certain merchants, and payment, the practice of reiterated exchanges of commodities which enables the distancing in time and space of the purchase and the reimbursement of the money due, create the historical conditions for defining the two social groups opposed by the loan mechanism, namely, those who offer and those who demand money.

With the division of tasks between these two groups, a new distribution of the economic surplus takes place effectuated by the interest by means of which the lenders take possession of a fairly considerable part of the trader's or producer's profit. In several text passages in *Capital*, Marx speaks of a 'division' [*Teilung*][31] between the two of the total profit or gross profit and even goes so far as to use the word 'split' [*Spaltung*][32] to characterise it more emphatically. Actually, in pre-capitalist times, the usurer's right could be charged in a brutal

breadth and depth, the more does *money* appear as wealth as such, wealth proper, wealth in general, as against its restricted form of appearance in use-values. *Hoard formation* depends on this'. (Marx 2016, p. 697 [1993, p. 650]).

29 Marx 2016, p. 698 [1993, p. 652].

30 Marx 2016, p. 697 [1993, pp. 650–1]. Regarding this point see also: 'Credit Money springs directly out of the function of money as a means of payment, in that certificates of debts owing for already purchased commodities themselves circulate for the purpose of transferring those debts to others. On the other hand, the function of Money as a means of payment undergoes expansion in proportion as the system of credit itself expands'. (Marx 1976a, p. 238 [1991, p. 129]).

31 The word 'division' appears as the title of the second topic of chapter five of the *1863–7 Manuscripts*, corresponding to chapter two of section five of *Capital* Volume III in Engels' edition. Afterwards it reappears in various passages, see, for example Marx 2016, pp. 460, 464, 472, 477, 483, 635 [1993, pp. 430, 433, 441, 446, 452, 596].

32 The word 'split' appears as the main title of chapter five of the *1863–7 Manuscripts* or the fifth section of *Capital* Volume III. It appears after that when Marx addresses the theme once more in the final part of the work dedicated to the 'Trinity Formula': Marx 2016,

manner both to the merchant and the direct producer according to the 'division' or 'split' between those social groups. Even afterwards, the 'division' takes on the aspect of a 'split' so that, following the path of the commercial capital in which it had its origin, interest-bearing capital presents itself as an autonomous form that seems to persist when it is submitted to the logic of industrial capital's valorisation. It is as if the modern banker were a parasite, just like the usurers of earlier times, piling his interest on top of the prices of the farmer and the manufacturer. What actually happens in capitalism, however, is something far more complex.

From a historical point of view, Marx states that '*the credit system* develops as a *reaction against usury*',[33] and not as an improved version of its practices. All the ruinous spoliation to which the usurer subjected trade and production until industrial capital came to predominate is inverted in functional form and organised by industry into a production credit 'system'. Marx continues, adding that 'the *banking system*, by its formal organisation and centralisation, is the most artificial and elaborate product brought into existence by the capitalist mode of production'.[34] Credit granted by banks is no longer an element external to production because it expands in accordance with the accumulation of productive capital and obtains its interest from the surplus value created in that sphere. This means that the total profit or gross profit has now to be shared into two parts, the interest due to those who lend the money capital and the net profit that remains with those who used that capital for production.

With regard to the articulation of the forms of sociability of the already constituted capitalism, the 'division' or 'split' separating profits and interest becomes a mode of operation of credit, autonomising a kind of task and a social group, but keeping both, task and group, harnessed to the valorisation logic. Although the concern of the money capital proprietor may oppose those of the entrepreneur, also called by Marx the 'functioning capitalist', it is the surplus value obtained by the latter that the former depends on to claim his share. Marx describes that general movement in this way:

> The owner of money who wants to valorise his money as interest-bearing capital, parts with it to someone else, puts it into circulation, makes it into a *commodity* as capital; as capital not only for himself but also for others.

pp. 896 and 889 [1993, pp. 851 and 899]. The English translation of the *1863–7 Manuscripts* translates both words as 'division' thereby effacing that remarkable difference between *Spaltung* and *Teilung*.

33 Marx 2016, p. 699 [1993, p. 652].

34 Marx 2016, p. 708 [1993, p. 661].

> It is not simply capital for the person who alienates it, but it is made over to the other person *as capital*, as *value* that possesses the *use-value* of creating surplus value, profit.[35]

Just like any other commodity, money has value and use value; except that, in its case, the use-value has a very specific meaning, that of 'creating surplus value, profit' for the industrial capitalist who invests it in production. When it is used to hire labour power, the lent money is realised as capital, a value that valorises itself and can then be distributed among the various branches of the system. The valorisation of money by its owner occurs when the 'other person' uses it to employ labour from which to extract economic surplus part of which will return into the hands of the original owner of the money in the form of interest.

Marx synthesises the process in his well-known formula: $M{-}\overbrace{M{-}C{-}M'}{-}M'$,[36] whose first movement M–M represents the loaning of the money and last one M'–M' the restitution of the loan money together with part of the surplus value in the form of interest M'. The indispensable investment in production M–C–M' lies between the two extremes and bracketed to call attention to its difference from the purely formal money movements at the two ends of the formula. However, it is the formal movement that is important for the lender of future capital, so that the process as a whole appears to him merely as M–M and M'–M', as if the part of the surplus value incorporated to the final M' had originated directly from the initial M, that is, the loaned money.

For Marx that *quid pro quo* implies the '*most externalised* and fetishised form'[37] of the capital relation whose nature, both real and illusory, it is necessary to understand.

To that end Marx begins by making a fundamental distinction:

> … the circumstances that determine the magnitude of the profit to be divided are very different from those that determine its distribution among those two kinds of capitalist, and often operate in completely opposite directions.[38]

35 Marx 2016, p. 449 [1993, p. 416].
36 Marx 2016, p. 446 [1993, p. 414].
37 Marx 2016, p. 492 [1993, p. 461].
38 Marx 2016, p. 463 [1993, p. 433].

While the 'magnitude of the profit' is based on conditions pertaining to the production sphere and is the result of the creation of surplus value by the real labour power that the entrepreneur puts to work, the 'division' of that profit into profit of enterprise and interest arises from the social form of property: the right of he who lends the future capital to a part of the returns provided by it derives exclusively from the title of ownership he holds. Unlike the division of profit into industrial profit and commercial profit, the division between interest and profit of enterprise rests only on a contract, a legal relationship.

Moreover, it is not a case of a mere division of the profit into various parts. Marx does not call the interest-bearing capital the 'most fetishised' form of capital because the autonomisation of the interest simply conceals its dependence on profit, he does so because the relation is inverted, and it appears as if the profit depends on the interest; that the profit is deducted from the interest. The conditions that 'determine its distribution' present themselves as those that 'determine the magnitude', the conditions that determine the production of the 'profit to be divided'. The complete form of fetishism that culminate in the Trinity Formula with which *Capital* Volume III closes consists precisely in this inversion of the principle of distribution of surplus value into the principle of production of surplus value. It is, however, with the interest-bearing capital that this *quid pro quo* experiences its decisive moment.

Going beyond the perspective of the economic agent, an aspect that could be called ideological, Marx describes a series of economic practices that sustain the inversion of the distributive principle into a production principle. The first practice concerns the legal relationship mentioned above: the fact that the right to receive interest rests on a legal contract requires that whoever borrowed money must comply with its terms, irrespective of whether the use made of the loan money was capable of creating surplus value or not. Although the entrepreneur can only pay interest with the surplus value obtained, he must pay it even before accounting for his own profit of enterprise. The second practice is based on the fact that in the money-form, capital is susceptible to a much faster and more intense centralisation on the part of the credit institutions. In the universal form of value, capital appears as an 'overall mass' compared to the industrial capital dispersed among raw materials and various types of equipment.[39] In this form of credit money, capital acquires greater force and social

39 The *1863–1867 Manuscripts* text say: '... because on the money market all loanable capital confronts functioning capital as an *overall mass* ... This is all the more true, the more the development and associated concentration of the *credit system* gives loanable capital a *general social character*'. (Marx 2016, p. 469 [1993, p. 438]).

impact than it does in the form of productive capital. The third practice follows from the fact that the interest rate fixed in the money market as a price has a patent and palpable aspect, despite its eventual fluctuations, whereas the '*general rate of profit* itself simply *appears* ... not as an empirical form of the actual profit rate'.[40] In other words, in contrast with the interest rate that the credit system establishes for all to see, the average rate of profit resulting from the equalisation of each capitalist's individual rates of profit is merely a guideline for the constantly changing individual profits and not an exact number. In that light Marx concludes that 'the general rate of profit in fact *appears* therefore as an empirical fact in the *average rate of interest*, although the latter is not a pure and reliable expression of the former'.[41]

These forms of effective economic practice explain why interest appears to be the legitimate remuneration for capital and profit appears to be a form derived from it. Interest is fixed by the credit institutions that centralise the 'overall mass' of social money; it seems to be independent of the vagaries of the effective production of commodities and surplus value and emerges as a given magnitude in the face of the ever-changing and uncertain average rate of profit. Thus, the conversion of the distributive principle in production principle is effectuated by the inversion of the nexus between the source of revenue and its division:

> *Capital – profit* (profit of enterprise plus interest) ... Since it is *interest*, as shown already, that appears as the specific and characteristic product of capital, with profit of enterprise appearing in contrast to this as a wage independent of capital, this first trinity form can be reduced to a more precise expression: *Capital – interest* ... where profit, the form of surplus value specifically characteristic of the capitalist mode of production, is fortunately set aside, removed from the scene, reduced to nothing.[42]

The profit of enterprise presents itself as what was left to the functioning capitalist after paying what was due to the one who would be the authentic capitalist, namely, the owner of money. It is as if this owner was the capitalist as such and the entrepreneur, in opposition to him, were a mere worker receiving a 'wage independent of capital'; that is, as if the profit of enterprise were a salary thereby placing the industrial capitalist alongside the workers he exploits. He

40 Marx 2016, p. 470 [1993, p. 440].

41 Marx 2016, pp. 468–9 [1993, p. 438]. For a more detailed discussion of those practices, see Grespan 2019.

42 Marx 2016, p. 888 [1993, p. 840].

actually thinks he is a member of the so-called producing class fighting against the abusive interest rates charged by the 'capitalist' who provides credit.

Thus, the formula 'capital – profit' transforms into the formula 'capital – interest' so that profit passes to a second plane and with it goes the surplus value 'specifically characteristic of the capitalist mode of production'. 'Fortunately' for the system, any vestige of exploitation of the labour, now situated alongside the entrepreneur in the production line, is 'set aside'. While in the Trinity Formula the relationship among the three sources and their revenues is, as we know, 'land – rent', 'labour – wages' and 'capital – profit', the passage from 'capital – profit' to 'capital – interest' removes the profit of enterprise from the 'capital' category to that of 'labour'. 'Capital' is now exclusively associated with interest, credit and money, and not with production and the labour exploited by the entrepreneur. Therefore, Marx declares that capital seeks to define itself not in opposition to labour 'but quite the reverse, with no relationship to labour at all, merely as a relationship between one capitalist and another'.[43] It would seem that '*Interest*, then, is the *net profit* yielded by property in capital as such'.[44] Indeed, interest emerges as the decisive variable because it stems from 'property in capital as such', and not from the performance of the entrepreneur.

As already stated, the inversion described by Marx is based on real economic practices that superimpose interest on the profit obtained by capital, so that:

> the question that now arises is this. How does this *purely quantitative division of profit into gross*[45] *profit and interest* turn into a *qualitative* distinction? In other words, how does it happen that even the capitalist who simply uses his own capital, and no borrowed capital, classes part of his gross profit under the special category of interest and takes particular account of it as such? And how, therefore, does it subsequently happen that *all* capital, whether borrowed or not, *distinguished* as *interest-bearing capital* from itself in its function as capital bringing a gross profit?[46]

43 Marx 2016, p. 484 [1993, p. 453].

44 Marx 2016, p. 481 [1993, p. 450]. In the final part of the *1863–7 Manuscripts*, Marx explains that: 'The division of profit into profit of enterprise and interest ... completes the autonomisation of the *form* of surplus value, the ossification of its form as against its substance, its essence. One portion of profit, in contrast to the other, separates itself completely from the capital-relation as such and presents itself as deriving not from the function of exploiting wage-labour (which is naturally inseparable from the activity of management), but rather from the wage-labour of the capitalist himself. As against this, interest then seems independent both of the wage-labour of the worker and of the capitalist's own labour'. (Marx 2016, p. 896 [1993, p. 851]).

45 Here, Engels corrected: 'net'.

46 Marx 2016, p. 474 [1993, p. 443].

The answer to these questions must begin by remembering that the contractual obligation to pay interest established so radically the practice of calculating part of the profits as fair reward for the loaning of capital, that all capital came to be considered in that way. Even when making use of his own capital, the entrepreneur would label 'part of his gross profit under the special category of interest', confusing interest-bearing capital with capital 'bringing a gross profit'. However, apart from this first answer, Marx presents a deeper reason for the transformation of the 'quantitative division of profit' into a '*qualitative*' division that redefines the very concept of capital.

In this second answer, once more two opposing totalities are in play just as in the case of substance and form, or of labour and capital, analysed in chapter 2, section 3.1. The substantial totality is made up of the gross profit or rather, the surplus value that the functioning capitalist extracts from the labour power. It is from the value produced by the labour-substance that the interest will be earned, and the profit of enterprise appropriated. Interest-bearing capital, however, also claims to compose a totality as if interest were a 'characteristic product of capital'. The first totality is 'substantial' because it refers to the labour and the surplus value without which interest could not, in the final analysis, be paid; the second is 'formal' because it is based on the entrepreneur's contractual commitment with the credit agent, irrespective of value's having been created and commodities produced, or not. According to the substantial totality, M–C–M' should subordinate the M–M at the beginning and the M'–M' at the end of the complete circuit of capital; but according to the formal totality, it is the credit represented by the M–M at the beginning of the circuit and the M'–M' at its end that is the dominant aspect of the process as a whole, inscribing within itself the M–C–M' of immediate production. For this reason, formality corresponds to the '*most externalised* and fetishized form' of capital relation.

Imposing M–M … M'–M' on M–C–M', that is, on production, is the economic practice by whose force interest-bearing capital endeavours to encompass industrial capital and compose a whole within which profit becomes a secondary form and surplus value disappears from view altogether. The formal totality opposes the substantial totality, thus lowering the latter to the condition of a mere stage or unessential aspect. It replaces profit with interest from which the profit of enterprise would be just a derivative or appendix. It presents the relationship of one individual capital to another as being more important than the opposition of capital to labour. Hence, the subordination of labour power to property, as capitalism's organising directive, is completed and disappears in the inversion of the principle of surplus value distribution into the principle of its creation. The legitimacy that this enormous *quid pro quo* acquires in the eyes of the economic agents originates from the fact that it represents the culmination of a series of practices, beginning with use of money in simple commodity exchanges and getting to the point where credit becomes the crucial means for conducting business and economic life.

Only a crisis would be capable of shaking this formal totality and exposing the substantial side that it conceals in its shadow. However, even in times of crisis, the mechanisms of real illusion are activated to continue concealing the sphere of productive capital and the exploitation of labour-power. Given that interest now takes the place of profit and surplus value through the fetishist inversion of interest-bearing capital and industrial capital, the financial appearance of the crisis seems to define the crisis in its entirety, as if it were its essence or at least the situation that triggers it. The capacity of this '*most* fetishized form' of capital relation to impose that real illusion will depend, in each case, on the intensity of the crisis itself.

2.2 *Financial Crisis*

The reference to crises related to interest-bearing capital occurs in the most fragmented part of the *1863–7 Manuscripts* consisting of Marx's notes on long quotations from texts of economists and minutes of the English parliament. This circumstance makes it difficult to conduct a systematic treatment of the crises called by Marx monetary crises and credit crises and, furthermore, has given rise to a multiplication of contrasting and unilateral interpretations among his commentators. Indeed, starting towards the end of the twentieth century and with the crisis of 2008, the idea was disseminated that financial dominance of contemporary capitalism would also mark the present-day crisis and define its nature.

In *The Negative of Capital*, however, I insist that, for Marx, the origin of crises can always be found in the movement of devaluation of productive capital. Already in *Capital* Volume 1 he states that:

> The superficiality of political economy shows itself in the fact that it views the expansion and contraction of credit as the cause of the periodic alternations in the industrial cycle, whereas it is a mere symptom of them.[47]

Leaving the discussion of the specific problem of industrial cycles and credit cycles for later on, it must be underscored here that in the cited text the 'expansion and contraction of credit' are 'symptoms' and not 'cause' of the industry

47 Marx 1976a, p. 786 [1991, p. 568].

movements. As is stated in my analysis in chapter 4, section 3.1 of *The Negative of Capital*, the crises that punctuate these movements have their origin in the irruption of capital's tendency to mismeasurement, that is, the incapacity of the valorisation process to measure and guide the continuity of the production process. It is the phenomenon of over-accumulation of capital which occurs when accumulation reaches a point at which any new investment of constant or variable capital would lead to a sudden drop in the average rate of profit.

Marx addresses the issue in chapter three of the manuscripts that would serve as the base for *Capital* Volume III according to his plan for categorial presentation: the impulses to valorisation or devaluation of capital have their roots in the production sphere itself, prior to appearing in the spheres of trade or of credit presented in chapters four and five of that work. Marx says that in the first phase of a crisis:

> part of the commodities on the market can complete their process of circulation and reproduction only by an immense reduction in their prices, i.e., a depreciation of the capital they present. The value of the fixed capital suffers more or less the same depreciation.

The text goes on to explain how it is only after the devaluation of the commodities brought about by the devaluation of the capital that:

> This disturbance and stagnation is made more acute by the development of money as a means of payment … and by the chain of payment obligations at specific dates. It is sharpened still further by the credit system which has also developed at the same time and the whole thing leads to severe crisis, sudden losses of value, actual stagnation and disruption in the reproduction process, and hence an *actual decline in reproduction*.[48]

Above all, the crisis consists of a 'disturbance and stagnation' that devalues products and capital and only later in the severing of the 'chain of payment' between producers and traders that culminates in the bankruptcy of the credit system. From this point on, 'the stagnation in production that has occurred increases the need for an expansion of production, within the limits set by capitalism'.[49] Accumulation tends to be resumed but always through the actions of

48 Marx 2016, p. 363 [1993, p. 328].
49 Marx 2016, p. 364 [1993, p. 329].

elements of the production sphere such as re-hiring labour at lower wages and the incorporation of constant capital with new technology.

The credit system is affected when the difficulty to produce commodities at a rate of profit that can ensure the reproduction of social capital and the valorisation of value prevents entrepreneurs to pay the interest due. They only do so constrained by contract, and then find the portion left to them with which to invest greatly reduced as well as the possibility of taking out new loans. The system is thus shaken as much at the end point represented by the reimbursement of the interest M'–M' as at the beginning of new loans M–M. At that moment, in the terms examined in the preceding item of this postface, the property of a title of right to a part of the surplus value, the principle on which the interest-bearing capital is founded, appears as a form that no longer corresponds to a substance, for the producers no longer manage to produce value and surplus value to the extent they did before. The totality that credit seeks to compose by encompassing production is no longer sustained, and the 'substantial' aspect of labour and surplus value imposes its reality on the merely 'formal' valorisation represented by interest.

In spite of all this, but also because of it, Marx explains that the phenomenon appears in an inverted form:

> It is self-evident that when the whole process rests on credit, a credit crisis, involving a lack of the means of payment, must break out if credit is withdrawn and only cash payment is accepted. The entire crisis must therefore present itself on the face of it [*prima facie*] as a crisis of credit and money.[50]

If the devaluation of capital is not sufficiently profound to reveal itself as over-accumulation of productive capital, then what persists is the formal totality intended by interest-bearing capital, that is, the appearance that 'the whole process rests on credit'; then the crisis arising from the excess of industrial capital 'presents itself *prima facie* as a crisis of credit and money', because the devaluation seems to come from the 'lack of the means of payment'.

This power of fetishist inversion of interest-bearing capital, the culmination of the fetishism of capital, develops through successive stages of dominance of the substance of value: the crisis appears to be a 'crisis of credit and money' and eventually appears as a crisis generated by financial speculation in which the determinant factor would be the risk taken by investors or the bad faith of man-

---

50 Marx 2016, p. 580 [1993, p. 543].

agers handling other people's capital. Throughout these stages, form gradually imposes itself on the substance of value, but always as an attempt to solve the problem of the recurrent mismeasurement, that is, to solve the failure to attune form to substance of value. In all cases, the decisive variable is the relation between rate of profit and rate of interest because it is the fall in profit that adjusts the fetishist illusion of credit and speculation to the limits of the value actually produced.

However, since the initial stage of credit, the relation between the rate of profit and the rate of interest is complex and articulated in two moments carefully distinguished by Marx. Before constituting an activity associated with banks to compose what Marx calls the 'banker's credit' system, the circulation of means of payment takes place among producers themselves and among producers and traders, defining a system of 'commercial credit'. In Marx's words:

> Commercial credit (i.e., the credit that capitalists involved in the reproduction process give each other) forms the basis of the *credit system*. Its representative is the *bill of exchange*, a promissory note or document of deferred payment. Each person gives credit with one hand and receives credit with the other hand. We shall start by completely ignoring *banker's credit*, which is an entirely separate and essentially different moment.[51]

Bankers' credit is based on the commercial system but 'essentially' separated from it because it forms a 'different moment', another level of activity constituted by the banks' mediation of the emission and circulation of bills of exchange among 'capitalists involved in the reproduction process'. Marx's conclusion is that:

> In fact one party lends another the money that he needs in the reproduction process. But this takes the form that the *banker* lends the money to the reproductive agents ... It is also an expression of the fact that disposal over this capital passes entirely into the hands of the bankers as intermediaries.[52]

The banker starts off as a simple 'intermediary' in the circulation of bills of exchange among the 'reproductive agents', that is, those involved in the activities of producing and trading commodities, but he soon comes to centralise the

51 Marx 2016, p. 572 [1993, p. 535].
52 Marx 2016, p. 623 [1993, pp. 584–5].

'disposal' of money capital in general, so that all the transit of bills of exchange and other negotiable instruments and mutual payments formerly undertaken by the commercial credit system pass through his hands. When this centralisation reaches a very high level it 'takes the form that the *banker* lends ... to the reproductive agents' the money retrieved from the bills of exchange and payment of debts due. In this way, the relation between commercial credit and banker's credit is inverted: it is no longer the circulation of bills of exchange between producers and traders that appear as 'the basis' of the system, but, instead, the mediation of the banks, which now lend to the capitalist the money with which to issue and honour the bills of exchange he needs. Bank credit now 'takes the form' of or presents itself as the basis of commercial credit. From then on, the growth and centralisation of the banking system itself makes productive capital increasingly dependent on the interest-bearing capital in an inversion typical of fetishism as a *real* illusion.

Nevertheless, in times of crisis the difference between commercial credit and bank credit is fundamental, for in each of the systems the relation between the rate of profit and the rate of interest is different. Marx explains that in 'the basis' of commercial credit 'by and large, therefore, the movement of moneyed capital (as expressed in the rate of interest) runs in the opposite direction to that of productive capital',[53] because credit dispenses with the banks' money supply and takes place directly among producers. Thus, whenever production expands, the increase in the rate of profit corresponds to the fluidity in the circulation of bills of exchange; producers are confident that the bill they receive will be paid at the end of the chain of mutual obligations, so that their demand for money to quit debt commitments is low and, accordingly, the rate of interest is low too. Marx insists that, in its turn, 'the rate of interest reaches its highest level during crisis, when people have to borrow in order to pay, no matter what the cost',[54] due to the rupture of the chain of payments which forces the demand for money up. The fall in the rate of profit now corresponds to the rise in the rate of interest charged by those who lend the money.

The domination of the credit system by banks, however, inverts that situation. With the exception of the actual moment when the crisis breaks out, when the sudden fall in the rate of profit also corresponds to an increase in the demand for money and with that, an increase in the rate of interest, the relation between the rate of profit and the rate of interest becomes a direct one. In times of expansion, the high rate of profit corresponds to a rate of interest that

53 Marx 2016, p. 579 [1993, p. 542]; my italics.

54 Marx 2016, p. 464 [1993, p. 434].

is also high due to the producer's greater demand for money from the banks for investment and working capital; in the times following a crisis, to the low rate of profit corresponds an equally low rate of interest, mirroring the producers' lower demand for bank money for their investment and working capital. Therefore, banks tend to take advantage of the general increase in profits to raise the part of surplus value to which they are entitled by contract and are only forced to reduce it when profits and surplus value remain stagnant after the peak of the crisis.

In the case of bank credit, this movement in the same direction on the part of the two rates contributes to making the interest seem to be the authentic remuneration for capital, taking the place of the profit obtained from the exploitation of labour power, as we saw in the preceding item, because it is not the industrial capitalist who appears to own the capital but, instead, the one who granted him a loan to start producing. The banker takes command of the process by creating financing mechanisms that make the producers less vulnerable to possible losses or delays in selling their commodities. Such mechanisms, however, also lead to serious problems should a crisis break out. In Marx's words:

> On the other hand, however, the situation is so much complicated by bill-jobbing, and by the sale of commodities simply in order to be able to draw bills of exchange, that the appearance of a very solid business with brisk returns can persist for a while even when the returns have in actual fact long been made at the expense of swindled money-lenders and swindled producers. This is why business always seems almost exaggeratedly healthy immediately before a crash.[55]

Banks now handle the bills of exchange and provide the bulk of the money advanced to producers for their investments. Thus, the 'returns' that the sale of products brings for their producers, enabling them to pay off their debts to the banks, seems to have been guaranteed by the earlier advance given by the banks themselves, that is, by the 'moneylenders'. If there is a drop in product sales, the credit system can 'crash' just as in the case of commercial credit, only that it takes longer to occur and to be perceived, a delay caused precisely by those bank money advances, whose flow may even continue for some time regardless of the effective 'returns' of the money. A drop in sales, felt immediately by commercial credit, is only perceived with some delay by bank credit

55 Marx 2016, p. 577 [1993, p. 540].

and usually when it is too late to avoid a crisis. In that regard Marx says: 'this is why business always seems almost exaggeratedly healthy immediately before a crash', surprising bankers, businessmen and economists, all of them dazzled by the fluidity propitiated by credit.

The interval that separates the effective 'returns' on investments and the continuous flow of bank advances creates a gap in which the domination of the substance of value by the form of value becomes even more sophisticated: the speculation. Marx locates the origin of speculation in credit because what credit makes possible is:

> *Acceleration, through credit,* of the various phases of circulation or commodity, then an acceleration of the metamorphosis of capital and hence an acceleration of the overall reproduction process. (On the other hand, credit also allows the acts of buying and selling to take a longer time, and hence serves as a basis for speculation).[56]

It is interesting to note how the speculation returns and responds to the simplest form of the crisis in the circulation of commodities, which consists in the spatial and temporal separation of purchase and sale, and adds to it the more complex forms of the commercial game of selling at a higher price than that for which the commodity was purchased, and the bankers betting on financing production to gain the right to appropriate part of it in the form of interest. The speculator makes money by betting on the uncertainties of business, an uncertainty that expands with the growth of the markets, and on the difficulty to forecast the future value of a commodity purchased or produced in the present. Then he begins to play with uncertainty itself, running the risk of a valorisation or a devaluation of capital or investment. From there it is just a small step to forecasting future values on the basis of the present one.

The well-known concept involved here is that of 'fictitious capital' which Marx closely associates with speculation as one of the more advanced stages of the imposition of formal totality on the substance of value. The concept appears in the *1863–7 Manuscripts* in formulations like the one I reproduce here:

> The formation [*Bildung*] of *fictitious capital* is known as *capitalisation* ... For example, if the annual income in question is £100 and the rate of interest is 5 percent, £100 would be the annual interest on £2,000, and

56 Marx 2016, p. 536 [1993, p. 501].

> this imagined [*eingebildet*] £2,000 is then taken as the *capital value* of the legal title (the title of ownership) to the annual £100. For the person who buys this title of ownership, the annual income of £100 does actually represent conversion of the capital he has invested at 5 percent. In this way, all connection with capital's actual process of valorisation is lost, right down to the last trace, confirming the notion that capital automatically valorizes itself.[57]

In Marx's example, what the proprietor of a contract that gives him the right to the future value of a commodity this will be produced or sold has in his hands is a simple forecast of that value. The forecast of the value is regulated by the interest rate with which the credit system remunerates the set of applications of their clients and that constitutes a basis for comparison of the yields of all the possible financial and speculative gains there could possibly be. If, following the example, this interest rate of five percent were to go up to ten percent, then the future value of the asset that the speculator holds the right to falls from two thousand to one thousand pounds sterling; if, on the other hand, it falls from five to two and a half percent, the future value goes up from two to four thousand pounds sterling. It is essential to perceive, in this case, that the future value basically depends on the fluctuations in the interest rate; it is always fixed in a provisional manner because the commodity it corresponds to may not even exist or come to be produced.

The meaning of 'fictitious' in the description of this kind of capital is quite clear in the words Marx uses in the original text cited above: this capital is 'formed' by being 'imagined'. These words announce that this capital is constituted by a value that is merely foreseen and conditional. By means of a fictitious valorisation process, according to the text, 'connection with capital's actual process of valorisation is lost, right down to the last trace'. Fictitious capital breaks off the 'connection' that even the monetary advances provided by bank credit still keep up with effective valorisation. While this credit depends ultimately on the returns obtained from the sale of the commodities produced, for fictitious capital only the reference to the rate of interest regulated by contract matters. In this respect, it is like an automaton that valorises on its own account; a 'representation' that consummates capital's pretension to autonomy from labour power, that is, the domination of substance by form.

57 Marx 2016, p. 558 [1993, p. 522].

In the system that develops from there, it is possible to accentuate both the elements of representation and fiction and those related to gambling and manipulation. On this point, however, speculation is in no way contrary to capitalist production. Marx underscores that:

> The credit system has a … character immanent in it … it develops the driving force of the capitalist mode of production, enrichment by the exploitation of other people's labour, into the purest and most colossal system of swindling and gambling.[58]

Ever since the simplest forms of its existence, capitalism has consisted of being a mode of 'enrichment by the exploitation of other people's labour' based on snatching the means of production away from the hands of the worker. The relation of one capitalist with another in industrial competition and then in the dispute of productive capital with commercial capital and interest-bearing capital for their shares of surplus value, represents a mere exteriorisation of the constitutive stripping of labour power, that is, of the primary negativity of labour power by capital. The 'exploitation of other people's labour' and its fruits does nothing but accentuate itself by composing the 'colossal system of swindling and gambling' that characterises speculation.

However, the swindle transformed into a 'system' shifts the problem of the crisis to the terrain of bad faith. When, Marx says, 'an immense quantity' of financial instruments 'represent purely fraudulent transactions, which now come to light and are exploded; as well as unsuccessful speculations conducted with other people's capital',[59] then it appears that the 'explosion' is some kind of punishment for the dishonesty of some interest-bearing capital dealers, a well-deserved retribution for the impudence with which they abused 'other people's capital'. On being attributed to speculation, the crisis appears to be merely a moral or subjective problem, a case of corruption which, if duly punished and corrected would make it possible for the mode of production to resume what was considered to be its normal healthy functioning. I will return to this issue later on in this postface.

In any event, the sequence of stages by which the form of value endeavours to gradually impose itself on its substance cannot be considered just a simple illusion. Capital's fetishism, even in its simplest configurations, always corresponds to real illusion processes because, while form is managing to impose

58 Marx 2016, p. 540 [1993, p. 505].

59 Marx 2016, p. 580 [1993, p. 543].

itself and cunningly avoid any manifestation of its contradictory nucleus, capital is creating values and use-values. Therefore, Marx states that:

> The credit system accelerates the material development of the productive forces and the creation of the world market … At the same time, credit accelerates the violent outbreaks of this contradiction, crisis, and with these elements of dissolution of the old mode of production.[60]

As long as the real illusion is in play, the fetishism of credit boosts the expansion of productive capital as a form suited to the substance. Even speculation cannot be viewed through a simple moral prism alone but rather in the light of the function it performs within the system, especially when the reproduction of capital needs to reinforce the negative traits that sustain it and guarantee its survival, namely, 'enrichment by the exploitation of other people's labour'. Nevertheless, illusion and reality split apart when a 'violent outbreak of the contradiction' between capital and labour occurs, that is, when the discovery occurs that form does not correspond to substance but imposes itself on it as a forgery. Crises, to some extent avoided or postponed by credit, manifest themselves in it with all the impetus of a repressed and held force that is suddenly liberated, but which credit and all the other instruments of the real illusion tried to control and overcome.

2.3 *The Modality of Financial Crisis*

After having stated that economic crises present themselves as credit crises and monetary crises, at a certain moment in the fifth chapter of the *1863–7 Manuscripts*, Marx insistently raises a question that reveals the other side of the bond between crises in the production sphere and in the monetary sphere. He asks:

> is the phenomenon of the so-called *plethora of capital*, an expression used only of moneyed capital, simply a particular expression of *overproduction*, or does it form a separate phenomenon alongside this?[61]

---

60 Marx 2016, p. 539 [1993, p. 505].

61 Marx 2016, p. 565 [1993, p. 529]. In the *1863–7 Manuscripts* the expression 'monied capital' appears in English, referring to the money capital that the banks have at their disposal for making loans. In his edition of *Capital* Volume III, Engels translates the English phrase into German as *Verleihbares Kapital*, which means capital for loaning, always in the form of money.

The question itself suggests the possibility that excess of moneyed capital is something different from an excess of productive capital. It could be that the 'plethora of capital', which refers to the 'monied capital', is not just a particular manner of overproduction but, instead, an independently determined phenomenon.

In principle, that possibility does not exist or is attenuated due to the close relations between the industrial cycle and the movements in the money and credit markets. Marx's answer to his own question would be that the excess of money placed at the disposal of the banks and credit agencies is nothing more than 'a particular expression of overproduction' on the part of industrial capital. Indeed, Marx explains that during the phase of production expansion, there is equilibrium between the industrialists' money deposits in banks and the loans that these industrialists request and receive, not only to conduct their businesses but also to invest in their further expansion. They purchase new equipment and hire more workers to satisfy capital's dominant drive to uninterrupted accumulation. The unbalance between money deposits and loans taken by industrialists only occurs with a crisis of overproduction when a lasting fall in rate of profit leads to an increase in deposits for lack of profitable investment opportunities. Marx explains how, in this situation, profit

> is transformed into *monied capital* only if it cannot be directly used to expand business in the sphere of production in which the profit has been made. This can happen for two reasons: either because this sphere is saturated and no more capital is required; or because before it can function as capital, the accumulation must first attain a certain volume, determined by the appropriate proportions for the investment of new capital in this particular business. It is therefore firstly transformed into *moneyed capital* and serves to expand production in other spheres.[62]

In the first case, the excess of accumulation in a certain branch of industry means that the profit cannot be invested in the same branch without making the rate of profit fall even more. This branch 'is saturated and no more capital is required' to produce in a profitable manner. Therefore, the capitalists operating in that branch stop requesting bank loans, albeit they continue depositing the profits that they still obtain and, in that way, contribute to the 'plethora of moneyed capital'. The second possibility for this 'plethora' is that the scale of production 'to expand business' in the chosen branch is too high, forcing capit-

62 Marx 2016, p. 624 [1993, pp. 585–6].

alists to deposit in banks, as capital funds, the profit obtained in another branch until such time as they can complete the volume needed for the investment. In this second case suggested by Marx, banks can count on more resources to lend to their clients in general. They manage funds that can serve 'to expand production in other spheres', but in the meanwhile they help to form the 'plethora of moneyed capital'. The text continues, with a warning:

> But if this new accumulation comes up against difficulties in its application, owing to a lack of spheres of employment ... this *plethora of moneyed capital* proves nothing more than the *barriers of the capitalist production process*. The resulting credit swindles demonstrate that there is no *positive* obstacle to the employment of this surplus capital, but rather an obstacle set up by its own *laws of valorisation*, by the barriers within which capital can valorise itself as capital.[63]

In other words, should there be a generalised overaccumulation and not one limited to some branch of production, then there will be no possibility of lucrative employment of any capital. The industrialists' money would go on piling up in banks without finding any 'sphere of employment' to invest in, a fact that merely indicates 'the *barriers of the capitalist production process*'; that is, it indicates the industrialist can only, and only want to produce in order to obtain profit. Hence, the 'obstacle' mentioned by Marx does not arise from any technical or material problem but, instead, from 'barriers within which capital can valorise itself as capital'. It is an obstacle created specifically by the capitalist mode of production.

Marx conceives the valorisation route of productive capital in its expansion, overaccumulation and stagnation, as the main determinant of the flow of moneyed capital available in banks and other credit institutions. This flow increases or diminishes according to the equilibrium, loss of equilibrium or regaining of equilibrium between, on the one hand, the deposits made by capitalists and, on the other, the loans they obtain. To this movement in the moneyed capital supply is aggregated that of the demand for money examined in the preceding item, thereby characterising a credit cycle guided by the relation between rate of profit and rate of interest. The combination of credit cycle and industrial cycle is described by Marx in the following terms:

> If we consider the turnover cycles in which modern industry moves – *state of quiescence, growing animation, prosperity, overproduction, crisis,*

63 Marx 2016, p. 624 [1993, p. 586].

> *stagnation, quiescence etc.* – (cycles which it falls outside the scope of our argument to analyse further) we find that a low level of interest generally corresponds to periods of prosperity or extra profits, a rise in interest comes between prosperity and its reversal, but that a maximum of interest up to extreme heights of usury corresponds to the crisis ... (Of course, low interest can also be accompanied by stagnation, and rising interest can be accompanied by growing animation).[64]

The industrial cycle is divided by Marx into six phases which he named in English, probably according to authors whose works he was reading and commenting on at the time. These phases are associated with the movement of the interest rate. What stand out in the quoted text, however, are the expressions that indicate the correspondence of the movements of the two rates as being merely possible. Marx says that not always but only 'generally', 'a low level of interest corresponds to periods of prosperity'; and at the end, that 'low interest *can* also be accompanied by stagnation, and rising interest can be accompanied by growing animation', instead of saying straight out, that they necessarily coincide.

Many pages farther on in the manuscript he again refers to the possibility of the two rates and the two cycles not being in step. More specifically, Marx addresses the excess of moneyed capital, resuming the question of a possible difference between this excess and the overproduction of productive capital.

> ... an accumulation (superabundance) of monied capital can take place which is connected with productive accumulation only relatively, i.e., it stands in inverse proportion to it. This is the case in the two phases of the industrial cycle, firstly at the time when productive capital has contracted (at the beginning of the cycle that follows the crisis) and secondly at the time when improvement sets in, but commercial credit still exerts very little pressure on monied credit ... The *superabundance of monied capital* expresses in the first case the stagnation of productive capital, in the second case the relative independence of commercial credit from moneyed credit.[65]

64 Marx 2016, p. 464 [1993, pp. 433–4].

65 Marx 2016, pp. 584–5 [1993, p. 547]. Afterwards Marx expresses that possibility in terms of its opposing modality: 'A plethora of moneyed capital as such does not *necessarily* signify overproduction, or even a want of spheres of employment for capital'. (Marx 2016, p. 624 [1993, p. 586]).

The excessive accumulation of moneyed capital for loans, says Marx, 'is connected with productive accumulation only relatively' and not in a way that could be considered 'absolute'. It should be noted that such 'relative' association 'can take place' but does not do so inevitably. Moreover, the 'relative' condition derives from the 'inverse proportion' between the two accumulations, according to which moneyed capital is abundant because, when the industrial cycle is in a contraction phase, there is no profitable employment for it and, in the phase when the industrial cycle is recovering, because bills of exchange of commercial credit are readily accepted so as to dispense with the use of the effective money loaned by the banks.

The text clearly takes up the fundamental distinction indicated in the preceding item between commercial credit and banking credit, now referred to as 'monied credit'. In spite of their being intermediated by banks there is still space for the circulation of bills of credit among producers and traders, and commercial credit can still affirm its 'relative independence' from banking credit. This was why in the preceding text Marx stated that 'low level of interest generally corresponds to periods of prosperity', a case typical of commercial credit although he did admit that 'a rise in interest' may correspond to a 'growing animation', a situation more typical of banking credit. In the texts cited above, the two credit systems exist side by side, even though the banking credit predominates.

However, given the inverse relation between the rate of profit and the rate of interest in each system, the final result is uncertain, that is, 'relative': if commercial credit manages to assert its 'relative independence' from bank credit, the tendency will be for the rate of profit to fall in times of prosperity; but if bank credit imposes its control on commercial credit, the tendency will be for the rate of interest to go up in times of prosperity. In both situations they are merely tendencies and the vector resulting from their clash is defined by the degree of autonomy of commercial credit and the degree of imposition of banking credit in each case.

The possibility that the industrial cycle may not determine the accumulation of monied capital absolutely is expanded in other passages of the *1863–7 Manuscripts*. In a generalised formulation Marx observes that:

> As long as the *social* character of labour appears as the *monetary existence* [*Geldsein*] of the commodity and hence as a *thing* outside actual production, monetary crises, independent of real crises or aggravating them, are unavoidable.[66]

66 Marx 2016, p. 633 [1993, p. 595].

The text makes explicit the possibility that monetary crises are 'independent of real crises', that is, of the crises that actually affect the reproduction of social capital. The basic condition of every mercantile economy – the opposition between the commodity's 'social character' represented in money and the private character of the immediate production of the commodity – makes money 'appear … as a thing outside actual production', outside capitalist reproduction itself.

Monetary crises 'independent of real crisis' usually stem from situations of fictitious valorisation and speculations with property securities. Although Marx admits that shares issued by joint-stock companies, for example, correspond to real capital, he considers the movement of their sale and purchase among the agents of its specific market to be speculative. Eventual modifications of their value motivated by changing expectations regarding the dividends they may eventually yield are not equivalent to effective capital. Their value may soar for a while, but if a sudden change in expectations brings them right down again, Marx adds that 'once the storm is over, these securities rise again to their former level, in so far as the undertakings they represent have not come to grief or turned out to be fraudulent'.[67] Undoubtedly, speculation can affect the effective reproduction of capital when, as the text says, the companies issuing the shares go bankrupt and cause a loss of real capital; or when, right from the start, they were 'fraudulent' companies created specifically to speculate and capture money from other speculators. Apart from these two situations, however, the pressure on the money market and monetary crises may very well be 'a separate phenomenon alongside' overproduction, as the first text cited in this item put it.

These possible mismatches between the movement of money and the course of effective reproduction confer an aspect of uncertainty and unpredictability on the crises. A violent devaluation of shares that represent value may perhaps not significantly affect the sphere of production but, on the contrary, crises can be set off by factors that seem to have their origin outside the production system in the narrowest sense, factors that present themselves 'as a thing outside actual production'. Such duplicity complicates the link between the industrial cycle and the credit cycle and casts a shadow of doubt on the very concept of cycle as a precise succession of phases in a process.

Nevertheless, various passages in Marx's Manuscripts assert the reverse, using explicit modal language. An example:

67 Marx 2016, p. 560 [1993, p. 524].

> But as soon as credit is shaken, and this is a necessary phase in the cycle of modern industry, all real wealth is supposed to be *actually* transformed into money … a crazy demand, but one that necessarily grows out of the system itself.[68]

According to the text, the phase in which a credit crisis breaks out is a 'necessary phase' in the industrial cycle and forces the sale of commodities at very low prices to pay off the bills of exchange and other debts due. A 'crazy demand', of course, but one that 'necessarily grows out of the system itself'. The modality associated to the cycle here is the necessity for the relationship between one event and the other to exist. There is no way to avoid 'credit' being 'shaken' and all the madness that ensues. In another passage Marx reinforces that idea:

> The very fact that the accumulation of moneyed capital is augmented by these elements that are independent of genuine accumulation, even if they accompany it, must lead to a constant plethora of the moneyed capital at certain phases of the cycle, and this plethora develops alongside the development of the credit system. Hence there develops at the same time a need to drive the production process beyond its capitalist barriers; overtrading, overproducing, and excess credit. This must always happen, however, in forms which bring about a rebound.[69]

The 'independent moments' to which Marx refers here are related to the increase in demand for labour by capitalists in the stage of recovery after a crisis; an increase that raises the wages of employees and employs new workers, swelling the deposits in banks. He explains that such deposits 'must lead to' an excess of moneyed capital 'at certain phases of the cycle', which leads to a 'need' for the system to overcome 'barriers' in trade, production, and credit. The final phase of this cycle, the rebound, the return to expansion, 'must always happen' as well. Once more, the modal status of the link between these two forms of accumulation is that of necessity, according to which, whenever an event occurs another event connected to it can 'always' be identified. In the text itself, however, there is a clause that weakens this strict connection. The entire movement begins when the accumulation of moneyed capital increases as a function of those 'independent moments' in the sphere of production which do not necessarily

---

68 Marx 2016, p. 671 [1993, p. 626].

69 Marx 2016, pp. 624–5 [1993, p. 586]; the translation replaces the word 'moments' (Momente, in the original) with 'elements', which makes my interpretation difficult.

occur together. It is thus a possibility, but one that necessarily precipitates the sequence of events examined above.

The simultaneous presence of this double modality in which a possible event necessarily triggers a succession of other events, clarifies the nature of necessity itself. As I explained in the course of this book, capital's immanent tendency to continuously valorise itself is a necessity that conflicts with its opposite tendency to devaluate. Given that both tendencies emerge from the contradictory core of the relation between capital and wage labour, both are necessary and neither one manages to impose itself on the other in an absolute way. The tendency to valorisation of value, which constitutes capital itself, and the tendency to devaluation of value, which defines crisis, are merely 'relative', in the sense that neither one manages to totally encompass the other and thus become absolute. This 'relative' nature of capitalist determinations also marks the industrial cycle, whose phases do not derive one from another in an absolute way. The conditions of the crisis are not entirely contained in those of the preceding expansion and do not contain the conditions for a posterior recovery. Therefore, the sequence and the cycle itself effectuate themselves in a relative, not absolute, mode.

This is also the nature of the credit cycle insofar as it is linked to production. In a text cited above, Marx says that the accumulation of moneyed capital 'is connected with productive accumulation only relatively'; this most certainly means that the phases of credit expansion and contraction, as well as the elevation and reduction of the rate of interest, are bearers of the same relative necessity as the production phases. Derived as they are from the latter, the opposing movements of credit do not correspond to a mere possibility but neither do they constitute an absolute, fatal necessity.

What is more important, however, is that the movement of moneyed capital, in the form of credit for production and financing in general, ends up obfuscating the movement of productive capital and attracting to itself the attention of the economic agents. After all, as Marx warns in the first chapter of *Capital* Volume II, due to its liquidity, moneyed capital is the most suitable form for the reproduction of capital; and interest-bearing capital in particular opens the door for more exacerbated forms of the representation of wealth, and especially for speculation with so-called fictitious capital. Thus, an acceleration in the rhythm of accumulation of productive capital, doubtless boosted by the credit system, seems to actually only stem from credit itself, and more, from credit in its craziest mode of financial speculation. The consequence of all this excess, the economic crisis, can therefore only be presented as if it were due to the credit system; in the best hypothesis, a problem with finance itself, or in the worst one, as the mere result of the madness and bad faith of certain speculators. The crisis could also present itself as a result of random events that shock the investment expectations of the economic agents or that heighten financing risks, such as changes in the political scenario or even natural disasters like epidemics, earthquakes, tsunamis.

In any case, the movement of productive capital will remain hidden. The necessity that leads its phases to succeed one another will appear to be a simple possibility, which can only become an effective reality through the intervention of events external to the dynamics of productive capital itself: accidental, unforeseeable events. It is important to emphasise that this appearance will not be a simple optical illusion nor even a deliberate fabrication, because it will always be the consequence of the way in which the capital reproduction system organises itself, and all the more so when the necessity in which its movement takes place is only a relative one, not absolute. The outbreak of a crisis actually requires the intervention of events external to the strict sphere of capital reproduction in the same way as does the exit from a crisis and the return to a period of accumulation considered normal. Nevertheless, such events will merely be triggers, mobilising systemic forces that lead to a crisis or to a resumption of production, and would never be capable of replacing the action of these forces. The fact that everything seems to be inverted and that the internal determining necessity of the crisis conceals itself in an external accident or an individual subjective disposition is yet another result of the subordination of social substance to social form, that is, the fetishism of capital.

Bibliography

Aglietta, Michel 1976, *Régulations et crises du capitalisme*, Paris: Calmann-Lévy.

Alcaly, Roger E. 1978, 'An introduction to marxian crises theory', *U.S. Capitalism in Crisis*, New York: Union for Radical Political Economics, 15–22.

Althusser, Louis 1965, Pour *Marx*, Paris: Maspero.

Althusser, Louis 1968, *Lire Le Capital*, Paris: Maspero.

Altvater, Elmar 2006, *Das Ende des Kapitalismus, wie wir ihn kennen*, Münster: Westfälisches Dampfboot.

Aristotle 1958, *Metaphysics*, Oxford: The Clarendon Press.

Arrizabalo Montoro, Xabier 2014, *Capitalismo y economia mundial*, Madrid: Roal.

Artous, Antoine 2006, *Le fétichisme chez Marx*, Paris: Syllepse.

Arthur, Christopher 1986, *Dialectics of Labour: Marx and his Relation to Hegel*, Oxford: Basil Blackwell.

Backhaus, Hans Georg 1969, 'Zur Dialektik der Wertform', *Beiträge zur Marxistischen Erkenntnistheorie*, edited by Alfred Schmidt, Frankfurt: Suhrkamp, 128–152.

Belluzzo, Luiz 1980, *Valor e capitalismo*, São Paulo: Brasiliense.

Benetti, Carlo, and Jean Cartelier 1980, *Merchands, Salariat et Capitalistes*, Paris: La Découverte.

Bensaïd, Daniel 1995, *Marx l'intempestif*, Paris: Fayard.

Berger, Johannes 1975, *Krise und Kapitalismus bei Marx*, Frankfurt: Europäische Verlagsanstalt.

Bober, Stanley 2008, *Marx and the Meaning of Capitalism. Introduction and Analyses*, New York: Palgrave.

Boccara, Paul 1973, *Études sur le capitalisme monopoliste d'État, sa crise et son issue*, Paris: Editions Sociales.

Boddy, Radford and James Crotty 1975, 'Class Conflict and Macro-Policy: The Political Business Cycle', *Review of Radical Political Economics*, Spring: 1–19.

Böhm-Bawerk, Eugen 1949 (1896), *Karl Marx and the close of his system*, edited by Paul M. Sweezy, New York: Augustus Kelley.

Breitenbürger, Gerd and Günter Schnitzler (eds.) 1974, *Marx und Marxismus heute*, Hamburg: Hoffmann und Campe Verlag.

Brenner, Robert 2002, *The Boom and the Bubble. The US in the World Economy*, New York: Verso.

Bresser-Pereira, Luís 1986, *Lucro, acumulação e crise*, São Paulo: Brasiliense.

Briaune, Jean-Edmond 1840, *Des crises commerciales, de leurs causes et de leur remèdes*, Paris: Bouchard-Huzard.

Bukharin, Nicolai 1972 [1924], *Imperialism and the Accumulation of Capital*, New York: Monthly Review Press.

Carchedi, Guglielmo 2011, *Behind the Crisis. Marx's Dialectics of Value & Knowledge*, London: Brill & Haymarket.

Carchedi, Guglielmo and Michael Roberts (eds.) 2018, *World in Crisis: a Global Analysis of Marx' Law of Profitability*, Chicago: Haymarket.

Castoriadis, Cornelius 1978, *Les carrefours du labyrinthe*, Paris: Seuil.

Chesnais, François (ed.) 2004, *La finance mondialisée: racines sociales et politiques, configuration, conséquences*, Paris: La Découverte.

Clarcke, Simon 1991, 'Overaccumulation and Crisis', *Science and Society*, 54/4: 442–67.

Colletti, Lucio (ed.) 1975, *Il marxismo e il 'crollo' del capitalismo*, Roma-Bari: Laterza.

Cutler, Tony et. al. 1977, *Marx's Capital and capitalism today*, London: Routledge & Kegan Paul.

Denis, Henri 1984 *Logique hégélienne et systèmes économiques*, Paris: PUF.

D'Hondt, Jacques 1980, 'L'histoire des sciences selon Marx et Engels', *Science et Dialectique chez Hegel et Marx*, Paris: Planty-Bonjour, CNRS, 57–67.

Dobb, Maurice 1937, *Political Economy and Capitalism: Some essays in economic tradition*, London: Routledge & Kegan Paul.

Dobb, Maurice 1973, *Theories of value and distribution since Adam Smith*, Cambridge: Cambridge University Press.

Engels, Friedrich 1961 [1859], 'Karl Marx, "Zur Kritik der Politischen Ökonomie"', *Marx Engels Werke* (MEW) 13, Berlin: Dietz Verlag.

Engels, Friedrich 1980 [1859], 'Karl Marx, "Contribution to the Critique of Political Economy"', *Marx Engels Collected Works* (MECW) 16, New York: International Publishers.

Fausto, Ruy 1986, *Marx, logique et politique*, Paris: Publisud.

Fineschi, Roberto 2001, *Ripartire da Marx. Processo storico ed economia politica nella teoria del 'Capitale'*, Napoli: La Città del Sole.

Foster, John Bellamy 1986, *The Theory of Monopoly Capitalism*, New York: Monthly Review Press.

Foster, John Bellamy and Robert McChesney 2012, *The endless crisis*, London: Brill & Haymarket.

Fulda, Hans Friedrich 1974, 'These zur Dialektik als Darstellungsmethode (im 'Kapital' von Marx)', *Hegel Jahrbuch*, Köln: Pahl-Rugenstein Verlag, pp. 204–210.

Gaskin, Richard 1995, *The Sea Battle and the Master Argument: Aristotle and Diodorus Cronus on the Metaphysis of the Future*, Berlin/New York: De Gruyter.

Giannotti, José 1971 [1966], *Origines de la dialectique du travail*, Paris: Aubier.

Giannotti, José 1984, *Trabalho e Reflexão*, São Paulo: Brasiliense.

Gordon, David 1978, 'Up and down the long roller coaster', *U.S. Capitalism in Crisis*, New York: Union for Radical Political Economics, 22–35.

Gordon, David 1980, 'Stages of accumulation and Long Wave economic cycles', *Process of the World System*, edited by Terence Hopkins and Immanuel Wallerstein, Beverly Hills: Sage Publications, 9–45.

Grespan, Jorge 2002, 'A Dialética do Avesso', *Crítica Marxista*, São Paulo: Boitempo, 14: 26–47.

Grespan, Jorge 2019, *Marx e a crítica do Modo de Representação Capitalista*, São Paulo: Boitempo.

Grossmann, Henryk 1992 [1929], *The Law of Accumulation and Breakdown of the Capitalist System*, London: Pluto Press.

Habermas, Jürgen 1973, *Theory and Practice*, Boston: Beacon Press.

Hansen, F.R. 1985, *The Breakdown of Capitalism. A History of the Idea in Western Marxism, 1883–1983*, London: Routledge & Kegan Paul.

Harman, Chris 2009, *Zombie Capitalism. Global Crisis and the relevance of Marx*, Chicago: Haymarket Books.

Hartmann, Karl 1970, *Die Marxsche Theorie*, Berlin: De Gruyter.

Harvey, David 1982, *The limits to capital*, Oxford: Basil Blackwell.

Harvey, David 2011, *The Enigma of Capital and the Crisis of Capitalism*, London: Profile.

Hecker, Rolf 2002, 'Einfache Warenproduktion oder einfache Warenzirkulation – die Debatte um die Ausgangskategorie des *Kapital*', Berliner Verein zur Förderung der MEGA-Edition (ed.), *In Memoriam Wolfgang Jahn*, Hamburg, 81–91.

Hegel, Georg 1955 [1837], *Die Vernunft in der Geschichte*, Hamburg: Felix Meiner.

Hegel, Georg 1975, Lectures on *the Philosophy of World History, Introduction: Reason in History*, Cambridge: Cambridge University Press.

Hegel, Georg 1986 [1812–16], *Wissenschaft der Logik I and II*, Frankfurt: Suhrkamp.

Hegel, Georg 1986b [1817], *Enziklopädie der philosophischen Wissenschaften, I, II e III*, Frankfurt: Suhrkamp.

Hegel, Georg 1986c [1837], *Vorlesungen über die Philosophie der Geschichte*, Frankfurt: Suhrkamp.

Hegel, Georg 2010, *Science of Logic*, Cambridge: Cambridge University Press.

Heidtmann, Bernhard 1974, 'Abstraktion und Dialektik in Marx' Erkenntniskritik', *Hegel Jahrbuch*, Köln: Pahl-Rugenstein Verlag, pp. 330–42.

Heinrich, Michael 1995, 'Gibt es eine Marxsche Krisentheorie?', *Beiträge zur Marx-Engels Forschung Neue Folge*, 1995: 130–150.

Heinrich, Michael 1996/97, 'Engels' Edition of the Third Volume of 'Capital' and Marx' original Manuscript, *Science & Society*, 60.

Heinrich, Michael 1999, *Die Wissenschaft vom Wert*, Münster: Westfälisches Dampfboot.

Hilferding, Rudolf 1985 [1910], *Finance Capital*, London: Routledge & Kegan Paul.

Hodgskin, Thomas 1969 [1825], *Labour defended against the Claims of Capital*, New York: A.M. Kelley.

Hof, Jan 2009, *Marx Global: zur Entwicklung des internationalen Marx-Diskurses seit 1965*, Berlin: Akademie Verlag.

Itoh, Makoto 1978, 'The formation of Marx' theory of crisis', *Science and Society*, XLII, 2, 129–155.

Itoh, Makoto 1980, *Value and Crisis: essay on Marxian Economics in Japan*, London: Pluto Press.

Juglar, Clément 1862, *Des Crises commerciales et leur retour périodique en France, en Angleterre et aux États-Unis*, Paris: Guillaumin et Cie.

Kant, Emmanuel 2009 [1781], *Critique of Pure Reason*, Cambridge: Cambridge University Press.

Kliman, Andrew 2011, *The Failure of Capitalist Production. Underlying causes and the Great Recession*, New York: Pluto Press.

Kocyba, Hermann 1979, *Widerspruch und Theoriestruktur: zur Darstellungsmethodik in Marxschen 'Kapital'*, Frankfurt: Materialis Verlag.

Koselleck, Reinhart 1988: *Critique and Crisis: Enlightenment and the Pathogenesis of Modern Society*. Cambridge, Mass.: MIT Press.

Koselleck, Reinhart 2006, 'Crisis', *Journal of the History of Ideas*, 67, 2: 357–400.

Koselleck, Reinhart, Otto Brunner and Werner Conze 1972–1992 (eds.), *Geschichtliche Grundbegriffe, Historisches Lexikon zur politisch-sozialen Sprache*, Stuttgart: Klett-Cotta Verlag.

Kotz, David 1987, 'Long waves and Social Structures of Accumulation: a critique and reinterpretation', *Review of Radical Political Economics*, 19, 4: 16–38.

Kotz, David 2015, *The Rise and Fall of Neoliberal Capitalism*, Cambridge: Harvard University Press.

Kotz, David et. al. 2010, *Contemporary Capitalism and its Crises. Social Structure of Accumulation Theory for the 21st Century*, Cambridge: Cambridge University Press.

Krätke, Michael 1999, 'Kapitalismus und Krisen: Geschichte und Theorie der zyklischen Krisen in Marx' ökonomischen Studien 1857/58', *Beiträge zur Marx-Engels Forschung Neue Folge*, 1998: 5–46.

Krätke, Michael 2001, 'Geld, Kredit und verrückte Formen', *MEGA-Studien*, 64–99.

Kühne, Karl 1974, *Ökonomie und Marxismus*, Berlin: Luchterhand, Volume II.

Kurz, Robert 1991, *Der Kollaps der Modernisierung. Vom Zusammenbruch des Kasernensozialismus zur Krise der Weltökonomie*, Frankfurt: Eichborn Verlag.

Kurz, Robert 2012, *Geld ohne Wert*, Berlin: Horlemann.

Kurz, Robert 2016, *The Substance of Capital* (*The Life and Death of Capitalism*), London: Chronos Publications.

Lange, Ernst 1978, 'Wertformanalyse, Geldkritik und Konstruktion des Fetischismus bei Marx', *Neue Hefte für Philosophie*, 13: 1–46.

Leibniz, Gottfried 1998 (1686), *Philosophical Texts*, Oxford: Oxford University Press. 250

Lenin, Vladimir 1979 [1917], *Imperialism, the highest Stage of Capitalism*, New York: International. 229

Lenin, Vladimir 1974 [1899], *The development of capitalism in Russia*, Moscow: Progress.

Lohmann, Georg 1991, *Indifferenz und Gesellschaft*, Frankfurt: Suhkamp.

Lukács, Georg 1976 [1923], *History and Class Consciousness: studies in Marxist Dialectics*, Cambridge: MIT Press.

Luxemburg, Rosa 1976 [1912], *The Accumulation of Capital*, London: Routlege and Kegan Paul.

McNally, David 2011, *Monsters of the Market*, Leiden: Brill.

Mandel, Ernest 1978 [1972] *Late Capitalism*, translated by Joris de Bres, London: Verso.

Mandel, Ernest 1980 [1978], *Long waves of capitalist development*, Cambridge: Cambridge University Press.

Mandel, Ernest 1984, 'Explaining long waves of capitalist development', *Long Waves in the World Economy*, edited by Christopher Freeman, London: Frances Printer Publ., pp. 195–201.

Marx, Karl 1961 [1859], *Zur Kritik der politischen Ökonomie*, Marx Engels Werke (MEW) 13, Berlin: Dietz Verlag.

Marx, Karl 1962 [1890], *Das Kapital. Erster Band*, Marx Engels Werke (MEW) 23, Berlin: Dietz Verlag.

Marx, Karl 1963 [1885], *Das Kapital. Zweiter Band*, Marx Engels Werke (MEW) 24, Berlin: Dietz Verlag.

Marx, Karl 1964 [1894], *Das Kapital. Dritter Band, Marx Engels Werke (MEW)* 25, Berlin: Dietz Verlag.

Marx, Karl 1965 *Theorien über den Mehrwert I*, Marx Engels Werke (MEW) 26.1, Berlin: Dietz Verlag.

Marx, Karl 1967, *Theorien über den Mehrwert II*, Marx Engels Werke (MEW) 26.2. Berlin: Dietz Verlag.

Marx, Karl 1968, *Theorien über den Mehrwert III*, Marx Engels Werke (MEW) 26.3. Berlin: Dietz Verlag.

Marx, Karl 1969a, *Theories of Surplus value I*, Moscow: Progress Publishers.

Marx, Karl 1969b, *Theories of Surplus value II*, Moscow: Progress Publishers.

Marx, Karl 1969c, *Theories of Surplus value III*, Moscow: Progress Publishers.

Marx, Karl 1974, *Grundrisse. Foundations of the Critique of Political Economy (Rough Draft)*, London: Penguin.

Marx, Karl 1976a, *Capital*, Volume I, London: Penguin.

Marx, Karl 1976b [1859] *A Contribution to the Critique of Political Economy*, Marx Engels Collected Works, New York: International Publishers.

Marx, Karl 1976c, *Ökonomische Manuskripte 1857–8. Teil I, Marx-Engels-Gesamtausgabe (MEGA)* II/1.1, Berlin: Dietz Verlag.

Marx, Karl 1978, *Capital*, Volume II, London: Penguin.

Marx, Karl 1980 *Urtext zur Kritik der Politischen Ökonomie, Marx-Engels-Gesamtausgabe (MEGA)* II/2, Berlin: Dietz Verlag.

Marx, Karl 1981, *Capital*, Volume III, London: Penguin.

Marx, Karl 1982 *Zur Kritik der politischen Ökonomie (Manuskript 1861–63), Marx-Engels-Gesamtausgabe (MEGA)* II/3.3, Berlin: Dietz Verlag.

Marx, Karl 1983, *Grundrisse der Kritik der Politischen Ökonomie, Marx Engels Werke (MEW)*, Volume 42. Berlin: Dietz Verlag.

Marx, Karl 1991 [1890], *Das Kapital. Erster Band*, in *Marx-Engels-Gesamtausgabe* (*MEGA*) II/10, Berlin: Dietz Verlag.

Marx, Karl 1993, *Marx Ökonomische Manuskripte 1863–1867. Teil II, Marx-Engels-Gesamtausgabe* (*MEGA*) II 4.2. Berlin: Akademie Verlag.

Marx, Karl 2008 *Manuskripte zum Zweiten Buch des 'Kapitals' 1868 bis 1871, Marx-Engels-Gesamtausgabe* (*MEGA*) II/11, Berlin: Akademie Verlag.

Marx, Karl 2012, *Marx Ökonomische Manuskripte 1863–1868. Teil III, Marx-Engels-Gesamtausgabe* (*MEGA*) II 4.3. Berlin: Akademie Verlag.

Marx, Karl 2016, *Marx's Economic Manuscript of 1864–1865*, Leiden/Boston: Brill.

Morf, Otto 1951, *Das Verhältnis von Wirtschaftstheorie und Wirtschaftsgeschichte bei Karl Marx*, Bern: Franke Verlag.

Moseley, Fred 2015, *Money and Totality*, Leiden: Brill.

Moseley, Fred and Tony Smith (ed.) 2014, *Marx's Capital and Hegel's Logic: a Reexamination*, Leiden: Brill.

Müller, Klaus 2009, 'Tendenzieller Fall oder Anstieg? Zur Komplexität ökonomischer Erscheinungen am Beispiel der allgemeinen Durchschnittprofitrate', *Marx-Engels Jahrbuch*, 47–75.

Müller, Marcos 1982, 'Exposição e método dialético no "Capital"', *Boletim SEAF*, 2: 15–41.

Murray, Patrick 2016, *The Mismeasure of Wealth*, Leiden: Brill.

Napoleoni, Claudio 1972, *Lezioni sul capitolo sesto inedito de Marx*, Torino: Boringhieri.

Okishio, Nobuo 1961, 'Technical change and the rate of profit', *Kobe University Economic Review*, 7: 85–99.

Okishio, Nobuo 1961, 'Notes on Technical Progress and Capitalist Society', *Cambridge Journal of Economics*, 1 (1): 93–100.

Pape, Ingetrud 1956–7, 'Zur Problemgeschichte der Modalität des Werdens', *Kant Studien*, 48, 1–4: 324–43.

Perelman, Michael 1987, *Marx's Crisis Theory. Scarcity, Labour, and Finance*, New York: Praeger.

Petry, Franz 1916, *Der soziale Gehalt der Marxschen Werttheorie*, Jena: Fischer.

Postone, Moishe 1993, *Time, Labour and Social Domination*, Cambridge: Cambridge University Press.

Reichelt, Helmut 1973, *Zur logischen Struktur des Kapitalbegriffs bei Karl Marx*, Frankfurt: Europäische Verlagsanstalt.

Reichelt, Helmut 2008, *Neue Marx Lektüre*, Hamburg: VSA-Verlag.

Reuten, Geert 2019, *The Unity of the Capitalist Economy and the State: a Systematic-Dialectical Exposition of the Capitalist Sysytem*, Leiden/Boston: Brill.

Ricardo, David 1951 [1817], *Principles of Political Economy and Taxation*, edited by Piero Sraffa, Cambridge: Cambridge University Press.

Riedel, Manfred 1969, 'Der Begriff der "Bürgerlichen Gesellschaft" und das Problem seines geschichtilichen Ursprungs', Böckenförde (ed.) *Staat und Gesellschaft, Wege der Forschung*, 471, 77–108.

Riedel, Manfred 1975, 'Gesellschaft, bürgerliche', Koselleck, Reinhart and Christian Meier (eds.) 1975, *Geschichtliche Grundbegriffe*, Stuttgart: Klett-Cotta, vol. 2.

Riedel, Manfred 1984, *Between Tradition and Revolution: The Hegelian Transformation of Political Philosophy*. Cambridge: Cambridge University Press.

Roberts, Michael 2016, *The Long Depression*, Chicago: Haymarket.

Robinson, Joan 1949, *An Essay on Marxian Economics*, London: Macmillan.

Robinson, William 2014, *Global Capitalism and the Crisis of Humanity*, New York: Cambridge University Press.

Robles Báez, Mario and Roberto Escorcia Romo 2015, *El tableau économique de François Quesnay y los esquemas de la reproducción del capital de Karl Marx*, México: Universidad Autónoma Metropolitana.

Rochabrún, Guillermo 2021, *El Capital de Marx, afirmación y replanteamiento*, Lima: Editorial Ande.

Rodbertus, Johann 2010 [1898], *Overproduction and Crisis*, New York: Kessinger Publishing.

Rogers, Chris 2014, *Capitalism and its Alternatives*, London: Zed Books.

Rosdolsky, Roman 1977 [1968] *The Making of Marx's 'Capital'*, London: Pluto Press.

Röttgers, Kurt 1975, *Kritik und Praxis. Zur Geschichte des Kritikbegriffs von Kant bis Marx*, Berlin: De Gruyter.

Rowthorn, Bob 1976, 'Mandel's Late Capitalism', *New Left Review*, 98: 59–83.

Rubin, Isaak Illich 1972 [1924], *Essays on Marx's Theory of Value*, Detroit: Black & Red.

Saad Filho, Alfredo 2002, *The value of Marx*, London: Routledge.

Sayer, Derek 1979, *Marx's Method*, Sussex: Harvester Press.

Shaikh, Anwar 1978, 'Political Economy and Capitalism: notes on Dobb's theory of crisis', *Cambridge Journal of Economics*, 2, 2: 233–251.

Shaikh, Anwar 1978b, 'An introduction to the History of crisis theory', *U.S. Capitalism in crisis*, New York: Union for Radical Political Economics, pp. 219–241.

Shaikh, Anwar 2016, *Capitalism. Competition, Conflict, Crisis*, New York: Oxford University Press.

Sherman, Howard 1964, *Macrodynamic Economics*, New York: Appleton-Century-Crofts.

Sherman, Howard 1991, 'Marx and the business cycles', *Science and Society*, New York, 31, 4: 486–504.

Schlesinger, Rudolf 1950, *Marx: his time and ours*, London: Routlege, Kegan Paul.

Schumpeter, Joseph A. 1954, *History of Economic Analysis*, London: Allen & Unwin.

Sismondi, Simonde 1971 [1827], *Nouveaux principes d'économie politique, ou De la richesse dans ses rapports avec la population*, Paris: Calmann-Lévy.

Smith, Adam 1965 [1776], *The Wealth of Nations*, New York: Modern Library.

Stamatis, Georgios 1977, *Die spezifischen kapitalistischen Produktionsmethoden und das tendenzielle Fall der Profitrate bei Karl Marx*, Berlin: Mehrwert Verlag.

Streeck, Wolfgang 2016, *How Will Capitalism End?*, London: Verso.

Streeck, Wolfgang 2014, *Buying Time. The Delayed Crisis of Democratic Capitalism*, London: Verso.

Struve, Piotr 1917, 'Past and Present of Russian Economics', *Russian Realities & Problems*, Cambridge: Cambridge University Press.

Sweezy, Paul M. 1942, *The theory of capitalist development*, New York: Oxford University Press.

Theunissen, Michael 1974, 'Krise der Macht. These zur Theorie des dialektischen Widerspruchs', *Hegel Jahrbuch*, Köln: Pahl-Rugenstein Verlag, pp. 318–329.

Tsuru, Shigeto 1993, *Institutional Economics Revised*, Cambridge: Cambridge University Press.

Tugan-Baranovsky, Mikhail 1913 [1901], *Les crises industrielles en Angleterre*, Paris: M. Giard, É. Brière.

Utz, Arthur F. 1982, *Die Marxistische Wirtschaftsphilosophie*, Bonn: WBV Wesskirch.

Vadée, Michel 1980, 'La conception de la théorie chez Marx', *Science et Dialectique chez Hegel et Marx*, Paris: Planty-Bonjour, CNRS, pp. 41–56.

Vadée, Michel 1992, *Marx penseur du possible*, Paris: Méridien Klincksieck.

Van Parijs, Philippe 1993, *Marxism recycled*, Cambridge: Cambridge University Press.

Vollgraf, Carl-Erich 1997, 'Kontroversen zum dritten Buch des *Kapital*: Folgen von und Herausforderungen für Edition', *MEGA Studien*, 1996/2: 86–108.

Vollgraf, Carl-Erich and Jürgen Jungnickel 1994, '"Marx in Marx' Worten"? Zu Engels' Edition des Hauptmanuskripts zum dritten Buch des *Kapital*', *MEGA-Studien*, 3–55.

Vuillemin, Jules 1984, *Necessité ou Contingence*, Paris: Minuit.

Weisskopf, Thomas 1978, 'Marxist perspectives on Cyclical Crisis', *U.S. Capitalism in Crisis*, New York: Union for Radical Political Economics, pp. 341–378.

Weisskopf, Thomas 1996, 'Marxian Crisis Theory and the Contradictions of Late Twentieth-Century Capitalism', *Radical Political Economy. Explorations in Alternative Economic Analysis*, edited by Victor Lippit, New York: Amonk.

Wildermuth, Armin 1970, *Marx und die Verwirklichung der Philosophie*, Haia: Martinun Nijhoff.

Wood, Ellen 2005, *The Empire of Capital*, London: Verso.

Index of Names

Printed in the United States
by Baker & Taylor Publisher Services